The Politics
of Modernization
in Eastern Europe

edited by
Charles Gati

With introductory essays by
Vernon V. Aspaturian and Cyril E. Black

Studies of the Institute on
East Central Europe, Columbia University

The Praeger Special Studies program—utilizing the most modern and efficient book production techniques and a selective worldwide distribution network—makes available to the academic, government, and business communities significant, timely research in U.S. and international economic, social, and political development.

The Politics
of Modernization
in Eastern Europe
Testing the Soviet Model

PRAEGER SPECIAL STUDIES IN INTERNATIONAL POLITICS AND GOVERNMENT

56239
0526163

Praeger Publishers   New York   Washington   London

Library of Congress Cataloging in Publication Data

Gati, Charles.
    The politics of modernization in Eastern Europe.

    (Praeger special studies in international politics
and government)
    Based on a conference held in Mar. 1973, sponsored
by the Institute on East Central Europe of Columbia
University.
    Includes bibliographical references.
    1. Europe, Eastern—Politics. 2. Europe, Eastern—
Foreign relations—Russia. 3. Russia—Foreign rela-
tions—Europe, Eastern. I. Columbia University.
Institute on East Central Europe. II. Title.
DR38.3.R8G37   320.9'47   73-15185
ISBN 0-275-28781-5

PRAEGER PUBLISHERS
111 Fourth Avenue, New York, N.Y. 10003, U.S.A.
5, Cromwell Place, London SW7 2JL, England

Published in the United States of America in 1974
by Praeger Publishers, Inc.

Second printing, 1976

All rights reserved

© 1974 by Praeger Publishers, Inc.

Printed in the United States of America

PREFACE
Charles Gati

This book is based on papers and commentaries presented at a conference, "Eastern Europe: The Impact of Modernization on Political Development," held at Columbia University on March 23-24, 1973. The conference was sponsored by the Joint Committee on Eastern Europe of the American Council on Learned Societies in order to encourage research on a neglected area of study. The editor of this book served as organizer and general chairman of the conference.

Perhaps it was the topic itself, perhaps it was the quality of the participants, or both, that led to an interesting and lively conference. Nearly all participants addressed themselves to the philosophical-methodological question at hand: Does the basically Western-made notion of modernization, which has been formulated and refined largely in response to developments in the Third World, provide an accurate or even helpful framework for the study of the socialist polities of Eastern Europe? On most questions, as the various chapters themselves reflect, disagreement prevailed. Some questioned, for example, the very meaning of "modernization" and "political development"; others expressed concern about the applicability of these concepts to Eastern Europe; some complained about the scarcity of reliable data that would permit significant generalization; and still others wondered whether this diverse region we call Eastern Europe or East Central Europe lends itself to comparative studies.

Many of these questions are explored in the introductory essays (Part I) by Vernon V. Aspaturian and Cyril E. Black. The four case studies in Part II, introduced by Robert Sharlet, deal with Hungary, Czechoslovakia, Romania, and Yugoslavia. Part III, to which I have written a brief introduction, explores the international dimension of modernization, examining the processes of interaction and influences between the Soviet Union and Eastern Europe as well as within Eastern Europe. Part IV, introduced by Istvan Deak, presents a variety of answers (and approaches) to the broad question of how tradition and modernity coexist in East European societies. An Appendix of statistical data on modernization and development, compiled by Vernon V. Aspaturian, constitutes the concluding part of the book.

On behalf of the contributors and myself, I am pleased to express my appreciation to those who made the conference

at Columbia University and this book possible: the Joint
Committee on Eastern Europe of the American Council of
Learned Societies and the Institute on East Central Europe
of Columbia University. For generous assistance, I wish to
thank the Institute's director, Istvan Deak, the Institute's
assistant to the director, Stanislaus A. Blejwas, and the
Institute's administrative assistant, Ms. Dorothy Roseman.
Those who participated in the activities of the conference,
chairing the various sessions or commenting on the papers,
included Seweryn Bialer, Zbigniew Brzezinski, Joseph Roths-
child, and Marshall D. Shulman, all of Columbia University,
and Jan Szczepanski of the University of Warsaw. I am grate-
ful for their contributions.

And finally, using the editor's prerogative, I wish to
dedicate this volume to Vernon V. Aspaturian, whose chapters
I am pleased to include here and whose friendship I cherish.

CONTENTS

56239
032616 3

LIST OF TABLES

xiii

TABLES IN THE APPENDIX

LIST OF FIGURES

MARXISM, MODERNIZATION, AND EASTERN EUROPE

**MARXISM AND THE
MEANINGS OF
MODERNIZATION**
Vernon V. Aspaturian

THE CONCEPT OF MODERNIZATION

The concept of "modernization," in spite of the vast
theoretical and empirical literature it has inspired, remains essentially an evanescent concept, largely because its
etymological reference point is temporal in character rather
than fixed and absolute. To be sure, current paradigms attribute a fixed definition to modernization, but this is
largely an arbitrary exercise designed to avoid the vexatious problems involved once the basic assumptions of the
paradigm are subjected to critical examination and its ideological or value-based parameters are questioned. Ideally,
the paradigm should be trans- or supravalue or ideological
in character, but this is rendered impossible because of the
historical association of modernization with "westernization," that is, the social, economic, and political value
systems and structures that originated in Western Europe in
the eighteenth century. These values and structures are
deeply imbedded in theoretical constructs of modernization
and manifest themselves most explicitly in both the empirical
indicators that are employed to measure the rate and level of
modernization in individual countries and the periodic visions of the "good life" generated by Western writers and
scholars.

Because of the inextricable connection between the concepts of modernization and westernization, modernization assumes a normative imperative that existing paradigms skirt
and is not simply an empirical concept. Substituting the
more neutral-sounding concept of modernization for the more
blatantly culture-bound and normative concept of westernization, however, does not solve the theoretical difficulties

involved; it merely serves to obscure and avoid them in the interests of rapid theoretical development. Important questions such as whether modernization is a fate or a choice, inevitable or optional, absolute or relative, remain unraised once westernization is objectified as modernization and decreed to be a desirable, inevitable, and universal phase of development.

In this manner, modernization becomes associated with another basic Western value concept, "progress," since modernization represents progress, just as westernization does. And thus the circle is completed: Progress is defined in terms of modernization, modernization is defined in terms of westernization, and westernization thus becomes the concrete empiricohistorical reference point for progress.

Whether one wishes to equate modernization with progress and westernization is beside the point. Existing paradigms of modernization are value-loaded paradigms and should be acknowledged as such so as not to preclude the possibilities of constructing other paradigms of development or simply existence (since development itself has assumed a strong normative coloration). Historically, westernization and modernization have been chosen as forms of social existence simply out of self-defense and security in a world of intense and predatory competition, rather than because of their value norms. The most emphatic illustration of this was the contrasting social decisions of Japan's elite to modernize and China's to imperiously disdain westernization. It would be plausible to assume that had not the West, with its modern technology and superior instruments of force, threatened the civilization of the Orient, neither Japan in the late nineteenth century nor China somewhat later would have abandoned their own forms of social existence and freely chosen that of the West. Unless one believes in the inevitability and eternity of the struggle for survival and existence, one must assume that some social orders might choose neither progress nor westernization nor modernization, with their promise of continuous turmoil, convulsions, anxieties, spiritual and moral uncertainties in return for their undoubted benefits. They might, instead, choose an existence that promises placidity, harmony, social equilibrium (even social stasis), and stresses the intuitive-esthetic aspects of existence, were they not threatened externally by other social systems. In Western terms (aside from cultural anthropologists), of course, such choices would be defined as stagnant (primitive), retarded (traditional), or retrogressive (reactionary).

The intellectual tradition of the West, including Marxism, blends two separate but now intertwined legacies, which distinguish it from other traditions, and both legacies are deeply structured in the concepts of progress and modernization. The first is the Greco-Roman rational-empirical strand with its emphasis on logical order and structure, systematic investigation, regularity, and certainty, which finds its contemporary culmination in modern science and technology. The second is the Judeo-Christian prophetic-messianic tradition, which is reflected in the periodic generation of utopias, visions of the good life, spiritual renewal and innovation, ecumenism, and universalism, and which finds its contemporary culmination in modern humanism. That these two strands of the Western tradition are in constant conflict and contradiction is more than obvious, but so is the symbiotic interdependence that has developed between them.

Contemporary social science, including its Marxist variants, evolved in the philosophical quest for a permanent, fixed, stable, and productive relationship between these two elements so as to minimize the destructive consequences of the contradictions and tensions between them. This has resolved itself in various epistemological and cognitive theories, philosophies of history, and theories of development in which the purposes, visions, and values of Western humanism will be achieved scientifically, thus simultaneously meeting the imperatives of both the scientific-rational and the prophetic-messianic components of the Western psyche. Kant, Hegel, Comte, and Marx emerge as the Western intellectual giants who have dealt explicitly with the problem of reconciling these two constituent strands in Western thought, and all contemporary Marxist and non-Marxist paradigms and theories of social development are eclectically derivative from their efforts.

Marxism, perhaps, represents the most ambitious and systematic attempt to reconcile the imperatives of both science and prophecy. Marx tried to solve the problem by converting messianic prophecy into scientific prediction, and most contemporary theories of modernization and development similarly attempt to provide a scientific-empirical rationalization for the acceptance or adoption of preferred and desired values and norms. In his Theses on Feuerbach, the young Marx, in an exuberant and combative mood, may have claimed too much for himself when he asserted that all previous philosophies sought to explain the world (the Greco-Roman scientific-rational-empirical strand), whereas his philosophy sought to change the world (the Judeo-Christian prophetic-messianic-utopian strand), since a substantial coterie of philosophers (the utopian thinkers, especially the utopian socialists and anarchists) also sought to change the world by providing alternative visions of the future to replace existing social systems. Lenin, among others, recognized Marx's debt to the utopian socialists, but it remains nevertheless true that Marx must be credited with the idea of attempting to place prophecy and utopia on a scientific foundation, by appropriating Hegel's dialectical method that enabled him to derive a logic and rationality from the contradiction of opposites that could transform chaotic vision into empirical order, convert prophecy into prediction, metamorphose utopia into reality, and transmute value into fact.[1]

Although Marx and his followers in the Soviet Union emphasize the deterministic and materialistic foundations of their ideology, in order to preserve its scientific credentials, Marxism, and in particular Marxism-Leninism, is emphatically more voluntaristic and nonmaterial in its dimensions than many non-Marxist theories of development.* Since neither Marx nor Lenin were scientists, but humanists, it is not surprising that the prophetic elements of Marxism subsumed the scientific; both were concerned primarily with social change not science, and the latter was subordinated to the former: Values and visions would determine the direction that science would take and not the other way around. Ideology thus plays an architectonic role in the Marxist-Leninist theory of development, and the generation of values and norms is not left to chance of spontaneity but is stringently controlled and directed by a special elite, the Communist Party, whose leaders shape and define the value parameters within which material development takes place, establishing purposes, goals, and priorities.

---

*The dichotomy between "Marxist" and "non-Marxist" theories of development and modernization employed here is purely for convenience. No precise dichotomization is intended, nor is it intended to convey the impression that all "non-Marxist" theories are identical, nor is the term "Marxist" designed to lump all Marxist theories together. Rather, the term "Marxist" should be understood as referring to those aspects of Marxist theory shared by Marx and Soviet theorists as well as those formulations extrapolated, modified, and developed in the Soviet Union and other communist countries. Furthermore, it should be recognized that Marxist-Soviet theories reflect a ruling ideology and constitute the basis of official policies and thus are not simply analytical theories, whereas "non-Marxist" theories are essentially analytical, unofficial formulations developed by independent scholars whose models and theories may or may not serve as inputs into official policy.

Non-Marxist theories of development, on the other hand, tend to be relatively unconcerned with values, goals, and ideology, since modernization is defined as an end in itself, is conceived as universal in time and space, and as impelled by automatic and impersonal forces. Values and goals are generated by the process itself and are thereby reinforced as societies move with mechanistic-like precision through successively higher stages of development, whose definitions are determined largely by quantitatively measured levels of achievement and performance called indicators and whose extrapolations become predictions of future levels and rates of development. The process of movement from one stage to the next is called "modernization," that is, progress, and its material development can be scientifically measured. When certain levels and rates of growth, approximating those of Western countries, are achieved, societies become "modernized," that is, westernized. Emphasis is placed on the process itself and the development of scientific-like methodologies that can generate hypotheses (values) and predictions (utopias); in this way new values and goals are churned up by the process of modernization, and these values and goals dimly outline the next stage of development. No special elite is required to maintain value control or prevent deviant development, although it is acknowledged that in underdeveloped countries and in communist countries "modernizing elites" exist who mobilize social and material resources, establish goals and priorities, and define the values and purposes of society. Whether "modernizing elites" are a necessary agent in the modernizing process, or merely optional and left to chance, is unclear in most non-Marxist theories of development.

Soviet and non-Soviet conceptions of development thus share a wide spectrum of common assumptions and values. Both Soviet and Western theories of development are infused with the notion of progress, dynamically reconciling prophecy and science, and view social development as a succession of increasingly higher stages of development. Neither allows much latitude for horizontal development, or the intensification of a particular phase, but stress movement from one stage to the next. This is considerably more emphatic in the Soviet scheme, which forces development through stages, telescoping or even skipping them, thus theoretically allowing considerable flexibility as it is applied to coexisting societies in various or uneven stages of development.[2] The Soviet concept of development is much more doctrinaire than Western concepts, because it is more purposive, explicit in its values and norms, conscious of its mission, and certain of its destination. Like its Western counterparts, the Soviet notion of development does not accept the equality of different stages of development, since development is viewed in vertical rather than horizontal terms. For communists, communism is the unambiguous highest stage of development in an absolute sense, whereas for Western theorists of modernization, industrial, postindustrial, or the high mass-consumptionist stage represents the highest current phase of development, which may simply be a stepping stone to a newer, higher, and as yet undisclosed phase. Thus, it is implicit in many Western theories that all countries will or ought to achieve this highest phase, just as Soviet writers posit socialism and communism as the highest stages of social development that all societies must inevitably achieve.[3]

Since both Soviet and non-Soviet theories of development derive from the same intellectual tradition, the two resemble each other in many respects and their schemes of developmental stages overlap considerably. Each has five stages, more or less: (1) "traditional primitive" vs. primitive communism, (2) "traditional civilization" vs. slave society, (3) "transitional society" vs. feudalism, (4) "industrial revolution" society vs. capitalism, and (5) "high mass-consumptionist" society vs. socialism-communism.[4] The two schemes are out of phase in a number of respects, since the Soviet categories are developed within a historical context and are sociohistorical stages, whereas the Western stages are ahistorical in character and are designed to empirically define existing types of societies. The Soviet scheme is far more dogmatic in this regard, as was reflected in its inability to deal effectively with various kinds of contemporary societies in underdeveloped countries that could not fit into the tightly closed, sacrosanct Marxist schema produced in the mid-nineteenth century. While Soviet scholars have done considered empirical investigation on underdeveloped countries, they have not yet dared to tamper with the five-stage sociohistorical scheme bequeathed by Marx, although they have generated a profusion of bewildering substages in an effort to accommodate an inflexible ascriptive doctrine.

(Especially confusing is the generalized Soviet catch-all cliché, "noncapitalist development," which is nonsocialist as well. Mongolia, supposedly an outstanding exemplar of "noncapitalist" development, has been noncapitalistically developing for nearly five decades. This concept, which is an exceedingly flexible one, is capable of being adjusted to fit any society whose development does not conveniently fit within the orthodox Marxist-Soviet frame; sometimes it is employed as a political device to honor or recognize anti-Western underdeveloped countries who claim or aspire to a variety of socialism that does not receive official recognition in Moscow. This catch-all concept as well as numerous substages, some of whose life span turns out to be very short, are designed to meet the deficiencies of the Marxist theory of development in underdeveloped countries, which received little attention from Marx except passing derision. Marx, however, appeared to recognize, at least implicitly, the inapplicability of his stages for some non-European societies by his intriguing and enigmatic references to "an Asiatic mode of production," which did not fit into his dialectical mold. Because Marx intimated that prerevolutionary Russia might plunge into such a state or become "semi-Asiatic" in its development, Soviet writers, until recently, were forbidden to explore the implications of what was condemned in 1931 as "the notorious Asiatic mode of production." Even today, the subject is approached gingerly and with considerable caution. While Soviet writers are not apt to develop new stages based on the "Asiatic mode" for underdeveloped countries generally, it should come as no surprise if Soviet writers discover that Mao's China represents a form of the "Asiatic mode of production.")[5]

Although Soviet and noncommunist theories of modernization and development are variants of the same Western tradition, this does not mean that the two are interchangeable or that they generate comparable and parallel institutions, structures, values, and social relationships. The Soviet theory of development is distinguished from other modern theories of development in a number of important dimensions:

1. Its value system, including visions of the future, are absolutized "progressive" values and utopias of the late nineteenth century and are deemed to be preemptive, exclusionary, and final. It signifies the end of prophecy and utopias, since Marx scientifically established his vision of a socialist and communist society as the historically predetermined end-product of development. Western stages of industrialization and modernization are designated an inferior stage of development--capitalism--that, while capable of many variants and susceptible to intensified horizontal development, remains nevertheless a simple milestone on the dialectical road to socialism and communism. Thus, mankind is deprived of the further need for prophets, and in accordance with an earlier tradition, Marx becomes the final and true prophet, not of God, but of history and science.

2. By specifying a particular social group, the proletariat, as the human fount of progress, Marxist theories of development are conspicuously voluntaristic and teleological rather than deterministic and open-ended in spite of

epistemological rhetoric to the contrary. The voluntaristic dimension of Marxism finds its exponential development in Marxism-Leninism, with the Communist Party acting as the necessary vanguard of the proletariat, the custodian of its values and aspirations, and the accelerating agent of development. In non-Marxist terms, the Communist Party is defined as a "modernizing elite," one among many, viewed as an optional convenience rather than a necessary prerequisite for development and modernization.

3. Within the context of Marxism, modernization has two aspects: (a) a qualitative sociopolitical dimension, defined in terms of superior and inferior values, norms, and social relationships, which are graded in reference to particular stages of development; and (b) a quantifiable material-technical dimension, defined and measured in terms of human capabilities and scientific, technological, and economic growth. In the Soviet context, the first aspect of modernization is paramount and decisive, while the second is ancillary and independent of the first and can take place within a lower order of values, norms, and social relationships that may equally serve the ends of injustice and reaction as well as justice and progress. Thus, one can distinguish between immature and modernized capitalism, but "capitalist modernization" is of a qualitative lower order than the modernization reflected by socialism and communism. No matter how highly developed (modernized) capitalism may be, in the second dimension it represents essentially the horizontal development of an inferior or lower phase of development. On the other hand, a socialist society--Bulgaria, for example--represents a higher form of modernization than the most highly developed capitalist society, in spite of its technological and economic inferiority, since its capabilities are designed to serve the ends of justice and presumably will be more rapidly and effectively developed than under capitalism.

This last point bears further examination for it highlights a basic deviation from orthodox Marxism, which originates in the historical fact that the first socialist state was established in an immature capitalist society (Russia), whereas for Marx, socialism was to be established initially in the most highly developed capitalist states. This meant that socialism in Russia was forced to assume the extra burdens historically assigned by Marx to capitalism, that is, the development of a scientific, technological, and industrial society. Socialism was not conceived by Marx to be a surrogate or alternative stage for capitalism, and in a passage that is framed within the context of a historical imperative, Marx issued a caveat against the usurpation of sociohistorical functions assigned to lower stages by higher stages of development:

> No social order ever disappears before all
> the productive forces for which there is
> room in it have developed; and new, higher
> relations of production never appear before
> the material conditions of their existence
> mature in the womb of the old society.[6]

And in specific reference to Russia, Marx again warned:

> If Russia is tending to become a capitalist
> nation she will not succeed without having
> first transformed a good part of her peas-
> ants into proletarians; and after that, once
> taken to the bosom of the capitalist regime,
> she will experience its pitiless laws like
> other profane peoples.[7]

But both Lenin and Stalin subsequently demonstrated that voluntaristic forces were superior to deterministic forces even in postcapitalist society, and Stalin set out to prove that capitalism need not be the only process for the transformation of peasants into proletarians and agrarian societies into industrial ones. The reality is that Stalin did create a new and effective alternative process of indus- trialization and modernization, and what is called "building socialism" is essentially a surrogate for capitalist devel- opment and modernization in underdeveloped communist coun- tries.

These three distinguishing characteristics of Soviet theories of modernization and development bring into sharp focus some of the difficulties experienced in establishing comparability in the modernization of communist and noncom- munist states. Noncommunist theories of modernization avoid the vexatious problem of dealing with the value purposes and goals of modernization, that is, its content and substance, and focus on the forms, processes, and indexes of develop- ment that are deemed to be universal in character and there- fore above ideologies, belief systems, and value norms. Uni- versally designed paradigms, by avoiding ideologies and val- ues, tend to produce extraparadigmatic impressions such as conclusions that all roads lead to modernization and eventu- ally convergence, implicitly decreeing that technology shapes ideology and values.

That there is a value dimension to modernization is in- escapable; this is often reflected in the inability of

11

existing paradigms to deal satisfactorily with political and social indexes of modernization, especially the former. Frequently, this difficulty is masked by complaints about the paucity, unreliability, or noncomparability of statistics as if it were a simple semantic or definitional problem. Rarely is it conceded that the problem transcends statistics and that statistical classifications often represent categories defined in terms of content and purpose. This difficulty is highlighted by the conceptual difficulties posed by the concept "political modernization," which is sometimes rejected as too explosively subjective and either inherently unmeasurable or noncomparable, insofar as it can be measured. (Samuel Huntington deals at length with the concept of "political modernization" within the overall concept of development, including decay as a possibility. In his conception, a society may be simultaneously "modernized" in a political dimension and at a lower stage of development in terms of human and material resources and capabilities, or the other way around. Furthermore, decay may transpire in one or the other dimension or in both. Although Huntington's criteria for political modernization or decay are not ascriptive in character as Soviet criteria tend to be, his conception is similar to the Marxist in that it allows for the possibility of differential modernization stages within a single society, not within the context of subsystem variations but in overall dimensions.)[8] This deficiency is particularly notable in various attempts to establish universal quantifiable indicators of "political participation" in terms of voter registrations, party membership, electoral behavior and outcomes, which frequently turn out to be meaningless because the prior assumptions concerning conclusions that can be drawn by such indicators in noncommunist countries are largely inapplicable to communist states.

These are not simple problems of semantics or methodology. Communist systems generate structures, institutions, groupings, and social relationships that do not have comparable, to say nothing of exact, counterparts in other countries. The words are often the same but they are infused with radically different meanings and this uniqueness is frequently reflected in the design of communist statistical categories, which are meaningful for them but not necessarily for other theorists of modernization. Thus, for communist systems, expanding the public sector, eliminating or reducing private property, eliminating, reducing, or enhancing certain social classes and groupings, circumscribing religious affiliation and institutions, expanding collectivization, etc., are important indicators of modernization, often more important to communist regimes than economic and

technological indicators. But where are their counterparts
elsewhere and what non-Soviet theories of modernization
would dignify some of these processes as indicators of modernization, although they are both measurable and quantifiable?

DETERMINISTIC AND VOLUNTARISTIC THEORIES
OF MODERNIZATION

Theories of modernization and development fall into two
broad types: deterministic and voluntaristic. Most current
Western theories fall into the first category, while the Soviet or communist theory falls into the second. The more
scientific, rigorous, and precise a theory claims to be, the
more deterministic its contours. Marxist theory emphasizes
the deterministic character of development up to and including capitalist society, but beginning with the development
of proletarian class consciousness and the revolution, deterministic development gives way to voluntaristic action;
analytical determinism is supplanted by normative voluntar-
ism; socialist and communist societies are built; capitalist
societies develop and evolve. The Soviet theory of modernization and development, as a voluntaristic theory, stresses
the decisive role of human consciousness in the building of
socialism and communism in contrast to the impersonal forces
of history that continue to function in capitalist and pre-
capitalist societies. Even the development of revolutionary
consciousness in nonsocialist societies is considered to be
the consequence of deterministic forces, whereas with the
advent of socialism and communism, human consciousness becomes detached from its material foundations and assumes an
autonomous and decisive role in development.

Voluntaristic theories of development have an ancient
and venerable pedigree. They all share a common emphasis on
the decisive role of human will and action, but they may
differ considerably in substance, purpose, and the identity
of the human modernizing agent. Some theories in the past
assigned the creative role of development and progress to
great personalities and individuals endowed with virtually
superhuman talents and abilities, whose vision provided the
targets for future development and whose energy and will to
action fueled the process. Other theories stress human aggregates as the impelling agents, whether they be a social
class (as in the case of Marxism), a national, religious, or
racial group, which constitutes a self-appointed or self-
realizing creative minority that provides a vision for the
future and the will and capability to achieve it.

Voluntaristic theories of modernization thus begin with people as the prime force in the developmental process; these theories require a human agent of modernization, that is, people who are capable of conceptualizing alternatives to existing social reality and who have the will and capacity to develop the capabilities to move society in the direction of the vision. The process is accelerated by enhancing the capabilities and developing the consciousness of the modernizing agent. Some modernizing agents may intensify their capabilities and simultaneously restrict recruitment of new members of the elite by various ascriptive criteria, while others may seek to expand their size through socialization and recruitment from the population at large on the basis of merit, commitment, performance, and achievement, although ascriptive criteria for membership may also be retained to a limited degree. The communist approach to modernization is of the latter variety. Although the Communist Party is a self-designated modernizing agent, it seeks eventually to modernize the entire population and assumes that all people are equally capable of modernization, an egalitarian assumption that is reflected both in the goal of a classless society and the elimination of all distinction between mental and manual labor.

Modernization derives from the word "modern," which means having the characteristics of the recent or, more pointedly, the present and thus by itself is devoid of normative or value content. Modernization, as noted earlier, however, appears to have been endowed with a normative meaning that strongly suggests that to acquire the characteristics of the present is both desirable and perhaps inevitable. Thus, modernization means the cutting edge of development, moving toward the most recent or the present, whatever that happens to be at any given point on the continuum of time. The Marxist theory of development explicitly allows for what might be called modernization in a relative sense as well as an absolute sense. Moving vertically from one stage of history to another constitutes modernization in a relative sense, while the culminating terminal goal of modernization is communism, defined at this point as not the present but the future. Societies moving from slave society to feudalism or from feudalism to capitalism, or capitalism to socialism, are all in the process of modernization in this relative sense. The movement is inexorable, but the pace and tempo can vary considerably and this accounts for the unevenness in development and the coexistence of societies in various stages of development at any given time in history. Thus, for Marxists and Communists, modernization means development in a particular direction, toward a predefined, indeed predetermined, social state. Thus, Marxists would have little difficulty in accepting Karl Deutsch's formulation of "social mobilization" as a process whereby "major clusters of old, social, economic and psychological commitments are eroded or broken and people become available for new patterns of socialization and behavior,"[9] which is a necessary prerequisite for modernization. But communists would part company with Deutsch in a number of particulars. In the first place, the process of "social mobilization" is neither passive nor automatic, but requires an active "mobilizer"; secondly, people do not become available simply for new--any new--patterns of socialization and behavior, but for specifically defined patterns of behavior and socialization that are defined, shaped, directed, and accelerated by the mobilizer--the human modernizing agent--which in communist countries is the Communist or Marxist-Leninist Party.

In its broadest abstract meaning, modernization is the creation of new choices and options in human development--psychological, intellectual, political, social, cultural, economic, and even emotional. It represents simply the pursuit of the new, sometimes infatuation with whatever is the most recent innovation in behavior, attitudes, beliefs, and patterns of social, economic, and political organization and relationships. Communists reject the notion that modernization can mean the open-ended selection of any new choices and options; the pursuit of any new horizon, vista, or utopia; the adoption of any new patterns of behavior and relationships. Rather they assume that innovation per se is not desirable in itself, since the new choices and options that are continually churned up by the ingenuity of man may allow for new forms of injustice, tyranny, oppression, and other antisocial and undesirable types of behavior. Consequently, while communists agree that modernization means the creation of new choices, options, horizons, and vistas, these must be carefully screened and classified into choices and options that are desirable and hence mandatory, those that are undesirable and therefore forbidden, and some that may be optional, depending upon circumstances.

At this point, it might be useful to issue a caveat with respect to the discovery of new indicators of modernization as the most advanced societies along the modernization continuum (the United States, Sweden, and other Western countries) develop new behavioral norms and institutional patterns, structures, and relationships. If one accepts the possibility of decay and decline as a phase in the developmental process, these changing patterns, quantified into indicators, may actually be indicators of decay rather than ultramodernization. This might particularly be the case where norms and types of behavior formerly considered to be socially deviant, pathological, or dysfunctional, and hence proscribed or circumscribed, become widely prevalent in advanced societies and are viewed as alternative rather than deviant behavior, optional rather than pathological patterns, polymorphously functional rather than dysfunctional, and hence no longer prohibited or circumscribed. Thus, indicators that demonstrate that many of the most modernized societies reflect increasingly higher rates and levels of crime, political violence, illegitimate births, abortions, homosexuality, pornography, and drug use, all of which were formerly considered to be symptoms of social pathology, that is, _anomie_, may inadvertently be quanitified into indicators of ultramodernization instead and become goals and targets for the less modernized societies trailing behind. This point also serves to emphasize the nexus between values and statistical indicators, that is, that theories and paradigms of modernization have value norms prestructured and processed into them, and betrays once again the basic circularity involved in many definitions of modernization, that is, modernization is the conceptualization of the characteristics of societies called modern.

The communist approach to modernization thus imparts an ethical and moral dimension to modernization that is normally absent or obscured in noncommunist theories of modernization, and indeed it insists that all approaches to modernization must have a substantive moral or ethical content. Modernization for what and for whom are important questions for communists, who reject the idea that modernization can be either nonteleological in its implications or above ideologies and values.

This view, of course, differs from what might be called liberal-democratic pluralistic theories of modernization on the one hand and the Nazi-Fascist approach to modernization on the other, although it shares important particulars with both. Liberal-democratic pluralistic modernization theories, despite their specific differences, tend to define modernization as a process that maximizes new choices and options, ideas, horizons, vistas, and utopias; they are loath to proscribe any innovation in advance, but allow the selection and choices to be determined by the marketplace of history as it were, rather than impose a path for history to traverse. Minimal restrictions are imposed upon the range of choices and minimal constraints are placed on their development. A few choices and options may be prohibited as being retrogressive and dysfunctional (namely, defining human aggregates into inferior and superior races and groups), but generally speaking, all that is not prohibited is permitted.

New choices and options are viewed as a spontaneous development, simultaneously polymorphic and multidirectional in character. Competing choices and options appear in the form of conflicting values, life styles, norms, behavioral patterns, and even coexisting alternative visions of how society should be reconstructed. Both culture and morality become relativized and give rise to competing and parallel processes and institutions of socialization. Purpose is dispersed and social will fragmented and fractionalized; as a central body of constraints disappears, private constraints develop as a result of what Herbert Marcuse has called "repressive tolerance," that is, the tolerance of negative, regressive, and antisocial choices and options.

The Soviet and communist approach to modernization, on the other hand, means to consciously mobilize human and material resources to maximize the opportunity to exercise permitted options and choices, to accelerate the eradication of old forbidden options, and to suppress undesirable new ones that are spontaneously generated. Thus, certain forms and processes of political, social, and economic behavior are made mandatory while a whole range of options and alternative patterns of activity are foreclosed.

Brief, digressive mention should be made here of nazism or fascism as a system of modernization. There is little doubt, as Geoffrey Barraclough and others have propounded, that the house that Hitler built exhibited many of the characteristics of what is defined as modernization.[10] He wrought a social revolution by destroying the power of the Junker class and opening up the social structure to new recruitment; he fostered upward mobility, widened participation through plebiscites, mass political and social organizations, catered to youth and women, eliminated unemployment through a vast program of public works, concerned himself with jobs, the eight-hour day, working conditions, culture, education, the arts, and above all, enhanced economic productivity. In the words of one writer, cited approvingly by Barraclough, Hitler dragged Germany "kicking and screaming into the century of the common man." Even Franz Borkenau was moved to concede in 1939 that under the Nazis, "some sections of the upper classes are directly destroyed. . . . There could be no more thorough-going revolution."[11] To be sure, nazism was chauvinistic rather than universalist, assumed human inequality rather than equality, and glorified war and violence rather than condemned them. All this, of course, raises in dramatic form the issue of the ethical content of modernization, or whether modernization can be defined in an amoral context. Communists, of course, have little difficulty in dealing with nazism as a system of modernization, since they concede the modernization of nazism in the economic and productive realm but deny it the credentials of modernization in the political and social realm.

FROM ECONOMIC MODERNIZATION TO POLITICAL DEVELOPMENT

The experience of modernization in Nazi Germany and prewar Japan, as well as in contemporary developing countries, convincingly demonstrates that political and socioeconomic development can proceed on separate tracks, one in the direction of economic and even social modernization and the other in an opposite or divergent political direction. Huntington makes the important distinction "between political modernization defined as a movement from a traditional to a modern polity and political modernization defined as the political aspects and political effects of social, economic and cultural modernization." The former, he writes, "posits the direction in which political changes theoretically should move," while "the latter describes the political changes which actually occur in modernizing countries," and "the gap between the two is often vast."[12] He further observes that "modernization in practice always involves change and usually the disintegration of a traditional political system, but it does not necessarily involve significant movement toward a modern political system," as defined by most writers on modernization. One might even add that in the case of prewar Germany, Hitler destroyed a modern political system, the Weimar Republic, in order to release new and innovating forces, open up new avenues, allow the choice of different options, etc., in order to accelerate the modernization of Germany within a different set of ideological and value parameters. Thus Huntington's point might be expanded to show that modern political systems can become obstacles to further modernization in much the same way that traditional regimes and societies might.

This point is particularly relevant to any examination of the course that modernization has taken in Eastern Europe. The prewar societies in Eastern Europe were by no means traditional or tradition-like societies in all cases; to be sure, some countries like Poland, Hungary, Romania, and Yugoslavia retained powerful residual elements of the social structure developed over a thousand years of development and could be described as semifeudal in character insofar as large parts of the countryside were concerned. To take Hungary as an example of where feudal magnates still dominated the rural areas, in 1935 no less than 54.6 percent of the total farming area was concentrated in only 1.7 percent of the farms, while at the other end of the spectrum 72.5 percent of the "dwarf farms" accounted for only 10.1 percent of the total farming acreage. Small and medium farms (25.8 percent) accounted for the remainder (35.3 percent).[13] But this condition was not true of prewar Czechoslovakia, which, in spite of its many flaws and the retarded development of Slovakia and Ruthenia, was by any scale of measurement in 1937 a modernized polity, and which under communist guidance was nevertheless indiscriminately subjected to the same type of social demolition and reconstruction as the semifeudal social and political order in Hungary in order to pave the way for new patterns and paths of development and modernization. Furthermore, in all of the countries, except Albania and perhaps Bulgaria, a modernized urban population existed that was growing in both numbers and influence and that participated widely and energetically in the political life of these countries before nazism and fascism started to cast their long shadows sometime in the mid-1930s. These modernized concentrations of people, mainly the bourgeoisie, the propertied classes and the professionals, had to be crushed in order to open up new vistas and horizons that the "old" orders were blocking.

Thus, we must srucuplously reexamine not only the actuality but even the plausibility of the well-known argument that the advent of Soviet power in the region performed the necessary and thankless Herculean task of sweeping away the social debris of a thousand years of accumulation. While Soviet power could be accurately described as Herculean in magnitude, its cleansing activities were often performed in the wrong stables, for not only social filth but valuable social and human resources were cast out indiscriminately as well. The new options that were opened up to the countries of Eastern Europe were not only externally chosen but extremely restricted and narrow as well. They turned out to be, unsurprisingly, the social, economic, cultural, and political institutions, structures, norms, values, processes, and sociopsychological attitudes of the Soviet Union, which became the model for the future development and modernization of the countries of Eastern Europe.

NOTES

1. For a fuller development of this theme by the author, cf. "The Contemporary Doctrine of the Soviet State and Its Philosophical Foundations," _American Political Science Review_, December 1954, pp. 1031-57.

2. Marx and Engels, of course, frowned on the idea of skipping or collapsing stages, although they recognized the possibility of accelerating development within stages. Thus,

Marx wrote: "When a society has got on the right track for the discovery of the natural laws of development . . . it can neither skip by bold leaps, nor remove by legal enactments, the obstacles offered by successive phases of its normal development. But it can shorten the birth pangs." Karl Marx, Capital, I (New York: Modern Library Edition, n.d.), pp. 14-15. While at one time Marx and Engels toyed with the possibility that Russia might skip the capitalist stage providing a socialist society had already been established in a more highly developed society, which could be employed as a model and as a source of support and sustenance, they subsequently withdrew this special indulgence. Thus, Engels wrote "No more in Russia than anywhere else would it have been possible to develop a higher form out of primitive agrarian communism unless that higher form was already in existence in another country, so as to serve as a model. That higher form being, wherever it is historically possible, the necessary consequence of the capitalist form of production." And he then told his Russian correspondents not to despair because of the inevitability of capitalism in Russia: "Capitalism opens out new views and new hopes. . . . Look at what it has done and is doing in the West . . . there is no great historical evil without a compensating historical progress. . . . Que les destinées s'accomplissent!" Karl Marx and Friedrich Engels, Selected Correspondence (New York: International Publishers, 1942), p. 515.

3. Samuel P. Huntington and Zbigniew Brzezinski are notable exceptions to these generalizations about non-Western theories of development. Neither accepts the proposition that "highest stages" of development are either inevitable for all societies or that all societies desire or are capable of achieving increasingly higher stages of developmental exhaltation. Huntington, furthermore, introduces the notion of "decay" as a possible stage of development for either developed or developing societies and thus rejects the inevitability of progress that underlies Marxist-Soviet and many non-Marxist theories of development. Cf. Samuel P. Huntington, Political Order in Changing Societies (New Haven, Conn.: Yale University Press, 1968); and Zbigniew Brzezinski, Between Two Ages (New York: Viking, 1970).

4. Cf., for example, Bruce M. Russett, et al., World Handbook of Political and Social Indicators (New Haven, Conn.: Yale University Press, 1964), pp. 293-303; the survey summary in Peter H. Merkl, Modern Comparative Politics (New York: Holt, Rinehart and Winston, 1970), pp. 23-90; and W. W. Rostow, The Stages of Economic Growth (New York: Cambridge University Press, 1960).

5. See Karl Wittfogel, <u>Oriental Despotism</u> (New Haven, Conn.: Yale University Press, 1957), for an elaborate attempt to derive a "hydraulic society" from Marx's "Asiatic mode of production" and apply it as an analytical concept to the Soviet and other communist systems.

6. Karl Marx, <u>Selected Works</u>, 2 vols. (New York: International Publishers, 1942), I, 356-57.

7. Marx and Engels, op. cit., p. 354.

8. Huntington, op. cit., pp. 32-39.

9. Karl Deutsch, "Social Mobilization and Political Development," <u>American Political Science Review</u>, September 1961, p. 494.

10. Geoffrey Barraclough, "Mandarins and Nazis," <u>New York Review of Books</u>, October 19, 1972; "The Liberals and German History," ibid., November 2, 1972; "A New View of German History," ibid., November 16, 1972.

11. See Walter Laqueur, "Rewriting History," <u>Commentary</u>, March 1973.

12. Huntington, op. cit., p. 35.

13. See Bela A. Balassa, <u>The Hungarian Experience in Economic Planning</u> (New Haven, Conn.: Yale University Press, 1959), p. 245.

2

EASTERN EUROPE
IN THE CONTEXT OF
COMPARATIVE MODERNIZATION
Cyril E. Black

THE OBJECTIVE OF MODERNIZATION STUDIES

In evaluating what has been done and what still needs
to be done in the study of modernization and political development in Eastern Europe, let us not lose sight of the
ultimate goal. The comparative study of modernization is
concerned with the policies that all countries must pursue
if their peoples are to attain the levels of political, economic, and social achievement made possible by the scientific and technological revolution. This field of study has
the humanistic purpose of contributing to the advancement of
knowledge called for by the opportunity for the first time
in history to bring to all peoples adequate health, welfare,
and education in an atmosphere of security, freedom, and
dignity.
Comparative modernization seeks to achieve this goal by
studying the similarities and differences in the development
of the countries of the world as a means of finding out what
levels of achievement are possible and what policies are
best suited to achieving them. The objectives of this search
are the same as those proclaimed by both doctrinaire liberalism and Marxism-Leninism, but the methods and assumptions are
different. Comparative modernization differs from them in
seeking to free itself from the many ethnocentric and eccen-
tric accretions that have come over the years to burden these
two nineteenth-century philosophies that were themselves
revolutionary at one time. Comparative modernization does
not assume either that the institutions characteristic of the
English-speaking and West European countries will predominate
or that the victory of the proletariat over the bourgeoisie
represents the ultimate goal of social development. It

assumes rather that certain levels of political, economic, and social achievement are possible as a result of the scientific and technological revolution, and it seeks to understand the policies by means of which these levels can be attained by peoples of differing institutional heritages.

It is easy to talk about levels of achievement, but difficult to define them. In the realm of health, welfare, and education, the inputs can be readily measured in terms of personnel and resources; and it is not difficult to define the desired objectives in terms of infant mortality, longevity, control of disease, and levels of accomplishment. In the realm of economic growth, the GNP per capita of the more advanced countries is still the accepted benchmark, but it is a matter of considerable controversy as to the effect on the levels that are possible or desirable of global limitations on resources. Even assuming agreement on a given level of achievement, many questions remain as to the policies called for in order to attain these levels.

The countries of Eastern Europe represent an interesting laboratory for the study of comparative modernization both because of their characteristic common heritage of institutions and problems and because of the variations among them.[1] It must be acknowledged that only a limited amount of the research available is directly pertinent to comparative modernization. Such studies combine new data on relevant topics and organization of the data for purposes of comparison among East European countries and between them and other countries of other regions.

In seeking to describe and compare the transformation of societies in the modern era under the impact of the scientific and technological revolution, it is useful to make a distinction between (1) the institutional heritage of countries and regions, (2) the nature of the requirements that societies must meet if they are to take advantage of the opportunities for development characteristic of the modern era, and (3) the international context of this process--in particular, whether a given society is relatively early or relatively late to modernize and under the influence of which foreign models. The first and third sets of distinctions refer in particular to Eastern Europe and will be discussed below. The second is of a more general character and deserves further comment.

Students of modernization seem to be accepting the view, after considerable trial and error, that it is possible to isolate certain preconditions and requirements that all societies must meet if they are to achieve the levels of political development, economic growth, and social mobilization made possible by the advancement of knowledge. It has

23

0526163

been noted, for example, that the early-modernizing Western societies, and the more or less successful latecomers such as Japan and Russia, shared certain preconditions before the modern era that greatly facilitated their later development. These preconditions include receptivity to foreign influences, usually due to an earlier history of borrowing; experience with centralized political leadership reaching down to the family level; a premodern economic system with a capacity for accumulating savings; a significant level of urban development; and the beginnings of an education system.

Societies undergoing the long and arduous process of transformation from a predominantly agrarian to a predominantly industrial way of life--after the seventeenth century in the case of the early modern societies, and after the 1860s in the case of Japan and Russia--have had to meet certain distinctive requirements that build on the capabilities developed during the premodern era. These include extensive borrowing from more modern countries, to the extent possible without the sacrifice of the national identity; aggressive political leadership designed to mobilize the resources of the country for development; a rechanneling of agricultural surpluses into manufacturing and transportation; and the capacity to mobilize the population through urbanization and education for the purpose of concerted efforts.

Modernization is generally seen as a process that is essentially continuous, extending into the indefinite future as long as knowledge continues to grow and thus to affect human actions. One cannot therefore speak of "modernized" societies in any terminal sense, since all societies are modernizing. One may nevertheless discern stages of modernization, and there is now rather general agreement that there is a stage following transformation that has characteristics almost as distinct as those that distinguish the period of transformation from the premodern. The early-modernizing societies entered such a stage after World War I and are being followed now by Japan and Russia. This stage is sometimes referred to as high or advanced modernization-- or even by such exotic terms as "postindustrial," or "postmodern." For our purposes, we may call such societies "advanced modernizing," and their requirements differ significantly from those of the preceding stage of transformation. In particular, this advanced phase requires a continuing and expanding need for borrowing and adaptability to change; new structures of political participation to accommodate the greatly enlarged role of central decision making; a transfer of labor force from manufacturing to the services, as dramatic as that from agriculture to manufacturing in the preceding phase; increased urbanization, with the many concomitant problems this produces; and large increases in expenditures for research and education.

The question of the ways in which the institutional heritage of Eastern Europe prepared the countries of this region for the task they were to face in the period of rapid transformation may be discussed under the heading of political culture--at the risk of some misunderstanding--in view of the various ways in which this concept has been employed.[2] The essence of political culture as the term will be used here is the learned patterns of behavior of the people of a country or region in regard to the relations of state and society, of individuals and groups within a society, and with other societies. These behavior patterns are learned over generations, and they change only with difficulty as the nature of these relations changes. They are expressed through institutions, but they have greater continuity. Institutions can be created and terminated by revolutions without much immediate effect on behavior patterns. Fundamental behavior patterns change in the long run only in response to fundamental changes in the conditions of life of a society, such as the change from a rural-agricultural to an urban-industrial way of life, or the change from a subordinate to an independent political status. Societies vary a great deal in their political culture, and these variations account for significant differences in the ways in which they react to common problems caused by the scientific and technological revolution. Indeed, this may well be the answer to the question posed by convergence theory. Levels of achievement certainly tend to converge in developed societies, but due to differences in political culture, modern institutions are likely to vary considerably.

One can argue about the components of a political culture but one can hardly deny the reality of such behavior patterns or their significance for modernization. For example, almost all the countries that have achieved a high level of development had political systems that were effective on a societywide level before the modern era. Germany, the one that did not, underwent the most traumatic experiences of any modern society in its efforts to achieve an effective political system. An ongoing comparative study of Japan and Russia reaches the conclusion that their premodern political cultures played a vital role in their later success.[3] Both countries had political systems that could act effectively on a societywide basis for some two centuries before the 1860s when modernizing leaders came to predominate. Both had a greater capacity to mobilize skills and resources than any societies except the English-speaking and West European. Both also possessed an ability to adapt foreign values and institutions to domestic needs that was relatively unique among later-modernizing societies.

These examples suggest ways in which a premodern political culture can have elements that facilitate the transition to modernity. Other, and equally ingrained, behavior patterns may well inhibit modernization. Absence of a political system regarded by members of a society as worthy of support is a characteristic of many countries. Such behavior patterns as the caste system in India, the Ottoman belief that the Christian infidels of the West were inferior, and the conviction of Chinese scholar-bureaucrats that theirs was the most cultured civilization are aspects of political cultures that represent serious obstacles to modernization.

With reference to Eastern Europe generally, if such a complex region may be said to have a political culture, two principal characteristics may be suggested. One is the marked absence before 1918 of widely supported political systems. This was due primarily to the political, ethnic, and religious fractionalization of the societies of this region, which led even after 1918 to the subordination of most other tasks to the achievement of national unity. This characteristic has been imaginatively described by Myron Weiner as the "Macedonian Syndrome" in an interpretation that suggests 16 ways in which the search for national unity has tended to forms of behavior antithetic to political, economic, and social development.[4]

A second general characteristic of the political culture of Eastern Europe, in this case supportive of modernization, is that by comparison with most later-modernizing societies these countries gained relatively early an understanding of the problems of economic and social development and in some cases of substantive development as well. Polish, Czech, and Hungarian scholars made significant intellectual contributions to the scientific and technological revolution in early modern times, and their leaders were relatively uninhibited in adapting Western models to local conditions. The Polish province was among the most industrialized in Russia, as were the Czech and Hungarian in the Hapsburg monarchy. The achievement of the Hapsburgs in the industrialization of Bosnia-Herzegovina after 1878 reflects a significant understanding of the problems of development long before economic theories were available to guide policy makers.[5]

The concept of political culture can be applied better to a single society than to a region, of course, and the recent Ph.D. dissertation by David W. Paul has interpreted Czechoslovak history in these terms.[6] He focuses attention in particular on three patterns that have had an important contemporary influence: "the search for a Slovak national identity," a high degree of pluralism (defined as the willingness to accept more than one political ideology and outlook), and a pattern of passive resistance when confronted with foreign rule.

There is no simple or generally accepted way of determining the relative level of development of societies. In the absence of more sophisticated methods of ranking, one may accept for this purpose the estimates of GNP per capita at market prices (1970) published by the World Bank. By this measure Czechoslovakia, with a GNP per capita of $2,230, ranks close to Austria ($2,010), Japan ($1,960), the USSR ($1,790), and Italy ($1,760)--just below the early-modernizing Western societies that by this indicator range from the United Kingdom ($2,270) to the United States ($4,760). Czechoslovakia is followed closely by Hungary ($1,600), and Poland ($1,400), and at a greater distance by Romania ($730), Bulgaria ($760), Yugoslavia ($650), and Albania ($600).[7]

THE COMPARATIVE APPROACH

The central concern of this volume is the relation of the policies characteristic of Marxism-Leninism to the ineluctable forces of change since World War II, and the succeeding chapters are concerned chiefly with the actions and interactions of individual countries. This introductory chapter will approach this problem in terms of selected examples of comparative research on political, economic, and social aspects of the central cluster of issues in the study of comparative modernization: levels of development, policies of modernization, and the role of political culture.

Political Aspects

One of the primary requirements of successful modernization is a government that commands the loyalty of the population and has the capability to mobilize and allocate resources on a societywide basis. As already noted, the societies that have modernized thus far had this capacity in the premodern era, and those that did not (Germany) experienced serious difficulties in political, economic, and social development.

There is no standard or fully accepted methodology for determining such governmental capacity, but one may take as a starting point the concept of political performance as

developed by Harry Eckstein. This study has been operation-
alized by Ted Gurr and Muriel McClelland for 12 nations including Yugoslavia, which is compared with the other countries in two periods: a decade in the 1920s and 1930s and
another in the 1950s and 1960s.[8] Their approach to political performance focuses on four dimensions: durability,
civil order, legitimacy, and decisional efficacy (as reflected in efficacy of budgetary decisions and maintenance
of authority). Each of these characteristics is analyzed in
terms of quantifiable indicators and standard scores.

Yugoslavia's performance as measured by these methods
is scored relatively low for the period 1927-36 and somewhat
higher for the period 1957-66. One may venture the estimate
that all of the East European countries except Czechoslovakia would probably reflect a similar pattern of performance.
(It would be interesting to have similar measures of performance for the late nineteenth and early twentieth centuries.) One problem with such efforts at measurement is
that the more measurable superficial variations may be emphasized at the expense of more profound and lasting, but
less measurable, qualities of a political system. This may
account for the fact that a country such as France rates below Yugoslavia in both periods. Such studies are nevertheless valuable as a means of complementing institutional
studies in the evaluation of the capacities of governments
to implement the policies called for by societal transformation.

Studies of leadership offer an alternative approach to
problems of political change, although most of the work is
relevant only to the last decade or two. A particularly impressive recent study of political leadership in Eastern Europe is that of Carl Beck in the symposium edited by Carl
Beck and others.[9] He focuses on the relationship to political change of 37 leadership attributes of a demographic and
career nature of the members of 16 Central Committees in
four time periods (1949, 1954, 1962, and 1968) in Bulgaria,
Czechoslovakia, Hungary, and Poland. He finds that these
leadership attributes correlated rather closely with the
relative stability of communist policies in Bulgaria, the
shift in policies in Poland and Hungary following the adoption of the New Course, and the more dramatic changes in
Czechoslovakia in 1968. On the basis of his extensive career data, Beck traces the initial trend toward bureaucratization of the four Party systems, followed by the increasing recruitment in recent years of personnel with a non-
Party technical and managerial background. He also delin-
eates the characteristic differences among Communist Party
elites in the four countries, with Bulgaria and Czechoslovakia

revealing the greatest contrasts. The former showed a basic stability in the gradual shift in its leadership from a strong "revolutionary activist" component to a more bureaucratized officialdom. The Czechoslovak leadership was dispersed and fragmented in its origins, becoming more Party-centered in the 1960s, and was then dispersed again in 1968. The Hungarian and Polish patterns fell between these two extremes, with a main emphasis on a "central official" component reflecting extensive experience with the party and government apparatus.

In a separate study of Yugoslavia in this symposium, Zaninovich takes a somewhat different approach and distinguishes between the political elite, the professional elite, and the workers and peasantry as a single group. He finds among other things that the political elites are older than the professional and more confident in the ultimate success of their revolution, while the professionals are less romantic and visionary, and more cynical, hard-headed, and pragmatic. Despite these differences, both elites share a modernizing approach to leadership that contrasts sharply with that of the worker-peasants. In addition to reflecting much more directly than the elites the ethnic and regional differences in Yugoslavia, the worker-peasants tend to be parochial, traditionally minded, and statist.[10]

Studies such as these of political leadership are complemented by related work in the field of political participation. Discussion of political participation has moved so far from the "cold war" simplifications of "free" vs. "captive" nations, or democracy vs. totalitarianism--or from the communist viewpoint as "democracies" vs. "imperialists"-- that it does not seem worthwhile to review these debates. Our concern here is rather to compare the influence of the various segments of society on the critical decisions that governments must make year in and year out--decisions that may be aggregated under the headings of welfare vs. growth.

In approaching this subject I should start out by expressing my own strong bias in favor of the view that all forms of government, premodern as well as modernizing, depend to a significant degree on political participation. The question is the relationship among the elements of a society engaged in this participation and the ways in which they influence decisions. Russia was certainly an autocracy under Nicholas I, for example, perhaps a reactionary autocracy, but this does not mean that there was not extensive political participation in Russia in the first half of the nineteenth century. Being an autocracy meant that no alternative political authority could challenge that of the central bureaucracy, but it did not mean that all decisions

56239

were made at the top. Russia in this period may be described as a corporate society formed by legally recognized interest groups--peasants, townspeople, merchants, clergy, noble landowners--that were to a very considerable extent autonomous and self-governing through village, municipal, provincial, and corporate institutions. When organic changes were made in the system, as in the 1860s, there was extensive consultation between the government and the relevant interest groups. Formal consultation with peasants no doubt played a relatively minor role in the debates leading to these changes, but an underlying motive of the emancipation was the fear that the peasants would revolt if their status was not altered--and revolt or the threat of revolt is certainly one of the more effective means of influencing decisions at the top.

The study of political participation has been one of the most beneficial results of the behavioral revolution against a purely institutional approach. We now recognize that electoral and legislative processes play only a limited, and perhaps not a dominant, role in the allocation of resources--or, to put it differently, that they legitimize these changes more often than they initiate them. Studies of political participation by Western scholars, however, are still concerned almost exclusively with Western political systems.

What we need now is an extension of this approach to Eastern Europe, with an emphasis on the types of data relevant to these societies. The electoral and legislative data that play such a large role in studies of political participation in the West are of little significance to the study of Eastern Europe. There is no point in comparing percentages of voters participating in elections, or types of legislatures, for these purposes. Similarly, the role of the communist parties in interest articulation and aggregation is comparable to the role of parties in Western Europe in only a limited degree. Where the two sets of systems overlap to a greater extent is in the competition for influence of major political, economic, and social interest groups--including the major units of the central bureaucracies in their function as interest groups.

An important start has been made in the study of political participation in communist societies with the study of the Soviet Union by Gordon Skilling and his colleagues, and similar work is needed in regard to the countries of Eastern Europe.[11] The essential point is that one of the principal roles of the communist parties is to negotiate among competing interest groups in the allocation of scarce resources. Centrally controlled, no less than pluralistic, political systems face decisions as to the long-term consequences of how resources are allocated at the highest level of aggregation between state consumption, private consumption, and investment, and at lower levels between defense, heavy industry, light industry, agriculture, consumer goods, health, education, and welfare, urban development, communications, research and development, and so on. It seems likely that even in the most centralized years of Stalinism there was extensive consultation among major interest groups before basic decisions were reached. The difference between the 1930s and the 1960s is that in the earlier period each player kept his cards close to his chest, for reasons that are well known, whereas today there are extensive debates in the press organs of the competing interest groups.

If we may extrapolate from these studies of the Soviet system, an informed intuition would lead one to expect that the various functional sections of the East European Central Committees would consult actively with leaders in the branches of the political and economic system for which they are responsible. The diverse demands of these groups would then have to be reconciled in deciding on the annual allocation of scarce resources. There would be a hierarchy of interest groups with defense, heavy industry, internal security, higher education, and research and development occupying a privileged position. Competition within and among these privileged interest groups would not infrequently be revealed to the public through their rival publications. Other interest groups, of which the largest and most important is formed by the worker-peasant consumer, would by contrast have little influence on the allocation of resources. The trade unions and organs of internal security would not represent their interests very forcefully, and would normally prevent their expression through strikes and more violent forms.

One of the few detailed studies of bureaucracy and interest groups in this region, by Andrzej Korbonski, is concerned with the debate on economic reform in Czechoslovakia in the 1960s. It reaches the conclusion that economists in the various relevant ministries--the Planning Commission, the Academy of Sciences, and other academic institutions-- engaged in an active debate on the issues relating to economic reforms. This debate "resembled closely the behavior of groups in Western societies despite the presence of a Party which for ideological reasons was firmly opposed to the existence of autonomous groups."[12]

Economic Aspects

In the economic realm, our principal interest is in the policies that the governments of Eastern Europe have pursued

in developing their economies. Before embarking on this subject, it would be well to recall that, with the exception of
Hungary, which ranks close to Austria and Germany, they are
substantially less urbanized than the West European countries.[13] The GNP rate of growth in Eastern Europe in the
period 1950-68 was about 5 percent, or about the same as
that of Western Europe.[14]

Turning now to our main concern, policies of income distribution, two generalizations are immediately apparent.
First, the proportion of the national income devoted to investment has been somewhat higher in Eastern Europe, rising
from 20 to 30 percent of GNP from the early 1950s to the
early 1960s as compared with 20 to 25 percent in Western
Europe.[15]

Second, the share of national income devoted to personal consumption has declined, although per capita consumption has increased due to the general growth of the economy.
The rate of growth of consumption has simply been slower.
The development policies of these countries thus continue to
require a significantly larger sacrifice by the consumer, although the extent of this sacrifice is much less than in the
1950s. This pressure on the consumer is reflected in the
fact that, as noted above, the consumer is the one interest
group that is not represented at the governmental level. It
is no doubt true that industrial workers have a much higher
degree of representation than agricultural workers (except
in Poland), but it is not institutionally effective. It
gains its influence, when it does, through threat of violence and other forms of bargaining and occasionally through
violence (as in Gdynia in 1970).

What is of particular relevance to the study of comparative modernization, as already noted, is the relation of political culture, levels of development, and policies of modernization characteristic of communist systems. We are fortunate to have in Frederic Pryor's volume one of the few
available comparative studies of Eastern and Western Europe
that confronts this issue directly. Most studies of this
subject are carried out in terms of aggregated figures--such
as total public expenditures--whereas this study is at a disaggregated level at which public expenditures are broken down
into their main component parts in a form suitable for comparison.

Pryor's principal conclusion in terms of the focus of
this chapter is that the influence of the economic system--
whether it is a market system as in Western Europe or a centrally planned system as in Eastern Europe--plays much less
of a role than one might expect. It "plays a statistically
significant role in the ratio of public consumption expendi-

tures to the GNP [only] for education, research and development, non-military external security, and possibly internal security excluding traffic control."[16] He concludes that these differences diminished between 1956 and 1962, that they existed for primarily political and social reasons, and that they could not have been predicted from purely economic considerations. In regard to public consumption expenditures for defense, welfare, and health, differences in economic systems between Eastern and Western Europe are not significant. More generally, "the policy dilemmas facing decision makers are quite similar in all nations regardless of system."[17]

The level of economic development is found to be significant for internal security, foreign aid, and research and development, in comparing the countries of Eastern and Western Europe in the same time period. When public consumption expenditures are studied in individual countries over time, however, there is a significant relationship with per capita income when it rises from about $200 to $600. Beyond that point, the relationship is more random.[18]

Also, the relation of centralization ratios (the share of total national consumption expenditures that is directly made at the central governmental level) shows no pattern in the nineteenth and early twentieth centuries. "From 1913 to the present, however, most countries have had a rising centralization ratio which has accompanied a rising per capita GNP and population."[19] The trend was mixed, however, in the period 1950-62. Finally, "in regard to public consumption expenditures there are few essential differences between nations of the two systems. . . ."[20] Differences are primarily those of policy, which nations in either system could adopt.

The general conclusion that planned economies are somewhat more effective in mobilizing resources but somewhat less efficient in using them is suggested in a careful study by Abram Bergson that compares the policies of economic development of the East European countries with each other and with those of Western Europe. More specifically, he finds that the rates of capital investment tend to be somewhat higher under socialism. The average annual rate of growth per worker is about the same as in Western Europe, however, and this is due to lower productivity per worker.[21]

Social Aspects

Social mobilization refers to that aspect of the general process of modernization that involves the transformation of human relations from the diffuse ones characteristic of premodern societies--in which the political, economic, and social commitments of most individuals are to the local community--to those characteristic of developed societies in which these commitments are predominantly at the national level before they take on transnational features as the world moves toward an ultimate global community. In relatively nonmodernized societies, production, economic mutual assistance, religion, and even defense are essentially tasks of the local community. Even language may be essentially of local concern, and dialects may vary sufficiently to hamper communication with neighboring communities.

The distinctive features of the policies of the East European countries in regard to social mobilization may be evaluated by seeing how they vary from the patterns of the more developed societies where the process of transformation was more gradual and less directed--less directed because there were no previous models to follow. Specifically, we wish to know in which respects the East European countries have gone further along these lines than those of Western Europe, despite their relatively lower level of development, and in which they are still relatively behind. To put it another way, which aspects of social mobilization have been assigned a higher priority and which a low--and what is the significance of this difference in emphasis?

In the centrally planned economies a much higher share of education is financed publicly, and probably a higher percent of working-class children enter into higher education than in Western Europe.[22] In terms of students per thousand of the relevant age group receiving degrees from institutions of higher learning, the ratio in 1962 is higher in Eastern (15) than in Western Europe (7), although not nearly as high as in the United States (43).[23] Public consumption expenditures devoted to research and development as a proportion of GNP were relatively higher in Eastern than Western Europe, although again much lower than in the United States.[24] There is a substantially higher ratio of defense expenditures to GNP in Eastern Europe than Western Europe, although all are well below the level of the United States and the USSR.[25]

The aspects of social mobilization that were similar in the two sets of countries include health services. Health inputs (doctors, dentists, nurses, hospital beds) were somewhat higher in Eastern than Western Europe, but outputs (infant mortality, life expectancy) were somewhat lower.[26] In the two sets of countries, the ratio of primary and secondary school teachers to the labor force was also about the same.[27]

Lower performance included ratio of teachers' salaries to blue-collar workers, much lower in Eastern Europe (80-100) except East Germany (192), than in Western Europe (160-180), although the U.S. ratio was only 105.[28] In regard to nourishment, Eastern Europe ate more potatoes, Western Europe more meat.[29] Construction of dwellings and of floor space per capita was significantly lower in Eastern Europe in the 1960s.[30] Similarly, in the realm of consumer goods (except motorcycles) the level in Eastern Europe was significantly lower.[31]

CONCLUSIONS

The evidence examined here in regard to the political, economic, and social aspects of modernization in Eastern Europe provides only limited answers to fundamental questions regarding the respective roles of political culture, level of development, and policies of modernization.

The institutional heritage of the East European countries no doubt accounts for the relatively low standard of political performance, and of productivity of labor and capital. The price paid for the degree of self-determination attained by these countries at the end of World War I has not been fully appreciated. It should be recalled that only Czechoslovakia among these countries surpassed the 1913 level of GNP per capita in the period 1918-39, and it maintained that level only for a short time. The economic nationalism of the 1920s, followed by the depression in the 1930s and World War II in the 1940s, prevented these countries (with the exception of Czechoslovakia) from developing the business and managerial skills required for high levels of productivity.[32]

Although communism was essentially imposed on these countries, their experience with free competition among political parties under reasonably stable conditions was severely limited. A generous estimate would include 1918-23 and 1931-34 in Bulgaria, 1918-26 in Poland, 1918-19 in Hungary, 1918-34 in Yugoslavia, 1925-28 in Albania, and 1918-37 in Romania. The case of Czechoslovakia is again exceptional in this regard. The success of the USSR in establishing an orbit of predominant influence may also be attributed in considerable degree to the political culture of this region. The successive failures of the French and German political hegemonies in Eastern Europe between 1918 and 1945 predisposed political leaders in this region to seek alternative solutions. Without discounting the role of Soviet military power, one should also note the different response of Finland to a Soviet pressure that was scarcely less powerful.

The level of development is of course an underlying factor in explaining the more general characteristics of the
East European countries as compared with the most developed
and the least developed. At a more detailed and specific
level, however, it does not explain a great deal. In the
economic realm, for instance, it is significant for public
expenditures for internal security, foreign aid, and research and development, but not for most of the other economic indicators.

Given this evaluation of the role of political culture
and the level of development, the policies of modernization
characteristic of the communist systems go far to explain
many of the more specific features of the system. The exclusive role of a single party; the system of political participation that excludes the influence of the greater part
of the population as citizens and consumers; the emphasis of
investment policy on heavy industry, and on higher education
and research--these policies reflect the characteristic communist pattern of mobilization.

The very sketchy answers provided in this chapter to
political, economic, and social aspects of comparative modernization reflect in considerable degree the limitations of
much of the published research on Eastern Europe and, by the
same token, the types of research that still need to be done.
Much of the scholarly work on Eastern Europe by social scientists, including that of political scientists, tends to be
more historical and descriptive than analytical. It answers
the question, what has happened?, rather than the more interesting question, what has been the relative success of
these countries in solving the characteristic problems of
the modern era? The studies cited in the main body of this
chapter are examples of what can be done. More and better
studies are needed along lines such as these.

One may question in this context the value of comparative communism as a focus of research. The question of the
varieties of policy among communist countries is an interesting one, but the answers are limited to a rather narrow
range of experience. If one is interested in learning about
the diversity of the institutional means by which certain
common policies can be implemented, it is more important to
compare the USSR with Japan or the United States than with
Czechoslovakia or even China.

Until recently, research in the West and in the East
has pursued separate paths, and the more ideologically oriented Marxist-Leninist social scientists have accused comparative modernization of the heresy of "teoriia edinogo
industrialnogo obshchestva"--the mistaken view that levels
of industrialization prevail over ownership of the means of

production as the determining factor in development. As
leadership in these countries has moved from "revolutionary
activist" to "managerial and technical," however, the human
sciences have come to prevail over ideology (at least in the
academies of science) to the extent that scholarly cooperation is now feasible.[33] An outstanding example of this is
the work of the European Coordination Centre for Research
and Documentation in the Social Sciences, in Vienna, under
whose auspices the impressive study of the Multinational
Comparative Time Budget Research Project under the direction
of Alexander Szalai was carried out.[34]

NOTES

1. Current work on Eastern Europe may be followed in
Bogdan Denitch, "Sociology in Eastern Europe: Trends and
Prospects," Slavic Review 30 (June 1971): 317-39; Jesse J.
Dossick's annual lists of doctoral dissertations in the De-
cember issues of the Slavic Review since 1964; Charles
Jelavich, ed., Language and Area Studies: East Central and
Southeastern Europe (Chicago: University of Chicago Press,
1969); Frederic J. Fleron, ed., Communist Studies and the
Social Sciences (Chicago: Rand McNally, 1969); Jerzy J.
Wiatr, ed., The State of Sociology in Eastern Europe Today
(Carbondale: Southern Illinois University Press, 1971);
Roger E. Kanet, ed., The Behavioral Revolution and Communist
Studies: Applications of Behaviorally Oriented Political Re-
search on the Soviet Union and Eastern Europe (New York:
Free Press, 1971); and the relevant periodicals, especially
ABSEES: Soviet and East European Abstracts Series, Canadian
Slavic Review, Newsletter on Comparative Studies of Commu-
nism, Osteuropa, Problems of Communism, Slavic Review,
Slavonic and East European Review, Sociology and Eastern
Europe, and Survey: A Journal of East and West Studies.
2. Lucian W. Pye and Sidney Verba, eds., Political
Culture and Political Development (Princeton, N.J.: Princeton, N.J.: Princeton University Press, 1965); Robert C.
Tucker, "Communism and Political Culture," Newsletter on
Comparative Studies of Communism 4 (May 1971): 3-12;
Dorothy Knapp, David W. Paul, and Gerson Sher, "Digest of
the Conference on Political Culture and Comparative Communist Studies," Newsletter 5 (May 1972): 2-17.
3. Cyril E. Black et al., The Modernization of Japan
and Russia (in progress).
4. Myron Weiner, "The Macedonian Syndrome: An Historical Model of International Relations and Political Development," World Politics 23 (July 1971): 665-83.

5. Peter F. Sugar, The Industrialization of Bosnia-Hercegovina, 1878-1918 (Seattle: University of Washington Press, 1963).

6. David W. Paul, "Nationalism, Pluralism, and Schweikism in Czechoslovakia's Political Culture" (Ph.D. dissertation, Princeton University, 1972).

7. International Bank for Reconstruction and Development, World Bank Atlas (Washington, D.C., 1972), p. 4.

8. Harry Eckstein, The Evaluation of Political Performance: Problems and Dimensions (Beverly Hills: Sage Publications, 1971); Ted Robert Gurr and Muriel McClelland, Political Performance: A Twelve-Nation Study (Beverly Hills: Sage Publications, 1971).

9. Carl Beck, "Leadership Attributes in Eastern Europe: The Effect of Country and Time," in Comparative Communist Political Leadership, ed. Carl Beck et al. (New York: David McKay, 1973), pp. 86-153.

10. M. George Zaninovich, "Elites and Citizenry in Yugoslav Society: A Study of Value Differentiation," in ibid., pp. 226-97.

11. H. Gordon Skilling and Franklyn Griffiths, eds., Interest Groups in Soviet Politics (Princeton, N.J.: Princeton University Press, 1971); see also Bohdan Harasymiw, "Application of the Concept of Pluralism to the Soviet Political System," Newsletter on Comparative Studies of Communism 5 (November 1971): 40-54.

12. Andrzej Korbonski, "Bureaucracy and Interest Groups in Communist Societies: The Case of Czechoslovakia," Studies in Comparative Communism 4 (January 1971): 57-59.

13. Frederick L. Pryor, Public Expenditures in Communist and Capitalist Nations (Homewood, Ill.: Richard D. Irwin, 1968), p. 31.

14. U.S. Congress, Joint Economic Committee, Economic Developments in Countries of Eastern Europe (Washington, D.C., 1970), p. 42.

15. Pryor, op. cit., p. 277.

16. Ibid., p. 284.

17. Ibid., p. 285.

18. Ibid., p. 288.

19. Ibid., p. 73.

20. Ibid., p. 310.

21. Abram Bergson, "Development Under Two Systems: Comparative Productivity Growth Since 1950," World Politics 23 (July 1971): 597-617.

22. Pryor, op. cit., p. 309.

23. Ibid., p. 195.

24. Ibid., p. 267.

25. Ibid., p. 91.

26. Ibid., p. 418.

27. Ibid., p. 430.

28. Ibid., p. 428.

29. Joint Economic Committee, op. cit., pp. 304-06.

30. Ibid., p. 311.

31. Ibid., pp. 311-14.

32. Frederick Hertz, The Economic Problems of the Danubian States: A Study in Economic Nationalism (New York: Fertig, 1947), pp. 218-23.

33. Cyril E. Black, "Marxism and Modernization," Slavic Review 29 (June 1970): 182-86 cites the relevant literature.

34. Alexander Szalai et al., eds., The Use of Time: A Cross-National Comparative Study of Daily Activities of Urban and Suburban Populations in Twelve Countries (forthcoming).

MODERNIZATION AND COMMUNIST POWER: FOUR CASE STUDIES

INTRODUCTION: COMPARATIVE POLITICAL DEVELOPMENT IN EASTERN EUROPE

Robert Sharlet

Rather than losing "Eastern Europe" in the terminological thickets, I am going to bypass the definitional problems of the term "modernization." Instead, I take the position that "the closure that strict definition consists in is not a precondition of scientific inquiry but its culmination,"[1] and will proceed directly to outline a framework within which to analyze the case studies in this section.

I would suggest the following agenda for the comparative study of political development in Eastern Europe: (1) a study of the changing roles of the Communist Parties in the development process; (2) an analysis of the varying modes of reception (and/or rejection) of the Soviet command model of development[2] in Eastern Europe; (3) a comparison of the Communist Party and/or party-state responses to the unwanted as well as the planned consequences of political development.[3]

CHANGING ROLES OF THE COMMUNIST PARTIES

There are three ideal-type roles for the Party in the development process. First, there is the Party as the independent variable, the causal agent of development. The Romanian case study in which the Party is characterized as the vanguard, armed with its ideology, which constantly strives to lead in the development process and direct the society, appears to offer the closest approximation in reality of this ideal type. However, whether the Romanian Party actually "leads" (or for that matter any other Communist Party) "is an empirical question, not an absolute given in the post-Stalin period."[4]

The second ideal-type role is best expressed by the anonymous statement that the Romanian Party leader Ceausescu "may be the last one in the bloc who thinks the party is shaping society. The others know it's the other way around."[5] The implication is that the Party is a dependent variable responsive to endogenous or exogenous independent variables (such as domestic strategic elites or the USSR respectively). The Hungarian case study, which examines the Party's dependency on the Soviet Union during the revolutionary phase in Hungary, suggests the second ideal type.

The Czechoslovak case study, especially in the discussion of the events of 1968, illustrates both variations of this role type. During the spring of 1968, social forces appeared to be shaping the Czechoslovak Communist Party. As the crisis grew, the Party seemed to be caught in a classic role conflict as contradictory internal and external forces both strove to influence its course of action. Finally, the invasion of August 1968 resolved the conflict in the direction of the stronger force and the Party became directly dependent upon the USSR.

A third ideal-type role for the Party in the development process is that of a noncritical variable--neither a hegemonial nor a client Party. Yugoslavia, which has been described as becoming a "non-Party system"[6] and even a "Rechtsstaat,"[7] has the only Party (or to be precise, "League") for which this category could be useful as a means of classification. The Yugoslav League of Communists neither decisively leads nor follows but, instead, appears to participate in the course of development through a legislative process that is far more highly articulated and significant in Yugoslavia than in any other East European state.

Each of the case studies in this section tends to illuminate one or more phases of the communist development process, therefore ideal typing of the Party's role in this process can be initially helpful as a preliminary means of classification. In reality, however, development is an ongoing process and a party's role accordingly changes over time and in conjunction with the circumstances of national political development. As a result, mixed types or hybrid categories (combining two or more ideal types) are likely to be far more useful in carrying out actual comparisons of the roles of different Communist Parties in the development of their respective societies. Below, I will sketch out two such hybrid roles that I would suggest the East European Communist Party fulfills in sequential order over a period of time.

After the successful attainment of power, the Party (subject to direct Soviet influence) serves as either the initiator or catalyst of change by setting in motion or accelerating the development process. This can be described as "directed development" or the "command phase" in which the Party acts directly upon the society by creating or "midwifing" new socioeconomic structures. In its preliminary role, then, the Party either initiates (say, in backward Albania) or catalyzes (as demonstrated in the Hungarian case study where the society was ripe for change) qualitative social change. In either instance, the Party soon becomes the principal agent of this change, utilizing its ideology to legitimatize (both for the mass public and the Party membership) its attainment of power and its subsequent disruption of the extant politicosocioeconomic order to make way for communist political development.

Once the development process is well under way in Eastern Europe (say after the short-term recovery plans and into the five-year plans), the Party gradually begins to transform itself into the role of the coordinator of development, the role implied in Jerry Hough's metaphor of the lower party secretary as "prefect."[8] This transformation is a slow process of adaptation as the Party assumes a lower profile in the development process by allowing for some interplay between itself and certain sectors of the society. The result is that social change now comes about less through unidimensionality and more through the codimensional efforts of Party and society. Simultaneously, the function of the Party's ideology undergoes change as it becomes more significant for the individual Party member's self-identification and as a device for the maintenance of intra-Party cohesion and less important as a message for public consumption and a means of mass mobilization.

It is difficult to forecast, but the ultimate role of the Party (stifled for the time being by the Soviet invasion of Czechoslovakia) may be a modified version of the familiar bargaining model with the Party "brokering" between competing interests in the development process while reserving the right to intervene, when necessary, in the national interest.

THE SOVIET COMMAND MODEL OF DEVELOPMENT

Turning to the question of the varying modes of reception of the Soviet command model of development, the point of departure is the initial post-World War II reception (or imposition) of the Soviet model throughout Eastern Europe in the form of a coherent body of ideas, institutions, and social processes for organizing, controlling, and developing a less-developed society. However, beyond the formative years, the reception (or rejection as in Yugoslavia) has varied considerably.

In Czechoslovakia, the Party, primarily fulfilling the role of a dependent variable influenced by an exogenous force (the USSR), applied the Soviet command model of development for two decades with the result of "overinstitutionalization."[9] As the Czechoslovak case study demonstrates in detail, a major dysfunction occurred to the point that Czechoslovakia represents a process of "demodernization."

The basic source of the problem, which has relevance beyond Czechoslovakia, was identified by a Western Marxist economist, the late Paul Baran, who wrote in 1962:

> The very system of extreme pressure on consumption, of unquestioned subordination to authority, and of rigidly dogmatic concentration on principal targets, which was imposed by Stalin and which enabled the Soviet Union to get over the "hump" of initial industrialization--this very system has turned, in the current phase of history, into a prohibitive obstacle to further economic and social growth.[10]

Since Czechoslovakia was already so highly developed at the time of the communist seizure of power, the Soviet command model has had especially negative consequences from the outset.

The Romanian case study suggests a very different mode of reception of the Soviet model, especially during the past decade. The Party, fulfilling much more the role of an independent variable (although subject to Soviet influence on the parameters of its actions), has filtered the Soviet command model of development through its cultural screen and thereby rejected, for example, the assimilationist tendencies implied in the corollary Soviet policy on nationalities. Although the Soviet model was received mechanically and uncritically in postrevolutionary Romania (as elsewhere in Eastern Europe), more recently the process of reception has become very selective and subject to modification by indigenous forces in Romania.

Yugoslavia represents the opposite end of the spectrum from Czechoslovakia in terms of the reception of the Soviet model. Very early in its postrevolutionary phase, the Yugoslav Communist Party rejected the Soviet model and embarked upon an effort (which continues until today) to fashion a political configuration perhaps unique unto itself among modern nation-states. The legislative process alone (which, unlike other East European states, is a significant factor in Yugoslav policy making) is exceptionally complex. The forthcoming new Yugoslav constitution is expected to further differentiate policy-making structures in the direction of greater decentralization with the intention of reducing or at least containing nationality tensions in contemporary Yugoslavia.[11]

In effect, the League of Communists in Yugoslavia has supplanted the Soviet model of development with one of its own. As such, the Yugoslav "model" includes the problem of an unresolved conflict between the often-contradictory imperatives of ideology and organization.[12] For example, as the Yugoslav case study implies, the ideological commitment to popularization or deprofessionalization of the economic and legislative processes conflicts with the need to institutionalize these processes to a degree consistent with the requirements of on-going macrodevelopment of the society. This inherent tension in the Yugoslav model manifests itself from the level of the enterprise (for example, the "self management" system) to the federal legislature (for example, the problem of turnover of legislators). On the positive side, the interaction of ideology and organization is reflected in the factionalism among the Yugoslav elites and, in this way, contributes to the dynamism of the Yugoslav system.[13]

RESPONSES TO THE CONSEQUENCES OF DEVELOPMENT

The final item on the agenda is the Party's and the party-state's responses to both the planned and unwanted consequences of the development process they initiated, directed, and coordinated. Taking first planned change, the economy has been the principal object of the Party's development efforts. In almost every East European country, the Party has been successful, to one degree or another, in bringing about significant economic development. The one exception has been Czechoslovakia, where, as the case study demonstrates, the planned application of the Soviet strategy for producing rapid, heavy industrialization to an already industrialized economy had the opposite effect of depressing economic growth and development.

As for the Party's coordination of economic development in other East European states, the question needs to be raised of whether or not they are merely "responding to economic forces which they only partially control, or to the economic-technical consequentials of the policies which they themselves decided. . . ."[14] In effect, the Party in Eastern Europe may no longer be able to cope effectively with the complex consequences of the economy it created (or in the Czechoslovak case, weakened).

A second important aspect of planned change provided in the Soviet command model is the commitment to education, which has, as its eventual consequence, feedback effects on the composition of the ruling elite. I am referring to education in the sense of a massive investment in specialized training that in the USSR over a period of time has yielded thousands of engineers and other specialists who have come to form strategic elites within and around the Party.

The pertinent question for Eastern Europe, where the commitment to education has only in recent years begun to yield specialized cadres in large numbers, is whether the Communist Party will respond to the subsequent feedback and allow the new specialists access to the policy-making process. The answers will no doubt vary from country to country. One point however is certain: Access by specialists to the decision-making process will be essential in the middle and long run if the Party with its first- and second-generation leadership of generalists or professional politicians intends to keep abreast of and remain in control of an increasingly complicated development process. The severe riots in Gdansk and other northern Polish cities of Christmas 1970, precipitated by certain ill-conceived and poorly timed economic decisions of an aging Party leadership, was an extreme result of one Party's failure to respond positively to the inevitable consequences of its own commitment to education.[15] The post-Gomulka leadership has wisely increased access to the policy-making process by the new generation of specialists in Poland.

The Romanian case study suggests that the problem of access to the decision-making process is very much at hand. The development process has begun to generate an educated society from which a series of specialized elites are emerging. The crucial question for the future is to what extent will the top leadership of the Romanian Communist Party increase access to its policy deliberations so that the specialists can assist in the more sophisticated coordination of advanced development.

In contrast, the question of access has already been settled in Yugoslavia, primarily through the decentralization and specialization of the policy-making process. The problem now is of a different nature--how to encourage turnover or renewal of elites congruent with the League of Communists' ideological commitment toward popularization of the political process. The present situation, as the Yugoslav case study indicates, tends to give precedence to institutionalization with the elites recirculating (rather than turning over) by "migrating" from one decision-making arena to another.[16]

In the area of the unwanted consequences of development, the Party and party-state in Eastern Europe is faced with some equally challenging problems. I will mention only two major problems briefly. First, there is the cluster of problems that are the familiar by-products of a rapid drive toward an urban-industrial society, namely acute housing shortages in the cities, the diminution of family authority

and the rise of juvenile delinquency, and a growing inci-
dence of crime. This cluster of problems is by no means
peculiar to Eastern Europe; one or more of them seem to be
concomitant with the general phenomenon of urbanization and
industrialization. However, their existence in Eastern
Europe will make it all the more imperative that the top
Party elites draw upon their cadres of specialists to deal
with these social problems.

A second unwanted consequence of communist political
development is the resurgence of ethnic nationalism that has
long been a traditional problem in Eastern Europe. The historic ethnic antagonisms, muted since the onset of communist
regimes throughout the region, have begun to reappear, at
least within Yugoslavia where the cleavages are becoming
more (rather than less) pronounced in the context of development (for example, ethnic disputes over the allocation of
investment capital and the distribution of foreign exchange
earnings). As is suggested in the Romanian case study, more
education and other aspects of social development may well
correlate with increased (rather than decreased) ethnic-
group cohesion and a heightened awareness of the group's
heritage. This, then, raises the question of whether Yugoslavia is the exception or a harbinger of renewed ethnic
conflict in Eastern Europe expressed in the vocabulary of
"development." If the latter turns out to be the case,
this could mean a serious crisis of authority in Eastern
Europe for the future.

This has been a preliminary agenda (with no intention
of being exhaustive) for the study of comparative political
development in Eastern Europe. Hopefully, it may be useful
by indicating the possibilities for systematic comparative
analyses of the East European communist systems.

NOTES

1. Abraham Kaplan, The Conduct of Inquiry (San Fran-
cisco: Chandler, 1964), p. 77.
2. For an outline of the "model," see Robert Sharlet,
"The Soviet Union as a Developing Country," Journal of Developing Areas 2, no. 2 (1968): esp. 273-76.
3. I am using Douglas Dowd's meaning for the term
"development": "growth is a quantitative process, involving
principally the extension of an already established structure, whereas development suggests qualitative changes, the
creation of new economic and non-economic structures."
Quoted in Karl de Schweinitz, Jr., "Growth, Development,
and Political Modernization," World Politics 22, no. 4
(July 1970): 518.

4. Milton C. Lodge, Soviet Elite Attitudes Since Stalin (Columbus, Ohio: Chas. E. Merrill, 1969), p. 30.

5. A young Pole in Warsaw quoted in James Feron, "Ideology on Decline in Eastern Europe," New York Times, March 22, 1973, p. 4.

6. M. George Zaninovich, The Development of Socialist Yugoslavia (Baltimore: Johns Hopkins University Press, 1968), p. 152.

7. Winston M. Fisk, "The Constitutionalism Movement in Yugoslavia," Slavic Review 30, no. 2 (June 1971): 296.

8. See Jerry F. Hough, The Soviet Prefects: The Local Party Organs in Industrial Decision-Making (Cambridge, Mass.: Harvard University Press, 1969).

9. This term is used in the following sense: "If the characteristic difficulty at the transitional portion of the development continuum is political decay--the result of a low level of institutionalization--the characteristic difficulty at the developed portion is political constraint, a result of overinstitutionalization." See Mark Kesselman, "Overinstitutionalization and Political Constraint: The Case of France," Comparative Politics 3, no. 1 (October 1970): 25.

10. Paul A. Baran, The Longer View: Essays Toward a Critique of Political Economy, ed. John O'Neill (New York: Monthly Review Press, 1969), p. 376.

11. See Paul Shoup, "The National Question in Yugoslavia," Problems of Communism 21, no. 1 (January-February 1972): esp. 25-27.

12. See William N. Dunn, "Ideology and Organization in Socialist Yugoslavia: Modernization and the Obsolescence of Praxis," Newsletter on Comparative Studies of Communism 5, no. 4 (August 1972): 21-56.

13. For a discussion of the factionalism over economic theory and policy, see Deborah D. Milenkovitch, Plan and Market in Yugoslav Economic Thought (New Haven, Conn.: Yale University Press, 1971), Chapter 12.

14. Alec Nove, The Soviet Economy: An Introduction, 2d rev. ed. (New York: Praeger, 1969), p. 17.

15. For a theoretical discussion of access and modernization with specific reference to the restricted access of specialists in Poland under Gomulka's leadership of the Party, see Dennis Pirages, "Modernization: New Decisional Models in Socialist Society," in Political Leadership in Eastern Europe and the Soviet Union, ed. R. Barry Farrell (Chicago: Aldine, 1970), Chapter 11.

16. This statement is based on the oral comments of Lenard J. Cohen at the conference "Eastern Europe: The Impact of Modernization on Political Development," Columbia University, March 23-24, 1973.

3

**HUNGARY: THE DYNAMICS
OF REVOLUTIONARY
TRANSFORMATION**
Charles Gati

This study seeks to modify Western interpretations of
the communist seizure of power in Hungary. It questions the
view that the communist coup in 1947-48 and the subsequent
political hegemony of the Communist Party of Hungary can be
explained exclusively in terms of external influences. Such
influences are generally identified as Western inaction and
indifference as well as persistent Soviet political and economic pressure. In particular, the presence of Soviet
troops on Hungarian soil is offered as conclusive evidence
that revolutionary change after World War II was imposed on
Hungary exclusively from without. Conversely, it is suggested that the communist coup, and presumably the modernizing process effected by the Communist Party subsequently,
basically lacked indigenous support both in Hungary and
elsewhere in East Central Europe, with the possible exception of Czechoslovakia.[1]
  Without denying the primacy of external influences and
the general validity of such interpretations, this chapter
seeks to focus on the internal background of communist hegemony in Hungary. It is not proposed here that communist
political success was not dependent on Soviet support; the
objective of this chapter is to suggest that fundamental
changes in the fabric of Hungarian society, particularly on
the eve of and during World War II, had set the stage for
the approaching revolutionary change. Indeed, the question

This chapter originally appeared in the East European
Quarterly 5, no. 3 (October 1971): 325-59. Reprinted by
permission. The author is indebted to Robert Sharlet and
Rudolf L. Tokes for their helpful criticism of an earlier
draft of this chapter. Original title: "Modernization and
Communist Power in Hungary."

after the war was no longer whether there would be change at all or whether the country could choose between evolutionary or revolutionary change; these questions had been settled--and settled primarily by previous economic, social, and political developments--in favor of further _and_ revolutionary change. The question actually facing Hungary, then, was the nature and direction of revolutionary transformation, with the choice in fact limited to two competing radical models of development--the populist-agrarian model and the communist-industrial model. In this context, the Soviet Union can be viewed as the catalyzer rather than the sole creator of revolutionary change.

The validity and implications of this interpretation are developed in the four sections of this study. In the first section, an outline is presented of the salient features of the modernizing process in Hungary, with some emphasis on the efforts and characteristics of Horthy's syncratic political system in the interwar period. The second section analyzes the two competing revolutionary (that is, populist and communist) formulas for Hungary's economic and political development. The third section deals with the results of the 1945 elections and with the respective positions of the prominent political parties at the time to ascertain the extent of popular support for the various models of development. Finally, a brief section at the end offers a few concluding remarks on modernization and communist power in Hungary.

STAGES OF MODERNIZATION

The process of modernization in Hungary might be divided into three stages of development.[2] The first or initial stage lasted from the second half of the nineteenth century, particularly from 1867, to the onset of World War I; the second or transitional stage occurred during the interwar period; the third or revolutionary stage began in 1944.*

---

*Further breakdowns of each stage of development can only be indicated here. The initial stage may thus be subdivided into the 1848-67 and 1867-1918 periods, the transitional stage into the 1920-33 and 1933-44 periods, and the revolutionary stage into 1944-56, 1956-66, and 1967 periods. Systematic elaboration on these subdivisions is beyond the scope of this chapter.

Initial Stage

If "modernization," in its most general meaning, denotes increasingly rapid political, social, and intellectual change under the impact of industrialization, Hungary had been barely touched by the wind of modernization until the second part of the nineteenth century. As late as the 1830s, the country's famous reformer, Count Istvan Szechenyi, still identified Hungary as his "great fallow-land." Less than 5 percent of the population lived in communities officially designated as towns or was employed in industry or trade. As of 1848, political rights, or rather certain political rights, were enjoyed by only 44,000 of the 136,000 "noble" families. Most functions of the courts were exercised by the landed aristocracy.

After the revolution of 1848-49 and particularly after the establishment of the Dual Monarchy in 1867, however, the challenge of modernization could no longer be denied. Economic retardation was increasingly becoming a source of embarrassment even for the landed aristocracy, and for this reason industrialization was stimulated by necessity as well as national pride. In the wake of Count Szechenyi, a small group of intellectuals, merchants, and artisans spearheaded the movement aimed at the adaptation of Western ideas and institutions. Progress was indicated by the decrease of uncultivated land from 22 percent in 1870 to 15 percent in 1890 to 5 percent in 1910. With the introduction, on a small scale, of fertilization and mechanization, the wheat crop per hectare* increased by nearly 60 percent between 1870 and 1890. The number of banks and savings and loan institutions grew from 41 in 1867 to over 600 by the early 1890s. The length of railways--an important prerequisite to, and indicator of, industrialization--was drastically extended from 1,350 miles in 1866 to 8,226 miles in 1896 to 13,625 miles in 1913. Trains that carried fewer than 3.5 million persons and less than 3 million shipping tons of goods in 1866 increased their capacity so that by 1894 the corresponding figures were 50 million persons and 27 million shipping tons of goods.

This intrusion of modernity, particularly during the last decade of the century, slowly began to leave its imprint on the country's social structure. The industrial population grew by 127 percent between 1870 and 1910 in contrast to a 36 percent increase of the whole population. By 1900, 16.7 percent of the population was employed in

---

*One hectare = about 2.5 acres.

transportation and industry (mainly the former) as opposed
to 13.8 percent in 1890; in the same period, the agricultural population decreased from 72.5 percent to 68.4 percent. Concurrently, the number of "large" factories, employing more than 20 workers, grew from 1,129 in 1890 to
1,756 in 1900 to 2,180 in 1910. Labor unions came into existence in 1899, and in the capital city of Budapest almost
one out of three workers joined the labor movement. The
scope of governmental activities was indicated by the growth
of the state bureaucracy:. The number of public servants increased from 25,000 in 1870 to 230,000 by the end of World
War I.

The government's growing interest in education was revealed by the budget of the Ministry of Religion and Education: It was increased from 0.82 percent of the total governmental budget in 1868 to 3.54 percent in 1900 to 5.54
percent in 1913. As a result, while about two out of three
Hungarians were illiterate in 1869, by 1890 it was less than
one out of two, by 1900 about two out of five, and by 1910
only one out of three. The output of graduates at the nation's universities also increased, although they still produced more lawyers than doctors, engineers, and scientists
together. Finally, the impact of modern culture was illustrated by the publication of Huszadik Szazad (Twentieth
Century) and of Nyugat (West) whose orientation clearly reflected the intelligentsia's growing interest in Western
culture.[3]

Such economic, social, and cultural developments obviously required, or should have required, political readjustments. On balance, however, the landed aristocracy and
the slowly emerging gentry, which dominated the top echelons
of the government after 1867, could not govern effectively,
let alone guide or direct the process of modernization.[4]
Specifically, the various governments of the 1867-1914 period
faced four crucial problems,[5] none of which did they seem
able to resolve or substantially mitigate.

First, the non-Magyar nationalities became increasingly
dissatisfied with their economic and political status during
this period, and their opposition to what they conceived to
be Hungarian domination remained complete. Their assimilation into and hence the integration of Hungarian society--
a major component of modernization--was left unresolved.
Second, the poverty and hopelessness of the agrarian population, if anything, continued to increase. As C. A.
Macartney noted,

It was calculated that by the end of the century [agricultural] laborers got enough to

feed themselves and their families adequately
only when the harvest had been "exceptionally
good"; another authority said that the conditions of the laborers had gone down by at
least 50 percent since 1848. Starvation dis-
eases were common. Hours of work had been
lengthened to the extreme limit. The agrarian
labor legislation of the period consisted almost exclusively of enactments designed to
prevent the laborers from defending their interests against those of the landlords.[6]

The third problem was that of the industrial proletariat.
Particularly after 1867, industrial growth was accomplished
overwhelmingly at the expense of the industrial working
class. The government in fact encouraged low wages, especially for unskilled labor, so as to develop native industrial strength in the face of competition from the great
manufacturing centers of Austria and Bohemia. The fourth
problem, persistent nationalist agitation against the Dual
Monarchy, provided for an acute crisis of the political
elites throughout the period as the country's two political
parties collided on the issue of Hungary's proper relationship with Austria: The Party of Independence considered
the Dual Monarchy a disadvantageous and dangerous arrangement, while the Liberal Party regarded it as a guarantee
of Hungary's undisturbed future.

    As Table 3.1 shows, the country's problems were re-
flected in the social composition of the Hungarian parliament. Of the six occupational groups identified here, four
were heavily overrepresented (that is, landowners, the intelligentsia, government bureaucrats, and the clergy); yet
the most vivid discrepancy was shown between the enormous
size of the laboring classes in the total population, on
the one hand, and their lack of political representation, on
the other. Two trends worth noting after 1920 were the
gradual decrease of the number of landowners and the slow
but steady increase of the number of entrepreneurs and members of the working classes in the legislature. These
trends, however, became evident only in the second or transitional phase of modernization; in the initial phase, the
political structure still reflected more continuity than
change as the country's landowners and lawyers continued to
occupy strategic positions in the political system.

    The available data on representation do not reveal yet
another trend within the political elite, that is, the rise
of the Hungarian gentry whose growing influence at the expense of the landed aristocracy was a development of major

TABLE 3.1

Social Composition of the Hungarian Parliament, 1887-1931

Election	Landowners		Intelligentsia (Lawyers, etc.)		Government Bureaucrats		Entrepreneurs		Clergy		Working Class	
	% of Repr.	% of Pop.	% of Repr.	% of Pop.	% of Repr.	% of Pop.	% of Repr.	% of Pop.	% of Repr.	% of Pop.	% of Repr.	% of Pop.
1887	31.3	19.6	33.4		26.0		5.8	6.6	3.5		--	72.5
1892	37.5	19.8	35.0	0.7	18.1	0.4	5.8		3.6	0.2	--	
1896	31.7		29.6		29.3		5.8	3.6	3.6		--	75.3
1901	34.8*		34.5		20.5		5.8		4.1		0.3	
1905	31.7	20.7	40.1	0.8	18.2	0.7	3.9	6.6	4.9	0.3	1.2	70.9
1906	33.7		41.0		10.8		5.3		8.0		1.2	
1910	36.8	21.1	33.9	1.0	18.3	1.1	6.8	7.6	3.1		1.1	68.9
1920	30.0		31.0		15.8		7.7		12.1		3.4	
1922	26.9	15.4	27.4		22.0	1.7	7.8	8.5	6.1		9.8	
1927	26.6		30.6	1.4	24.1		6.9		6.1	0.2	5.7	72.8
1931	22.5		32.2		26.1		8.6		3.7		6.9	

Source: Adapted from Rezso Rudai, "Adalek a magyar kepviselohaz szociologiajahoz 1887-1931" [Data on the social composition of the Hungarian Parliament 1887-1931], Tarsadalom-tudomany [Social science] 13 (1933): 218-19.

significance. The gentry, to be sure, was divided: Its
lower stratum--economically less privileged, culturally deprived, and fearful of losing untenable prerogatives--al-
lied with the aristocracy against modernization and argued
for closer ties with Vienna. However, the higher stratum
of the gentry--educated, quite well-to-do, distinctly cos-
mopolitan and urbane--offered itself as a substitute, as it
were, for the urban middle class and welcomed Western influences. Thus the Hungarian political elite was becoming
rather evenly divided between the conservative aristocracy
and the poorer segment of the gentry, on the one hand, and
the progressive well-to-do segment of the gentry, on the
other. Accordingly, it showed a casual attitude toward industrialization: It neither impeded nor guided it.[7]

As a result, the tempo of industrialization was moderately slow, with the rate of economic growth reaching 3.0
percent in agriculture and 4.4 percent in mining and manufacturing by 1910.[8] A genuine opportunity for more rapid
modernization was missed in view of what has been called the
"uniquely favorable institutional and economic setting for
the development of both agriculture and industry" provided
by the economic setup of the Dual Monarchy, that is, a
guaranteed market for Hungary's agricultural exports coupled
with administrative measures protecting the emerging Hungarian industry.[9] The opportunity was missed largely because
the transfer of power from traditional to modernizing leaders had only begun and no decisive break with a predominantly agrarian life as yet occurred. In the countryside,
practically all of the country's cultivable land remained
in a few hands and land ownership remained a determining
factor in both politics and social advancement. Indeed,
social mobility lagged behind Hungary's economic development. Such early channels of social mobility as the civil
service and the military were still closed to members of
the lower classes.

Nonetheless, in a casual, almost haphazard fashion,
the feudal features of Hungarian society were being left
behind. The influence of a progressive gentry increased
and that of the landed aristocracy declined. Railroads
were built. Illiteracy was significantly reduced and the
country's school system was expanded. Western ideas im-
pregnated Hungary's intellectual life. In short, the
socioeconomic foundations of traditional society were being
undermined even if the intrusion of modernity did not as
yet cause social upheaval or political transformation.

Transitional Stage

The casual but steady process of modernization, which had characterized the first stage of development, led to a serious and largely successful attempt by the landed aristocracy to slow down the pace and ease the consequences of change during the premiership of Count Istvan Bethlen (1921-31). However, a dramatic reversal occurred in the 1930s; so much so, in fact, that by the eve of World War II Hungary became "industrialized" as illustrated by the fact that less than 50 percent of the country's population engaged in agricultural pursuits (see Table 3.2).

TABLE 3.2

Occupational Distribution in Hungary, 1900-41
(in percent per year)

Economic Branch	1900	1910	1920	1930	1941
Agriculture, forestry, and fishing	59.4	55.8	58.2	54.2	50.0*
Mining, metallurgy, manufacturing, commerce, transport, and communications	23.0	26.9	26.3	30.4	32.6
Government, community, business, and recreational services	4.6	5.7	6.1	7.7	8.0
National defense	1.7	1.6	2.4	1.0	3.2
Domestic service	6.2	5.7	4.3	4.5	3.7
Other	5.0	4.3	3.6	3.2	2.8

*Without forestry and fishing, 48.7 percent.

Source: Alexander Eckstein, "National Income and Capital Formation in Hungary, 1900-1950," in Income and Wealth, ed. Simon Kuznets, ser. V (London, 1955), p. 182.

This was the setting: Hungarian political life in the interwar period centered around two major questions. First, the regime of Regent Miklos Horthy (1920-44), which came into being after the collapse of the revolutions of 1918-19, was so repulsed by the revolutions that it allowed if not encouraged the notorious White Terror of 1920-21 to run its course, during which hundreds of communists, socialists,

and Jews were murdered without trial. Subsequently, the
Horthy regime failed to come to terms with the revolutions'
modernizing alternatives. Clearly, the Karolyi experiment
in 1918 offered a bourgeois-democratic model of industrialization and political development whose substance, meaning,
and appeal the Horthy regime could have utilized; in its
abhorrence, it spent its time and energy denouncing them.

Second, the Horthy regime was equally vehement in its
desire to revise the terms of the Treaty of Trianon which,
it claimed, represented a national defeat for Hungary. Indeed, when the new boundaries were drawn, only 28.6 percent
of the old kingdom remained as Hungary proper, with the
rest being assigned to the neighboring countries. As a
consequence of the new boundaries, Hungary's population decreased by over 60 percent. More than anything else, the
breakup of the Dual Monarchy and the dismemberment of Hungary was caused by the unjust Hungarian nationality policies
of the pre-1914 era, and the Treaty of Trianon expressed
the profound bitterness of the repressed nationalities who
had long opposed Hungarian rule and sought independence and
statehood. Supported by all shades of political opinion,
the Horthy regime argued, of course, that the punishment
meted out to Hungary was too severe and that the new boundaries were not well drawn. It claimed that more than half
of the 3.5 million Hungarians now separated from Hungary
lived in areas contiguous to their homeland and thus a more
equitable and just arrangement would have been possible.
Indeed, the new states of Czechoslovakia and Yugoslavia
were not homogeneous either; both were composed of several
different nationalities. At any rate, the Horthy regime
kept the question of revision alive at least partly in
order to divert attention from economic stagnation, social
injustice, and political regression.

To be sure, economic and fiscal reconstruction after
the war ran into serious obstacles. The currency was rapidly depreciating, and the budget was unbalanced. It was
clear from the beginning that reconstruction depended overwhelmingly on the government's ability to secure financial
assistance abroad; mainly for political reasons, however,
foreign loan was not available until 1924.[10] With the pro-
tection of the Dual Monarchy removed, moreover, the economy
was now dependent on foreign markets and foreign supplies,
and the country faced a serious balance of payments problem
as well. Since Hungary's major product for export was
wheat, whose world price tended to fluctuate, each time the
price of wheat fell the whole economy was affected. In
short, disruption and destruction inflicted by the war and
readjustment necessitated by the boundary changes made rapid
reconstruction exceedingly difficult.

Yet, World War I and the boundary changes effected by the Treaty of Trianon were not without potential benefits to economic and social change in Hungary. First, Trianon provided the basic conditions for the creation of national unity--a primary prerequisite for further modernization-- since it led to the disappearance of the divisive separatist movements of the ethnic minorities. Because of ethnic homogeneity, the Horthy regime could have attained firm political authority more easily and used it for the encouragement of the process of modernization. Second, the war had accelerated the development of industrial production in general and of the metal processing and engineering industries in particular; Hungary emerged from the war with an enlarged industrial capacity. The horsepower capacity of large-scale manufacturing, for example, had increased by 50 percent between 1913 and 1921, from about 400,000 to 600,000.[11] Moreover, the largest Hungarian manufacturing centers--Budapest, with its industrial suburbs, in particular--were not detached from the country. The largest financial and cultural centers also remained within Hungary and so did most of the trained personnel needed for industrialization. Third, the proportion of "very large" holdings in the countryside-- those over 1,000 hold (1,420 acres)--did increase somewhat, but the proportion of "very small" and thus uneconomical holdings--those from 0 to 10 hold (0 to 14.2 acres)--declined to 30 percent of what they had been prior to World War I.[12]

In short, while difficult and costly economic readjustments undoubtedly had to be made after the war, what added up to a temporary halt in the modernization process was caused primarily by the political leadership's determination to circumvent the consequences of modernization. Let us emphasize: Trianon offered a combination of opportunities, as well as impediments, for modernization; under Count Istvan Bethlen's premiership in the 1920s the opportunities were deliberately ignored. As a representative of his class, Bethlen sought order and stability at the same time that he longed for a return to the undisputed rule of the landed aristocracy.

The political system to serve such objectives can best be identified as a syncratic political system, using A. F. K. Organski's conceptual framework.[13] The system was characterized by the common or shared rule of the landed aristocracy and the lower segment of the gentry, on the one hand, and the upcoming industrial elite and the upper segment of the gentry, on the other. As elsewhere, too, syncratic politics occurred in Hungary during the transitional stage of modernization, at a time when the goal of industrialization had not yet been attained and when the industrial elite was still weaker than the old agricultural elite. Syncratic government, then, expressed the desire of the landed aristocracy "to slow the pace of industrialization and to control its consequences. . . . Faced with certain defeat, they nevertheless managed to maximize their power and postpone its final shift into other hands."[14]

As Table 3.3 illustrates, the Bethlen regime did not seek to stop the trend of industrialization altogether; it sought to control the processes of industrialization and to slow its pace without completely disrupting its cordial relationship with the largely Jewish financial and industrial elite. Unable and unwilling to stop industrial expansion, the government aimed at the conservation of the balance of power between the old agricultural and new industrial elites. If the latter, however slowly, still continued to gain ground, it was because the government feared economic isolation and because the possibility of another war, this time with Hungary's neighbors, required larger industrial capacity and advanced know-how.

TABLE 3.3

Rates of Economic Growth in Hungary,
1899-1901 to 1940-41 and 1942-43
(in percent per year)

Period	Mining and Manufacturing	Agriculture
1899-1901 to 1911-13	4.4	3.0
1911-13 to 1928-29 and 1930-31	1.7	-0.7
1928-29 and 1930-31 to 1940-41 and 1942-43	5.7	-1.5
1934-35 to 1939-40	10.8(!)	2.0

Source: Alexander Eckstein, "National Income and Capital Formation in Hungary, 1900-1950," in Income and Wealth, ed. Simon Kuznets, ser. V (London, 1955), p. 176.

What were the consequences of such "syncratic balancing"? Organski's apt generalization applied to the Hungarian case:

The main effect of syncratic government is typically to exempt the agricultural elite

61

from paying the economic and social cost of industrialization and to lessen the cost paid by the peasantry. Though their life remains hard and their exploitation at the hands of their landlords is often great, the peasants do not suffer the brutal displacement and abrupt change that afflicted their brothers in bourgeois Europe or in stalinist Russia and China. . . . Under a syncratic system, the savings for investment in industry are squeezed primarily out of the industrial sector itself, not gathered from the entire country. To a very large extent, the savings in the industrial sector are created by increases in productivity in the modern portion of the economy and by decreases in the living standard of the industrial proletariat.[15]

A second consequence of such "balancing" was growing social unrest as expressed in the intensification of the three major conflicts of the Hungarian, as of all, syncratic political systems: (1) the conflict, already mentioned, between the old agricultural and new industrial elites; (2) the conflict between each of the elites and their respective employees; and (3) the underlying urban-rural dichotomy.[16]

The latter, urban-rural tension, was particularly acute in Hungary where urban civilization became identified with foreign civilization; a sizable proportion, perhaps two-thirds, of the ambitious urban middle class was of Jewish and German extraction. This growing middle class of the cities, estimated to make up from 8 to 10 percent of the population, was not the enterprising middle class of the Anglo-Saxon world; it consisted of relatively few entrepreneurs but many professionals. Its special character was indicated by the fact that, in order to qualify for membership, it was normally sufficient to possess a university degree. Not surprisingly, the city's conception of rural life was at best condescending, at worst hostile. Primitive life in the countryside became a source of mockery. The prevailing image of the peasant was that of an uneducated, uncultivated, unsophisticated, and simple soul, respectful though often sly. The city appreciated folk music, witness the acceptance of Bela Bartok and Zoltan Kodaly, but this attitude was marred by the enormous popularity of folksy, Viennese-type operettas which caricatured the peasant way of life.

Conversely, the city seemed strange, alien, non-Magyar, and on the whole unacceptable for traditionally rural

Hungary. In a sense, the city was attractive and dangerous: It offered both somewhat higher wages and the ills of urban civilization, that is, slums, concentrated unemployment, loneliness. At best, it was a place to visit. Also, the average peasant or small farmer who had always marketed his own produce considered it rather odd, if not outright immoral, for a city merchant to make a living by simply buying and selling that which he himself did not produce. Preferring conditions prevalent prior to the advent of industrialization, then, rural Hungary did not conceive of some of the advantages of industrialization and modernization: better schools and hospitals, advanced methods of agricultural production, and the like. Also, rural resistance to modernity was exacerbated by bitter anti-Semitism, diligently promoted by the lower stratum of the gentry whose members found it uncomfortable, even degrading, to deal with Jewish financiers in the 1920s; even worse, their declining estates tended to drift into Jewish hands after the economic crisis of 1929-31. Rightly or wrongly, rural Hungary identified Jewish influence with industrialization and blamed the Jew for the real or imagined humiliation it was suffering. In short, as rural Hungary was being bypassed, a stubborn and provincial opposition set in against the outward-looking urban society of the cities.*

As to the political conflict between the industrial and agricultural elites, on the one hand, and their respective employees, on the other, Horthy's syncratic regime sought to secure its hegemony by placating, indeed paralyzing, the two political parties expressing and representing the interests of the agricultural and industrial proletariats: the Smallholder Party and the Social Democratic Party.

The Smallholder Party had attained some recognition during World War I, and at the first national elections in 1920 it sent a surprisingly large group of 91 representatives to the legislature in contrast to the 59 of the establishment's Christian National Party (as it was called at the time). Led by Istvan Nagyatadi Szabo, a farmer, the Smallholder Party won the election on a platform of land reform, secret ballot, and progressive taxation. Count Bethlen, a nonparty deputy then with close ties to the Christian Nationals, recognized that Szabo would probably prefer to share his power (he was somewhat "frightened by the responsibility of creating a new state"[17]) and approached

---

*It was this nostalgic yet militant spirit which provided the source material and contributed to the inspiration for the emerging populist movement of the 1930s. See next section, "Two Revolutionary Models of Development."

him with the idea of working together in a united party. He
suggested that the Smallholder Party's platform could be
carried out more effectively by a new party which would undoubtedly obtain more than sufficient majority in the legislature.[18] The apparently naive and definitely inexperienced
Szabo agreed and became Minister of Agriculture in a cabinet
dominated by the Christians; indeed, the Smallholder Party
was soon swallowed up in the new United Party. Its program,
too, was disregarded: The secret ballot, already in force,
was withdrawn; the pseudo land reform--with only about 1.5
million acres or about 5 percent of the arable land distrib-
uted--did not meet the needs of Hungary's landless population; and progressive taxation was simply forgotten. By the
time of Szabo's death in 1924, the Smallholder Party no
longer retained its former political strength and appeal and
it was only in the 1930s that the new Independent Smallholder Party made a renewed attempt to represent the political and economic interests of the peasantry.

Bethlen also succeeded in curtailing the activities of
the Social Democratic Party and of the trade unions. Although the social democrats had greatly suffered during the
White Terror and many of their best leaders were forced to
escape to Western Europe, the party's moderately socialist
program retained a degree of popularity among the industrial
proletariat. The aim of the Social Democratic leadership
was to gain more freedom of action from the government in
order to expand socialist activity at least in the industrial centers. Bethlen's primary goal was to prevent the
trade unions and the Social Democrats from organizing the
peasantry. The compromise between the government and the
socialists became known as the Bethlen-Peyer Pact.[19] The
parties, inter alia, agreed that the Social Democratic Party
would not attempt to organize among the peasants, trade
unions would deal only with economic, not political, issues,
and the socialists would cooperate with the government in
presenting Hungary's case in the West. The government, in
turn, agreed to permit the publication of socialist propaganda, the party was allowed to organize industrial workers,
and it could once again be represented in the legislature.

The cleverly manipulated and balanced syncratic political order thus established could not withstand the enormous
impact of the economic crisis of 1929-31. Factories idled
and the number of employed workers dropped (see Table 3.4),
while the price of most agricultural produce diminished.
What amounted to a social and economic upheaval, then,
forced Bethlen to resign in 1931. He was first replaced by
another member of the landed aristocracy, but in 1932 Gyula
Gombos, a former officer in the army, took over the premiership (1932-36). Gombos' program contained something for all,

and in this respect at least he emulated fascism from the beginning. His program was carefully phrased so that the first part of a particular statement usually neutralized the second part. He announced, for example, that the "safeguarding of the liberty of the press is a national asset," but he added: "so long as the press faithfully serves the nation." In another passage, Gombos called for the reintroduction of the secret ballot, adding, however, that "at the same time the great national ideals of the Hungarian people must be safeguarded."[20]

TABLE 3.4

Workers in Hungarian Industry and Craft, 1929-43

Year	Number	Index (1929 = 100)
1929	613,300	100.0
1930	559,800	91.3
1931	508,500	82.9
1932	447,600	73.0
1933	451,300	73.6
1934	489,900	79.6
1935	526,900	85.9
1936	581,100	94.7
1937	638,000	104.0
1938	688,800	112.3
1939	759,700	123.9
1940	794,100	129.5
1941	853,600	139.2
1942	872,700	142.3
1943	919,000	150.0

Source: Bela Kovrig, Magyar Szocialpolitika (1920-1945) [Hungarian social policy (1920-1945)] (New York: Hungarian National Council, 1954), p. 39.

Of course, Gombos was a demagogue, at best a sincere demagogue, and so it is tempting to dismiss or underestimate him. Nevertheless, two major developments occurred during his premiership, each of which pointed to far-reaching consequences. First, he succeeded in curtailing the influence of the old agricultural aristocracy. Second, his definitely pro-German foreign policy resulted, inter alia, in German economic and political penetration, with German economic

influence becoming a decisive stimulus for Hungarian industrialization and modernization.

As for the first development, Gombos was acutely aware
of the lack of a Western-type middle class in Hungary. He
was also aware of the apparent inability of Bethlen's syncratic coalition to govern effectively, let alone guide the
seemingly inevitable economic and social transformation of
Hungary. "Mind you," he repeated time and again, "there
isn't a single count in my government." Antagonistic to the
vested interests of the 1920s, Gombos altered the syncratic
balance created and cherished by Bethlen. His new coalition
relied heavily on the gentry, the army, the bureaucracy, the
industrial elite, and only after that on the landed aristocracy. In short, he changed the character and orientation of
the governing elite, the latter becoming less cautious and
more radical, pro-Italian and pro-German, less nostalgic and
more outward-looking, anti-Semitic, somewhat vulgar, but
more receptive to change. To be sure, some of this "change"
was to lead Hungary to political catastrophe in World War II,
but it also led to rapid industrialization under German tutelage. At any rate, Gombos finally concluded the transfer
of power from a traditional to a modernizing leadership.
Indeed, the political system Gombos built, to use Edward
Shils' category, was a modernizing oligarchy strongly motivated toward economic development.[21] Its impulse for modernization stemmed from the system's concern for efficiency,
its dislike for traditionalism, and its correct appraisal of
the depth and extent of social and political disaffection
and economic deprivation. The system was further characterized by its verbal commitment to democratization, something,
however, that it opposed in practice.

The second major development associated with Gombos'
premiership was the aggressive German economic penetration
of Hungary. As Table 3.5 shows, Germany's share in Hungarian foreign trade rapidly increased in the 1930s. Of Hungary's total export in 1930, for example, only 10.3 percent
went to Germany; the corresponding figure in 1939 was 52.2
percent. Of Hungary's total import in 1930, 21.2 percent
came from Germany; the corresponding figure in 1939 was 52.5
percent.

At the same time, as Table 3.6 illustrates, Hungary's
foreign trade with its five traditional trading partners
(Austria, Czechoslovakia, Romania, Yugoslavia, Poland) seriously declined. Of Hungary's total export in 1922, 76.9
percent went to these five countries; by 1935 it was only
31.6 percent. Of Hungary's total import in 1922, 67.5 percent came from the five countries; by 1935 it was only 44.1
percent. Traditionally, of course, Germany had always

TABLE 3.5

Germany's Share in Hungarian Foreign Trade, 1920-39

Year	Import (% total)	Export (% total)
1920	8.4	11.1
1921	12.9	9.3
1922	16.6	9.1
1923	14.3	6.2
1924	12.5	7.9
1925	15.0	9.9
1926	16.6	12.9
1927	18.2	13.3
1928	19.5	11.7
1929	20.0	11.7
1930	21.2	10.3
1931	24.1	12.7
1932	22.5	15.2
1933	19.7	11.2
1934	18.3	22.2 (!)
1935	22.7	23.9
1936	26.0	22.8
1937	26.2	34.1
1938	NA	NA
1939	52.5 (!)	52.2 (!)

Source: Ivan T. Berend and Gyorgy Ranki, Magyarorszag a fasiszta Nemetorszag "elettereben" 1933-1939 [Hungary in the "living space" of fascist Germany 1933-1939] (Budapest, 1960).

TABLE 3.6

Hungarian Foreign Trade with Neighboring Countries,
1922, 1928, and 1935
(Austria, Czechoslovakia, Poland, Romania, Yugoslavia)

Year	Import (% total)	Export (% total)
1922	67.5	76.9
1928	55.6	68.4
1935	44.1	31.6

Source: Adapted from Frederick Hertz, The Economic Problems of the Danubian States: A Study in Economic Nationalism (London, 1947), p. 82.

tended to sell more to Hungary than to buy from it; beginning with 1934, however, an approximate balance over the
years appeared between German exports to and imports from
Hungary. In other words, Germany was now willing to purchase Hungarian agricultural products in larger quantities,
a development of definite interest to the struggling and
capital-lacking Hungarian economy.

Economic growth thus stimulated by Germany was only
barely short of being phenomenal. To begin with, the rate
of industrial growth between 1934-35 and 1939-40 reached an
impressive 10.8 percent per year as Table 3.3 shows. The
up-to-then declining agriculture also began to grow, at the
more modest rate of 2.0 percent. The number of workers employed in industry more than doubled during the decade between 1933 and 1943 (see Table 3.4). Conversely, the number
of people employed in agriculture further declined to 48.7
percent of the total population by 1941 (see Table 3.2).
For the first time, then, the majority of the working population was engaged in nonagricultural pursuits which, by
most standards, qualified Hungary as an industrial country.*

Unfortunately, reliable social indicators pointing to
the full impact of industrialization are difficult to come
by. The available data, however, clearly illustrate the
profound social impact of industrialization. Illiteracy,
for example, declined to about 7 percent by 1941 (see Table
3.7). The number of secondary schools increased by nearly
60 percent in four years, from 167 in the 1934-35 academic
year to 262 in 1938-39. The general improvement and extensive utilization of communications was indicated by the fact
that about 4.5 million long-distance telephone calls were
made in 1932 and nearly 8 million in 1939.

Some of the most profound modernizing measures were
initiated during the premiership of Pal Teleki (1939-41).
First, Teleki sought to reform the country's antiquated
bureaucracy. Concerned about widespread corruption, he
wanted to eliminate the traditional practice of protekcio, a
system of special advantages or "pull," whereby political
paternalism and family patronage served as the necessary prerequisite for holding a position and for advancement in the
bureaucracy. He was hoping to introduce objective entrance

---

*It should be pointed out that the indicator frequently
used for industrialization is the percentage of economically
active males engaged in nonagricultural pursuits. In the
Hungarian case, the difference between economically active
males and economically active males and females engaged in
nonagricultural pursuits was negligible.

examinations to bring competent and qualified personnel into state administration. Under his premiership, bureaucrats were reminded of their primary function which was to serve the general public, rich and poor alike. As Bela Kovrig pointed out, Teleki did not pursue these objectives because of any deep commitment to democratic principles, a commitment he was probably lacking, but because of his conviction that without a thorough reform of the bureaucracy the integration of Hungarian society was not possible.[22]

TABLE 3.7

Rate of Illiteracy in Hungary of People
over Seven Years of Age, 1900-49

Year	Illiteracy (% population)
1900	40.7
1910	33.3
1920	15.2
1930	9.6
1941	7.0 (approx.)
1949	5.0

Source: Adapted from The Statesman's Year Book and Zoltan Horvath, Magyar Szazadfordulo [Hungary at the turn of the century] (Budapest, 1961), p. 591.

Second, Teleki sought to improve the esprit de corps of the Hungarian people by initiating a number of cultural and educational programs. He encouraged the establishment of about 20 so-called popular colleges whose purpose was the education of poor, mainly peasant-born youth. He commenced the publication of Hungarian classics in inexpensive paperback editions and organized a speakers' bureau which provided large and small communities around the country, free of charge, with qualified scholars who lectured on cultural and historical subjects. To bring knowledge and current information into the often remote villages of Hungary, Teleki initiated a program of wall-newspapers which carried apolitical and topical news, and an executive order from the Ministry of Internal Affairs required local, that is, country and village, political leaders, who disliked the idea, to prominently display such wall-newspapers.

Again, Teleki's objective was to fight traditional provincialism and narrow perspectives and to overcome the knowledge gap between city and countryside.[23]

Teleki's suicide in 1941, in protest against Hungary's forced participation in the German attack of Yugoslavia, marked the conclusion of the transitional stage of modernization. Hungary, in a sense, became industrialized. The state bureaucracy had established nearly uniform practices and procedures throughout the country. The knowledge gap between urban Hungary and rural Hungary had narrowed. Ethnic divisions no longer inflicted major damage to the fabric of society. The steady modernization of social relations was clearly in evidence, particularly just prior to and during World War II. Extensive kinship units began to lose their pervasiveness. As illiteracy significantly diminished, the number of qualified men with productive skills increased. The movement of people from the countryside into urban centers assumed considerable proportions. In the political realm, this phase of development witnessed the conclusion of the rule of the landed aristocracy as the syncratic balance gave way to the modernizing leadership.

Revolutionary Stage

The passing of traditional society, combined with the most unsettling impact of World War II, created a revolutionary situation: too many old problems had remained unsolved and too many new problems had come to the surface. Specifically, no genuine land reform had taken place until 1944-45; less than one-tenth of one percent of the landowners still owned 24.5 percent of the land in the 1930s, while 45.9 percent of the "landowners," that is, small farmers, owned only 19.3 percent of the land (see explanation under Table 3.8). Also, in terms of improvements in the general standard of living, the benefits of industrialization were not discernible. The otherwise improved state bureaucracy could not rid itself of traditional habits and customs, and it was still used to protecting old privileges. In addition, national unity had suffered as the country lined up behind Germany's war effort, a development opposed both by Bethlen's conservative group of politicians and by radical populist and communist intellectuals. Above all, destruction and dislocation caused by World War II inflicted heavy damage on the whole country and the whole population.

Thus, the Horthy regime collapsed in 1944, well before the arrival of Soviet troops, but not only because Hitler no longer needed or supported Horthy. As Horthy remained

TABLE 3.8

Size Distribution of Farms in Hungary, 1935

Size Class in Hold[a]	No. of Farms in Each Size Class		Area of Farms in Each Size Class	
	No.	% Total	Area (hold)	% Total
0-1[b]	776,487	41.0	312,403	1.9
1-5	664,263	35.1	1,620,942	10.1
5-10	204,471	10.8	1,477,376	9.2
10-20	144,186	7.6	2,025,946	12.6
20-50	73,663	3.9	2,172,300	13.5
50-100	14,895	0.8	1,008,597	6.3
100-500	10,669	0.6	2,251,629	14.0
500-1,000	1,816	0.1	1,274,054	7.9
1,000-3,000	1,254	0.1	2,053,766	12.7
Over 3,000	306	neg.	1,908,328	11.8
Totals	1,892,010	100.0	16,105,341	100.0

[a]One hold = 1.42 acres.

[b]As Professor Eckstein points out, the picture is distorted by the inclusion of holdings with less than one hold because a number of these holdings, though not the majority, were owned by people who operated them only to supplement their income.

Source: Alexander Eckstein, "Land Reform and the Transformation of Agriculture in Hungary," Journal of Farm Economics 31 (1949): 458.

rather agreeable even as late as 1944, Germany in fact still needed him. However, Hitler did help to oust him because the Horthy regime was disintegrating. Such disintegration was taking place, first, because of internal pressures generated by the disequilibrated social system: The population was exhausted by war at the same time that it vainly sought further change on the road to modernity. Second, the political system was no longer able to initiate a process of resynchronization.[24] The political elite was sufficiently disgruntled to refuse to mobilize the political system's coercive forces against either external, that is, German, or internal pressures. By 1944, therefore, Hungarian society was both disequilibrated and had an ineffective and discredited political base of authority;[25] with this internal disintegration it was ripe for revolution. But

what direction would the revolutionary transformation take
after the war?*

TWO REVOLUTIONARY MODELS OF DEVELOPMENT

Not considering the various radical groupings of the
right,[26] two revolutionary movements of the left--the populist and the communist movements--possessed qualities for
the leadership of the revolutionary transformation to come.
As Horthy's political system was disintegrating, both presented alternative platforms for the future political and
economic development of Hungary. Their appraisal of the
immediate past was similar in that they saw no merit in the
modernizing attempts of the 1930s and early 1940s. Their
appraisal of the country's immediate objectives also coin-
cided as they agreed that the restoration of old privileges
was undesirable, land reform was imperative, the social immobility of the past had to be erased, and the overhaul of
the bureaucracy was overdue. On the other hand, their appraisal of future economic development differed in that the
populists preferred a predominantly agrarian, small-scale,
village-based, and decentralized economy, while the communists advocated rapid, centralized, and thorough industrialization, including the development of heavy industry.

Main Features of Populist Thought

As the war was coming to a close, the populists' ideas
were widely known and probably widely shared. A prominent
sociologist, Janos Kosa, observed in 1942 that virtually the
entire Hungarian youth identified itself with populism.[27]
The British historian C. A. Macartney noted that populism
was "genuinely native" and it was "destined to have a not
unimportant future" in Hungary.[28] The chief Hungarian communist ideologist, Jozsef Revai, in one of the first full-
scale studies on the populist movement in 1938 called it
"the most important intellectual current of the last two
decades in Hungary."[29]
In its basic platform and attitudes, Hungarian populism[30] differed little from Russian populism and from populism in the developing countries.[31] It was more an attitude

---

*For a further discussion of the revolutionary stage
of development, see next section, "Parties and Development
after the War."

and a state of mind than a coherent and ordered set of specific ideas. It is nevertheless possible to extricate certain commonly held propositions from the voluminous populist literature.

In the economic realm, populism was an "ideology of delayed industrialization."[32] As a movement, it emerged in the 1930s in response to the impact of the economic crisis and renewed industrialization. In their economic (as in their political) program, the populists subscribed to a "third road" position--neither capitalism nor communism, neither West nor East. Capitalism and large-scale industrialization were considered beneficial for others, that is, the West, but largely harmful for Hungary. This was so, first, because industrialization required foreign assistance and investment which would place the country at the mercy of foreigners. Second, industrialization would definitely be uneven, they maintained, because the controlling foreign interests would neither understand nor appreciate tradition; they would be guided exclusively by profit considerations. Third, the populists feared the social and cultural consequences of industrialization; they were concerned, in particular, about the uprooting of peasant youth whose life in the "sinful" and alien city would turn him against native values and culture.

Thus, the Hungarian populists opted for an agrarian-oriented economy. Laszlo Nemeth, a leading populist writer and ideologist, for example, advocated the creation of cottage industries or what he called a "garden-Hungary." In his conception of the good economic system, emphasis was not on mass production but on creativity, handicraft, light industry. Perhaps a small furniture factory here and there, utilizing local talent for wood-carving, food processing plants, catering to regional tastes and eating habits, or factories producing farm machinery that would ease the heavy workload of the peasant. The populists opted for small-scale production because it would bring industry to the countryside and thus the movement to the already overgrown cities would stop. In addition, they sensed that the development of heavy industry was extremely costly and the peasantry would likely carry the main burden of it. In short, they would have fully agreed with Stuart Chase who once advised Mexican peasants, "If I were you, when and if the new highway comes looping over the mountains into your village street, I would buy all the boxes of extra-sized carpet tacks I can afford."[33]

As to agriculture, the populists focused on the plight of the peasantry and advocated a radical land reform. Much of the best populist literature was devoted to the description and analysis of the misery and exploitation of the peasantry. The publication of Pusztak nepe (People of the Puszta), by Gyula Illyes, became both a literary bestseller and a political event in 1936, as did Imre Kovacs' Nema forradalom (Silent revolution), Zoltan Szabo's Tardi helyzet (The situation at Tard), and Geza Feja's Viharsarok (The stormy corner), all of which have since been reissued in numerous editions and translated into several languages. In these partly sociological, partly impressionistic studies the populists sought to reveal the intolerable conditions of the peasantry and to express their uncompromising demand for a radical land reform, even though they could not always agree on the step beyond land reform. Most of them, like Feja, Illyes, and Veres, envisaged a social system of peasant communities with voluntary cooperatives, that is, agrarian socialism. Others, like Erdei, Kovacs, and Szabo, opted for the utilization of modern technology in farming: Large-scale agricultural production on the advanced Western pattern, they thought, would eliminate the misery and retardation of the peasantry.

In the political realm, the populist platform was blurred by the basic eclecticism of Hungarian populism. Rudolf L. Tokes identifies the main Western ingredients or sources of Hungarian populism as the German school of sociological positivism, Marxism, West European reformist socialism, West European leftist radicalism, peasant romanticism, Rosenberg's race myth, the fascist corporate system, and Scandinavian socialism;[34] and the list may be even extended to include Eastern influences. At any rate, eclectic though the Hungarian populist political platform was, it definitely included, first, the notion of nonalignment, a kind of "third road" foreign policy to be steered between Germany and the Soviet Union. As Nemeth explained the meaning of "third road" in an oft-quoted analogy, "Let us suppose that there is a political party in New Guinea which maintains that New Guinea should belong to the British. According to another party, New Guinea could be happy only under the Dutch. Then someone stands up and asks, 'couldn't New Guinea belong to the [native] Papuans?' This is the third road."[35]

Second, Western-style political democracy and freedom were not in the populist platform. To be sure, the populists often demanded the "democratic reorganization of the country," "freedom of thought, speech, press, assembly, and organization," or "universal, equal, and secret suffrage,"[36] and the like; yet they were also apprehensive about the misuse of freedom in a democratic political system. Illyes, for example, once remarked that his commitment to freedom of the press was limited because, as he put it, "when the press was genuinely free, it freely prostituted itself."[37] Indeed, the populist notion of freedom and democracy meant, above all, freedom for the peasantry to possess land and it meant the "democratic," perhaps equal, distribution of wealth in society. On the whole, the populists were prepared to accept almost any form of government so long as it served the interests of the peasantry, their assumption being that the interests of the peasantry were strictly identical with those of the nation. Put differently, the populists concluded that the socioeconomic transformation of Hungary, and of the peasantry in particular, had priority over the development of a democratic political order. Very much like present-day leaders in the developing world, the populists believed that political democracy might well be used against the interests of the people by foreigners or by seminative, that is, Jewish, industrialists.

Finally, the <u>cultural</u> platform of Hungarian populism can best be characterized by emphasizing its nationalist and historical perspective. The populists were proud of indigenous talent, of folk music and folk art, of those Hungarians of the past who had shown courage, of the ostensibly uncorrupted simplicity of primitive culture. They looked <u>up</u> to "the people" and <u>down</u> on "the masses."[38] Depending on the need of the moment, they glorified one or another period of Hungarian history--once it was a war of independence, to demonstrate bravery and sacrifice, then it was clever and wise political maneuvering between wicked foreign powers, to demonstrate the overriding value of survival for the nation. The uses of the past were many. History served for national self-assurance to prove that the West was not superior; after all, didn't Hungary defend the West time and again against Eastern hordes? In a psychological sense, history served for escape from the undesirable present into an ostensibly "golden age" in the past.

To sum up, the Hungarian populists offered both an attitude and a platform. Their orientation was eclectic in its foundations; romantic in tone; nationalist in cultural outlook; archaic in its attempt to resurrect the "golden age" of the past; utopian in its hope for moral regeneration to combat the perversions of modern life; negativistic in its anticapitalist, antiurban, anti-German, anti-Semitic, and anticommunist sentiments; emotional in its search for foreign conspiracies and scapegoats; sentimental in its absolute commitment to the cause of the peasantry; calculating in its foreign policy orientation; anarchic in its distaste for organization; conservative in its hatred of advanced social differentiation and division of labor; progressive in

its belief in the value of education and in its deep commitment to social equality; and irrational in its contradictions. Above all, the populist orientation was revolutionary yet Hungarian. The populists were prepared to turn
society upside down--redistribute the land, provide educational opportunities for all, exclude the old elites from
positions of influence and replace them with "the people,"
and defy the great powers. In a sense, populism was also a
microcosm of Hungary:[39] It mirrored the confusion and contradictions of the country's struggle with, and for, modernization. Significantly, the populists lacked the attributes
required for further modernization once the war was over:
an organizational base, the acceptance of the necessity of
industrialization, and a wider, less provincial, indeed international perspective.

The Communist Preparation for Development

     The other revolutionary movement of the left, the com-
munist movement, possessed qualities the populists lacked
and lacked what the populists possessed. Specifically, the
outlawed and illegal Communist Party enjoyed little or no
popular support. It was not considered an indigenous movement with an indigenous ideology. Its best leaders were in
exile, in Moscow and in Western Europe, and some of them had
not been in direct touch with Hungarian reality since 1919.
Those who were in Hungary engaged in underground activities
which seldom went beyond journalistic and polemic endeavors,
even though during World War II there were a few demonstrations with communist participation as well as isolated instances of sabotage. Unlike the populists, however, the
communists paid attention to organizational matters, possessed an ideology which embraced industrialization and urbanization, and showed great familiarity with international
politics.[40]
     The Communist International's 1935 resolution, which
called on all communists to work together with socialists
and others against the rise of fascism in Europe, represented an impossible assignment for the Communist Party in
Hungary since, after the arrest of its leadership in January
1936, it consisted of a small group of largely inexperienced
men. Their objective was the creation of a Popular Front;
however, the Social Democratic Party rejected any cooperation with the communists initially and the communists did
not even approach the Smallholder Party at this time. By
necessity, therefore, it was the populist movement which
represented the greatest attraction for the communists.

First of all, the populists also pursued revolutionary objectives. Second, the communists could reasonably expect
that, given the populists' political dilettantism, leadership within the movement would easily slip into their hands.
Third, as most populists were known noncommunists, this was
an ideal "front," a convenient hiding place. Finally, the
communists were naturally attracted by the populists' popularity and national appeal.

At any rate, the communists' flirtation with the populist movement marked the beginning of their alliance policy
between 1936 and 1944. The objective was clear: the penetration of noncommunist groups and organizations. On assignment from the party's leadership in Prague and later in
Moscow, they cooperated with almost any movement or group
opposed to Hitler or Horthy or the war. Yet, on balance,
their immediate accomplishments were minimal. A few communist journalists were able to join the staff of <u>Nepszava</u>,
the daily of the Social Democratic Party. They later participated in a number of antiwar demonstrations and issued,
together with the socialists and the Smallholder Party,
antiwar manifestos. The Communist Party's membership, however, did not increase during the war, nor could it organize
a single effective strike against the government or against
Hungary's participation in the war.

The party's leaders (Kallai, Sagvari, Losonczy, Rajk,
Kadar) succeeded, however, in making the Communist Party a
palatable, if not quite desirable, political ally. By the
last years of the war, the Social Democrats, the populist
National Peasant Party, the Smallholder Party, and nonparty
intellectuals found it possible to make common appeals with
the communists against the war. After all, they agreed with
the communist program which at this time was strictly limited to the goals of independence from Germany, peace, and
social and political equality. Indeed, the party's spokes-
men did not offer anything specific or detailed to counter
the populist platform; they emphasized "broad" agreement on
"fundamental" issues. As a result, the indigenous communist
leadership became part of the antiwar effort and made useful
contacts with the democratic left, but its program was
vague, superficial, and elusive.

In the meantime, the party's politically more sophisticated leaders in Moscow (Rakosi, Gero, Revai, Imre Nagy,
Farkas) were preparing for their imminent return to Hungary.
While most of them had left the country decades ago, their
commentaries published in the periodical <u>Uj Hàng</u> (New voice)
and broadcast by Radio Moscow revealed that they were exceedingly well-informed about Hungarian developments. Particularly after the Soviet victory at Stalingrad, they were

also cognizant of the role they were to play in Hungarian politics. In addition, looking at the war from Moscow, they knew of the strains and tensions between the Soviet Union and its Western allies and understood their meaning and possible consequences for East Central Europe. Finally, their experience and training had taught them about the relevance of political organization and about what they considered the inevitability of industrialization in Hungary after the war.

Therefore, when the new postwar government came into being in the East Hungarian city of Debrecen in the fall of 1944, the Communist Party possessed much more than the support of the Soviet Union, however decisive that support was. It possessed a leadership with an international outlook, trained in the worst kind of political infighting in the Soviet Union, lacking in any great concern about the brutal impact of social and economic dislocation that was to come, and unhesitatingly committed, as was to be seen later, to the twin goals of forced industrialization and political hegemony. Second, the Muscovite leadership was reinforced and complemented by the Party's indigenous leaders who, through an elusive program which emulated populism, had partly destigmatized the communist name within the new postwar democratic political elite. Third, the Communist Party faced a divided opposition, made up of the large Smallholder Party, the Social Democrats, and the National Peasant Party. Each of these parties possessed a few gifted leaders (Tildy, Bela Kovacs, and Ferenc Nagy; Kethly; Imre Kovacs, Bibo, and Erdei, respectively), but their political perspective was provincial in comparison with that of the communist leaders now returning from Moscow. The latter understood the revolutionary momentum caused by the war and by the process of modernization in the 1930s. They were skilled politicians and professional revolutionaries. Slighted within Hungary, the Communist Party also had an economic program of development which went beyond reconstruction and land reform: It was, of course, the program of industrial socialism. In short, the Communist Party was prepared to carry the process of modernization to its ultimate conclusion, irrespective of cost and consequences, through revolution if necessary.

PARTIES AND DEVELOPMENT AFTER THE WAR

After the war, the immediate objectives of modernization were self-evident. Aside from creating order and fiscal stability, the most pressing task of the new coalition government was to realize the age-old dream of land reform, which was largely completed in 1945 (see Table 3.9).[41]

TABLE 3.9

Size Distribution of Farms in Hungary in 1947,
by Number of Farms and Area in Each Size Class

Size Class in Hold[a]	No. of Farms in Each Size Class		Area of Farms in Each Size Class	
	No.	% Total	Area (hold)	% Total
0–5	1,406,325	68.1	2,871,958	17.9
5–10	388,179	18.8	3,388,857	21.1
10–20	175,428	8.5	2,789,353	17.3
20–50	71,164	3.4	2,359,004	14.7
50–100	14,864	0.7	1,295,506	8.1
100–200	5,525	0.3	714,512	4.4
200–1,000	4,034	0.2	1,352,728	8.4
1,000–3,000[b]	504	neg.	796,007	4.9
Over 3,000[b]	91	neg.	513,919	3.2
Totals	2,066,114	100.0	16,081,844	100.0

[a]One hold = 1.42 acres.
[b]These were state holdings.

Source: Alexander Eckstein, "National Income and Capital Formation in Hungary, 1900-1950," in Income and Wealth, ed. Simon Kuznets, ser. V (London, 1955), p. 464.

In addition, the new regime sought to reduce the size and change the social composition of the bureaucracy. The government's first measures also included the improvement of the country's communications network, the expansion of educational opportunities (by giving preferential treatment to the so-called popular colleges), the betterment of the social security system, the enlargement of health services in the countryside, and the like.

Differences within the coalition government during the first year or so were mainly political. The country's future relationship with the Soviet Union caused division and there was intensive competition for governmental portfolios. The question of Hungary's relationship with the Soviet Union was not resolved, of course, until the Communist Party secured its political hegemony in 1948. For the time being, however, the government's composition was settled by the national parliamentary election of 1945. The results of this free and secret election showed the Smallholder Party (SP) with 57 percent of the vote, the Social Democratic

Party (SDP) with 17.4 percent of the vote, the Communist
Party (CP) with 17 percent of the vote, and the National
Peasant Party (NPP) with 7 percent of the vote.[42] This convincing victory of the SP can be explained by the party's
opposition to Soviet pressures. The party also demonstrated
its political acumen by appealing to divergent elements in
the Hungarian electorate. Indeed, the SP was eclectic and
its positions on the prominent issues of the day were often
contradictory. It supported the land reform, but it courted
the Catholic church which sought to retain some of its large
holdings; its top leaders were prepared to cooperate with
the Soviet Union, others in the party remained vehemently
anticommunist; it approved the political trials of wartime
high officials, but it did not fully repudiate the past; it
received the support of agricultural laborers and small
farmers, yet it was the overwhelming choice of their former
landlords as well; it flirted with antiurban sentiments, yet
it was clearly the most bourgeois party on the political
scene. Accordingly, the Smallholder Party was a coalition
in itself, a broker party, as nonideological as any in Hungarian history; indeed, as a whole entity, in contrast to
its components, it was more committed to winning elections
than to any particular program of action.

The 1945 elections were decided on a number of exceedingly complex issues, of course, including the country's
proper relationship with the Soviet Union, the desirable extent of land distribution, the nature of the Horthy regime,
the scope of change in the bureaucracy, and the future of
modernization and economic development. If, however, one
had been able to isolate the issue of modernization and economic development alone, support for the Smallholder Party
on this issue only would have been less convincing. Consider the following: Broadly speaking, Hungary could pursue
one of three alternative paths of development after the war:

 1. the bourgeois-democratic path, characterized by its
objective of measured modernization through evolution and
the democratic political process, continued industrialization without the significant disruption of the country's social and economic structure, and an agriculture based on the
independent small farmer; or

 2. the populist-agrarian path, characterized by its
emphasis on light or cottage industries, an agricultural
policy leading to a vaguely defined agrarian socialism, the
revolutionary eradication of social immobility still in-
fecting the fabric of Hungarian society, and by a willingness to accomplish these objectives through almost any form
of government; or

 3. the communist-industrial path, characterized by its
commitment to one-party rule, the rapid development of heavy

industry, the establishment of cooperatives and state farms in the countryside, and the breakup of the social structure to give way to members of the industrial and agricultural proletariat.

Needless to say, the electorate's precise choice among the three alternative models of development cannot be ascertained. However, it is possible to extrapolate from the results of the 1945 elections the voting public's probable preference. Considering, moreover, the substance of some 250 interviews in the Columbia University Research Project on Hungary,[43] it may be postulated that the bourgeois-democratic path was probably supported by approximately two-thirds of the SP vote (38 percent of the total) and half of the SDP vote (8.7 percent), representing 46.7 percent of all votes cast. The populist-agrarian model was probably supported by the remaining one-third of the SP vote (19 percent) and the full NPP vote (7 percent), for a total of 26 percent. Finally, the communist-industrial model was probably supported by the remaining half of the SDP vote (8.7 percent) and the full CP vote (17 percent), for a total of 25.7 percent. Considering the first model evolutionary and the other two revolutionary, the figures therefore indicate that the voting public was rather evenly divided between evolutionary and revolutionary change, with 46.7 percent of the electorate opting for the former and the majority (51.7 percent) for the latter (see Tables 3.10 and 3.11 for the actual results of the election and for our extrapolated calculations).

TABLE 3.10

Results of 1945 Elections in Hungary

Party	% Total
Smallholder Party (SP)	57.0
Social Democratic Party (SDP)	17.4
Communist Party (CP)	17.0
National Peasant Party (NPP)	7.0
Others	1.6
Total	100.0

Source: Agnes Sagvari, Tomegmozgalmak es politikai kuzdelmek Budapesten 1945-1947 [Mass movements and political struggles in Budapest 1945-1947] (Budapest, 1964), p. 181.

TABLE 3.11

Extrapolation of Results of 1945 Hungarian Elections
Based on Three Models of Development

Models of Development	SP Vote (% total)	SDP Vote (% total)	CP Vote (% total)	NPP Vote (% total)	Evolution or Revolution
Bourgeois-democratic	38.0	8.7	--	--	46.7
Populist-agrarian	19.0	--	--	7.0	51.7
Communist-industrial	--	8.7	17.0	--	
Totals	57.0	17.4	17.0	7.0	98.4

These calculations are based on the following assumptions: First, neither the Communist Party nor the National Peasant Party were divided on the question of development; the former supported the communist-industrial model, the latter the populist-agrarian model. Second, not unlike socialist parties in other parts of the world, the Social Democratic Party was evenly divided between supporters of evolutionary and revolutionary change, some therefore approving the deliberate pace of bourgeois-democratic development, others opting for rapid industrialization advocated primarily by the communists. Third, the solid majority or about two-thirds of the supporters of the Smallholder Party endorsed the bourgeois-democratic path of measured modernization, independent agriculture, and democratic procedure, while the remaining minority approved the more radical solutions contained in the populist-agrarian model.

If so, two questions may be raised: why did the one-third minority of the smallholders vote for the Smallholder Party and not the National Peasant Party? And why did the more radical half of the socialists vote for the Social Democratic Party and not the Communist Party? The answer to both questions is that the election was not decided on the issue of development alone. Specifically, the Smallholder Party won the election primarily because of the prevailing belief that its leaders would more firmly resist Soviet pressures than those of the other parties. More than any other single factor, apprehension over foreign, that is, Soviet, domination assured the victory of the Smallholder Party. In addition, there were many who did not want to

"waste" their vote on the National Peasant Party despite
their known populist preference. Indeed, such leaders of
the SP as Bela Kovacs, Ferenc Nagy, Ortutay, Dobi, and
others had intimate ties to, or were in fact, populists;
they joined the Smallholder Party because it was more a
"governing" party than the somewhat disjointed populist
National Peasant Party. As to the reluctance of some socialists to vote directly for the Communist Party, it can
be explained largely by their unwillingness to endorse the
party's Soviet orientation and its desire for political
hegemony. These voters seemed satisfied that the left wing
of their own party would press for rapid modernization without succumbing to foreign rule or political dictatorship.

To sum up, the preceding analysis of the 1945 elections
points to a more widespread popular acceptance of revolutionary change in Hungary than previously assumed: a slight
majority of the electorate was probably prepared to accept
either the communist-industrial or the populist-agrarian
model of development. The two parties directly and decisively promoting these models (CP and NPP) were somewhat
more cohesive and united than the two parties favoring evolution (SP and SDP). Given this support for the radical
models of development, then, coupled with the path-breaking,
modernizing trend of the previous decade, revolutionary
transformation was unavoidable. The choice under the circumstances was in fact reduced to one between industrial
and agrarian socialism. That the former prevailed was due
to the Communist Party's professional leadership, the inadequacy of populist socialism as a model of development at
this particular juncture, the eclecticism of populist ideology, and the divided agrarian movement. Last, but certainly
not least, the Soviet Union provided its determined support
to those pursuing revolutionary change in the direction of
industrial socialism.

CONCLUSIONS

In Hungary as elsewhere, the process of modernization
was uneven. Initial progress after 1867, mainly in terms of
industrialization, was followed by the syncratic reaction of
the 1920s when the political system sought to curtail the
pace of modernization. Tension and discontent built up at
this time burst into the open after the economic crisis, resulting in unprecedented economic growth and the further intrusion of modernity just prior to and during World War II.
The impact of rapid change, in turn, created a revolutionary
situation embraced by the populist and communist movements.

In addition, revolutionary change enjoyed widespread, perhaps majority, support and hence only the direction of such change remained in doubt. Rooted in long-standing values and tradition, the populists offered a revolutionary program of national rejuvenation including social equality, some sort of agrarian socialism, and antiurbanization. Rooted in the recently acquired trend of modernization, the communists offered a revolutionary program of industrial socialism. Opposed to urbanization and heavy industrialization, the populists sought to circumvent the processes of modernization, while the communists were prepared to carry on with the timely tasks of industrialization and modernization.

The stage for revolutionary change was thus set: With the "dysfunctions"[44] of revolution in evidence, competing revolutionary ideologies appeared on the scene. The final trigger or "accelerator" to "catalyze . . . the already existent revolutionary levels of dysfunctions"[45] was then provided by the Soviet Union. The catalyzer rather than the creator of revolutionary change, it naturally opted for the communist model of modernization.

NOTES

1. Outstanding studies of this kind include Hugh Seton-Watson, The East European Revolution (New York: Praeger, 1951); Zbigniew K. Brzezinski, The Soviet Bloc: Unity and Conflict, rev. ed. (New York: Praeger, 1961); Stephen D. Kertesz, Diplomacy in a Whirlpool: Hungary between Nazi Germany and Soviet Russia (Notre Dame, Ind.: University of Notre Dame Press, 1953).
2. This is a modified version of the periodization offered by C. E. Black in his The Dynamics of Modernization: A Study in Comparative History (New York: Harper and Row, 1966), pp. 67-94. Black's study also includes an excellent bibliographical essay on the literature of modernization.
3. Most of the preceding data has been derived from Zoltan Horvath's informative and colorful Magyar szazadfordulo: A masodik reformnemzedek tortenete 1896-1914 [Hungary at the turn of the century: history of the second reform generation 1896-1914] (Budapest, 1961). For a thorough and important study of the social composition and growth of the industrial proletariat, see Miklos Lacko, Ipari munkassagunk osszetetelenek alakulasa 1867-1949 [Development of the composition of our industrial proletariat 1867-1949] (Budapest, 1961).
4. For the social background of high government officials, see Erno Lakatos, A politikai magyar vezetoreteg [The Hungarian political elite] (Budapest, 1942).

5. C. A. Macartney, October Fifteenth: A History of Modern Hungary 1929-1945, 2d ed., vol. I (Edinburgh, 1961), pp. 8-13.

6. Ibid., p. 10.

7. See Table 3.3.

8. Alexander Eckstein, "National Income and Capital Formation in Hungary, 1900-1950," in Income and Wealth, ed. Simon Kuznets, ser. V (London, 1955), p. 176.

9. Ibid.

10. As quoted in Macartney, op. cit., pp. 61 ff.

11. Eckstein, op. cit., p. 177.

12. Macartney, op. cit., p. 26.

13. A. F. K. Organski, The Stages of Political Development (New York: Knopf, 1965), pp. 122-56. The word "syncratic," Professor Organski explains, is derived from the Greek syn which means "together" and from cratic which, of course, means "rule."

14. Ibid., p. 155.

15. Ibid., p. 155, p. 139.

16. Ibid., pp. 125 ff.

17. Ferenc Nagy, The Struggle Behind The Iron Curtain (New York: Macmillan, 1948), p. 14.

18. Several documents related to the establishment of the United Party are reproduced in Dezso Nemes, ed., A fasiszta rendszer kiepitese es nepnyomor Magyarorszagon, 1921-1924 [Development of the fascist system and destitution in Hungary, 1921-1924] (Budapest, 1956), pp. 255-332.

19. Karoly Peyer was the head of the Social Democratic Party throughout the interwar period--its Norman Thomas. A detailed, though exceedingly biased study of the agreement is Laszlo Reti, A Bethlen-Peyer paktum [The Bethlen-Peyer Pact] (Budapest, 1956).

20. Macartney, op. cit., p. 148.

21. Edward Shils, "Political Development in the New States," Comparative Studies in Society and History 2, no. 3 (April 1960): 265-92, and no. 4 (July 1960): 379-411.

22. Bela Kovrig, Magyar szocialpolitika (1920-1945) [Hungarian social policy (1920-1945)] (New York: Hungarian National Council, 1954), pp. 174-79.

23. Ibid., pp. 179-83.

24. Chalmers Johnson, Revolutionary Change (Boston and Toronto: Little, Brown, 1966), pp. 90-91.

25. Ibid., pp. 98-99.

26. A judicious treatment of the radical right is Istvan Deak, "Hungary," in The European Right: A Historical Profile, ed. Hans Rogger and Eugen Weber (Berkeley and Los Angeles: University of California Press, 1965), pp. 364-407. Cf. Macartney, op. cit. See also, Miklos Lacko, Nyilasok, nemzetiszocialistak 1935-1944 [Arrow-Crossists, National

Socialists 1935-1944] (Budapest, 1966); Kalman Szakacs, Kaszaskeresztesek [Scythe-Crossists] (Budapest, 1963).

27. Janos Kosa, "Magyar tarsadalomkutatas" [Hungarian social research], Magyar Szemle (1942), p. 260.

28. Macartney, op. cit., p. 156.

29. Jozsef Revai, "Marxizmus es nepiesseg" [Marxism and populism], reprinted in his Marxizmus, nepiesseg, magyarsag [Marxism, populism, Hungarianism], 4th ed. (Budapest, 1955), p. 298.

30. On Hungarian populism, see Charles Gati, "The Populist Current in Hungarian Politics 1935-1944" (Ph. D. diss., Indiana University, 1965). Cf. Rudolf L. Tokes, "The Hungarian Populist 'Third Road' Ideology--Three Case Studies: 1932-1943 (M. A. thesis, Columbia University, 1961). For a contemporary account, see Geza Juhasz, Nepi irok [Populist writers] (Budapest, 1943). The most important contemporary (1938) communist appraisal of populism is Revai, op. cit., pp. 297-466. The renowned Hungarian Marxist Gyorgy Lukacs also published several studies of Hungarian populism on the eve of and during the war in Uj Hang [New voice], the Moscow-based Hungarian periodical; his studies were reprinted later in Irastudok felelossege [The responsibility of intellectuals] (Moscow, 1944), pp. 79-94. More recent communist appraisals include an official policy evaluation by the Communist Party, "A 'nepi' irokrol" [On the "populist" writers], Tarsadalmi Szemle [Social review] (June 1958), pp. 38-69; Ferenc Poloskei and Kalman Szakacs, eds., Foldmunkas es szegenyparaszt-mozgalmak Magyarorszagon 1848-1948 [Movements of agricultural laborers and poor peasants in Hungary 1848-1948] (Budapest, 1962); Magda K. Nagy, A Valasz [The answer] (Budapest, 1963).

31. Cf. David Mitrany, Marx Against the Peasant: A Study in Social Dogmatism (New York: Collier Books, 1961); Franco Venturi, Roots of Revolution: A History of the Populist and Socialist Movements in Nineteenth Century Russia (New York: Knopf, 1962); Avram Yarmolinsky, Road to Revolution (New York: Collier Books, 1962); James H. Billington, Mikhailovsky and Russian Populism (London and New York: Oxford University Press, 1958); Richard Wortman, The Crisis of Russian Populism (Cambridge, Mass.: Harvard University Press, 1967). See also Isaiah Berlin, Richard Hofstadter, Donald MacRae, Leonard Schapiro, Hugh Seton-Watson, Alain Touraine, F. Venturi, A. Walicki, Peter Worsley and others, "To Define Populism," Government and Opposition 3, no. 2 (Spring 1968): 137-79.

32. Mary Matossian, "Ideologies of Delayed Industrialization: Some Tensions and Ambiguities," Economic Development and Cultural Change 6, no. 3 (April 1958): 217-28.

For the populist critique of capitalism and industrialization in Russia, see in particular Solomon S. Schwarz, "Populism and Early Russian Marxism on Ways of Economic Development of Russia (the 1880's and 1890's)," in Continuity and
Change in Russian and Soviet Thought, ed. Ernest T. Simmons
(Cambridge: Harvard University Press, 1955), pp. 40-62.
　　33. As quoted in John Kenneth Galbraith, Economic Development in Perspective (Cambridge, Mass.: Harvard University Press, 1962), p. 9.
　　34. Tokes, op. cit., pp. 33-38.
　　35. Szarszo [an incomplete but exceedingly informative
record of a major populist gathering at the resort town of
Balatonszarszo in 1943] (Budapest, 1943), p. 54.
　　36. See the 12 points of the populist March Front of
1937, for example: "A Marcius Front kialtvanya" [The manifesto of the March Front], Valasz (1937), p. 697.
　　37. As quoted in Lukacs, op. cit., pp. 90-91.
　　38. Matossian, op. cit., p. 227.
　　39. Cf. Paul E. Zinner, Revolution in Hungary (New
York: Columbia University Press, 1962), p. 16.
　　40. There is no English-language history of the Hungarian Communist Party. The only significant work relates
the very beginning of socialist and communist activities to
about 1920; see Rudolf L. Tokes, Bela Kun and the Hungarian
Soviet Republic: The Origins and Role of the Communist
Party of Hungary in the Revolutions of 1918-1919 (New York:
Hoover Institute Publications, Praeger, 1967). For an official survey, see A magyar munkasmozgalom tortenete, 1867-
1945 [The history of the Hungarian labor movement, 1867-
1945] (Budapest, 1962-63). Detailed and analytical works on
the decade prior to 1945, all vastly exaggerating the role
of the Communist Party, include Gyula Kallai, A magyar
fuggetlensegi mozgalom 1939-1945 [The Hungarian independence
movement 1939-1945], 4th rev. ed. (Budapest, 1955); Erno
Zagoni, A magyar kommunistak a munkasegysegert 1939-1942
[The Hungarian communists for labor unity 1939-1942] (Budapest, 1963); Henrik Vass, ed., A kommunista part szovetsegi
politikaja 1936-1962 [The alliance policy of the Communist
Party 1939-1962] (Budapest, 1966); Istvan Pinter, Magyar
kommunistak a Hitler-ellenes nemzeti egysegert, 1941 junius-
1944 marcius [Hungarian communists for anti-Hitler national
unity, June 1941 to March 1944] (Budapest, 1968).
　　41. Many important documents related to the planning
and execution of the 1945 land reform are included in
Foldreform 1945 [Landreform 1945] (Budapest, 1965), which
contains an informative introduction by Magda M. Somlyai.
Cf. Paal Job and Antal Rado, eds., A debreceni feltamadas
[Resurrection in Debrecen] (Debrecen, 1947). See also Imre

Kovacs, Im Schatten der Sowiets (Zurich, 1948) and Ferenc Nagy, op. cit. For the actual results of the land reform, see Table 3.9.

42. For an informative, though biased, analysis of the elections, see Agnes Sagvari, Tomegmozgalmak es politikai kuzdelmek Budapesten 1945-1947 [Mass movements and political struggles in Budapest 1945-1947] (Budapest, 1964), esp. pp. 146-84. Cf. Kovacs, op. cit.; Nagy, op. cit.; and Job and Rado, op. cit.

43. The author wishes to thank Columbia University and Professor Henry L. Roberts, former director of its Institute on East Central Europe, for their permission to study the rich data collected by Columbia's Research Project on Hungary.

44. Harry Eckstein, "On the Etiology of Internal Wars," History and Theory 4 (1954): 140.

45. Chalmers Johnson, Revolution and the Social System (Stanford, Calif.: Hoover Institution, 1964), p. 12.

4

CZECHOSLOVAKIA:
THE GREAT LEAP BACKWARD
Otto Ulc

In 1968 Czechoslovakia celebrated the fiftieth anniversary of her foundation. This half century of statehood consisted of 20 years of pluralistic democracy (1918-38), 20 years of totalitarian dictatorship (1948-68), 6 years of Nazi occupation (1939-45), and 4 years of transition.

Accordingly, a person born during World War I may claim an exposure to a record variety of modes of government. The 50 years include two generations of political prisoners--the first, foreign made; the second, homemade--and two traumatic experiences with colossal betrayal. In 1938, the Western allies sold out the country to the aggressor. In 1968, the Eastern allies were the aggressors. In neither case did Czechoslovakia attempt to defend her sovereignty.

Czechoslovakia may thus be regarded as an exception in the East European orbit on many counts. If the classification of political systems is applied according to the degree of structural differentiation and cultural secularization, the country would fall under the category of democratic systems with limited subsystem autonomy and participant culture. In contrast, Albania, Bulgaria, Hungary, Poland, Romania, and Yugoslavia maintained authoritarian regimes of a rather conservative variety.

The stability of a system, in respect to the chances of its successful restructuring, depends to a large degree upon the types of problems faced by the elites. It may be argued that the protagonists of Czechoslovak change were quite fortunate compared with conditions elsewhere.

─────────────

This chapter is based on material from the author's forthcoming Politics in Czechoslovakia, to be published by W. H. Freeman.

First, Czechoslovakia has the record of being the only Versailles-created state whose democratic form of government was not destroyed from within. While the East European proletariat lived in semifeudal conditions, with their leaders in jail or in exile, the interwar Czechoslovak socialist movement was strong and the Communist Party was a legitimate political participant. Socialism—though not Stalinism, to be sure—was a matter of choice by the majority of the population, and not an unwanted import sustained by the presence of alien military force.

Second, the country was economically developed, with her non-Slovak part claiming a high level of industrialization and standard of living. Furthermore, the land was only a little scarred by the havoc of World War II.

Third, despite the wartime pro-Nazi puppet regime in Slovakia, the victorious powers considered Czechoslovakia as an ally, with no burden of reparations or permanent presence of foreign troops.

Fourth, the country was free of anti-Russian sentiment. On the contrary, the nineteenth-century Panslavic movement had left its imprint.

Finally, Benes's was the only exile government of the Communist-bound part of Europe that was allowed to return, at least as a symbol of statehood and preservation of its continuity.

PRESSURES FOR POLITICAL CHANGE

Stimulus toward political change may emanate from (1) the political system itself, notably its elites; (2) social groups in the domestic environment; and (3) political systems in the international environment. These forces of change do not operate independently of each other. Rather than being influenced by only one of the stimuli at a given time, it is the interaction of the three elements that determines the intensity and course of such a change. By way of an example, let me mention Czechoslovakia as of 1968:

Time	Dominant Stimulus toward Change
Preceding January 1968	2
January–August 1968	1
Following August 1968	3

Stimulus 2 (economic crisis and the pressure of restive intellectuals in particular) led to the overdue changes within the political leadership. The liberal wing of the Party (1) then proceeded toward reforming the system until this program was stopped by the August invasion of the Warsaw Pact

forces (3). It should be stressed that stimulus 2 (domestic
social forces) exercised a vitally important pressure upon
the political elite in the preinvasion period as to the direction and speed of the liberalization reforms. This pressure deprived the Party of playing the leading role, or indeed taking the initiative. In the postinvasion period,
stimulus 2 (the nation's unity in anti-Sovietism) delayed
the anticipated restoratory results of stimulus 3 for almost
a year.

The third stimulus then became dominant, as exemplified
by the Prague joke: "Czechoslovakia is the most peaceloving
country on earth. She does not even interfere in her own
affairs." The remaining stimuli atrophied: the second because of the loss of legitimacy, the first because of the
loss of integrity. This atrophy then became prevalent for
all systems--political, economic, and social.

The application of the term "state building" in the
period of constructing a people's democracy must not be
taken literally. An existing state had preceded this construction effort, but it was a "wrong" state. Hence, state
building in this situation had to be preceded by "unbuilding" the capitalist state. This process of "unbuilding"
involved manifold restructuring efforts:

1. Some formerly unknown structures, such as the Soviet products of prokuratura (Prosecutor's Office) and
arbitrazh (Arbitrating Agency), were imported and planted
in alien soil.
2. Some structures were totally, unconditionally abolished (for example, administrative courts).
3. Some structures were retained in form though not in
content (for example, the judiciary, adopting the concept of
"class justice" and explicitly rejecting equality before the
law).
4. Some structures, primarily of a technical nature,
were retained in both form and content.

Imposition of the backward Soviet system on the more
advanced, differentiated, and secularized system of Czechoslovakia resulted in a transformation, but as far as "development" was concerned, this was a development in reverse.
If secularization is understood as a process of increased
rationality in men's political behavior, imposition of a
state doctrine, of a monopoly of creed, could mean nothing
but a setback. The Stalinist political system thus led to
the "desecularization" of political culture as it reversed
the previous process of secularization in many ways, that
is, abandonment of the merit system in the recruitment process and reliance on ascriptive criteria, notably the

91

socioeconomic profile of the candidates. Furthermore, both traditional and ideologically oriented attitudes ruled out certain alternatives of political decision making. Law and its decline in clarity and binding force provided another example of this process of deterioration. Accordingly, if the shift from traditional to constitutional restraints on political action is considered one of the most important turning points in the development of political systems, the transformation of the pluralistic society of prewar Czechoslovakia into a Stalinist one must be viewed a great leap backward.

If we turn from secularization of culture to differentiation of structures, we find strains of irrationality, waste, and overextension. Instead of enhancing smooth operations, devices of mutual control were imperiled by deadlocks, overlapping, and the absence of identifiable responsibility--the obezlichka, as the Russians call it. The boundaries of the political system were subjected to relatively large fluctuations whose extent appeared in inverse proportion to the level of strains generated from within or outside the systems. In the case of Stalinism, then, it was a matter of prime ideological significance to view the political system as one with all-embracing access and substitution for any role and function, irrespective of its nature. Accordingly, the Party Secretariat was not inhibited from pondering about the political significance of sauerkraut or encroaching upon the management prerogative of the State Retail Sauerkraut Organization.

Moreover, both unintentional and at times deliberate confusion existed within such a political system, leading to and emanating from the substitutionality of roles and structures. Even the anti-Stalinist political elite of 1968 suffered from blurred vision in these matters. For example, Alexander Dubcek, as the first secretary of the Communist Party (a voluntary organization), along with Premier Oldrich Cernik signed a treaty of friendship with Bulgaria, while the head of the state, Ludvik Svoboda, stood idly by. Thus, decades of constitutional neglect were to leave many marks, from the remuneration for political engagement from the state treasury to the existence of the Workers Militia, a private army under the sole command of the Party's first secretary.

To sum up: Rather than enhancing development and state building, the Stalinist variety of cultural secularization and structural differentiation led to a rather complex setback. The dubious achievements in modernization will be illustrated with examples from the economic (welfare) and political (responsiveness) spheres.

Faithful to the Soviet pattern, Czechoslovak Marxists declared that their country, too--in its transition from capitalism to socialism--contained three economic sectors with three corresponding social classes: (1) the socialist sector--the working class; (2) the sector of small-scale production--the petite bourgeoisie, mainly the peasantry; and (3) the capitalist sector--the bourgeoisie.

The period of the dictatorship of the proletariat had resulted in a thorough transformation of the society's social composition. The 1968 Statistical Yearbook illustrated this transformation as shown in Table 4.1.

TABLE 4.1

Social Composition in Czechoslovakia,
1950, 1961, and 1967

Social Groups	1950		1961		1967	
	000s	%	000s	%	000s	%
Workers	6,950	56.4	7,738	56.3	8,319	58.3
Other employees	2,028	16.4	3,834	27.9	4,212	29.5
Collectivized farmers	2	0.0	1,466	10.6	1,186	8.3
Other cooperative producers	0	0.0	164	1.2	166	1.2
Small (private) farmers	2,510	20.3	484	3.5	332	2.3
Free professions			9	0.1	11	0.1
Craftsmen; entrepreneurs	470	3.8	51	0.4	45	0.3
Capitalists	378	3.1	--	--	--	--
Total	12,338	100.0	13,746	100.0	14,271	100.0

Source: Statisticka rocenka CSSR 1968 (Prague: SNTL, 1968), p. 93. Cf. Ladislav Hrzal, Nova mysl, no. 11 (May 31, 1966), p. 25.

The forcible vertical mobility, whereby some 300,000 loyal and largely unqualified proletarians[1] replaced the holders of roles in both the political and economic systems, was accompanied by a thorough restructuring of the economy itself. The "iron concept of socialism" put emphasis on heavy industry with a corresponding neglect of light, in particular consumer, industries. In effect, this preference sacrificed lucrative foreign markets in the hard currency areas. While in 1947 the Soviet Union and the rest of the new socialist camp absorbed only 19 percent of Czechoslovakia's export, a year later this percentage jumped to 39.6 percent and reached 78.5 percent by 1953.[2] In 1969, except for Bulgaria among the Comecon countries, Czechoslovakia had the lowest share of foreign trade with Western countries.

Erroneous structure of the economy, erroneous foreign market orientation, inefficiency, obsolescence, neglect of agriculture, of services and the infrastructure in general, overemployment, a decline in working morale and in the standard of living, along with other negative after-effects were the price to be paid for Stalinist follies. Some additional data will be offered to substantiate the charges: The emphasis on quantitative expansion of the national economy led to 75 percent of investments to be allocated in the production sphere against a mere 25 percent left for the nonproductive, notably the service, sector. (In comparison, the correlation in the USSR was 65.4:34.6; in France 58.3:41.7; and in the United States 38.4:61.6.)[3] Stanislav Razl, then premier of the Czech national government, conceded in 1969 that in many respects the economy was "living off the substance," meaning thoughtless, reckless concentration on superficial goals and neglect of the country's real riches and potential.[4] Striving after the unachievable went hand in hand with a neglect of the achieved. For example, no new machinery was installed for 30 years in the Bata Industries, the famous prewar shoe producer. According to Premier Razl, housing in particular exhibited signs of neglect and deterioration; as of the late 1960s, over 50 percent of all housing units in Czechoslovakia were 40 years old and older, with 12 percent exceeding one century.[5]

Stress on quantitative expansion was accompanied by a steady increase in employment. Instead of modernizing equipment and management, idle manpower--women and the aged--was brought into the productive process. Although this economically damaging state of affairs has been lately criticized as "overemployment," in the Czech lands the economy still employs half a million pensioners, with nearly half of the total labor force composed of women--allegedly a world record. According to figures for 1966, women dominated the following spheres: agriculture, 51.2 percent of the total labor force; municipal services, 54.3 percent; communication, 51.1 percent; education and culture, 60.4 percent; retail trade and restaurants, 71.7 percent; and social services, 77.5 percent.

For Czechoslovak Stalinism the ideal man was one of hard, physical labor, highly motivated and politically engaged. Every worthy citizen was expected to approximate this goal, given of course the deterministic limits of his class identity. The primitive glorification of the proletariat was heralded in 1948 along with the imposition of collective guilt on every nonmanual laborer (except for the bureaucrats who had imposed such criteria). The intelligentsia was the scapegoat for all seasons, a whipping boy to be held on short lead in an environment in which the values of the less cultured part of the proletariat were made binding for all. For many of the uneducated political elite, including Novotny, this militant antiintellectualism was revenge and cure for their apparent inferiority complexes. The members of the intelligentsia, as one writer put it, "have to purify themselves, continuously, from the presumption of hostile and almost saboteur-like activity, when their fate was often decided by people with an instinctive or artificially implanted hatred of everyone who surpassed them in education."[7]

Class criteria deteriorated into what Frantisek Samalik once called "social racism"[8]--a primitive feeling of superiority on the part of the proletariat in compensation for gratifications the revolution had promised but did not deliver. From the viewpoint of the Stalinist bureaucracy, the implantation of such social racism into the consciousness of the proletariat was an important political achievement, for the proletariat's insulation from and antagonism vis-à-vis its natural ally, the intelligentsia, only enhanced the tenure of the Stalinist bureaucracy. It should be added, however, that the antiintellectualism of the working class was not a pure Stalinist import as it received auxiliary nourishment from the traditional Czech understanding of democracy. The "little Czech man" had habitually used plebeian egalitarianism as an excuse for envy and social jealousy and Stalinism successfully exploited his frame of mind.

Marxist socialism, rather than a model for human emancipation and self-realization, thus became a tool of the so-called nivelizace, meaning equalization of incomes. Czechoslovakia's underrating of qualified work must be close to a world record. Even now, the lifetime earnings of highly trained specialists are still behind those of a laborer with average skills. The predicament of physicians, lawyers, and teachers earning less than streetcar drivers and the like has become a distinguishing mark of the Czechoslovak socialist landscape. For example, a comparative study of remuneration of medical personnel--prepared by British economist Brian Abel Smith for the World Health Organization--showed Czechoslovakia to be second to last (followed by the then Tanganyika) of the 17 countries compared.[9] In

1964 the relation of average incomes among blue collar laborers, technicians, and white collar workers was 100:130:84.[10]

The protagonists of economic reform in Czechoslovakia were well aware of the debilitating impact of this egalitarianism. Material incentives were recognized as a necessity for energizing the economy. It was pointed out, for example, that in the case of the Trinec complex of steel mills, 93 percent of each worker's wage was fixed and secured by his mere physical presence at the plant. Only the remaining 7 percent was determined by worker's own initiative and actual performance, in consequence of which even the ambitious individuals would avoid undue exertion and rely instead on either overtime work or the employment of other family members.[11] Another solution found by the ambitious was the so-called black denivelization, meaning illicit work for private customers with the use of stolen material from state supplies. This activity served to meet public needs not satisfied by the socialist sector.

The equalization trends progressed throughout the years of Novotny's rule. While in 1959, 75.6 percent of all employees in the national economy earned between Kcs 1,000-2,500* a month, the proportion grew to 81.8 percent by 1964.[12] Interestingly, the first known in-depth study of the nation's earning pattern was completed only in 1967.[13] Among the first concessions to reality by its authors--a scientific team led by Pavel Machonin--was the admission that the tripartite division of society into workers, peasants, and working intelligentsia was antiquated: "Czechoslovak society is vertically differentiated according to the type of work, education, and way of life in one's spare time. . . . This is all the more surprising as far as differentiation in the way of life is concerned, for we had anticipated it to be far more uniform." The surprised authors revealed that the leveling of incomes did not lead to the leveling of way of life and thinking; the latter remained very much determined by one's type of work and education.

In the study, the vertical social differentiation of the Czechoslovak population was presented as a six-layer pyramid. Going from the top to the bottom, these are:

---

*Kcs denotes the local currency unit called koruna. One U.S. dollar was equal to Kcs 7 at that time and at the official tourist rate of exchange for westerners; however, for Czech citizens the rate was as high as Kcs 35 for $1. Thus the rate varied from 7 to 35!

1.   2.3 percent engaged exclusively in nonmanual labor,
with professionals from within the industries heavily represented. The majority live in cities, in Czech lands rather
than ·Slovakia; the generation between the ages of 31 and 45
prevails. 75 percent of this first category are Party members.
2.   8.0 percent predominantly nonmanual employees.
Composition is similar to that of the first layer, though
with an increasing influence of small-town individuals and
younger generation. Half of the group are Party members.
3.   15.0 percent urban stratum, in which 40 percent are
technicians. Skilled workers are also included in this
group and so are the young.
4.   26.2 percent, representing the national average,
dominated by skilled labor and by white-collar employees,
and other than big-city dwellers.
5.   30.4 percent, the worker-peasant stratum, with
lower qualifications, and a 40 percent share of Slovaks and
other minorities. Small-town and village people are most
numerous. 75 percent are non-Party members, 80 percent
hold no offices and functions, that is, have no access to
political participation.
6.   18.1 percent composed of unskilled laborers and
peasants. The rural stratum and the aged prevail. Only
14.3 percent are Party members, and only 6.4 percent have
any functions in public life.

The report expressly stated that it did not include
the political elite in its study, further failing to define
this omitted component. It may come as a surprise to some
that the regime's social policies, adjusted by and to the
political character of the Czechs, became viewed by the majority of the people as synonymous with socialism and as
worthy for preservation.
Among the numerous writers who touched upon the subject in 1968 was the young economist Vaclav Muller in his
study "What Is Socialism."[14] Muller finds Czechoslovak
society ridden with economic, political, and moral crises.
Increased production does not generate betterment in living
conditions. Under less artificial conditions of economic
planning, the current overemployment would turn into unemployment. Whereas in capitalist economic systems mechanisms have been developed for averting long-term recession
and technical stagnation, in socialism such mechanisms,
though badly needed, are both absent and unknown.
For Muller the political crisis is self-evident when
he states, "Never again shall I believe that the domination

by one Party offers a guarantee of democracy." Moral crisis, in Muller's opinion, is the heaviest burden. Stalinism was a system of mediocracy "where the average people ruled and the below-average played havoc," permitting the unworthy to compensate for their deficiencies through the officially condoned abuse of power. Yet, despite the sorry record of two decades of socialism, the Czechoslovak people do not reject basically this experiment. Muller finds the explanation in the nation's preference for social security.

Factories, offices and other institutions of the state are the only sources of livelihood, Muller noted. Employment and remuneration--once essentially economic categories --acquired the qualities of a guaranteed social pension. In pursuit of "tenured citizenship," the man in the street is likely to prefer social security to legal order and civil rights. Such "total security" can become an obstacle to economic progress and lead, after the moral stimuli generated by the revolution have been exhausted, to the total extinction of all stimuli. A further step is economic stagnation and the impossibility of guaranteeing social security in the first place. This trend was felt in Czechoslovakia mainly by senior citizens and young couples.

Thus, when it comes to matters of social welfarism, Czechs are quite prepared to settle for less, provided that one's neighbor's lot is no better.

Muller put it in these words: "The unique aspect of our situation is our willingness to be satisfied with low wages--on the assumption that the other people's income will not rise beyond certain limits either. This way of thinking has grown in our country to absurd proportions."

In addition to social security and egalitarianism, the gentle pace of work is an additional key characteristic of Czechoslovak socialism. Contrary to the glorification of Stakhanovites in the early Stalinist era, a malaise of tardiness has developed

> to exert only as much energy and effort as
> have been tacitly and with absolute solidarity
> accepted in a given place of work as a kind of
> collective norm. As a rule it is not the able
> and the efficient who raise to their level the
> average and below average workers but vice
> versa, it is the mediocre who set the norm.[15]

Actual performance is far below potential performance. According to a Unesco account, the Czechoslovak working morale is among the lowest in Europe. Actual utilization of working hours expressed by the coefficient 1.4 contrasts

with 4.2 for West Germany and 6.0 for Japan.[16] The following episode reported in the Czech daily press is rather il-
luminating in this context: "A certain Western businessman
who had visited several of our industrial plants was asked
about his view on Czechoslovakia's standard of living. He
responded: "Considering the way you work, you live exceedingly well indeed."[17] It is customary for a worker to chan-
nel his energy saved through the slow pace of his effort
into illicit ventures in his spare time and to consider such
activity a legitimate compensation for the poor rewards received from the state.

Living well means that the national average daily ca-
loric intake is 3,150 calories, thus exceeding by 250 calories the average of other industrial societies. Czechoslovak culinary habits are reminiscent of one of the characteristics of Stalinist economy--emphasis upon quantity rather
than quality. The average citizen eats plenty but not well.
Of the population, 77 percent suffer from protein shortage,
caused no doubt by the state-imposed price structure: While
1,000 calories in flour cost a mere Kcs 1.0 and in sugar
Kcs 2.23, in the case of eggs the price is Kcs 12.04 and for
meat it is Kcs 14.29. This heavy diet, with predominance of
starches over protein (together with costs for drinks and
tobacco) accounted in 1962 for 51.6 percent of the population's total expenditures.[18]

Backward housing contrasts with impressive cultural
opportunities in urban areas. A state-subsidized repertory
opera house, for example, exists even in a provincial town.
However, it is the automobile that exemplifies the Czechoslovak imitation of the affluent society. Since 1953--the
year of monetary reform, which in practice meant abolishment
of savings and a fresh start for the pauperized nation--the
sales of new cars were as follows: 1953--74; 1954--211;
1957--over 20,000; 1961--29,500; 1966--47,500; 1968--75,000,
with estimated sales of 100,000 in 1969 and 200,000 customers remaining on the waiting list.[19]

The automobile saturation in socialist countries as of
1966 is shown in Table 4.2. Absence of distinction between
state and private ownership of cars diminishes the value of
the data. Nonetheless, the distance between the two industrialized countries and the rest--with the Chinese added,
it appears, with tongue in cheek--is all too apparent. Yet,
in the Czech case, the privately owned automobile is an unreliable measure of the standard of living; it is a reflection of the craving for a status symbol for which other
amenities of life have to be sacrificed. Miroslav Holub, a
well-known poet and scientist, after his prolonged sojourn
in the United States touched upon this theme when he wrote

about "the paradox . . . that whereas for an American property is a rather utilitarian tool, for us property, a cottage, an icebox, a carriage is a value in itself, a value
measured not by advantages to the man but by all the hard-
ship required for the sake of acquisition and maintenance."[2]
The price for this petit bourgeois Czech folly is five years
of an average person's income, inferior diet, denial of
other pleasures, and additional years on a waiting list for
an inferior vehicle. After this austerity, the socialist
bliss of owning a car is reached. However, it is beyond
one's means to maintain it and the automobile becomes a
rather immobile status symbol. Social value prevails over
economic value in this environment more reminiscent of
Emperor Franz Josef than Josef Stalin.*

TABLE 4.2

Automobile Ownership in Socialist Countries, 1966

Country	Number of Cars	Population (in 000s)	Population per Car
East Germany	661,600	17,011	25.7
Czechoslovakia	521,163	14,240	27.3
Yugoslavia	237,200	19,511	82.2
Poland	234,100	31,420	134.2
Soviet Union	1,000,000	230,508	230.5
Hungary	40,000	10,146	253.6
Romania	29,000	19,027	704.7
Bulgaria	11,000	8,144	740.4
China	17,400	686,400	39,444.3
(United States	78,672,100	194,583	2.5)

Source: Halo-Sobota, March 8, 1969.

---

*High gasoline price, for example, rules out the use of
a car for commuting. However, with the gradual saturation
of the market, this particular status symbol has passed its
peak and has been to some extent replaced in the midst of
the 1960s by travel abroad as the mark of social distinction
The travel categories, in increasing order of importance,
are: socialist bloc, Yugoslavia, developing countries--
Soviet-oriented, developing countries--Western-oriented,
Western Europe, overseas capitalist, especially the United
States.

THE POLITICS OF ECONOMIC REFORM

Czechoslovakia in the 1960s provided a textbook example
of interaction and mutual conditioning of the political and
economic systems. The stultifying inefficiency that was
characteristic of the political environment spilled over
into the economic realm. The nadir was reached in 1963, the
year of absolute decline in production. In the fall of the
same year, wide discussion on the national economy opened.
This exchange of views--which, however, appeared as a one-
way dialogue with the economists proposing and the practi-
tioners disposing--evolved around the issue of the command
system. Some sought to replace the central plan, as the
main motivating force, with the market system and to grant
autonomy to economic units. This challenge to the outdated
model also threatened the parasitic bureaucratic layer that
the command system sustained and that in turn made the sustenance of the command system possible. It appeared that
termination of the bureaucracy's role was the price for economic recovery.

The political elite consented to economic experimentation with great reluctance. In 1964 the draft principles of
the reform were made public and in early 1965 were adopted
by the Central Committee of the Party. Meanwhile, the economists proceeded with detailed work on the New Economic
Model (NEM). The year 1966 and early 1967 were then the
period of "the start of the NEM and creation of conditions
for its full functioning."[21]

Novotny and his colleagues were caught in a dilemma.
As enemies of NEM by conviction and its temporary allies by
recognition of necessity, they realized that sincere implementation of the reform would render the current mode of
governing impossible. Conversely, total boycott of NEM
would aggravate the economic crisis and bury them all under
the fallen roof of the totalitarian edifice. Therefore, the
leadership settled for a compromise of selective implementation of less substantial remedies, not allowing for a thorough structural and functional transformation--without which
the success of NEM was beyond reach. Procrastination and
half measures contributed to the fall of the Novotny regime.
The new leadership showed their determination in the Action
Program of April 1968 to put the economy on rational, market-
oriented foundations. The Action Program promised gradual
removal of protectionism and subsidies in order to bring
prices closer to the world market, to decentralize the system of economic management, and to dispose of the hierarchical bureaucratic structure.

In 1968 a new dimension was added to the NEM issue, notably democratic participation and comanagement by employees.

The reformist economists proposed the establishment of Workers Councils (rady pracujicich), to be elected by the labor force and scheduled to function above and over the management. In July of that year the trade unions incorporated the proposal in the draft of their new charter; preparatory work on the workers councils and their establishment in several plants were under way.

Simultaneously, a complex debate erupted among the advocates of change. While they were in agreement about the necessity of rescinding the command economy in favor of the market economy, they differed on other issues; it was a conflict between the "democratic" and "technocratic" schools of reform. They both seemed to view freedom and efficiency as two mutually exclusive values. Advocates of the former school feared perpetuation of dictatorial practices, while their opponents pointed out that democratic Schlamperei will feed or clothe no one. At times, polemics over the virtues of the technocratic, managerial solution as opposed to the democratic idea of self-government were differences of degree rather than irreconcilable points of view.[22]

The Soviet and East European economic scene is often viewed in terms of conflicts between parasitic Party bureaucrats and rational, educated, competent technocrats. It is our contention that such a view is not applicable to Czechoslovakia. In this country the issue of NEM never became a clear-cut conflict between managers as supposed partisans of economic reforms and apparatchiks as its foes. As a result of the recruitment patterns over the past 20 years, the purges of old personnel, and the promotion policies based predominantly on political merits (aided by frequent interchangeability of political and economic roles), the managers and the apparatchiks, by virtue of their background training, and political motivation, have to be viewed as close relatives and not hostile neighbors. Thus the conflict has not been between "political managers" ("politocrats" rather than technocrats) and the apparatchiks, but rather between these two groups on the one hand and the emerging, well-trained professionals challenging the formers' qualifications for leadership on the other. To put it differently, the conflict over NEM was not one between economic roles and political roles but between competence and political loyalty.

The inadequate qualification of the managerial group can be documented as follows: According to data released in 1966, of 11,941 (factory) directors and their deputies only 2,822 were university educated and 2,265 did not go beyond grade school. On the whole, only 45 percent satisfied the qualification requirements.[23] Qualification, it was established at the time, was in inverse proportion to one's position on the managerial ladder: the higher the position, the greater the probability of deficient educational background. Thus, whereas only 29.7 percent of the top executives in industry fulfilled the qualification requirements, the ratio of their deputies was as high as 48.4 percent. Of the total of the managerial group only 11.9 percent were university trained. Of the managers, 70 percent were 45 years of age or younger and had ample opportunity in the previous 20 years to remedy their educational shortcomings. Their failure to do so may be attributed to lack of motivation or talent, or both. Preference for loyalty is clearly indicated when one considers that of the 657,000 individuals with higher education in Czechoslovakia between the ages of 25 and 59, only 11.3 percent were being utilized for management roles appropriate to their training.[24]

Reluctance of the economic bureaucrats toward educational improvement contrasts with their eagerness for political participation. According to a 1965 survey, higher-echelon managers held, on the average, three political roles, requiring six hours a week. In the case of directors, the amount of time spent on this type of political involvement was nine hours.[25] Data covering 1967 shows that the absolute majority of Czechoslovak managers were also Party functionaries. Only 21.57 percent of the respondents were not members of the Party and another 21.9 percent, though members, held no political role.[26] This symbiosis and multifunctionality of roles presents the typical economic bureaucrat as also a Party activist. Considering the profile of the executive stratum, then, the emancipation of the economic system from within was rather unlikely.

Under the threat of NEM the economic bureaucrats and their counterparts in the Party were drawn together into a mutually protective alliance. In a public opinion survey, between 80 and 90 percent of respondents in all walks of life favored abolishment of discrimination against noncommunists and the introduction of competence and education as the sole criteria in cadre work. The only group in disagreement was the economic bureaucrats, prompting the rather cautious comment that "an idea comes to one's mind if this tendency is not acceptable only to those officials in the economy who feel threatened in their careers by the introduction of such attitudes and criteria."[27]

Corollary to such views was the managers' hostility toward comanagement or workers' participation in any form. In 1968 the antagonism reached its peak. Numerous strikes were reported and other pressures were exerted in order to achieve the removal of incompetent executives. Not infrequently, the Party apparatus intervened on behalf of the victim of public wrath and ordered his reinstatement.

Stalinist managers could offer neither democracy nor efficiency. In a significant twist of irony, the Workers Councils, which bureaucrats called a pseudodemocratic trick and threat to efficiency, became the vehicle of rational changes opting for removal of dilletantism of the old management and introduction of professional competence. These councils, elected by popular vote, had a higher ratio of specialists and highly trained people than that found in management.[28] To repeat, the issue was not democratization versus efficiency, as the Stalinists asserted, but an attack on a system that was neither democratic nor efficient.

It was not the intention of the Workers Councils to substitute for management but rather to formulate the basic orientation of the given enterprise. This function was explicitly likened to that of a board of directors in a capitalist firm. According to a poll by the Academy of Sciences, the idea of Workers Councils was received with sympathy: 53.3 percent of respondents were in favor, with only 9.9 percent opposing.[29] The size of the negative vote corresponded to the estimated strength of conservative sentiment in the country. The most resolute hostility toward the councils was demonstrated by the economic bureaucrats on the higher level of the so-called general directorates. They either forbade the elections for the councils to take place and/or refused to acknowledge the results of the election held.

By the time of the Warsaw Pact invasion, only 15 percent of the total future councils were established. Realization that the Soviets were hostile to this innovation and that time was running out accelerated the foundation efforts. By October 1968 the councils operated in 70 enterprises (about 10 percent of the total), with the preparations in advanced stage in 267 others. By March 1969 the councils functioned in 114 Czech and 6 Slovak enterprises.[30] The political and economic significance of this novelty was underlined by the weight of industries involved. The key industries, including the protégés of the Stalinist Iron Concept such as Skoda Industries in Plzen (Pilsen), were the most active council builders rather than a marginal textile factory with its underpaid female labor force in the borderland province.

It was at Skoda in Plzen that the new director-general was chosen in an open contest publicized in classified ads, all in violation of 20 years of nomenklatura restriction (cadre ceiling) and monopoly of Party apparatus over appointments of this magnitude. Also at Skoda, the members of· councils from 182 enterprises, representing a labor force 900,000 strong, assembled for their first nationwide conference.[31]

In the meantime the popularity of the experiment grew in inverse proportion to the probability of its implementation. The postinvasion leadership, due to Soviet pressure and also as a reflection of their own genuine preference, changed from an unenthusiastic onlooker to a force patently hostile to workers' participation. First the Party declared further exploration of the idea undesirable and forbade formation of new councils without, however, dissolving the old ones. Next followed the work on different drafts of the Socialist Enterprises Act, viewed as an attack on the emancipation of the labor force. With the ascendancy of Husak to power, the work on the law and hence the ratification of the councils' legitimacy was postponed indefinitely. By the end of 1969, the purge of liberals among the trade union leadership was accomplished and the experiments with the Workers Councils were denounced as a demagogic, rightist, antisocialist trick.[32] All the councils were disbanded in the status quo ante drive, including the dismissal of the director-general of the Skoda industries.

Husak, in his policy statement, vowed for the return to the decisive role of the state plan in the management of the economy and abandonment of what he labeled romantic notions about the omnipotence of the market. The protagonist of totalitarian restoration condemned the NEM in terms undreamed of in Novotny times. The main Party daily, Rude pravo, even published an indictment to the effect that no NEM has even existed.[33] Equally authoritative sources condemned Ota Sik and all those who fought against the role and rule of dysfunctional bureaucracy in the economic sphere. It was charged that Sik and his school had denied the decisive role of the state in the economy and thus had destroyed the latter's socialist character.[34] Thus, in the economic system the call for Stalinist restoration has been explicit and unabashed. Both the democratic and the technocratic reformers lost.

THE PARTY'S ROLE AND INTEREST REPRESENTATION

Decision makers occupy themselves with the perception of consequences of their rejection or accommodation of particular demands. The interest of Stalinist rulers and the ruled are likely to be in fundamental conflict, and nonresponsiveness to demands is among the preconditions of the perpetuation of such a political system. To a Stalinist mind, particularly sensitive about the leading role of the Party, compliance to outside initiative would appear as a surrender, a characteristic of a weak leadership.

Emphasis on the leading role of the Party and its monopoly of initiative relegated other forces to the role of supporting actors to add desired folkloristic flair to the background setting. Appropriately, the organizations that would be referred to in a pluralistic system as associational interest groups were known as "voluntary mass organizations," the instrument of socialization and control of the noncommunist majority of the populace. Gradually, however, the adjective zajmovy (interest) did lose its satanic connotation and was reluctantly readmitted to the political realm. On the other hand, the expression natlakova skupina (pressure group) has remained synonymous with the subversion of socialism.

In the Novotny era the Party distinguished between obedience and passivity. Quite frequently the mass organizations were requested to comment on prepared legislative measures. The Party solicited the judgment of scientific institutions on pending policy measures. It befits the nature of the matter that both obligation and inclination to follow the expert advice were absent.

Of all the transmission belts, the trade unions were able to approximate closest the interest articulation function. In the early years of the People's Democracy the regime seemed to entertain the notion of the withering away of the state and the transfer of its functions to social organizations. The trade unions were entrusted with coadministration of social welfare. The acquired rights were poorly utilized, as we can detect from the tone of 1968 unionist self-criticism: "The trade unions were the initiators of social welfare laws. But their deputies in the National Assembly acquiesced to all the objections raised against such bills by the government and other state organs. They were quite willing to listen to state bureaucrats and ministers while turning a deaf ear to factory workers."[35] Leadership of the trade unions included some of the most notorious Stalinists in the country. They put great effort in preventing differentiation in a movement in which the interests of physicians and garbage collectors were ordered to be identical.

Professional organizations existed either in name only or not at all. The fate of what ought to be the bar association was such a case. Known as the Union of Czechoslovak Lawyers (JCSP), its function was exhausted with public relations for the political system, addressed to the sympathizers in capitalist countries. Dissatisfaction of the rank and file was unlikely for the excellent reason that the JCSP enjoyed the status of "voluntary selective organization" and appeared to have no membership whatsoever. In 1968 the bar repudiated its past pseudoexistence and declared the determination to become a professional organization open to all law school graduates, irrespective of their present occupation. The new program of JCSP was concerned with the fight for the economic, political, and social betterment of the legal profession, along with demands for substantive changes in the legal order.

The medical profession experienced similar emancipatory trend. In 1968 the autonomous Union of Czech Physicians was founded for the purpose of defending and furthering the interests of 23,000 physicians in Czech lands.[36] The Union also addressed itself to issues of general sociopolitical impact, as exemplified by their demand for the abolition of capital punishment.

In addition to emancipation and differentiation, in this brief posttotalitarian period the earlier-established associational interest groups gained in stature. For instance, the rather dormant Czechoslovak Scientific and Technological Society became a member of the National Front and a mandatory consulting body on matters affecting the material and social interests of technical intelligentsia.[37] The Society of Human Rights, established under Dubcek--and banned by Husak in 1969--provided an example of an interest group that despite its marginal political recognition and stigma of "bourgeois class appeasement," exhibited a surprising political agility. The organization responded to legislative proposals and submitted its own recommendation to the draft law on rehabilitations, and in an effort that could be described a classic case of lobbying, secured with the minister of education the inclusion of the United Nations Declaration of Universal Human Rights into the school curricula.[38]

Only an extensive quotation can give the flavor of the posttotalitarian change, as provided in the Rude pravo interview with Bohumil Simon, the head of the Prague municipal Party organization. His rejection of "pressure politics" and acceptance of "interest pressure," without explaining the difference between the two, was symptomatic of the reformers' lack of terminological and conceptual clarity in these untested grounds. The discussion before us revolved around Prague's housing shortage, obsolete communication, and need for priority funding from the state coffers.

Q: Isn't such a demand for these funds considered an expression of the so-called pressure politics?

A: To articulate reasonable demands and to forward substantiated proposals to higher organs for the solution of problems that are beyond the power of the city, district, or province, cannot be-- I hope--considered an expression of pressure politics. . . . The appropriate Russian word <u>nazhimat</u> (to press, or to lobby) is likely to be most often used in this connection.

Q: Was this something you learned during your recent stay in Moscow?

A: Yes, the Moscow Party organization, it seems, <u>nazhimat</u> on the central organs frequently and effectively. This can be confirmed--among other things--by two facts: In the capital of the USSR no solid fuels are used any more (only gas, oil, and electricity)--and in this is the secret of Moscow's clean air--and housing construction is relatively four to five times greater than in Prague.

Q: Thus, we too will <u>nazhimat</u> more strongly. . . . [punctuation in orig.] But to understand each other properly: Do you or do you not exclude the existence of a certain interest pressure from below represented by individual interest groups?

A: I do not exclude the existence of such an interest pressure--on the contrary, I consider it an inseparable part of politics.[39]

The centrifugal trend toward differentiation and autonomy was marked by ideological uneasiness of the reformers, amateurism of the spokesman for the emerging units of interest articulation, and last but not least, by considerable disparity in their activities. In contrast to the energetic start of the individual professions, other interests, notably those of peasantry lagged far behind.

Perhaps it is useful to comment here on the citizen's relation to his lawmaker. We shall not delve into absurdities such as the absence of secret ballot for the voter and the exercise of secret ballot by his representative in the Parliament. Of more interest to us at this moment is the heterogeneity of styles and responses among the deputies toward their constituents. The data published in 1968 ampl documented this unintentional defiance of totalitarian uniformity. The contributing factors were the deputies' political weight, engagement in other roles, nature of articulated demands, degree of Stalinist aloofness of the deputy,

and even his eventual vanity. For example, the Rude pravo
report on the activities of the Deputy Ondrej Sulety, member
of a puppet Slovak party, is a pathetic account of rustical
peregrinations and missionary fervor.[40] In contrast, Jiri
Hendrych, the man second only to Novotny in power, and the
nominal deputy for Southern Bohemia, did not face the voters
for an entire year and neither did he bother even to acknowledge their letters.[41]

Another member of the same National Assembly, Jan
Sejna--a fellow Stalinist, political general, pro-Novotny
plotter, and defector to the United States--conceived his
duty to his constituents in what may add color and charac-
terization of truly Czech totalitarian values. This role
was described in these words:

> The voters liked him, they often turned to him
> for help and he would constantly take care of
> something. But he would never do it the legal
> way or through proper use of his parliamentary
> mandate, but exclusively through his acquaint-
> ances, nepotist ties, and complicated counter-
> services. If, let us say, a village voter
> would ask him for help in the matter of allo-
> cation of cement, it would never occur to
> Sejna to think about any legal procedure, but
> quite naturally he would start to search for
> information, where and how one could get cement
> on the black market; then he sends to the fore-
> man a bottle of cognac from the supplies of
> the Ministry of National Defense, and the
> stolen cement he orders to be delivered in the
> Tatra limousine to the voter in question.[42]

Even in the period of peak Stalinism, variables affecting the elite's responsiveness, such as petty animosity,
bidding for popularity or other facets of human frailty,
could not be ruled out. The case of Vaclav Talich provides
for such an example.[43] This famous conductor was accused
of collaboration with the Nazis, and he further suffered
because of personal vendetta of the patriarch music scholar,
Minister of Education Zdenek Nejedly. But because of
Talich's great prestige in artistic circles, the Minister
of Propaganda Vaclav Kopecky, one of the most obnoxious
Stalinists in the land, managed to restore the conductor's
honor and his nomination as "National Artist."

In the beginning of 1968 the National Assembly remained
a prominent symbol of the deposed order. Owing to the im-
munity rule, the legislature was a Stalinist preserve.

Bohumir Lomsky, to cite one case of many, lost his role as minister of defense, resigned his seat in the Central Committee of the Party, but stayed as an unassailable parliamentarian. This was also the turn of all prominent personalities of the Novotny regime--except for Novotny himself--such as Hendrych, Lastovicka, Dolansky, Simunek, Fierlinger Neuman, and Plojhar. The National Assembly of 300 deputies elected in 1964, turned into a Stalinist white elephant in the preinvasion period of 1968 and only due to the totalitarian practice of legislative impotence did this animal remain a nuisance rather than a real danger.

Josef Smrkovsky, one among the most prominent Communis reformers, became the speaker of the Assembly. This body, after two decades of mortifying unanimity, started to experience a process toward diversity that had already been under way in the Party and the society at large. The public and the mass media began to pay attention to what was prematurely written of as a hopeless Stalinist relic. Whether for sake of conviction, expiation, strategic calculation, political self-realization, or bid for popularity, the tranquillity under the parliamentary roof vanished. This political cemetery turned into a battleground of polarized forces, upon whose formation Party allegiance had little influence. Thus, communist deputy Vilem Novy, an exponent of the most primitive variety of Stalinism, would cross swords with the communist deputy Gertruda Cakrtova-Sekaninova, a proponent of liberalization. Members of the puppet parties, too, used the opportunity to shed off the stigma of servility. Among the most energetic was Jan Subrt, a deputy for the Czech Socialist Party. Together with the Communist Cakrtova-Sekaninova he sponsored--but failed to carry through--a bill on legal responsibility of persons guilty of Stalinist terror in the past. Subrt also openly endorsed the 2,000-word manifesto that General Samuel Kodaj, a fellow-lawmaker, declared a call for counterrevolutionary uprising.[44] The same deputies who in 1967 adopted unanimously the new censorship law, in 1968 rescinded the act by a vote of 184 to 30 (with 17 abstentions).[45]

The parliamentarians were accused of hypocrisy and schizophrenia. After August 1968 even the most vociferous critics referred to the National Assembly with respect betraying both admiration and disbelief. In embattled Prague the Parliament went into continuous session in a gesture of patriotic defiance. Female deputies, some with an uninterrupted record of Stalinism, and the proletarian generals, no doubt humiliated by the surprise fraternal invasion, were particularly noticed for their stand.

Perhaps the most illustrious incident of emancipation was the clash of the Czech legislators with Minister of

Interior Groesser regarding his Stalinist words and deeds. Groesser was summoned to answer sharp questions and the inquiry resulted into a mild censure, duly publicized to the nation. Deputy Wichterle, when asked about this affair, responded: "There is nothing worse than when the people are afraid of the Minister of Interior."[46]

The eventful year of 1968 provided also for a rare test of the representative system. In several areas the voters took their Constitution seriously and decided to apply the provision on the recall of their deputy. According to the Constitution a request carrying signatures of at least one-third of voters registered in the given constituency would lead to new election within one month. These measures were taken both before the invasion (case of M. Pastyrik, the former trade union head) and after the invasion (case of D. Kolder, a Stalinist apparatchik), but both deputies in the best totalitarian tradition and understanding of their roles refused to surrender _their_ seats. Theirs was also the final decision. The late-1969 amendments calling for expulsion of numerous deputies, and co-option of new Party nominees, further degraded this representative system. The only form of dissent left to the deputies has been their widely practiced physical absence from the chambers. The flair of Stalinist restoration was aptly expressed in the vow of the Deputy Machacova-Dostalova in the 1969 Federal Assembly: "Never again must the parliament be allowed to degenerate into a political arena. . . ."[47]

Political participation in the East European political systems seems to generate particularly interesting themes. Among these one may mention the relation between potentiality and actuality of participation, the boundaries of participation, permissibility of political engagement, legitimacy of political neutrality, and the like.

The Czechoslovak case may offer some ground for illustration. Except for the parochial subculture of nomadic Gypsies, the citizen was forced into overt, active participation without, however, contributing to the input effect upon the decision-making process. Three modes of participation may be identified, listed in the descending order of acceptability in a totalitarian model: (1) manipulated participation; (2) nonparticipation; (3) authentic participation. Only the first variant--and, in effect, a contradiction in terms--is considered legitimate and a passing mark for proper citizenship. The second variant must not be confused with indifference or abdication. Exactly the opposite may be true. A great deal of courage may be required _not_ to join the only sacred church. The indifferent do not stand aside but are in the very midst of the anonymous tranquillity of manipulated participation. During 1968, nonparticipation lost its aura as the ultimate frontier of political daring and instead attempts at authentic participation were made. Proposed remedies appeared as a three-step progression in rehabilitating political processes: (1) rehabilitation of the legitimacy of participation, followed by (2) legitimacy of dissent, and finally by (3) legitimacy of an alternative. Of course, foreign intervention destroyed all such possibilities.

The pluralistic trends and the corresponding degree of displeasure between both the domestic and foreign defenders of totalitarian monolith may be viewed through these concentric circles:

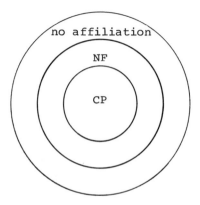

The inner circle is monopolized by the ruling Communist Party. The middle circle represents the confines of the National Front, that is, all authorized structures except the Communist Party. The outer circle is left for the remaining political behavior, if any. The National Front, rather than a structure in its own right, was first of all a concept of vassalage, a common denominator for obedient pseudoparticipation. It is also an instrument of political and economic blackmail: The applicant for membership pledges good behavior in exchange for toleration and material amenities. A suspected troublemaker is denied membership, such as was the case of the Federation of Locomotive Crews; a misbehaving member shall be expelled as happened to the Union of Film and Television Artists.

Among the first acts of the postinvasion order was the elimination of all the components of the outer circle, notably the preparatory committees for the Social Democratic Party KAN (Club of Politically Engaged Non-Party People),

and K-231 (Organization of Former Political Prisoners).
After this elimination, the purification drive reached the
middle circle, that is, both the puppet parties and the mass
organizations in the National Front. A rule of proportion
was established whereby the less the political nature of the
organization applying for a permit and thereafter for admission into the National Front, the less obstacles will hamper
such an effort. Accordingly, the ministry of interior declined to accredit the Christian organization called Work of
Council Revival (DKO) but had no objections to the establishment of the Czech Teetotalers Union.

With the components within the outer circle eliminated
and the middle circle brought to obedience, the ruling Party
as the inner circle became the focus of purification. The
year 1968 provided the opportunity for the pluralistic tendencies in the essentially nonelitist Communist Party of
Czechoslovakia to surface. Proposals were openly offered
for the creation of two Communist Parties, one reflecting
the modern trends of democratic socialism and the other ad-
hering to the traditional Bolshevik style.

The mass rather than elitist base of the ruling Party
deserves a comment. Absolute and relative figures of enrollment and voting patterns would indicate that Italy is
"more communistic" than, say, Ireland. Once such a Party
becomes the monopolist of political power, it invalidates
the correlation between the strength of membership and the
nature of the society. The direct opposite may come closer
to the truth: the larger the Party, the more diluted and
less elitist, and in effect the less suitable an instrument
of totalitarian rule. The size of the ruling entity is in
inverse proportion to the character of its policies--"the
less totalitarians, the more totalitarianism," so to speak.
In such a situation the Party is endangered by the tendency
of reflecting the heterogeneous interests of the broad membership. Rank inflation may be cured either by a purge or
by dual elitism; a minority of authentic participants and a
majority of nominal participants.

Not surprisingly, among the first Soviet postinvasion
demands was a call for the reduction of the Czechoslovak
Party's membership from the then 1.6 million to some 300,000.
This figure is the estimated strength of the conservative,
pro-Soviet forces.

The 1968 attempt at genuine participation in political
processes has been short-lived. The legitimacy of different
paths to socialism--sanctioned by Lenin, lifted by Stalin,
revived by Khrushchev, only to be once again suspended by
his successors--received in Czechoslovakia in 1968 a promise
of qualitative refinement--legitimacy of different paths to
socialism within one country.

SOME CONCLUDING REMARKS

The time factor remains a crucial variable affecting the militancy of demanding social systems. Passage of time corroded the commitment of a great many authentic totalitarians. Two decades of revolutionary dedication leave the practitioner with strained vocal cords and sore feet. Invocation of a 20-year-long dream that fails to bear tangible results ends in fatigue. Determination turns into improvisation, zeal into hypocrisy, and the Marxist writ becomes as impractical and misplaced a source of inspiration as a Gideon Bible in a brothel.

The ineffectual regime of Novotny in its closing period may perhaps be called "totalitarian immobilism." The capabilities of the system were in steady decline. The program of postinvasion "normalization" is conceived as the restoration of the pre-1968 order without its defects and weaknesses. Yet this neo-Stalinist counterreformation of the 1970s will fail to revive the totalitarian order. Instead, a weakened, exhausted system will emerge, possessing the characteristics of what may be termed a posttotalitarian system—an involuntary, partial retreat toward classical dictatorship, or, to use the terminology of Gabriel Almond and G. Bingham Powell, Sr.,[48] a move to a conservative authoritarian system. Soviet power prevents the regime from falling apart, but at the same time the nonexistent mass support and thorough alienation, especially of the young, deprives this regime of the fresh vigor it had enjoyed in and immediately after 1948. The power composition and the location and sympathy in August 1968 was akin to the situation in Poland in 1956: The nation rallied around the Party against the Soviet Union. In 1969 the Czechoslovak scene started to resemble Hungary of 1956: The nation turning its back on the Soviet Union and its own discredited Party.

The resultant system, further mutilated by cadre turnover in favor of incompetent opportunists, will have a low performance capability and mobilizational capacity. Conserving and not innovative, such a system will hardly be capable of imposing mandatory mobilization and involvement of all citizenry.

NOTES

1. <u>Rude pravo</u>, May 11, 1967.
2. Vaclav Prucha, <u>Nova mysl</u>, no. 7 (July 1968), p. 842; <u>Halo-Sobota</u>, supplement to <u>Rude pravo</u>, March 13, 1969, p. 3.
3. <u>Prace</u>, July 5, 1967.

4. Lidova demokracie, February 14, 1969.

5. Vladimir Pribsky, Svet prace, no. 27 (July 9, 1969), p. 17; Rude pravo, February 14, 1969.

6. Nova mysl, no. 2 (January 24, 1967), pp. 14-17;

7. Oto Schmidt, Zitrek, no. 4 (October 30, 1968), pp. 6-7. Cf. Zitrek, no. 6 (February 12, 1969), p. 7; Nova mysl, no. 4 (April 1968), pp. 461-65; no. 5 (May 1968), pp. 637-45; no. 2 (February 1969), pp. 184-93.

8. Frantisek Samalik, Literarni listy, no. 17 (June 20, 1968), p. 16, and no. 20 (July 11, 1968), p. 5.

9. Milan Skaryd, Czechoslovak Life, April 1969, pp. 30-31.

10. Prace, March 16, 1966.

11. Prace, November 10, 1966; Rude pravo, June 14, 1968.

12. Pavel Machonin, Nova mysl, no. 12 (June 14, 1966), p. 20; Prace, May 25, 1966 and June 29, 1967.

13. Pavel Machonin, Nova mysl, no. 4 (April 1968), pp. 466-74, and no. 1 (January 1969), pp. 67-71; Alena Cechova, Reporter, no. 19 (May 15, 1969), pp. 23-24, Miloslav Petrusek, Sociologicky casopis, no. 6 (December 1969), p. 574.

14. Literarni listy, no. 13 (May 23, 1968), pp. 1, 3.

15. Ibid.

16. Radio Prague, July 23, 1968, quoted by FEC Situation Report, no. 61 (July 24, 1969), p. 3.

17. Svobodne slovo, March 22, 1969, p. 1.

18. Zdenek Urbanek, Rude pravo, August 13, 1966; Bohumil Simon et al., "Standard of Living," Nova mysl, no. 1 (January 1968), pp. 34-45; Lidova demokracie, July 26, 1969.

19. Lidova demokracie, June 9, 1967 and November 19, 1968; Rude pravo, June 21, 1967; Halo-Sobota, February 8 and April 12, 1969.

20. Miroslav Holub, Literarni listy, no. 16 (June 13, 1968), pp. 7-8.

21. Bohumil Simon et al., Nova mysl, no. 26 (December 28, 1967), p. 8.

22. Petr Pithart, Literarni listy, no. 23 (August 1, 1968), p. 4; Vladislav Chlumsky, Literarni listy, no. 25 (August 15, 1968), p. 5; Rudolf Slansky, Reporter, no. 21 (May 22-29, 1968), p. 10; Miroslav Jodl, Reporter, no. 24 (June 12-19, 1968), p. 7; Vaclav Klaus, Reporter, no. 23 (June 5-12, 1968), p. 10; Jan Zoubek, Reporter, no. 30 (July 24-31, 1968), p. 9; Otakar Turek and Miroslav Toms, Reporter, no. 32 (August 7-14, 1968), p. 15; Ivan Svitak, Prace, May 19, 1968.

23. Prace, January 15, 1966; Czechoslovak Life, no. 10 (October 1968), p. 2.

24. J. Klofac and V. Tlusty, "Socialism and Just Reward," Reporter, no. 43 (November 6-15, 1968), pp. v-xii.

25. Jiri Camra, Nova mysl, no. 26 (December 28, 1967), p. 6.

26. Jaroslav Kolar and Alena Kunstova, Nova mysl, no. 4 (April 1969), p. 480.

27. Ladislav Koubek, Nova mysl, no. 1 (January 1969), p. 80.

28. Reporter, no. 5 (February 6, 1968), p. iv.

29. Prace, August 13, 1968; Dragoslav Slejska, Reporter, no. 16 (April 24, 1969), pp. 25-26.

30. Politika, October 10, 1968; Nove slovo, March 13, 1969.

31. Rude pravo, December 18, 1968 and January 11, 1969

32. Prace, November 15, 1968; Rude pravo, October 25, 1968; October 2 and 25, 1969.

33. Jiri Smrcina, Rude pravo, May 23, 1969.

34. Rude pravo, July 23, 24, 25, 1969.

35. Vaclav Kraus, Czechoslovak Life, no. 6 (June 1969) pp. 8-9.

36. Literarni listy, no. 22 (July 25, 1968), p. 2; Svobodne slovo, March 29, 1969, p. 3.

37. Prace, October 31, 1968, pp. 4-5.

38. Czechoslovak Life, no. 3 (March 1969), p. 28.

39. Rude pravo, December 7, 1968, p. 2.

40. Rude pravo, November 9, 1968, p. 2.

41. Jiri Seydler, Reporter, no. 11 (March 20, 1969), p. 14.

42. Pavel Juracek, Mlady svet, no. 13 (March 29, 1968), pp. 8-9.

43. Frantisek Cervinka, Listy, no. 11 (March 20, 1969), p. 9.

44. Literarni listy, no. 20 (July 11, 1968), p. 2, and no. 22 (July 25, 1968), p. 14.

45. FEC Situation Report, no. 72 (June 28, 1968), p. 1; also see no. 56 (May 16, 1968), p. 2.

46. Reporter, no. 19 (May 15, 1969), p. 8. For details of the Groesser case, see Rude pravo, April 30, 1969.

47. Zivot strany, October 8, 1969.

48. Gabriel Almond and G. Bingham Powell, Jr., Comparative Politics: A Developmental Approach (Boston: Little, Brown, 1966), pp. 256, 280ff.

5

ROMANIA: PROBLEMS
OF THE MULTILATERALLY
DEVELOPED SOCIETY
Trond Gilberg

One of the most important developments in political
science during the last decade has been the increased interest in the study of modernization. As early as 1961, Karl W.
Deutsch outlined the major elements of social mobilization
and political modernization as he saw them.[1] Subsequent
works in this field have by and large accepted his categories and concepts, and many scholars have proceeded to examine economic and political modernization comparatively and
in one-country studies.[2]

Among students of communist political systems, the decline of "totalitarianism" as an explanatory concept has
resulted in increased awareness of other main elements of
political life in such societies. There is now considerable
interest in the relationship between modernization, both
economic and political, and communist power. The basic
problem confronting scholars in this field is essentially
this: How can a political elite, often made up of old
apparatchiks with limited technical knowledge handle the
complex problems arising from economic modernization, a
process they themselves have started? What will be the nature of political power in such systems, given the systemic
requirements of modernization? These crucial questions will
remain the major focus of this study.

According to Deutsch, social mobilization and political
development, crucial elements of the more general modernization process, can be identified by the following developmental factors: industrialization, urbanization, increased
literacy, income growth (both totally and per capita), and
growth of mass media and their audiences. Political development can be measured through increased voting, expanded participation in groups and other structures, and linguistic,

cultural, and political assimilation of subgroups in society.[3] The process as outlined appears unilinear: Societies will experience industrialization, thus shifting the working force from primarily agricultural to industrial; this process will foster urbanization, with increased opportunities for better education (which in turn is needed for the industrialization process); this process will result in higher incomes, both totally for society and also for individual citizens. Politically, social mobilization as described above will result in higher participation ratios in terms of voting and other political activity in various groups. The modernization process in the economic field will tend to unify society, thus reducing the viability of regional, cultural, and linguistic particularities, which will in turn lead to assimilation in cultural, linguistic particularities, which will in turn lead to assimilation in cultural, linguistic, and political terms.[4]

The unilinear dimension of the modernization and mobilization process, as described above, causes some important problems in substantive research. It is at least conceivable that industrialization and urbanization will not result in higher educational achievements; at least in the early stages of industrial development, it may be feasible or even rational for political and economic elites to maintain a low level of literacy among the urban, unskilled proletariat.[5] Similarly, industrialization will not yield higher per capita income as a matter of course, although total national income is likely to rise in this process. (Part of the increase in GNP, for example, may temporarily be produced by higher exploitation of labor, not added income for individuals.) As the modernization process progresses, it is indeed likely that improved literacy standards and higher per capita income will result, but an examination of countries undergoing various phases of uneven modernization, such as Romania, Bulgaria, and other countries in Eastern Europe, may indeed show them to be at a stage where the unilinear tendency described above is not that clear.

Important as some of the modifications listed above may be, they still represent cases that can ultimately be fitted into the scheme devised by Deutsch and others. A much more fundamental problem arises when the student of modernization attempts to examine countries that remain relatively low on such indicators as industrialization but can show impressive figures for literacy, mass media circulation, GNP, and per capita income. Should such a society be classified as premodern or traditional? The analytical problem arising in this context has not been satisfactorily solved in the Deutsch model or in many other works on modernization.

One of the sources of difficulty in classification encountered in this field stems from the inherent tendency in
Deutsch's model to classify societies or states as modernized rather than the populations inhabiting such units. It
seems necessary at this point to examine not only the gross
categories of industrialization, urbanization, population
flow, and educational achievement, but also the skill levels
achieved by the population groups within each occupational
and educational category. Thus it would be possible to
speak of a modernized economic system in which the overwhelming majority of the population would be engaged in
agricultural pursuits, but where high yield ratios, mechanization, and sustained high productivity indicate skill
levels that can reasonably be categoriezed as "modern."*
For this reason this study will include an examination of
productivity and other skill measures in each major occupational category as well as the gross indicators of the
Deutsch model.

While the most common scholarly model of modernization
requires modification, the communist model, in practice in
Eastern Europe for the last quarter century, deviates from
the Deutsch scheme in some crucial aspects. The modernization efforts launched and carried out in Eastern Europe
during Stalinism did not follow a unilinear trend, but must
rather be characterized as a wholesale onslaught on this
massive problem on a broad front. Thus, the goals were not
only industrialization and transfer of population masses
from rural to urban areas, but also mechanization and organizational reform in agriculture, a process that was
forcefully pushed simultaneously with the industrialization
process. Similarly, the Stalinist leaders in Eastern Europe,
clearly men in a hurry, launched a campaign designed to
eradicate illiteracy at a time when rapid economic trans-
formations in urban and rural areas were putting severe
strains on the entire societal fabric. It is this wholesale
onslaught on "backwardness," this concerted, broadly based
push for modernity, that to some extent sets the communist
systems of Eastern Europe apart from the Western-based
Deutsch model.[6]

The political effects of social mobilization and political development toward modernization, as set forth in much
of the literature on the subject, will not necessarily

---

*One such country may be Denmark, which has a high
proportion of the population in agriculture, but with high
scores on modernization indexes such as productivity, education, social services, and political participation.

follow in the communist-led modernization process. Political activity, such as voting, cannot be properly described as participation in communist systems; it is rather a form of political mobilization, designed to lend an aura of legitimacy to a political system that cannot be classified as democratic. The student of modernization in communist systems must therefore look to other indicators of political activity in the stage of modernity; important fields of examination would include interest group and "grouping" activity, political recruitment patterns that deviate from the traditional norm of Party dominance, and increased pluralism in the decision-making process itself.

Finally, the unilinear assumption of political integration and assimilation of subgroups into a dominant national culture as a result of the modernization process may not apply in multiethnic societies. Some studies have shown that ethnic minorities develop increased cohesion as a result of improved education and other processes of modernization, partly as a defense mechanism against the drastic change associated with rapid socioeconomic development, but partly because of greater awareness of the ethnic heritage in social, economic, and cultural fields.[7] The possibility of a reversal of unilinear development must be watched closely in a multiethnic state such as Romania.

The limited criticism of Deutsch, outlined above, is not intended to eliminate the general modernization model from the current research project. Rather, it is envisaged that the Deutsch model will remain as a general framework, but with modifications introduced (as indicated above). In this way it is hoped that some of the ambiguities in the model itself can be dealt with while at the same time the communist model of modernization can be incorporated as a focus for research.

THE ROMANIAN DEFINITION OF MODERNIZATION

Any study of modernization in Eastern Europe must of necessity deal with the self-definition of this process as expressed by the political leaders in any one time period. The regimes of this area came to power with an express goal of propelling their societies into the ranks of modernity after World War II. An evaluation of regime performance in this field must clearly deal with the perceived goals of the political leadership as well as the objective standards posited by the scholarly model outlined above.

The evaluative process is somewhat enhanced by the fact that the regime definition of modernization in many respects

coincides with the Deutsch model. In the case of Romania,
"modernity" throughout the last decade has been defined by
the RCP (Romanian Communist Party) leadership under Gheorghe
Gheorghiu-Dej and Nicolae Ceausescu as a two-pronged development toward a "multilaterally developed society." One of
the two major thrusts is social and economic, the other political. In socioeconomic terms, the "multilaterally developed society" would have the following major characteristics:

    1. High level of industrialization. Romania in this
stage would be predominantly industrialized (that is, industry would be the primary employer for a majority of the
work force). The structure of industry would show very high
development levels for both the heavy and light branches,
with a high technological level of automatization, rationalization, and electronics. Because of the modern equipment
in all fields of industry and the superior training of the
work force, output figures and productivity would be comparable to that of the contemporary United States and West
Germany, two of the countries most frequently used as examples of modernized societies.[8]
    While the end result of the multilaterally developed
society would be high levels of development everywhere, the
road to this goal is to be primarily through the process of
heavy industrialization, which would in turn provide the
base for rapid and sustained improvements in the consumer-
goods field. This two-step process of industrialization
has been even more heavily emphasized by Ceausescu during
the past few years, when he has repeatedly scolded the economic planners for their tendency to import technology from
abroad without laying a domestic base for its use. Ceausescu
is now emphasizing the need to build a base domestically,
including a technological foundation.[9]
    The industrialization process will also include urban-
ization, which will take place under controlled circumstances, ensuring planned growth, limitation of size, and
regional center development designed to offset problems of
rapid growth. It is envisaged that 65-70 percent of the
total population would be living in urban areas by the
1990s, the official "target decade" for the multilaterally
developed society.[10]
    2. A highly productive agriculture. The Ceausescu
concept of modernization includes a major function of agriculture even within the multilaterally developed society.
A substantial number of people will remain in this employment category, and the regime envisions agriculture as one
of the economic cornerstones of society. The most important

developmental factors in agricultural modernization are technological improvements and better utilization of raw materials and manpower, which can significantly raise the output and productivity in this sector. Once again, the Romanian planners heavily emphasize skill levels within any given economic sector as a measure of modernization. The ratio of employment between such sectors is only one of the developmental goals established.[11]

3. _An educated and highly cultured citizenry._ A constant theme running through major speeches and policy statements during the last decade has been the need to raise the cultural level of the citizenry to a higher stage in the multilaterally developed society. This level will include "virtually universal" intermediate education for the entire population, with ample possibilities for specialization and on-the-job training. At the same time, the modernized citizen will have full access to the cultural productions of the socialist society in such fields as the arts, literature and sports. Furthermore, "culture" in the multilaterally developed society also connotes a set of interrelationships in which the individual will use his acquired skills for societal purposes, rather than for petty, selfish gain. The cultured citizen, then, is well educated, well trained in his profession, so that he can perform necessary economic functions and at the same time interact with others in the social setting of high development. Above all, the modernized citizen would discard traditional ways of thinking and would leave behind old superstitions and prejudices. The most immediate payoff of such a development is expected to be much closer functional integration of ethnic groups into the mainstream of economic life. This concept of culture clearly has important political connotations as well.[12]

4. _Continued emphasis on central planning and management._ Although the final goal of socioeconomic modernization is to lay the material base for a communist society, the multilaterally developed society will continue to be managed by political and economic experts, with a continued centralizing emphasis (although practical decentralization will take place wherever needed for efficient carrying out of the economic plans, which will continue to be centrally determined). Modernity, in this context, essentially means a well-organized, smoothly functioning bureaucracy with skill levels sufficient for high-level performance in all fields of the economy. This element has strong political connotations, insofar as the planners and managers will continue to be Party leaders.[13]

The RCP leadership is engaged in a complicated task of political mobilization, which goes hand in hand with the socioeconomic goals outlined above. Thus, the highly literate, well-trained, and socially conscious population in the multilaterally developed society must also act politically, but in carefully prescribed ways, chief of which are the following:

1. Acceptance of the Communist Party as the supreme force, politically and in socioeconomic leadership, in society. The citizen in the multilaterally developed society will be a conscious and willing participant in the political process guided by the RCP. This form of participation clearly differs drastically from activities subsumed under the same heading in a Western democratic society; since there is no possibility for any political actor to challenge the leadership in society, opposition cannot become establishment, and "participation" remains political mobilization, an important lubricant in the well-oiled machinery of modernity.

2. Acceptance of the right of the Communist Party to mobilize the citizenry for regime goal fulfillment at any time. The communist elite in Romania envisions a modern society as one where the citizenry willingly forsakes privacy, abstains from group activity designed to isolate individuals from the top political leadership, and enthusiastically undertakes duties laid upon them by that leadership in its capacity as societal leader. In a word, the modernized citizen is easily mobilizable and will frequently volunteer his services for the fulfillment of leadership goals.[14]

3. Acceptance of a Romanian communist system, with equal rights and duties for all "cohabiting nationalities."[15] This concept is of the greatest importance in a multiethnic society such as Romania, where nationalities at times have engaged in considerable political controversy. Modernity, on the other hand, is seen as the great equalizer of all ethnic groups, thus destroying old, parochial allegiances and providing a new, higher commitment--to the multilaterally developed society.[16]

4. Acceptance of the principle that modernized citizens will act politically to help eradicate "traditional" and "old-fashioned" political views that may remain in sectors of the population during the modernization process and in some pockets even after the process is essentially completed. In addition, the modernized citizen must be on

guard against occasional elite mismanagement, even in the
multilaterally developed society, so that such mistakes can
be dealt with. It would clearly be a great advantage for
the top Party leadership if the citizenry would become
highly expert at performing this watchdog function, especially vis-à-vis the bureaucratic and technical executors
at all levels of government.[17]

    5. <u>A high level of anticipatory political activity</u>.
The modernized citizen is so well integrated into society
and the policies to be carried out by the political regime
that he will anticipate elite actions and reactions. In
this manner, the cumbersome control functions, now occupying much of the elite's time, could be dispensed with, to
the great benefit of society in other fields.[18]

    6. <u>Universal acceptance of the end result--a commu-
nist society</u>. One of the sources of regime legitimacy in a
communist system is its claim that is working in close conjunction with history for a highly desirable end result--a
communist society. In this context, the Ceausescu regime is
striving to prevent the socioeconomic modernization process,
with its increased social stratification and diversification, from producing "bourgeois" values and attitudes among
the citizenry. A concerted effort of political socialization, with emphasis on socialist "morality and consciousness," is under way among the masses of the population, the
technical and artistic intelligentsia, the peasantry, and
Party cadres. Political modernization, when successful,
will reduce the danger of "embourgeoisement" in this field,
and will eventually eliminate such old values altogether.[19]

SOCIOECONOMIC MODERNIZATION IN ROMANIA, 1950-70

Industry

    Both the modified Deutsch model and the Romanian "self-
definition" of modernization specify industrialization as a
major element in this process. Table 5.1 shows the process
of industrialization in Romania in the period 1950-70.
Table 5.2 indicates the relative weight of various branches
of the national economy in the same period.

    The massive, sustained industrialization drive in Ro-
mania during the last quarter century has also resulted in
an increasingly sophisticated mix of finished products, as
illustrated by Table 5.3. It shows an impressive overall
growth of total industrial production, but the bulk of this
increase stems from the regime's emphasis on Group A (heavy
industry). An analysis of the subgroups shows the increasing

Principal Indicators of Economic Development in Romania, 1955-69
(1950 = 100)

	1955	1958	1960	1963	1965	1969
Population	106.2	110.7	112.8	115.3	116.7	122.7
Population occupied in the economy	112	113	114	115	116	118
Number of wage earners	139	139	153	185	203	234
Volume of investments	238	276	431	655	788	12*
Social product	186	215	263	338	414	582
National income	192	214	268	338	413	561
Total industrial production	202	267	340	502	649	10*
Group A	217	299	397	620	823	13*
Group B	185	229	277	373	457	674
Total agricultural production	162	141	171	170	193	223

*Number of times of 100 percent increase over base year.

Source: Anuarul Statistic, 1970, pp. 104-05.

TABLE 5.2

Weight of Various Fields of Production in the Total Social Product
and National Income of Romania, 1938-69

Year	Industry	Construction	Agriculture and Forestry	Transportation and Telecommunications	Other Fields
			Percent of Social Product		
1938	39.0	5.4	30.2	6.4	7.8
1950	46.6	7.4	25.8	4.2	8.1
1955	44.9	7.9	30.5	3.9	6.1
1960	52.4	9.7	24.6	3.5	5.2
1963	56.2	9.9	21.6	3.5	3.7
1965	57.3	9.4	21.7	3.3	3.7
1969	62.7	9.9	18.2	3.3	3.2
			Percent of National Income		
1938	30.8	4.4	38.5	6.5	4.9
1950	44.0	6.0	28.0	4.3	5.9
1955	39.8	5.6	37.6	3.7	4.1
1960	44.1	9.0	33.1	3.8	3.5
1963	46.9	8.3	29.8	4.2	2.9
1965	48.9	8.0	29.3	4.0	2.6
1969	57.4	9.0	24.1	3.9	2.5

Source: Anuarul Statistic, 1970, p. 109.

TABLE 5.3

Total Industrial Production in Romania, Groups A, B, and Subgroups, 1948-69
(1938 = 100)

	1948	1950	1955	1960	1963	1965	1969
Industry—total	85	147	299	502	741	957	15*
Group A	92	167	363	664	10*	14*	22*
Group B	79	129	240	358	483	591	872
Electrical and thermal energy	156	248	576	11*	17*	27*	52*
Combustibles	76	98	182	263	351	387	476
Coal	87	137	207	283	359	400	567
Petroleum	72	87	171	232	306	333	395
Ferrous metallurgy (including extraction of ferrous metals)	121	193	294	726	10*	12*	20*
Nonferrous metallurgy (including extraction of nonferrous metals)	68	137	293	532	809	998	17*
Machine construction and metal finishing	87	179	496	10*	17*	23*	41*
Chemical industry	101	171	502	11*	23*	35*	74*
Extraction of nonmetalliferous minerals and production of abrasive substances	131	108	392	865	15*	19*	28*
Construction materials	117	273	686	11*	18*	23*	38*
Exploitation and processing of wood products	99	136	247	363	526	672	870
Cellulose and paper (including exploitation of reeds)	120	165	226	379	658	910	16*
Glass, porcelain, pottery	133	229	482	794	12*	14*	20*
Textiles	91	172	299	404	553	663	981
Ready-made clothes	123	319	478	770	10*	13*	21*
Leather goods, fur, footwear	102	175	299	432	555	702	10*
Food industries	62	107	181	254	319	382	500
Soap and cosmetics	84	129	291	358	440	538	771
Polygraphic industries	131	147	308	515	822	10*	15*

*Number of times of 100 percent increase over base year.

Source: Anuarul Statistic, 1970, pp. 158-59.

emphasis on electrical energy, machine building, and the chemical industry, with construction materials, ferrous and nonferrous metallurgy experiencing somewhat lower growth rates. Among the consumer-goods industries, only ready-made clothing can compete with heavy industry indicators in terms of growth rates.

Part of the industrial development in Romania has been brought about by added manpower, more technical experts, and more sophisticated machinery; part of the increase has come from increased productivity per employee. Table 5.4 shows the total rise in the industrial work force, as compared to other major economic categories. Table 5.5 illustrates the increase in all major industries, 1938-69; and Table 5.6 analyzes the rise in productivity per employee in selected industries.

The evidence presented in Tables 5.4-5.6 clearly shows an impressive achievement in the industrialization of Romania during the last 25 years. Total output has gone up significantly in all major industrial subfields, with the strongest showing in such high-priority fields as chemicals, machine building, electrical energy, and metallurgy. The wood processing industry also remains strong. Much of the output increase stems from added manpower, but an overall rise in productivity per worker has also been an important factor, as shown by Table 5.6. The RCP elite's emphasis on introducing better general education and improved facilities for specialized training on a mass basis thus appears to have paid off in terms of higher production output.

A very significant element in raising the skill levels in industry has been the constant increase in highly trained supervisory personnel in this branch of the economy. Table 5.7 shows the rising number of technical specialists in the major industrial subfields examined above.

The evidence presented in Table 5.7 clearly illustrates the frontal attack launched by the Romanian modernizers, the RCP elite, in the field of multilateral development. Industrialization can only become possible when the skill levels of both workers and the industrial managers and technicians are high enough to absorb the requirements of advanced technology and an increasingly complex capital plant. The Romanian modernizers have therefore expanded the numerical base of industrial workers, introduced new machinery, and trained the rank and file as well as the technical experts simultaneously. It is this major overall attack on underdevelopment (as defined by the modernizing elite), fueled by the will to develop and a simultaneous development of the capabilities of the citizenry that sets the communist model of modernization apart from Deutsch's scheme.

TABLE 5.4

Economically Active Population in Selected Fields in Romania, 1956 and 1966

	1956	Percent of Total	1966	Percent of Total
Total	10,449,128		10,362,300	
Industry	1,478,025	14.1	2,013,525	19.4
Agriculture and forestry	7,278,518	69.7	5,920,327	57.1
Construction	265,513	2.6	536,519	5.2
Transport and telecommunications	297,025	2.8	391,236	3.8
Commerce and trade	257,946	2.5	387,759	3.7
Health care	128,112	1.2	199,066	1.9
Education	178,034	1.7	340,088[a]	3.3
Science, culture, and the arts	83,277	0.8	51,805[b]	0.5
Administration (center, local, and cooperative)	194,141	1.9	146,996	1.4
Political, cultural, and societal organizations	38,782	0.4	29,062[c]	0.3

[a]Some of the science personnel were counted in "Education" in 1966, but not in 1956.

[b]Reduced number in this category due to (a).

[c]In 1966 only Party cadres were counted in this category, while in 1956, administrators were also included.

Sources: 1956, Recensamîntul Populatiei din 21 Februarie 1956; 1966, Recensamîntul Populatiei si Loquintelor din 15 Martie 1966.

Number of Workers on Active Payrolls in Romanian Industry, 1950-69
(in thousands)

	1950	Per-cent of Total	1955	Per-cent of Total	1960	Per-cent of Total	1963	Per-cent of Total	1965	Per-cent of Total	1969	Per-cent of Total
Industry—total	640.4		916.4		1,067.9		1,318.4		1,441.0		1,730.6	
Electrical and thermal energy	4.9	0.8	9.6	1.0	11.7	1.1	21.3	1.6	26.3	1.8	29.8	1.7
Combustibles	49.0	7.7	70.0	7.6	72.6	6.8	77.0	5.8	82.6	5.7	81.6	4.7
Coal	25.5	4.0	42.1	4.6	41.1	3.8	41.3	3.1	45.7	3.2	47.6	2.8
Petroleum	21.9	3.7	25.7	3.0	28.0	3.0	31.0	2.7	31.8	2.5	28.9	1.9
Ferrous metallurgy (incl. extraction of ferrous metals)	27.0	4.2	35.7	3.9	48.7	4.6	57.4	4.4	59.8	4.1	67.9	3.9
Nonferrous metallurgy (incl. extraction of nonferrous metals)	12.7	2.0	17.1	1.9	28.9	2.7	42.2	3.2	46.2	3.2	49.0	2.8
Machine construction and metal finishing	131.1	20.5	195.5	21.3	237.5	22.2	299.8	22.7	334.4	23.2	432.4	25.0
Chemical industry	15.6	2.4	30.0	3.3	42.7	4.0	61.0	4.6	74.3	5.2	104.5	6.0
Extraction of nonmet-alliferous minerals and production of abrasive substances	2.3	0.4	3.9	0.4	4.6	0.4	5.9	0.4	6.7	0.5	7.9	0.5
Construction materials	36.3	5.7	57.8	6.3	60.3	5.6	80.8	6.1	80.4	5.6	92.8	5.4
Exploitation and processing of wood products	118.1	18.4	179.5	19.6	181.7	17.0	219.9	16.7	241.2	16.7	258.5	14.9
Cellulose and paper (incl. exploitation of reeds)	7.0	1.1	7.5	0.8	11.3	1.0	17.3	1.3	21.5	1.5	25.8	1.5
Glass, porcelain, pottery	8.3	1.3	10.6	1.2	15.7	1.5	20.0	1.5	20.6	1.4	23.1	1.3
Textiles	85.0	13.3	111.9	12.2	128.6	12.0	153.1	11.6	159.1	11.0	194.8	11.3
Ready-made clothes	27.3	4.3	39.0	4.3	54.5	5.1	68.6	5.2	76.0	5.3	103.4	6.0
Leather goods, fur, footwear	35.4	5.5	40.1	4.4	50.6	4.7	56.6	4.3	58.8	4.1	75.4	4.4
Food industries	67.7	10.6	89.7	9.8	94.3	8.8	110.5	8.4	125.5	8.7	153.4	8.9
Soap and cosmetics	0.9	0.1	1.1	0.1	1.4	0.1	1.6	0.1	1.7	0.1	2.0	0.1
Polygraphic industries	8.5	1.3	13.1	1.4	15.8	1.5	18.3	1.4	18.6	1.3	18.6	1.1

Source: Anuarul Statistic, 1970, pp. 218-19.

TABLE 5.6

Productivity of Labor (per worker) in Selected Industries in Romania, 1955-69

(1950 = 100)

	1955	1960	1963	1965	1969	Average Annual Increase 1951-69 (in percent)
Industry--total	160	237	291	343	456	8.3
Electrical and thermal energy	183	362	443	562	980	12.8
Combustibles	133	178	225	232	295	5.9
Coal	91	130	164	166	228	4.4
Petroleum	171	216	262	279	371	7.1
Ferrous metallurgy (incl. extraction of ferrous metals)	121	229	283	325	448	8.2
Nonferrous metallurgy (incl. extraction of nonferrous metals)	119	150	158	176	284	5.6
Machine construction and metal finishing	219	392	504	615	875	12.1
Chemical industry	170	276	400	502	766	11.3
Extraction of nonmetalliferous minerals and production of abrasive substances	240	481	726	824	10x	13.2
Construction materials	179	282	352	455	636	10.2
Exploitation and processing of wood products	146	205	254	293	362	7.0
Cellulose and paper (incl. exploitation of reeds)	139	166	198	222	333	6.5
Glass, porcelain, pottery	178	229	285	320	408	7.7
Textiles	143	172	202	231	282	5.6
Ready-made clothes	160	212	244	276	341	6.7
Leather goods, fur, footwear	184	237	283	349	414	7.8
Food industries	138	185	202	224	252	5.0
Soap and cosmetics	233	228	247	287	364	7.0
Polygraphic industries	149	208	285	346	483	8.7

Source: Anuarul Statistic, 1970, p. 228.

Number of Engineers and Technicians in Subsections of Romanian Republican* Industry, 1960-69

	1960	Per-cent of Total	1963	Per-cent of Total	1965	Per-cent of Total	1969	Per-cent of Total
Total	75,675		88,498		102,258		123,648	
Electrical and thermal energy	2,454	3.2	3,668	4.1	4,479	4.4	5,200	4.2
Combustibles	6,040	8.0	6,108	6.9	6,772	6.6	7,516	6.1
Coal	2,408	3.2	2,380	2.7	2,736	2.7	3,230	2.6
Petroleum	3,235	4.8	3,270	4.2	3,541	3.9	3,760	3.5
Ferrous metallurgy (incl. extraction of ferrous metals)	3,760	5.0	3,940	4.5	4,617	4.5	6,355	5.1
Nonferrous metallurgy (incl. extraction of nonferrous metals)	2,493	3.3	3,277	3.7	4,016	3.9	5,110	4.1
Machine construction and metal finishing	27,297	36.1	33,163	37.5	37,189	36.4	47,805	38.7
Chemical industry	4,469	5.9	6,141	6.9	7,922	7.7	11,260	9.1
Extraction of nonmetalliferous minerals and production of abrasive substances	439	0.6	433	0.5	517	0.5	626	0.5
Construction materials	2,104	2.8	2,478	2.8	3,101	3.0	3,718	3.0
Exploitation and processing of wood products	8,992	11.9	9,499	10.7	11,666	11.4	12,073	9.8
Cellulose and paper (incl. exploitation of reeds)	697	0.9	997	1.1	1,336	1.3	1,807	1.5
Glass, porcelain, pottery	693	0.9	835	0.9	930	0.9	1,140	0.9
Textiles	5,011	6.6	5,381	6.1	5,925	5.8	6,981	5.6
Ready-made clothes	651	0.9	771	0.9	912	0.9	1,172	0.9
Leather goods, fur, footwear	1,435	1.9	1,536	1.7	1,728	1.7	1,956	1.6
Food industries	7,606	10.1	8,736	9.9	9,484	9.3	8,925	7.2
Soap and cosmetics	153	0.2	162	0.2	161	0.2	178	0.1
Polygraphic industries	920	1.2	1,016	1.1	1,275	1.2	1,535	1.2

*Under direct national supervision.

Source: Anuarul Statistic, 1970, pp. 220-21.

Agriculture

As indicated above, the Romanian political and economic leaders envision agriculture as an important part of the economy in the multilaterally developed society. This economic branch will be significantly smaller than hitherto in terms of total manpower employed, but the reduction in this field is to be offset by increased skills in the remaining agricultural population, which will in turn result in higher output. Significant improvement will also be achieved through mechanization and injection of large numbers of specialists (agronomists, zootechnicians, etc.). Table 5.8 illustrates the trend of mechanization in agriculture since pre-World War II times; Table 5.9 shows the output of specialized personnel working in agriculture; and Table 5.10 shows the increases in output of total agricultural production, 1938-69.

Education

A major objective of the Romanian modernizing elite has been to raise the general level of education of the population, while at the same time producing the mix of experts needed for sustained economic growth and, presumably, political modernization. In this respect, considerable achievements have been recorded by the Romanian regime during the last quarter century. Table 5.11 illustrates the developments of professional schools, 1948-70; Table 5.12 shows the rise in the general educational levels, 1938-70; and Table 5.13 examines higher educational development, 1948-70.

The achievements of the Romanian modernizers are perhaps more impressive in the educational field than in any other area posited as crucial in the modernization process. There is now universal elementary education, which has resulted in the final eradication of illiteracy; specialized schools yearly turn out a large number of cadres for the ever-expanding industry; and the impressive production of people with higher education is one of the main factors in continued high growth rates in the economy. The RCP leadership has clearly put a major emphasis on the most crucial element in the modernization process--the achievement of requisite skills among the citizenry at all levels.

TABLE 5.8

Tractors and Major Agricultural Machinery in Romania, 1938-69

	1938	1948	1950	1955	1960	1963	1969
Tractors							
in physical units[a]	4,049	10,189	13,713	23,033	44,194	65,351	101,906
in conventional units of 15 HP[b]	4,858	12,227	16,746	30,488	65,290	100,894	177,464
Ploughs for tractors	--	8,606	13,642	25,613	46,130	70,809	95,015
Mechanical cultivators	--	560	1,343	7,787	20,667	20,808	28,037
Rotating hoes	--	--	--	--	6,784	11,612	16,041
Mechanical sowing machines	--	5,100	6,350	12,454	33,948	63,118	55,040
Spreaders for fertilizers	--	--	--	--	3,182	1,895	13,757
Irrigators	--	--	--	--	2,864	5,328	8,752
Combines for cereal	--	45	118	1,535	17,577	32,493	48,368
Threshers for cereal	15,161	16,320	14,251	15,467	12,660	8,919	--
Combines for corn	--	--	--	--	846	77	4,591
Combines for silo plants	--	--	--	--	920	5,232	7,224
Cultivated area per tractor (in hectares)	2,493	957	684	420	222	151	96

[a]Refers to actual number of all tractors.

[b]Refers to tractors in 15 HP units (for example, a 30-HP tractor will be classified as two "conventional" units).

Source: Anuarul Statistic, 1970, pp. 268-69.

TABLE 5.9

Specialist Cadres in Romanian Agriculture, 1961, 1964, and 1968

	1961	Percent of Total	1964	Percent of Total	1968	Percent of Total
Agricultural specialists--total	17,453		23,428		33,412	
With higher education--total	7,909	45.3	12,476	53.3	16,087	48.1
thereof:						
Agroengineers	4,588	26.3	7,467	31.9	8,601	25.7
Zootechnicians	794	4.5	1,571	6.7	1,406	4.2
Veterinarians	1,726	9.9	2,224	9.5	3,596	10.8
Mechanical engineers	547	3.1	953	4.1	1,156	3.5
With middle-level education--total	9,544		10,952		17,325	
thereof:						
Agronomists	5,523		5,451		3,863	
Zootechnicians	1,077		1,586		1,415	
Veterinarians	1,586		2,390		6,797	
Tractor drivers	56,427		75,890		104,521	

Source: Anuarul Statistic, 1970, p. 441.

TABLE 5.10

Total Agricultural Production in Romania, 1948-69
(1938 = 100)

Year	Total Production	Vegetable Products	Animal Products
1948	62	55	76
1950	74	65	94
1955	120	119	123
1960	126	118	145
1963	126	121	136
1965	143	133	163
1969	165	154	191

Professional Schools and Students by Category in Romania, 1948-70

	1948/ 1949	1950/ 1951	1955/ 1956	1960/ 1961	1963/ 1964	1969/ 1970
Schools--total thereof:	511	546	402	519	459	410
Mining and petroleum	23	11	12	16	17	22
Electrical energy and electronics	9	12	11	2	3	13
Metallurgy and machine construction	277	264	76	72	69	59
Chemistry	16	15	11	14	23	20
Wood processing	26	21	22	16	16	20
Light industry	29	40	25	63	58	28
Food industries	12	31	2	3	7	6
Construction and construction materials	6	13	22	32	42	43
Agriculture and forestry	49	72	142	251	172	111
Transport and telecommunications	32	34	35	22	24	32
Commerce	19	26	2	28	27	31
Health	--	--	29	--	--	24
Graduates--total thereof:	6,058	24,783	26,320	30,236	65,166	79,492
Mining and petroleum	395	730	663	1,535	3,199	4,391
Electrical energy and electronics	277	883	1,777	106	553	2,980
Metallurgy and machine construction	3,334	9,578	8,391	6,060	12,860	17,275
Chemistry	88	450	831	606	2,678	4,889
Wood processing	93	1,993	1,010	1,173	1,651	1,621
Light industry	--	3,290	3,711	4,431	9,305	8,538
Food industries	--	537	113	209	1,400	1,364
Construction and construction materials	--	881	2,228	4,195	7,642	9,089
Agriculture and forestry	--	1,045	4,193	8,860	19,524	17,541
Transport and telecommunications	1,243	3,993	2,229	954	2,189	4,538
Commerce	310	1,068	52	2,107	4,165	2,873
Health	--	--	875	--	--	4,021

Source: Anuarul Statistic, 1970, pp. 598-601.

135

TABLE 5.12

Education in Romania, 1938-70

	1938/1939	1950/1951	1955/1956	1960/1961	1963/1964	1969/1970
Preschool education						
Kindergartens	1,577	4,435	6,422	7,375	7,633	10,032
Registered students	90,787	199,096	275,433	354,677	372,430	428,480
Teachers	1,819	5,826	9,623	12,533	13,404	18,257
General schools and general lycées						
Schools	13,865	15,556	15,893	15,638	15,469	15,500
Registered students	1,604,481	1,846,890	1,732,160	2,587,861	3,058,339	3,323,603
Teachers	45,359	70,282	83,510	103,669	125,199	149,604
Art schools						
Schools	--	19	11	45	49	57
Registered students	--	1,527	2,879	14,530	19,292	22,098
thereof: registered also in general schools	--	--	2,137	12,535	15,082	11,594
Teachers	--	281	126	1,082	1,541	2,738
Professional schools						
Schools	224	546	402	519	459	410
Registered students	39,250	99,257	94,409	127,224	188,287	202,048
Teachers	896	7,808	5,564	7,330	9,431	11,527
Education at place of employment: registered students	--	--	--	--	--	61,318
Pedagogical schools and pedagogical institutes (2-year duration)						
Schools	55	110	38	25	17	--
Registered students	5,537	33,046	6,955	9,271	10,498	3,787
Teachers	1,076	1,710	602	666	472	--
Specialty lycées						
Lycées	--	--	--	--	--	217
Registered students	--	--	--	--	--	108,988
Teachers	--	--	--	--	--	5,780
Technical education, postlycée specialization and maistri*--total						
Schools	142	358	180	246	358	322
Registered students	14,746	95,373	20,281	42,212	71,925	44,903
Teachers	3,871	5,644	1,226	2,913	4,195	2,585
Higher education						
Colleges	33	136	127	131	171	192
Registered students	26,489	53,007	77,633	71,989	112,611	151,705
Teachers	2,194	8,518	8,369	8,917	11,965	13,166

*Maistri indicates level of skill reached after a period of training and a formal examination ("apprentice").

Source: Anuarul Statistic, 1970, pp. 592-95.

TABLE 5.13

Higher Education by Specialty in Romania, 1948-70

	1948/ 1949	1950/ 1951	1955/ 1956	1960/ 1961	1963/ 1964	1965/ 1966	1969/ 1970
lleges--total	129	136	127	131	171	183	192
ning	3	3	5	2	2	2	2
troleum	2	3	4	4	4	4	4
ectrical energy and electrotechniques	3	3	6	5	5	6	8
tallurgy and machine construction	7	9	11	8	10	11	11
dustrial chemistry	3	3	3	3	3	3	3
mber industry	2	1	1	1	1	1	1
ght industry	1	1	1	1	1	1	1
od industry	2	2	1	1	1	1	1
ansport and telecommunications	1	5	4	1	1	1	1
chitecture and construction	5	6	9	8	9	10	10
riculture	12	13	15	8	8	8	12
terinary science	2	2	2	1	4	4	4
restry	2	2	2	1	1	1	1
uman medicine"	20	20	12	7	7	11	11
armacy	3	4	3	3	3	4	4
ilology	4	4	5	6	7	7	7
ilosophy	4	4	2	1	4	4	4
story, geography, geology	4	8	4	1	1	1	1
tural-biological sciences	4	4	4	3	3	3	3
emistry	4	4	3	3	3	3	4
thematics, physics	4	4	4	3	8	8	9
dagogy	6	9	4	43	65	69	65
w	4	4	4	3	3	3	3
onomics	5	5	6	3	5	5	10
ysical education and sports	1	1	1	1	1	1	1
ulptural and decorative art	3	2	3	3	3	3	3
eatre and cinema arts	5	5	3	2	2	2	2
sic	5	4	4	5	6	6	6
her specialties	8	1	1	--	--	--	--
Total registered students	48,676	53,000	77,633	71,989	112,611	130,614	151,705

Source: Anuarul Statistic, 1970, pp. 612-13.

Expansion of Mass Media

One of the principal indicators of modernization as posited by Deutsch was expansion of the mass media to a truly national scale. The Romanian leadership is also quit conscious of the importance of information distribution, both as a vehicle designed to raise the general cultural level of the population and also as an important socializa- tion agent with a political bent. Table 5.14 shows the ex- pansion of the Romanian press, 1949-69, while Table 5.15 in dicates the emergence of radio and television as major dis- seminators of information in contemporary Romania. It should be emphasized here that the expansion of the mass media can be seen as an indicator of political modernizatio as well as socioeconomic development; as such, Tables 5.14 and 5.15 will be discussed and further amplified in the sec tion, "An Attempted Overview."

Urbanization

Continued industrialization has also brought with it rapid urbanization in Romania, as indicated by Table 5.16. Urbanization has been rapid and sustained since 1948, and this trend continues unabated. Even more conspicuous rates of urbanization would appear if residence in suburban commu nities still classified as rural were to be included. (For further information on this topic, see the 1956 and 1966 census figures, quoted elsewhere in this chapter.)

TABLE 5.14

The General Press in Romania, 1949-69

Year	Titles (total)	Circulatio (000s)
1949	57	501,407
1950	64	555,470
1955	78	738,117
1960	75	870,525
1963	76	1,012,143
1965	57	995,316
1969	76	1,106,759

Source: Anuarul Statistic, 1970, pp. 644-45.

TABLE 5.15

Radio and Television in Romania, 1938-69

Year	Broadcasting Stations	Subscribers--Radio (in 000s)	Television Stations	Subscribers--Television (in 000s)
1938	2	252	--	--
1948	6	258	--	--
1950	7	300	--	--
1955	15	654	--	--
1960	19	1,283	6	55
1963	22	1,711	19	245
1965	30	1,920	26	501
1969	41	2,204	83	1,288

Source: Anuarul Statistic, 1970, pp. 640-41.

TABLE 5.16

Urban-Rural Distribution of the Romanian Population, 1930-69

	Total	Total Number		Percent of Total	
		Urban	Rural	Urban	Rural
December 29, 1930*	14,280,279	3,051,253	11,229,476	21.4	78.6
January 25, 1948*	15,872,624	3,713,139	12,159,485	23.4	76.6
February 21, 1956*	17,489,450	5,474,261	12,015,186	31.3	68.7
1960	18,403,414	5,912,011	12,491,403	32.1	67.9
1963	18,813,131	6,234,217	12,578,914	33.1	66.9
March 15, 1966*	19,103,163	7,305,714	11,797,449	38.2	61.8
1969	20,010,178	8,096,261	11,913,917	40.5	59.5

*Official census.
Source: Anuarul Statistic, 1970, p. 64.

THE PROBLEMS OF DIFFERENTIAL MODERNIZATION:
SOCIOECONOMIC DEVELOPMENT AMONG NATIONALITY GROUPS

The Deutsch model predicts that as the modernization
process progresses, regional and ethnic subcultures will
become increasingly assimilated into the "mainstream" of society (in Romania this would presumably mean "Romanianiza-
tion" of other nationalities). Several scholars have examined this proposition and have concluded that assimilation
in socioeconomic terms may indeed take place (that is, the
processes of industrialization, urbanization, and higher
educational achievement may produce such assimilation) but
cultural assimilation will be a much slower process, if it
takes place at all. Table 5.17 shows the distribution of
occupational categories within the five largest ethnic
groups in Romania, 1956 and 1966; Table 5.18 examines educational achievements within the same groups; and Table 5.19
illustrates the effect of urbanization on the same ethnic
groups. Table 5.20 attempts to measure one element of cultural assimilation by examining the extent to which each of
the major nationality groups continues to use their native
tongue as the chief means of verbal communication.

TABLE 5.17

Occupational Distribution within Nationalities
in Romania, 1956 and 1966
(percent of total nationality engaged in selected occupatio

	Workers		Functionaries		Collective Farmers		Individu: Farmers	
	1956	1966	1956[a]	1966[b]	1956	1966	1956	19(
Romanians	21.6	38.9	13.1	12.3	2.9	39.7	54.3	5.:
Hungarians	32.6	45.9	12.7	11.6	5.7	34.2	40.1	2.(
Jews	25.3	29.0	53.4	59.4	0.0	0.3	0.7	0.(
Gypsies	40.4	47.3	0.6	0.5	6.7	30.4	16.4	2.(
Germans	57.1	58.5	13.8	13.6	10.9	19.6	10.4	1.(

[a]Includes engineers, technicians, and specialized personnel.
[b]Includes "intellectuals and functionaries."

Sources: 1956: Recensamintul, 1956, p. 563; 1966:
Recensamintul, 1966, p. 157.

TABLE 5.18

Romanian Nationalities in Educational Categories, 1956 and 1966

	Romanians	Hungarians	Germans	Gypsies	Jews
		1956			
otal population years and over	14,426,484	1,358,256	345,015	76,485	131,172
-year schools (not inished) and iscellaneous schools	1,414,641	137,584	12,297	14,307	11,587
ercent of A	9.8	10.2	3.5	18.7	9.2
-year schools	8,053,413	955,479	252,143	32,837	60,998
ercent of A	55.8	70.3	73.0	42.9	46.6
-year schools	884,488	156,048	57,663	484	24,884
ercent of A	6.1	11.5	16.8	0.6	19.1
iddle level schools	532,101	53,271	15,327	9	19,153
ercent of A	3.7	3.9	4.4	0.0	14.5
igher schools	183,299	13,391	3,629	1	10,454
ercent of A	1.3	1.0	1.2	0.0	7.6
		1966			
otal population 2 years' and over	13,253,588	1,339,716	315,345	42,581	40,258
rimary	10,047,710	961,202	215,681	41,139	16,270
ercent of A	75.8	71.7	68.6	96.6	40.4
eneral	1,413,357	195,067	46,531	1,236	5,124
ercent of A	10.7	14.6	14.9	2.9	12.7
rofessional	624,074	72,467	23,997	179	2,252
ercent of A	4.7	5.4	7.6	0.4	5.6
iddle technical nd special	393,090	40,985	11,399	11	2,910
ercent of A	3.0	3.1	3.5	0.0	7.2
ycées	484,251	49,806	12,044	15	6,621
ercent of A	3.6	3.7	3.8	0.0	16.4
igher education	291,106	20,189	5,693	1	7,081
ercent of A	2.2	1.5	1.9	0.0	17.6

Sources: 1956: Recensamintul, 1956, pp. 576-77; 1966: Recensamintul,), p. 115.

141

TABLE 5.19

Urban-Rural Distribution of Nationalities
in Romania, 1956 and 1966
(in percentages)

| | 1956 | | 1966 | | Increase/Decrease |
	Urban	Rural	Urban	Rural	in Urbanization
Romanians	29.2	70.8	36.9	63.1	7.7
Hungarians	41.1	58.6	47.6	52.4	6.2
Germans	50.1	49.9	53.8	46.2	3.7
Jews	95.2	4.8	97.8	2.2	2.6
Gypsies	17.3	82.7	26.5	73.4	9.2

Sources: 1956: Recensamintul, 1956, p. 556; 1966: Recensamintul, 1966.

TABLE 5.20

Use of Native Language as Chief Means of
Communication in Romania, 1956 and 1966
(in percentages)

| | Total Population | Native Language | | | | |
		Romanian	Hungarian	German	Yiddish	Gypsy
		1956				
Romanians	14,996,114	99.4	0.3	0.1	0.01	0.1
Hungarians	1,587,675	1.2	98.6	0.2	--	--
Germans	384,708	2.1	1.6	96.1	--	--
Jews	146,264	57.5	15.8	4.8	21.9	--
Gypsies	104,216	45.2	8.6	--	--	46.2
		1966				
Romanians	16,740,310	99.7	0.2	0.04	--	0.1
Hungarians	1,619,592	0.9	98.9	0.1	--	--
Germans	382,595	1.6	1.0	97.4	--	--
Jews	42,888	65.0	18.2	5.0	11.0	--
Gypsies	64,197	30.8	10.2	--	--	58.8

Sources: 1956: Recensamintul, 1956, p. 562; 1966: Recensamintul, 1966, p. 113.

The evidence presented clearly shows that the general modernization process has had a very uneven impact on the various ethnic groups in Romania. For some, such as the Gypsies, modernization has only recently affected traditional life styles; it is only since 1956 that this group has become "domesticated" and has settled on collective farms and to some extent in industrial occupations. Furthermore, widespread illiteracy (37.7 percent in 1956)[20] has only recently been overcome. The overwhelming majority of Gypsies still have only a basic education, and only one member of this group has managed to get into an institution of higher education as late as 1966.

Other groups, such as Jews and Germans, and to a lesser degree Hungarians, must be considered relatively modernized (both according to the Deutsch model and in terms of the Romanian elite's self-definition of modernization) even at the beginning of the communist regime in Romania. For these groups, the modernization process has simply reinforced group characteristics already in existence, and at the same time competition for specialized jobs, etc., has become much more pronounced, insofar as other groups now approach modernized standards of skills and other characteristics.

The chief beneficiaries of the modernization process on a mass scale have naturally been the Romanians; after all, this group constituted the overwhelming majority of the population in 1956 and 1966 and consequently stood to gain most significantly from the processes examined above. The Romanians nevertheless have a long way to go before they reach the modernization standards of groups such as Jews and Germans in many fields.

While all nationalities have been involved in socioeconomic modernization during the years of communist rule, this process has not resulted in significant cultural assimilation of minorities. Germans and Hungarians still overwhelmingly continue to use their mother tongue as the chief vehicle of communication and thus have not accepted Romanian as a matter of convenience. There are some linguistic assimilationist tendencies among Gypsies and certainly among Jews, but in the latter case this process has been underway for decades, if not centuries, and therefore cannot be ascribed to the modernization process in socialist Romania per se. All in all, the evidence of ethnic groups in the modernization process casts significant doubts on one of the major contentions of the Deutsch model and certainly indicates that the Romanian-dominated regime will meet with massive problems if it earnestly undertakes major cultural assimilationist efforts.

AN ATTEMPTED OVERVIEW

The figures presented above clearly indicate that the Romanian modernizing elite, made up primarily of the top RCP leadership, has made considerable strides toward achievement of the modernization goals established. There have been major gains in industrialization, both in terms of total output, the mix of that output, and productivity in the work force. There are still many problems in this field, including insufficient and inefficient use of existing capital plant and natural resources, and in this respect Romania is far from the achievement levels of other countries that are considered modernized, such as the United States or West Germany. Problems such as these nevertheless cannot obscure the fact that major achievements have been made in this field.

One of the main reasons for such progress toward the multilaterally developed society appears to be the expansion of the educational system. The RPC elite has clearly perceived the crucial need for developing requisite skills among the masses of the population and also producing a large reservoir of highly skilled experts, especially engineers of all kinds, who can perform the tasks of running and supervising an increasingly sophisticated economy. The Ceausescu regime is clearly aware of the continued need for investment in people in this field, as the current five-year plan allocation for education indicates.[21]

Achievements in agriculture continue to lag significantly behind those in industry; major reasons for this are the lack of investments and inadequate educational emphasis on this branch of the economy. Considerable mechanization has nevertheless taken place here, and there is currently greater emphasis on educational programs that can furnish experts in this field.[22] Despite more interest in agriculture during recent years, it seems necessary that the modernizing elite concentrate more on this branch in the future if multilateral development is to be achieved.

Industrialization has resulted in rapid urbanization in Romania. This trend has been so overwhelming that there is now considerable official concern over such well-known problems as urban sprawl, rising crime, and pollution.[23] The massive move to the cities has also widened the gap between urban and rural areas in terms of standard of living, social services, and cultural and artistic offerings. The RCP is aware of this problem and is determined to reduce the difference between the city and the village by raising the socioeconomic and cultural level of the latter to a stage approaching that of the former. This is an important element of multilateral development.

Another field where socioeconomic modernization has had
a differential impact is in various ethnic groups, as shown
by Tables 5.17-5.20. Once again, the Romanian modernizers
are committed to achieving approximately equal services and
opportunities for all nationalities in the multilaterally
developed society. This is indeed a massive task that might
take another generation, although the current long-range
plans for this achievement are kept to an approximate dead-
line of 1990.[24]

Modernization, as defined above, has resulted in two
major societal developments in Romania. First of all, social stratification and hierarchy have developed. Ceausescu
expects this condition to continue into the multilaterally
developed society, especially with reference to the leading
role of the Communist Party. The RCP will continue to lead,
thus to provide the motor for, continued modernization. One
of the major theoretical issues in RCP publications is the
question of how this hierarchical, multilaterally developed
society can be transformed into the communist stage, which
continues to be envisioned as a classless society. A thorough discussion of this problem would be outside the scope
of this study; suffice it to say that the regime's definition of multilaterally developed is of necessity a major
theoretical problem for those concerned with the transition
to the final stage of historical development.

The second major societal result of modernization has
been a significant increase in individual choice, both concerning availability of material goods and services and also
career opportunities. The standard of living, although modest, is rising every year.[25] New careers open up continuously, especially in technical fields. The RCP is committed
to continued diversification in this respect; in fact, it is
this trend that the communist elite in Romania emphasizes as
a major element of personal freedom. Freedom, it is said,
is the ability of each individual to realize his fullest potential, no matter what his skills; it is the responsibility
of the political leadership to provide the means whereby
such self-realization can be completed. This, then, is
socioeconomic freedom; the ability to choose alternative
political paths is specifically denied, as we shall see below. The definitions of multilateral development, personal
freedom, and indexes of modernization currently espoused by
the RCP seem to fall neatly into a general pattern in Eastern Europe and the Soviet Union. They provide a major force
for continued development in the economy, but serious political ramifications will also follow, as discussed below.

While the socioeconomic effects of modernization in Romania can be measured with some element of accuracy through the indexes found in statistical yearbooks, political modernization is much less clearly identified. As stated above generally accepted indexes such as increased voting, more participation of the general public in the decision-making process, and increased group activity usually will not hold in a system of mobilization, where virtually 100 percent of the electorate repeatedly returns the Party-dominated ticket with equally substantial margins, and where group activity is severely regulated by the omnipresent Party. Any meaningful study of this subject must therefore look for other indexes. One of these is increased subgroup activity in the political realm. This phenomenon, now clearly visible in all of the modernizing systems of Eastern Europe, strongly impinges upon one of the main elements of the Romanian modernization goals: universal acceptance of the Communist Party as the supreme force, politically and in socioeconomic leadership.

Acceptance of the Communist Party as the
Sole Legitimate Leader of Society

The RCP has been faced with increasing complexities in the decision-making process in the 1960s and 1970s. The rapid economic development, illustrated above, has resulted in the emergence of several socioeconomic elites, or apparat whose crucial functions in the economy have also furnished political influence of some magnitude. The Communist Party has been faced with the constant need to control and manipulate such elites, thereby maintaining the principle of unquestioned Party supremacy in decision making. During the last decade, serious problems have developed in Party relations with elements of the economic managers and specialists some academic personnel and also scientists, a section of the military, and artists and writers.

The very modernization process, set in motion by the Party, has clearly established the need for large numbers of economic managers, planners, and other specialists. This principle has been readily accepted by the RCP, which has furnished the funds and commitment for education of such cadres, as illustrated statistically above. The political problems of this process appear when technical specialists become involved in political decision making. Since the RCP is in charge of economic planning and management, it will

invariably be involved in making decisions that clearly belong in the realm of economics, and this fact has in turn
increased the risk of confrontation with the experts. This
process is clearly more complex than a mere conflict between
two apparats; there are "technicians" within the top RCP
leadership and "apparatchiks" among the managers, and
clashes of various factions produce a complex quilt of hast-
ily established, temporary coalitions that may be dismantled
as quickly as they were formed. Throughout the 1960s, however, more lasting coalitions were apparently formed around
the apparatchik-manager dichotomy, and the confrontation apparently escalated to a point where Party leader Nicolae
Ceausescu found himself confronted by a manager-oriented
group within the RCP Executive Committee that seriously challenged his right to unquestioned decision making in economic
matters. The chief Party spokesman for the managers was
Premier Ion Gheorghe Maurer, by background a technocrat.*
A series of confrontations developed: One of the most significant of these was a major controversy over budget allo-
cations in the 1971-75 five-year plan.[26] Ceausescu's answer
to the challenge was occasional shake-ups internally (as was
the case at the Tenth RCP Congress, where personnel changes
in some top Party positions were made which strengthened
Ceausescu's hand)[27] and a major confrontation with economic
experts, academic personnel, artistic intelligentsia, and
parts of the RCP apparatus. This major showdown started in
the summer of 1971 and lasted for approximately one year.
In the West, this political crisis has become known as the
"Little Cultural Revolution."[28]

The Little Cultural Revolution was officially inaugurated by Ceausescu at a meeting of the RCP Central Committee
in June 1971 and was formally confirmed and expanded at another Central Committee meeting in November of the same year.
At the November meeting, Ceausescu detailed his criticism of
the problems arising from the modernization process and outlined his program for remedying the situation. The main
points were:

1. Major mistakes in ideological education could be
found in the mass media, especially radio and television,
and also in the arts and literature.

---

*Maurer's position within the Party seems to have been
weakened as a result of the "Little Cultural Revolution."
Maurer was also involved in a serious automobile accident
that severely weakened him physically.

2. Educational institutions at all levels had been extremely lax in ideological training and had fallen back on formalism and abstract formulas without practical meaning.

3. Many Party cadres had permitted the same kind of formalism and sloganeering to penetrate ideological work.

4. The modernization process, with its social stratification and differentiation, had resulted in some leadership groups acquiring undue advantages.

5. Because of the major problems outlined, a massive attack had to be launched on the old, "bourgeois-landowner" mentality, with a view toward furthering "socialist ethics and morality" in modern Romanian society.

6. The ideological offensive would first and foremost be carried forth through increased Party activity at all levels and in all fields.[29]

The November speech epitomizes the problems of strict Party control in an increasingly pluralistic society. Ceausescu in effect admitted that some groups had challenged the supremacy of the Communist Party and had only paid lip service to ideology, the moral-political mainstay of RCP claim to unquestioned leadership in society. The Party leader furthermore tied this deficiency to the modernization process. The remedy was seen as increased emphasis on "socialist morality and ethics," whose main political content is acceptance of Party supremacy in all fields. The November speech is an extremely frank admission of the problems arising from the "pluralization" of a society undergoing rapid and fundamental modernization.

The Little Cultural Revolution gradually engulfed most of the socioeconomic elites of Romanian society as well as the Party itself. By the winter of 1972 the process had resulted in important purges in the Party, in the military, among writers and artists, and in some economic ministries and planning agencies. Thus, in April several members of the RCP Central Committee, including the first RCP secretaries of the Caras Severin and Covasna regions, were dismissed from their Party posts. The same fate befell Dimitru Popa, head of the Bucharest Party Committee. Vasile Patilin one of the members of the RCP Secretariat, was demoted, apparently because of his close connection with recalcitrant elements within the military establishment. Severe purges shook parts of the military; it was rumored that a faction closely associated with Patilinet had opposed Ceausescu's foreign policy as too nationalistic, and one official, Ion Serb, was jailed, possibly executed, for spying for the Soviet Union. Purges also shook some of the economic ministries, and Ceasescu, through decentralization measures of all kinds, attempted to reduce the influence of the economic managers, even at the plant level, where the trade unions were entrusted with some of the planning and supervisory functions previously carried out by the management.[31]

Significant problems also developed in relations between the RCP and the artistic and literary elite of the country. The artists and writers had been entrusted with a major educative task in a society moving toward multilateral development; it was expected of this elite that it would wholeheartedly support the goals and leadership of the Communist Party and would inspire the citizenry to act in accordance with the major goals established by the political elite. Instead of such compliance, many artists and writers started describing the less flattering sides of reality in modern Romania. The frontal attack against incorrect literary and artistic production launched by Ceausescu in 1971 merely served to bring out more opposition from this elite. Some writers even went so far as to question the need or advisability of establishing socialism or a multilaterally developed society or redefined these societal stages in such a fundamental fashion that they bore few resemblances to the Party's program.[32] Some of the more daring oppositionists frankly stated that "freedom" meant personal freedom to choose socialism or any other political form,[33] while yet others stressed the view that individuals should have the right to "opt out" of the developmental process as defined by the Party.[34] This alternative view on modernization, development, and progress clearly represented a major challenge to continued Party supremacy, and the battle was joined. By the summer of 1972 the inevitable outcome of such an unequal struggle was manifested in major purges of the Writers' Union and other formal organizations of the intelligentsia. But critical voices continue to be heard among the elite, and currently the Party seems to have retreated somewhat from its attacks on this stratum.[35]

"Mobilizability" of the Masses of the Population

As mentioned above, one of the major political goals of the Romanian modernizers in the multilaterally developed society is to gain acceptance from the population of the principle that each citizen is available for political mobilization at any time. Indeed, part of this mobilization goal envisions a high degree of anticipatory political action on the part of the citizenry in this field, a state of affairs that would in effect reduce the need for the massive and cumbersome control system now in existence in the country.

Political mobilization is also an integral part of the modernization process as seen by Deutsch and others. Deutsch is primarily concerned with the increased political activity of citizens, including oppositional activity, but he also emphasizes that, in a modernized society, citizens are generally more aware of political matters than in more traditional systems and thus "available" for activization in political terms.[36] This emphasis on mobilization by communist leaders and Western scholars alike warrants closer scrutiny in the Romanian case.

Most scholars and many communist commentators agree that the principle of political mobilization, actual or potential, has not been accepted on a massive scale by the citizens in Romania or elsewhere in Eastern Europe. In fact, the RCP press is constantly full of exhortations to increased societal and political activity among average citizens as well as Communist Party cadres.[37] One of the main goals of the Little Cultural Revolution was to reduce the apathy and lethargy in political matters that apparently permeates important strata of Romanian society. Ceausescu has repeatedly emphasized that without political commitment people cannot be expected to fulfill their socioeconomic tasks, and the entire process of "building Socialism" is in dire jeopardy.[38] The massive ideological campaigns that have been carried out during the last few years in Romania have clearly been designed to halt the trend toward "depoliticization" and "privatization" at all levels. So far, serious shortcomings continue to exist; the Romanian population is not easily aroused for mobilization purposes, and anticipatory political and economic action is still a long way off, to paraphrase Ceausescu.[39]

The pervasive apathy is perhaps most noticeable among youth, the very segment of the population that is expected to complete the transformation to a multilaterally developed society and in effect preside over that societal stage. At the Ninth Congress of the Communist Youth Organization UTC (Uniunea Tineretului Comunist) in February 1971, Ion Iliescu, then Secretary General of the UTC, highlighted the problems encountered in this field:

> The propaganda work should bear the hallmark
> of creative, innovating spirit, should stimu-
> late vivid political thinking, by tackling
> all questions in a concrete way, closely con-
> nected to reality. Nevertheless, in the
> propaganda work of some organizations, in
> the politico-ideological study, manifesta-
> tions of formalism, inertia keep persisting,
> as well as an abstract character, manifest

in the mere statement of some general theses
and principles, the utilization of some already known stock phrases and clichés, the
use of a limited range of ways of addressing
the youth, a flat, dull approach to problems,
lack of courage in tackling highly topical
problems requiring thorough analysis and
scientific arguments. There are still a
large number of UCY organizations which over
a long period of time do not start any actions in support of keeping the youth politically informed, especially the young people
in enterprises and villages. The active
forms of propaganda activities with the direct participation of young people, forms of
activity that should appeal to their thinking abilities, have not been adequately extended.

The analysis of these deficiencies in
the context of the present and long-term requirements of the youth education, of the
dynamic development of socialist building in
our country as also the complexity of contemporary international life--characterized
by sharp ideological confrontations--ask for
the UCY organizations to continuously improve the form and contents of political-
ideological training. We should particularly insist on the continuity of actions, the
capacity of permanently adapting oneself to
the concrete necessities and conditions,
highly varying from one organization to the
other, depending upon the categories of
young people on their age, training and
concerns.[40]

Similar comments were made by Iliescu's successor Martian
Dan at the RCP Central Committee Plenum, November 1971.[41]
Dan's speech was made in support of Ceausescu's scathing attack on widespread apathy in the Party, in the UTC, and
among several other societal elites.[42] The subsequent ideological campaign apparently failed to achieve the desired
results in this field; at the RCP National Conference in
July 1972, Ceausescu returned to the problem of apathy and
the many mistakes committed in mass work designed to mobilize both rank and file and Party cadres for the implementation of major political and socioeconomic goals:

The improvement of the ideological and educational activity must be a permanent pre-
occupation of the Party organizations and
bodies, whose duty it is to ensure that the
best use is made of all the means at the
disposal of our society for increasing the
socialist consciousness of the working
people. Starting with the schools--the decisive factor in education--and ending with
the modern mass media--radio, television,
and the press--everything must be subordinated to the implementation of the tasks set
forth by the November 1971 Plenary Meeting
of the Central Committee. Similarly, the
mass and public organizations, the trade
unions, the Union of Communist Youth, the
unions of creative artists must pay greater
heed to educational activities. The Socialist Unity Front will have to act with a view
to rallying the efforts of all these organizations, to coordinating their activities
devoted to the cultivation of the socialist
consciousness of the entire people. It goes
without saying that the whole ideological-
educational activity must be under the permanent guidance of the Party bodies and organizations. Wherever they live and work, the
communists must actively militate for the
assertion in life of the philosophical concepts of our Party, of the principles of
communist ethics.

We must pay more attention to theoretical work. In this respect it is imperative
that the Academy of Social Sciences improve
its activity by taking a more active part--
as was indicated to it as far back as its
inception--in the overall ideological and
educational activity. I think it is necessary that the workers in the field of ideology participate more intensely in the practical activities going on in various spheres
of work. It is particularly imperative that
the research work in the field of economic
sciences and of the science of management be
improved.[43]

On virtually every occasion, Ceausescu has made it
plain that the concept "multilaterally developed society"
implies political development as well as socioeconomic

modernization, and that citizen activity and participation, both anticipatory and in response to elite-initiated campaigns, is an indispensable part of this developmental stage. Without this kind of carefully controlled participation, neither material plenty nor "socialist morality" can be achieved.[44] Romania is thus clearly in a "premodern" stage in this field as of today.

Ethnic Groups and the Struggle Against Old-fashioned Values

Both Deutsch and the Romanian modernization model consider some form of assimilation of regional and ethnic groups to the "mainstream" of societal development an important by-product of the modernization process. For Deutsch, "assimilation" apparently means relative cultural integration, in which minorities gradually accept some form of national political system that will in any case be strongly influenced by the largest group. The Romanian definition no longer posits cultural assimilation as a prerequisite for the multilaterally developed society; the current elite view on this recognizes the right of each nationality to maintain its cultural traditions. It is nevertheless expected that minority group life be "socialist in content"; this in effect means that all ethnic groups must accept the leadership position of the RCP and the other basic requirements of the multilaterally developed society, as outlined above. By the same token, outmoded values, especially "bourgeois-landowner" outlooks on personal achievements and relations between citizen and state, must be eradicated before one can truly speak of a "modern" society.[45] One of the old-fashioned values that has thus been assigned to the scrap heap of history is "bourgeois nationalism," which is, in essence, the political expression of ethnic particularities. The multilaterally developed society specifically precludes this form of nationalism.[46]

There is considerable evidence indicating that ethnic problems continue to play a part in contemporary Romanian political life. The Hungarian minority has on occasion caused considerable concern in Bucharest, notably in the fall of 1956, when events in Hungary proper had a profound impact on the Magyars in Transylvania and elsewhere.[47] There were demonstrations in many Transylvanian cities and also in Bucharest, and the RCP, still quite weak in mass support, was forced to undertake stringent security measures. The invasion of Czechoslovakia in 1968 was another occasion upon which Bucharest voiced concern over possible repercussions among ethnic minorities in Romania. The post-1968 nationality policies of the Ceausescu regime have been markedly less "Romanian" in content and have increased the possibilities for national expression in arts, literature, and to some extent even in education, where teaching in the native tongue of Hungarians has been somewhat expanded as compared to the mid-1960s. Certain problems still exist, particularly since the Hungarian nationalists in Transylvania have found a measure of encouragement in official policies emanating from Budapest. This situation inaugurated an angry exchange between Romania and Hungary in 1971, in which the Romanian spokesman charged Budapest with interference in domestic Romanian affairs. Implied in the official statement from the Romanian capital was also the contention that such interference was bound to cast doubts on the function of the RCP as the sole legitimate ruler in the country--a point that is of the utmost importance and has been made on various informal occasions later.[48]

It is doubtful that the Hungarian minority represents any threat to the rule of the RCP, but it is also clear that little cultural assimilation has taken place during the period of socialism, and the ethnic particularism that exists in cultural terms is clearly seen as a potential threat to the rule of the current political elite, which is overwhelmingly Romanian ethnically.[49]

Other ethnic groups also produced certain difficulties for the regime in Romania during the 1960s. During that decade, the Jewish minority was drastically reduced through outmigration. A limited degree of emigration has also been allowed for Germans, although this has now been reduced to a trickle. Ceausescu has repeatedly emphasized that the homeland for the Swabians and Saxons is Romania, where these groups have lived for centuries; there can be no question of Romanian Germans going "home" to the Federal Republic.[50] The Party leader has also repeatedly appealed to the German minority to work closely together with the Romanians and other "cohabiting nationalities" to fulfill the five-year plans and thus help propel Romania into the stage of multilateral development.[51] During the last few years, some concessions have been made concerning native language teaching and other matters of concern to the German minority in an obvious effort to harness this group as well for a modernization process essentially conducted by Romanians.

Other nationality groups may also have certain reservations about the main policies of the RCP, although evidence is largely lacking here. It is certainly conceivable that an ethnic group such as the Gypsies, who have only recently been "domesticated" and consequently have had only relatively minor payoffs from socioeconomic modernization, would be less than enthusiastic about the policies carried out, especially since the process of development has seriously disrupted traditional and accepted ways of life. Romania is a country in rapid transformation, and the major socioeconomic changes now taking place in the country are essentially pushed forward by leaders dedicated to Romanian nationalism. In this context, socioeconomic modernization may not produce automatic integration of other groups, especially ethnic subcultures, despite obvious economic gains for all strata of society. Politically, continued ethnic particularism in a setting of high economic development would be a measure of failure in the political mobilization efforts considered so crucial by the current RCP modernizing elite. The Romanian experience of modernization therefore casts serious doubts on Deutsch's assumption of assimilation as a natural concomitant of socioeconomic development.

The evidence presented above clearly illustrates the problems associated with political mobilization and development in an emerging pluralistic society such as Romania. The fundamental question of continued Communist Party monopoly of political power in the face of emerging social and economic elites is now in the forefront for all of the East European communist systems. Considerable controversy exists within the academic community concerning the final outcome of this dichotomic controversy between society as a whole and the political subsystem; some scholars predict a breakdown or significant transformation of communist rule, while others have confidence in the ability of communist political elites to maintain control over other apparats for a long period of time.[52] I shall not attempt to join this particular battle at this point. My prediction for the future of communist rule in Romania is of a more general, and hence perhaps safer, nature. It seems likely that continued socioeconomic modernization will result in political diversity that will complicate the decision-making process rather than simplifying it, so that the RCP elite must contend with political controversy rather than political synchronization. Or, to put it differently, in terms of the regime's self-definition of socioeconomic and political modernization: Socioeconomic modernization will not result in the desired political modernization, but will create a momentum of its own that is likely to result in increased political activity in the lower ranks for specific goals rather than dedication to grand societal goals defined by the Communist Party as a matter of right. Thus, Ceausescu and his successors will be continuously faced with the need to control the "beast" of modernization that they themselves begat and nurtured along.

CONCLUSION

The relationship between communist power and modernization in Romania is relatively clear. The Communist Party
elite provided the will to modernization and the power to
carry it out. Some scholars have argued that modernization
(essentially as defined above) would have taken place in
Eastern Europe no matter what kind of political elite came
to power; the area was simply ready for such development in
societal terms. This may have been true in Romania as well,
but the point here is that the RCP elite did in fact set
this process in motion and supervised its execution up to
the present time, with clear goals as to the further progress toward the end result--a Communist society. A fundamental point about modernization in Romania is that someone
willed it and took measures to carry it out--it did not just
happen. The fact that it was a communist elite that supervised the modernization process provided it with certain
special features, first among which were the frontal attack
on all areas of backwardness simultaneously, and also the
emphasis on people and their skills as crucial ingredients
in the process. To this day, these two major elements are
clearly visible in the RCP quest for the multilaterally developed society.

Just as communist power has been instrumental in shaping the scope and direction of modernization in Romania, the
process itself has had a profound impact on that power.
Socioeconomic modernization has produced a new managerial
class whose indispensable functional skills are beginning to
have some political impact. Continued stratification and
diversification of the citizenry have increased the potential for a political pluralism of sorts. At the same time,
the Communist Party has experienced some difficulty in its
attempts to mobilize the masses of the population for societal goals established by that political elite; this problem is clearly related to the "pluralization" of the population, so closely a result of the modernization process. For
the present political leadership in Romania, the relationship between modernization and communist power at this stage
of societal development constitutes the most fundamental
problem to be confronted on the threshold of the multilaterally developed society.

A NOTE ON ROMANIAN STATISTICS

As noted by John Michael Montias and other prominent
students of Romanian politics and economics, official statistics of that country can be misleading, contradictory,

and internally inconsistent on some occasions. There seems
to be a consensus among scholars in this field that such
shortcomings are unintentional, or based on classifications
unfamiliar in the West, or with built-in biases. The scope
of this research effort prevents a detailed discussion of
validity and reliability of statistics. Suffice it to say
that I have proceeded on assumptions similar to those of
Professor Montias in this chapter, accepting official statistics as at least indicative of major trends. An understanding of such trends is considered sufficient for the
tasks at hand.

One field in which intentional distortions may exist is
in figures on ethnic minorities (it is at least conceivable
that statistics on such a sensitive political topic would be
manipulated). Even if this were the case, the official figures are not very flattering in regard to assimilation and
integration of minorities, and the most critical comment
that could be made would be a contention that there is even
a lesser achievement in this field than we would assume from
looking at rather bleak figures (from the RCP point of view).
I have therefore chosen to use official statistics in this
field as well, with the caveat outlined above.

NOTES

1. Karl W. Deutsch, "Social Mobilization and Political
Development," American Political Science Review, September
1961, pp. 493-515.
2. One major study that deviates somewhat from the
Deutsch model is Samuel P. Huntington, Political Order in
Changing Societies (New Haven, Conn.: Yale University
Press, 1968).
3. Deutsch, op. cit.
4. Ibid.
5. Findings of this nature are reported in several
chapters of Erich Goldhagen, ed., Ethnic Minorities in the
Soviet Union (New York: Praeger, 1968).
6. For a discussion of this aspect, see, for example,
Ghita Ionescu, The Politics of the European Communist
States (New York: Praeger, 1967).
7. Some of these factors have been discussed by Vernon
V. Aspaturian in Allen A. Kassof, ed., Prospects for Soviet
Society (New York: Praeger, 1968), pp. 143-201.
8. See, for example, Nicolae Ceausescu's speech to the
RCP Tenth Congress, 1969, in Congresul al X-lea al Partidului
Comunist Roman (Bucharest: Editura Politica, 1969), pp.
19-91.

9. Ceausescu in his report to the RCP National Conference, July 1972, in National Conference of the Romanian Communist Party, July 19-21, 1972. Report Presented by Comrade Nicolae Ceausescu, General Secretary of the Romanian Communist Party, Supplement to Romania Today, no. 8/213 (1972) (Bucharest), pp. 10-11.

10. Ceausescu in Congresul al X-lea, op. cit., pp. 24-33.

11. Ibid., pp. 33-37.

12. National Conference, op. cit., pp. 13-14, and also Ceausescu's speech to the RCP Central Committee, November 1971, in Scinteia, November 4, 1971.

13. National Conference, op. cit., pp. 14-27, 28-36.

14. Scinteia, op. cit.

15. Ceausescu's nationality policies have been well documented in formal statements, for example, in Scinteia, April 28, 1971, and Scinteia Tineretului, May 4, 1971.

16. Ibid.

17. National Conference, op. cit., pp. 36-40.

18. Ceausescu outlined this prospect in his report to the Tenth Party Congress, in Congresul al X-lea, op. cit., pp. 64-91.

19. Ibid.

20. Recensamintul--1956, pp. 576-77.

21. A detailed breakdown of the 1971-75 five-year plan can be found in Scinteia, October 21, 1971.

22. National Conference, op. cit., pp. 8-9.

23. These problems have been discussed on numerous occasions, for example, G. Iftodi, "The 1971-1975 Five-Year Plan," in Viata Economica, no. 49 (1971).

24. E. Mesaros, "Demographic Forecasts and Economic Development in Romania up to the Year 2000," Probleme Economice, no. 7 (1971).

25. For a discussion of planned increases, see 1971-1975 Five-Year Plan in Scinteia, October 21, 1971.

26. Ceausescu came out ahead here, insofar as the plan as finally promulgated contains most of his projects. For a full text of the plan, see Scinteia, October 21, 1971.

27. The staffing of top Party bodies at the Tenth Congress is reported in Congresul al X-lea, op. cit., pp. 751-58.

28. See Trond Gilberg, "Ceausescu's 'Kleine Kulturrevolution' in Rumanien," Osteuropa (Aachen), October 1972, pp. 717-28.

29. Ibid.

30. Ibid.

31. Ibid.

32. See, for example, articles by the poet Adrian Paunescu in Romania Literara in the period 1968-70; furthermore, see novels such as Animale Bolnave [Sick ani-

mals] by Nicolae Breban, Absentii [The absent ones] by
Augustin Buzura, and Ostinato, by Paul Goma.
33. The writer Augustin Buzura in the literary journal Tribuna (Cluj), January 13, 1972.
34. Ibid.
35. The developments at the 1972 Writers' Conference
were reported in detail in Le Monde (Paris), May 26, 1972.
36. Deutsch, op. cit.
37. See, for example, the campaign that was started
after the November 1971 Central Committee meeting and that
ran as front page material in Scinteia for several months
thereafter.
38. For example, Ceausescu at the November 1971
"Ideological Plenum," in Scinteia, November 4, 1971.
39. See especially his speech to the November 1971
RCP Central Committee Plenum, in Scinteia, November 4, 1971.
40. The statement is found in Romania's Youth 1 (1971):
21. (Romania's Youth is a "review edited by the Central Committee of the Union of Communist Youth and the Council of
the Union of the Students' Associations of Romania." The
English-language version uses the English abbreviation UCY
for the Union of Communist Youth; I have used UTC, for the
Romanian title, which is Uniunea Tineretului Comunist.)
41. Scinteia, November 7, 1971.
42. Ceausescu's speech in Scinteia, November 4, 1971.
43. National Conference, op. cit., pp. 32-33.
44. For example, in Congresul al X-lea, op. cit., pp.
64-74.
45. Ceausescu on numerous occasions--for example,
Scinteia, November 4, 1971, where he repeatedly and forcefully made this point.
46. Congresul al X-lea, op. cit., esp. pp. 57-60.
47. For example, Stephen Fischer-Galati, Twentieth
Century Rumania (New York: Columbia University Press, 1971).
48. The Romanian reply was given by Paul Niculescu-
Mizil, member of the RCP Politburo and a Party secretary in
charge of international communist relations (Scinteia, July
9, 1971). The Hungarian charges were launched by Zoltan
Komocsin, Niculescu-Mizil's counterpart in the Hungarian
Party, in a review of foreign relations before the Hungarian
Parliament on June 24, 1971.
49. For a list of the top RCP officials elected at the
Tenth Party Congress, see Congresul al X-lea, op. cit., pp.
751-58.
50. For example, Ceausescu in Scinteia, February 21,
1971.
51. Ibid.
52. See, for example, a collection of essays on this
topic in R. V. Burks, ed., The Future of Communism in Europe
(Detroit: Wayne State University Press, 1968).

6

YUGOSLAVIA: THE POLITICAL ROLE OF THE ADMINISTRATIVE ELITE

Lenard J. Cohen

The political power of administrative officials holding
high-level positions in the public or state bureaucraoy has
been a subject of vital concern to contemporary social scientists. Through their location in the governmental structure of most political systems, and particularly their involvement in key stages of the process of formulating and
executing public policy, professional civil servants have
the potential ability to initiate, modify, or even completely sabotage the decisions taken by those individuals who
claim the right to exercise political authority. In addition to their responsibilities for the preparation and implementation of policies, an important source of bureaucratic power derives from the specialized training of administrative personnel. Max Weber suggested that "under normal
conditions, the power position of a fully developed bureaucracy is always overtowering. The 'political' master finds
himself in a position of a 'dilettante' who stands opposite
the 'expert' facing the trained official who stands within
the management of administration." In Weber's view, "the
question is always who controls the existing bureaucratic
machinery. And such control is possible only in a very limited degree to persons who are not technical specialists."[1]
One of the most important issues that may be raised
with respect to bureaucratic influence in the political process concerns the impact that senior civil servants have on

The research related to this study was supported by the
Foreign Area Fellowship Program of the American Council of
Learned Societies and the Social Science Research Council,
and the International Study of Opinion-Makers project.

the process of modernization, that is, the capacity of a society to successfully adapt its political, economic, and social institutions in order to control the rapidly and continuously changing conditions of its environment.[2] The
skills, outlook, and behavior of administrative functionaries can prove to be a decisive factor either facilitating
or impeding the adoption and execution of modernizing programs. Appointed officials in the government bureaucracy,
for example, may perform an innovative role by formulating
measures to deal with crucial societal problems or by supporting such policies that are introduced or advocated by
political decision makers. In contrast, such officials may
behave as a bastion of conservatism endeavoring to obstruct
what they regard to be departures from traditional practices
and routine procedures. Whether or not administrators will
actually have any influence on the process of modernization,
to what end, and with what degree of success is an empirical
question that must be examined in each society.[3]

Although the pivotal role that top administrative functionaries may play in shaping the outcome of political decisions is frequently acknowledged, students of communist political systems have devoted relatively little attention to
the attitudes and behavior of administrative officials in
the state bureaucracy. Beyond the difficulty of conducting
systematic research in communist systems, an important factor accounting for this situation has been the general feeling among students of these regimes that the political control exercised by the party organs over government agencies
and organizations, including the state administration, did
not warrant consideration of the activities of civil servants as a distinct or significant factor influencing political development. Studies of "bureaucracy" in communist
systems have tended to focus exclusively on the party bureaucracy, or to treat party leaders and government functionaries as indistinguishable parts of a single "bureaucratic" elite or stratum. Carl Beck, for example, in one of
the few studies of communist administrative development published in the 1960s, observed that

> it is impossible to pinpoint a formal state
> bureaucracy in Eastern Europe in the sense
> one can do so in describing politics in
> Great Britain or France. The course of ad-
> ministration is not determined by a bureau-
> cracy in the sense of a formal state admin-
> istrative system that is independent and
> instrumental, but is determined instead by
> the interplay between the leaders, the

movement, and a series of administrative organizations. The latter because of the
power of the party to intrude at any time
displays few of the functional and behavioral
characteristics that are ascribed to classical bureaucracy.[4]

While the primacy of the party apparatus over the top
echelons of the governmental structure remains an essential
feature of all of the East European communist states, events
in recent years have tended to enhance the political importance of the state bureaucracy in many of these countries.[5]
The most explicit case of such development, as in so many
other areas of change in this region, has occurred in Yugoslavia. The growing importance of the state administration
in the Yugoslav political process stems in large part from
the convergence of two closely related changes that have
taken place over the last two decades: (1) the growing autonomy of governmental institutions from direct party control, and (2) the emergence of Yugoslav parliamentary assemblies as important arenas for political decision making.

The transformation of the Yugoslav Communist Party from
a command-oriented instrument of revolutionary change into
an "ideological-guiding force" (reflected in its designation
after 1952 as the League of Yugoslav Communists) provided
the major impetus to the appearance of the state administration as a meaningful "political" institution. Beginning in
the early 1950s, as part of the institutional reorganization
that followed in the wake of the rift with the Soviet Union,
the Yugoslav leadership embarked on a policy of gradually
upgrading the political status and influence of the formal
structure of state institutions. In an effort to combat the
"bureaucratization" of society, the Yugoslav regime acted to
sever the close relationship between the party apparatus and
the state administration that is characteristic of other communist political systems. After 1953 the Party (League) apparatus no longer maintained special organizational units
for the control of administrative agencies. Party cells
within governmental organizations were also disbanded, and
the practice of political leaders simultaneously holding
high-level positions in both the Party organs and the state
administration (the so-called personal accumulation of functions) was strongly discouraged, although not totally eliminated. As early as 1956 one Yugoslav specialist noted the
growing division between professional Party workers and administrative personnel in the state bureaucracy: "Many politically educated administrative cadre left the administrative service only because they were in some allegedly polit-

ical functions, and others would feel that there isn't a
place for them in the state administration. The idea began
to create differences in everyday social relations between
personnel in our state organs."[6]

The emancipation of the state administration from direct
party tutelage, together with.such other measures as the
sharp reduction of the number of administrative personnel and
the decentralization of the functions of federal agencies to
the regional and local level, succeeded in eliminating many
of the cumbersome and dysfunctional aspects of bureaucratic
control over the economy and society. At the same time, however, these changes also allowed the remaining administrative
agencies and personnel considerably more latitude for independent action than they had previously enjoyed. Character-
izing this development in conceptual terms, we can say that
as the partisanship of state administrators diminished during this period, their level of politicization markedly increased. As Fred Riggs has pointed out,

> politicization involves a heightening of the
> influence of officials, both military and
> civil, in the making of policies for a whole
> polity. Such officials may not also be ac-
> tive in a political party or take part in
> electoral and legislative politics. To the
> extent that public officials are associated
> with a political party, they may be called
> "partisan." [The] degree of partisanship
> provides no measure of bureaucratic power.
> Some spoilsmen in a bureaucracy, having been
> rewarded for party work, may hold unimpor-
> tant positions and exercise no significant
> influence, either inside or outside the bu-
> reaucracy. However, other political ap-
> pointees, holding high office, may exercise
> significant power. Thus bureaucratic par-
> tisanship may be high while degree of bu-
> reaucratism varies from high to low. Con-
> versely, we can find systems in which a low
> degree of partisanship is associated with a
> wide range of variation in degree of politi-
> cization.[7]

Thus, while during the height of the so-called bureaucratic
or administrative period of Yugoslav socialism from 1945 to
1951, it was the party bureaucracy that dominated political
life; during the subsequent phase of Yugoslav development
the state bureaucracy has become a more important political
force.[8]

In addition to the changes made with respect to the control of the administration, the withdrawal of the League of Communists from operational management over broad areas of social and economic activity also stimulated the develop ment of parliamentary assemblies as focal points for the adoption of political decisions. After 1963, and the estab lishment of a new constitutional system, many key issues that had previously been considered exclusively by top part bodies were transferred to the jurisdiction of legislative representatives serving in the structure of parliamentary assemblies on the federal, republican-provincial, and local levels.[9] (See Table 6.7 for some empirical indicators of parliamentary development.)

One result of this development has been that Yugoslav representative bodies, which had formerly enjoyed only nom- inal authority over the state bureaucracy, have gradually assumed practical responsibility for the political control of administrative functionaries. In practice this has mean that the task of recruiting senior civil servants, monitor- ing their activities, and holding them "accountable" for th performance of their duties now falls largely within the do main of elected parliamentary deputies. The organs of the League of Communists continue to exercise an influence on the selection and behavior of administrative officials in Yugoslavia, but far less directly and extensively than in the other communist states, and typically by means of very different methods. As a consequence of these changes, the relationship between elected legislative representatives an appointed officials in the state administration, which has drawn so much attention in studies of noncommunist regimes, has become an interesting area for political inquiry with respect to the Yugoslav political system.

Thus, the major aim of this study is to explore the po litical influence of senior civil servants in Yugoslavia on the process of legislative decision making. Three factors affecting the extent of administrative involvement in the legislative process on the top (federal) level of governmen tal authority have been selected for consideration: (1) th attitudes of higher civil servants regarding their own ac- tivities in the policy-making process, that is, their role orientations; (2) the pattern of interaction between senior state administrators and elected parliamentary deputies; an (3) the pattern of influence between administrative officia and parliamentary deputies.

An underlying assumption of the study is that the atti tudes and activities of higher administrative functionaries can have a significant influence in determining what kinds of legislative decisions are formulated and how, or indeed

if, such decisions are implemented. The way in which administrative officials view their own responsibilities, and the
nature of their relationship with elected political officials, is therefore an important factor in understanding the
overall process of modernization in Yugoslavia. Moreover,
an examination of the role played by administrative officials
in the legislative process can also help shed some light on
the capacity of Yugoslav representative institutions to control and delimit activities of the state bureaucracy. In
that sense the following discussion is part of a broader inquiry by this author into the political institutionalization
of the parliamentary system in Yugoslavia between 1953 and
1973, a development that has been a major aspect of political modernization in that country.[10]

The data for this study derives primarily from survey
interviews with Yugoslav federal administrators and federal
legislators conducted from March 1968 to January 1969 by the
International Study of Opinion-Makers project. The project
was cosponsored by the Bureau of Applied Social Reserach at
Columbia University and the Institute of Social Sciences in
Belgrade, and it was directed by an interdisciplinary team
of social scientists from the United States and Europe.[11]
In addition to the analysis of survey interview data, this
study also incorporates the results of field research conducted by this author on parliamentary and administrative
development in Yugoslavia.

The survey carried out by the International Study of
Opinion-Makers project included interviews with Yugoslav
leaders in six institutional sectors: federal legislators,
federal administrators, Party and mass organization leaders,
economic leaders, mass communications, and intellectuals.
Since the major focus of this study concerns the involvement
and political influence of senior civil servants in the legislative process, a subject that primarily includes the relationship between administrative officials and elected parliamentary representatives, only the first two subgroups--
federal legislators and federal administrators--are discussed in the following pages. Table 6.1 includes a breakdown of the types of positions included in the two subgroups
and the composition of the sample.

THE ROLE ORIENTATIONS OF HIGHER
ADMINISTRATIVE OFFICIALS

One of the few beliefs that appears to be shared by
elites and citizens alike in most political systems is that
administrative officials should be subject to the control of

TABLE 6.1

The Composition of the Sample and Universe List in Yugoslavia,[a] 1968-69

	Basic Universe List		Sample Respondents		Sample Respondents as a Percent of Universe
	Number	Percent	Number	Percent	Percent
I. Federal administrative functionaries					
A. Senior civil servants in the federal assembly (secretaries of the chambers, committees, commissions, advisors, assistants, etc.)	37	24.5	26	32.1	70.3
B. Senior civil servants in the federal administration					
1. in the Federal Executive Council[b] (secretaries, undersecretaries, assistants, advisors, etc.)	23	15.2	15	18.5	65.2
2. in the state secretariats, federal secretariats, councils, commissions, administrations, etc. (secretaries, undersecretaries, deputy-secretaries, directors, advisors, assistants, etc.)	91	60.3	40	49.4	44.0
Total federal administrators	151	100.0	81	100.0	53.6
II. Deputies in the Federal Assembly					
A. Deputies in the "political chambers"					
1. Chamber of Nationalities	70	28.6	16	24.6	22.9
2. Federal Chamber	120	49.0	38	58.5	31.7
B. Top-ranking deputies in the functionally specialized chambers[c]	55	22.5	11	16.9	20.0
Total deputies	245	100.0	65	100.0	26.5

ᵃThe "universe list" of Yugoslav opinion makers was initially defined in terms of a set of positions in six institutional sectors: federal legislators, federal administrators, federal party and mass organization leaders, economic leaders, mass communicators, and intellectuals. It comprised a total of 1,413 positions occupied by 1,290 individuals. A sample of 517 individuals occupying 569 of these positions was interviewed in the period from March 1968 to January 1969 and included the two subgroups being analyzed in this study. The choices made outside of the "universe list" generally refer to individuals nominated by the respondents who hold positions on the republican-provincial and communal levels of authority. Since this study is concerned primarily with administrative-legislative relations on the federal level, a detailed analysis of these responses is not included in the following pages.

ᵇThe 17 members of the Federal Executive Council (FEC) during 1968-69 are not treated as "administrative functionaries" in this study. During the period covered by this analysis the president and members of the council were elected by the deputies of the Federal Assembly from among their own ranks, that is, elected legislators, and functioned very similarly to a cabinet or ministerial council in parliamentary systems. According to Yugoslav constitutional theory the members of the FEC were entrusted with the "political-executive" function rather than "administrative-technical" duties. The members of the council were almost exclusively important personalities in the League of Communists and other mass sociopolitical organizations. We have chosen to exclude the members of the FEC from the "administrative elite" because we are primarily concerned with the way in which appointed officials formally charged with administrative tasks view their own duties and how they interact and perceive other actors in the governmental process. From 1956 on, however, appointed civil servants working within the organizational framework of the FEC have been considered both structurally and functionally as part of the Federal Administration (Savezna uprava) and are therefore included along with other senior officials in subgroup "B." For a detailed discussion of the problems involved in defining the composition of the administrative elite, see Radomir Lukic, "Hauts Fonctionnaires et Hommes Politiques en Yugoslavia" (unpublished paper presented at the Eighth World Congress of the International Political Science Association, 1970), and Jovan Djordjevic, "The Executive in Yugoslavia," in Decisions and Decision-Makers in the Modern State, ed. Jean Meynaud (Zurich: Unesco, 1967), pp. 99-114.

ᶜThis subgroup includes deputies in the Social-Health Chamber, Educational-Cultural Chamber, and Organizational-Political Chamber of the Federal Assembly who served as members of Assembly commissions, the presidents of committees in these chambers, and the presidents and vice-presidents of these chambers. Top-ranking deputies in the Economic Chamber of the Federal Assembly were treated as part of the "economic" rather than the "legislative" elite by the International Study of Opinion-Makers project in the compilation of the "basic universe list" of Yugoslav leadership (along with economic planners and industrial directors) and are therefore not included in the total number of deputies from the functionally specialized chambers included in this table.

"political" authorities. "With few exceptions," writes one
student of comparative administration, "there is common
agreement, transcending differences in political ideology,
culture, and style, that bureaucracy should be basically instrumental in its operation, that it should serve as an
agent and not as a master."[12] No matter in what institution
or group political authority may happen to be vested at a
particular time (a legislature, party, military, etc.), "administrators" are expected to develop a self-image, or conception of their role in accordance with this norm and to
behave accordingly.[13]

The Yugoslav case is no exception in this respect. According to constitutional theory and administrative law, the
administrative function consists of two basic activities:
(1) the implementation and enforcement of the laws, regulations, and policies adopted by representative institutions;
and (2) the provision of specialized assistance to elected
decision makers in carrying out their duties, such as the
detailed preparation of legislation, drawing up reports,
providing information, and various other forms of "technical
consultation." A handbook for employees in the state administration emphasizes that the legislative process involves a
combination of rules that are designed to

> secure the complete and absolutely decisive
> role of the competent legislative organs in
> the adoption of laws and other regulations,
> and in that way their responsibility for the
> laws which are adopted. In addition, it is
> the aim of these rules to achieve: the full
> consideration and evaluation of all possible
> solutions and alternatives, the participa-
> tion of political and other legislative fac-
> tors, the confrontation of various interests
> in the solution of special social problems,
> as well as consultation with representatives
> of different interests and opinions, etc.
> . . . However, the particular aim of the
> rules of legislative procedure is to insure
> the complete freedom and all other condi-
> tions for the realization of the rights of
> members of representative bodies, to express
> their will, and unhindered participation in
> this procedure.[14]

An examination of the attitudes expressed by higher administrators in Yugoslavia regarding the duties they consider most important in carrying out their jobs reveals a

close correspondence between their own role orientations and the official conception of the administrative function (Table 6.2). Of 81 federal administrators interviewed in 1968 and 1969, the largest number (38 percent) indicated that professional assistance in policy making was the most important aspect of their responsibility. About 25 percent of the administrators regarded the implementation of policies adopted by the Federal Assembly and the members of the Federal Executive Council as the chief feature of their work. A smaller, although not insignificant, number of the respondents expressed a more participatory definition of their roles, indicating their most important task to be participation in the formulation of the long-term goals and policies for society (14.8 percent), or the presentation of new ideas that contribute to the efficiency and modernization of society (8.6 percent). Only five (6.2 percent) of the higher administrators regarded responsiveness to the public as the most important aspect of their duties.

It seems rather clear from these responses that most of the Yugoslav administrators interviewed tend to emphasize those facets of their work that are formally prescribed, and that are frequently stressed by official norms. They are the same type of answers given by many administrators in other countries when presented with similar questions about their activities.[15] The tendency of Yugoslav civil servants to give "correct" responses is even greater given the politically sensitive environment in which they labor and the relatively unusual nature of survey interviews being conducted in their midst. While there is always a natural temptation either to question seriously or completely reject the validity of such survey data, particularly with respect to the much maligned and usually suspect activities of "bureaucrats," one interesting pattern does emerge from the above responses. Namely, the administrators interviewed tended to place a much greater emphasis on the professional-advisory, or consultative aspects of the administrative function than on the implementation of policy. Although policy counsel is an officially acceptable administrative function, it is the execution of laws, that is, policy implementation, that is usually given priority in Yugoslav constitutional theory.

The strong orientation toward policy counsel among administrative functionaries working in the Federal Assembly is not surprising given the fact that they are required to assist elected officials in the preparation of legislation. The professional-advisory or policy-counsel orientation of federal administrative officials working outside of the legislature, however, is also very high. One factor that may explain this pattern of responses is the changing functions

TABLE 6.2

The Role Orientations of Higher Administrative Functionaries in Yugoslavia

Question: Which of the following duties do you consider most important in your work? Choose three and rank them.

Role Orientation[a]	First Choice of Administrative Functionaries in the					
	Federal Administration		Federal Assembly		Total	
	Number	Percent	Number	Percent	Number	Percent
Policy counsel (professional assistance in the formulation of decisions of federal legislative and executive organs)	18	32.7	13	50.0	31	38.3
Policy implementation (the precise implementation of the decisions and policies of federal legislative and executive organs)	14	25.1	6	23.0	20	24.7
Program formulation (participation in the formulation of the long-term goals and policies of society)	9	16.4	3	11.5	12	14.8
Innovation (the presentation of new ideas that contribute to the efficiency and modernization of society)	5	9.1	2	7.7	7	8.6
Administrative efficiency[b] (ensure effective and rational administration, check waste, and avoid unnecessary expenditures)	5	9.1	1	3.9	6	7.4
Responsiveness to the public (ensure the influence of citizens and the publicity of administrative work)	4	7.2	1	3.9	5	6.2
Total responses	55	100.0	26	100.0	81	100.0

[a]The description of each role orientation in parentheses is a translation of the choices offered to the respondents in the questionnaire.

of the federal administration in recent years. Very briefly,
the decentralization of numerous governmental functions to
the republican and communal levels has considerably diminished the responsibilities of the federal administration for
the direct implementation and enforcement of laws. Moreover,
a great many federal administrative tasks have also been
transferred to various "self-managing institutions" that
have a quasi-independent position (for example, federal institutions for banking, insurance, employment, etc.), and
therefore these matters are no longer directly within the
jurisdiction of senior civil servants. As a result of these
changes, the activity of federal administrators has been increasingly directed toward the provision of professional
staff service for legislators rather than toward the execution of laws and regulations. This development is particularly significant given the fact that one of the principal
avenues by which administrative officials influence the content and outcome of political decisions in any regime is in
the area of "professional," "technical," or "specialized assistance" in the formulation of politics.[16] While it is impossible to determine the extent and nature of this influence simply from the attitudes of administrative officials
concerning their most important duties in response to survey
interviews, the importance and prospect of some type of administrative involvement in legislative decision making is
clearly evident in the minds of Yugoslav civil servants.

Thus, nearly two-thirds of all the administrators interviewed emphasized either the consultative aspect of their
duties, direct participation in policy formulation, or the
presentation of new ideas. The responses tend to confirm
the observation made by many Yugoslav authors that higher
state functionaries spend a major portion of their time providing assistance to elected officials and give relatively
little attention to the implementation or enforcement of
laws. As one administrator observed when answering criticisms that senior civil servants are too deeply involved in
the formulation of policy and neglect their duties imple-
menting decisions:

>   Although the primary task of the administra-
>   tive organs is to implement laws and regula-
>   tions, these organs, according to some analy-
>   ses, spend 60 to 80 percent of their effec-
>   tive working capacity, especially the lead-
>   ing personnel, in the preparation of analy-
>   ses and proposals for representative bodies
>   and their organs. . . . one only needs to
>   stroll through the halls, for example, of

the Federal Assembly and see how many professional employees and functionaries of
the administration are engaged in the work
of different committees, commissions, and
chambers at the request of these organs of
the Assembly, <u>and not on the initiative of
the organs of the administration</u>.[17] (Emphasis added.)

THE PATTERN OF INTERACTION

The frequency and character of interaction between legislators and administrators is an important factor effecting
the extent of administrative influence in the legislative
process. A high rate of communication and contact between
the two groups may facilitate the ability of the legislature
to control the administration by allowing elected deputies
to oversee the work of civil servants and question them concerning their activity. Interaction with elected officials
may also provide an opportunity for administrators to advance their own beliefs in the framing of policy. Whatever
the outcome may be, a close working relationship between administrators and legislators promotes a mutual awareness of
each others' problems, strengths, and weaknesses.[18]

How extensively do Yugoslav legislators and administrators interact with one another? An analysis of the responses of Yugoslav federal administrators and members of
the Federal Assembly, who were asked about their contacts in
their respective fields of work, can help to illustrate the
network of contacts between the two groups. The specific
question put to federal servants and legislative deputies
during 1968-69 was: "During the past month, who are the
three people with whom you have most often had discussions
about problems in your own field?" The responses are presented in Table 6.3, and again schematically in Figure 6.1,
in order to indicate the pattern of interaction between different institutional sectors of the political system on the
federal level.

The responses of administrators appear to confirm their
close working relationship with deputies in the Federal Assembly, which also emerge from the analysis of their attitudes concerning the administrative role. Of the 55 persons
named by administrative officials in the Federal Assembly as
"discussion partners" on matters in their own field, the
majority (41.9 percent) were deputies in the Federal Assembl
The fact that 15 out of 23 of the legislators named by administrators in the Federal Assembly as discussion partners

The Pattern of Interaction between Federal Administrative and Legislative
Elites in Yugoslavia
(in percents)

Question: During the past month, who are the three people with whom you
have most often had discussions about problems in your own field?

Persons Named by Institutional Sector	Sector of Elite Respondents		
	Administrative Functionaries in the		Federal Legislators (N-57)
	Federal Administration (N-46)	Federal Assembly (N-22)	
Administrative functionaries in the Federal Administration	34.4	10.9	2.2
Administrative functionaries in the Federal Assembly	--	20.0	1.0
Members of the Federal Executive Council (the cabinet)	13.8	1.8	4.5
Federal legislators	16.2	41.9	33.1
Party and mass organization leaders*	9.2	5.5	10.5
Other/nonpolitical or non-administrative individuals	4.6	7.3	8.2
Outside of universe list	21.8	12.7	41.3
Total persons named as interaction partners	100.0 (N-87)	100.0 (N-55)	100.0 (N-133)

*The "party" refers to the central organs (federal) of the Yugoslav League of Communists.
Mass organizations include the Socialist Alliance of the Working People of Yugoslavia, the Trade
Union Federation, the veterans' association, and the organizations for women and youth on the
federal level.

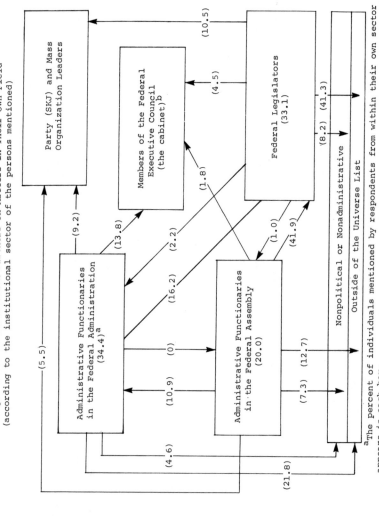

FIGURE 6.1

Percent of Different Persons Mentioned by Yugoslav Federal Administrators and Legislators as Interaction Partners on Matters in Their Own Field (according to the institutional sector of the persons mentioned)

Party (SKJ) and Mass Organization Leaders

Members of the Federal Executive Council (the cabinet)[b]

Federal Legislators (33.1)

Administrative Functionaries in the Federal Administration (34.4)[a]

Administrative Functionaries in the Federal Assembly (20.0)

Nonpolitical or Nonadministrative

Outside of the Universe List

(10.5)
(4.5)
(1.8)
(9.2)
(13.8)
(2.2)
(16.2)
(1.0)
(41.9)
(8.2)
(41.3)
(5.5)
(0)
(10.9)
(7.3)
(12.7)
(4.6)
(21.8)

[a]The percent of individuals mentioned by respondents from within their own sector appears in each box.

[b]See Note 3 in Table 6.1.

174

were elected officials in the Assembly (presidents of the chambers, presidents of various committees and commissions, etc.) illustrates the point at which administrative involvement in the legislative process takes place. Direct contacts between administrative functionaries and deputies serving in the Federal Assembly appear to be much more extensive than the degree of interaction among the various parliamentary administrators themselves (20.0 percent of the responses). Administrative functionaries working for a particular committee or commission are more likely to develop a closer working relationship with those legislators who either preside over or are intimately involved in the work of these bodies than with fellow administrative officials who perform tasks on other matters in the legislative process. This situation is a natural consequence of the functional and topical division of labor among various committees and commissions in the Federal Assembly, and it probably tends to undermine the solidarity and cohesiveness of the parliamentary administrators as a group.

Administrative functionaries working outside of the parliament tended to choose a much higher level of their interaction partners from within their own ranks (34.4 percent). The fact that federal administrative agencies are either directly within the organizational framework of the Federal Executive Council (the rough equivalent of the cabinet, or "government," in other parliamentary systems), or are under its direct supervision explains the high rate of interaction between senior civil servants and members of the Council (13.8 percent of the nominations). Federal administrators also indicated some interaction with deputies in the Federal Assembly (16.2 percent), usually with legislators holding key parliamentary functions such as the presidents of various committees. The data on interaction does not, however, reveal a very high rate of contacts between federal administrators and higher party officials. While undoubtedly a close relationship continues to persist between top administrative officials and some high-ranking members of the League of Communists (due to common experiences, social affiliations, etc.), the frequency of direct contact between individuals holding positions in these two institutional sectors does not appear very great today. In contrast to earlier years when the Communist Party exercised close supervision over the state administration, these findings suggest a growing differentiation between the party and the state apparatus.

While Yugoslav administrators, particularly those serving in the Federal Assembly, claim to have a major portion of their working discussions with federal legislators, this pattern of interaction is not indicated by the deputies

themselves. When questioned about the most important discussion partner in their "own field," federal legislators typically chose other members of the Assembly (33.1 percent), or
in most cases (41.3 percent) individuals completely outside
the "universe list" of federal leaders. One effect of the
decentralization of governmental authority in the Yugoslav
system has been to "territorialize" political power and
therefore make both the members of the Federal Assembly and
the federal administration more responsive to interest
groups and elites on the regional and local level. The high
level of persons named outside the "universe list" reflects
the close ties that legislators maintain with various individuals and groups on the republican-provincial and communal
levels of the federation. The large number of interaction
partners chosen by legislators from among their own colleagues in the Federal Assembly (33.1 percent) rather than
from among party leaders may reflect the increasing organizational vitality of the parliamentary system as an independent component of the political system in recent years (see
Table 6.7). The line separating legislators serving in the
"political chambers"* of the Federal Assembly from functionaries working in the party and in mass organizations remains
a rather thin one, however, since most individuals in both
subgroups share a common background in professional "sociopolitical activity" (Party-League, mass organization, and
government).

The most important finding with respect to our discussion, however, is the fact that federal deputies report very
little interaction with administrative officials. Part of
the reason for this may be explained by the fact that only
a small portion of the legislators interviewed held those
positions in the Federal Assembly in which they would be
most likely to have frequent contact with administrators
(for example, heads of committees and commissions who constantly deal with administrative officials during the preparation of legislation and various other aspects of parliamentary activity). As mentioned earlier, the responses of
administrators regarding their contacts in the Federal Assembly seem to illustrate that their pattern of interaction with
deputies, while very frequent, was limited to particular legislators holding key positions in the Assembly. It is not

---

*The term "political chambers" during the period in
which the survey was carried out (1968-69) refers to the
Federal Chamber and the Chamber of Nationalities. Of the
65 deputies interviewed, 83 percent were in these chambers,
which were composed almost entirely of professional politicians.

entirely surprising, therefore, that when asked to name the people with whom they most frequently discussed matters in their "own field," most federal legislators would name a relatively small number of administrative officials. Although the data on interaction cannot help to specify the precise nature and extent of administrative involvement in the formulation of policy, it does suggest that such activity occurs with respect to specific issue areas and phases of the legislative process rather than a diffuse pattern of frequent contacts between administrators and parliamentary deputies.

THE PATTERN OF INFLUENCE

While sociometric data on interaction patterns can shed some light on the frequency of contacts between legislators and administrators, there is no way of knowing, at least from the data available, how such behavior affects the distribution of influence between these two groups. Knowing that communication exists between certain individuals suggests the extent to which potential for the development of influence exists, in one way or another, but offers little insight into how that influence is structured, or if any influence relationship actually exists at all. A second sociometric question from the International Opinion-Makers study of the Yugoslav elite offers some additional insight with respect to the pattern of influence between federal administrative officials and elected deputies. The question reads: "Could you tell us the names of the three people who have had the greatest influence on your opinions, concerning the most essential problems in your field?" The responses by both federal administrators and legislators (Table 6.4 and Figure 6.2) reveal a significantly different pattern than the data on interaction. For one thing, while the rate of response was only slightly lower than for the question on interaction, the number of individuals nominated as influential was considerably smaller. On the question of interaction, the responses were widely diffused among a variety of individuals, with most respondents naming different people as discussion partners. The responses to the question of influence, however, centered on a more limited number of individuals, most of whom were named by several of the respondents. It has been suggested that this type of result derives from the general tendency of elite studies using a reputational approach (of which the above question on influence is one variant) to reveal a narrower spread of leadership than studies that focus on the involvement or interaction of elites on specific issues or decisions.[19]

TABLE 6.4

The Pattern of Influence between Federal Administrative and Legislative
Elites in Yugoslavia
(in percents)

Question: Could you tell us the names of the three people who have had the
greatest influence on your opinions, concerning the most essential
problems in your field?

| | Sector of Elite Respondents | | |
| | Administrative Functionaries in the | | |
Persons Named by Institutional Sector	Federal Administration (N-43)	Federal Assembly (N-18)	Federal Legislators (N-52)
Administrative functionaries in the federal administration	15.1	11.5	3.4
Administrative functionaries in the Federal Assembly	--	--	--
Members of the Federal Executive Council (the cabinet)	13.2	7.7	6.8
Federal legislators	20.8	23.1	18.6
Party and mass organization leaders	20.8	27.0	25.4
Other/nonpolitical or non-administrative individuals	3.7	11.5	10.2
Outside of universe list	26.4	19.2	35.6
Total persons named as influentials	100.0 (N-53)	100.0 (N-26)	100.0 (N-59)

Percent of Different Persons Mentioned by Yugoslav Federal Administrators and Legislators as Having an Influence on Their Opinions Concerning Matters in Their Own Field (according to the institutional sector of the persons mentioned)

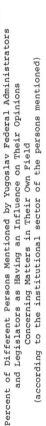
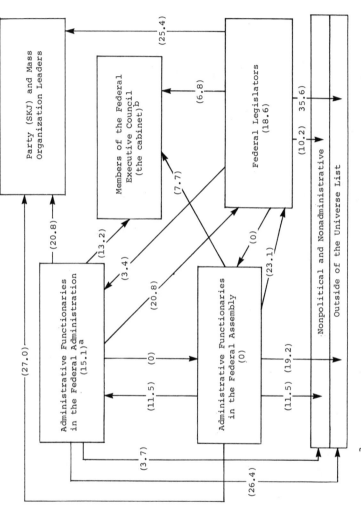

[a] The percent of individuals mentioned by respondents from within their own sector appears in each box.

[b] See note a in Table 6.1.

179

In terms of our interest here, however, a more important question than the number of persons nominated as influ entials is the source of that influence. This also differs considerably from the responses on interaction. What emerges most clearly about the type of individuals nominate as influential is the importance accorded to high-ranking members of the League of Communists and other mass organiza tions. Of the persons named by administrative functionarie in the Federal Assembly as having the most influence on opinions in their field, the largest number (27.0 percent) were party and mass organization leaders. This group also made up a large proportion (20.8 percent) of the individual named as influential by functionaries in the federal admini tration, although the close connection between these civil servants and officials on the republican-provincial level a counted for a greater number of responses (26.4 percent) ou side the "universe list." In addition, both subgroups of a ministrators also nominated a large number of legislators a influential on opinions in their field.

What is surprising is that the number of the legislato named was not even greater, given the formal accountability of the administration to members of the Assembly and the growing activity of the parliamentary system after 1963. The fact that a large proportion of the legislators named are professional politicians by occupation and are members of the Central Committee of the League of Communists makes it difficult to determine whether their influence derives mainly from their positions as elected members of the parliament or because they are generally influential "socio-political workers" who happen to be in the parliament. It would seem likely that a combination of both institutional affiliations--League and Federal Assembly--provides a basis for their influence over the opinions of administrative officials.

The continued significance of the League and other mass sociopolitical organizations as the locus of political powe in the Yugoslav political system emerges even more clearly, however, from the responses of legislators themselves. Leav ing aside the large number of persons nominated as influential by deputies in the Federal Assembly who are outside the universe list of the federal elite (that is, regional and local leaders), the greatest percentage of their choices are among leaders in the League of Communists and the mass organizations (25.4 percent). This reflects the fact that, although Yugoslav parliamentary deputies have displayed increasing independence in recent years, the overall "guidance" of the League of Communists is still acknowledged as an essential feature of the legislative process.[20] When it

comes to choosing influentials in their own "field," the
legislators quite naturally also name a large portion of
their fellow deputies in the Federal Assembly (18.6 percent).
It is necessary to emphasize again, however, that Yugoslav
legislators who are professional politicians by occupation
(as most of the deputies in the sample are) make very little
distinction between political leaders serving party organizations, mass organizations, and the parliamentary system.
Legislators consider activity in each of these institutional
sectors as closely related and largely interchangeable facets of "sociopolitical work." To distinguish, therefore,
between persons nominated by legislators who are involved in
one or another sphere of "political" activity may be more of
an analytical than a real distinction. What appears more
clearly is that only a fraction of all the persons named by
legislators as having an influence in their own field were
civil servants in the state administration (3.4 percent).
If high administrative officials have any influence in the
policy-making process, it certainly is not apparent from the
responses of the federal legislators.

The reputed influence of a small number of party and
mass organization leaders on both legislative and administrative matters emerges even more noticeably by comparing
the number of nominations received by individuals in various
organizational sectors (Table 6.5). If those persons who
received five or more nominations (that is, who were named
by five or more respondents as having an influence on opinions in their field) are considered as highly influential,
then--according to the perceptions of both federal legislators and federal administrators--a relatively small number
of party and mass organization leaders at the summit of the
Yugoslav political system appear to have the most influence.
It should be emphasized, however, that this finding in no
way suggests that the direct intervention of party leaders
in the activities of state institutions is of the same magnitude or has the same consequences as in earlier years,
particularly before 1963. In the case of routine decisions,
which constitute the overwhelming portion of decision making, both federal civil servants and legislators have considerable latitude for independent action.

The major aim of the preceding discussion has been to
examine the evidence from survey interview data gathered by
the International Study of Opinion-Makers project concerning
the influence of Yugoslav administrative officials on political decision making. The findings from the analysis are
both suggestive and limited in their usefulness. They reveal that the way in which administrators perceive their
roles corresponds closely to the official-legal conception

TABLE 6.5

Persons Mentioned by Yugoslav Federal Administrators and Legislators as Having an Influence on their Opinions Concerning Matters in Their Own Field (according to the number of nominations received by persons in each institutional sector)

	Institutional Sector of Respondents								
	Administrative Functionaries in the						Federal Legislators		
	Federal Administration			Federal Assembly					
Sector of Persons Nominated	High[a]	Medium[b]	Low[c]	High	Medium	Low	High	Medium	Low
Administrative functionaries in the federal administration	--	1	--	--	--	3	--	--	1
Administrative functionaries in the Federal Assembly	--	--	7	--	--	--	--	--	--
Members of the Federal Executive Council (cabinet)	1	3	3	--	1	1	1	--	3
Federal legislators	--	2	9	--	2	4	1	2	8
Party and mass organization leaders	3	3	5	3	1	3	4	4	7
Other/nonpolitical and non-administrative individuals	--	--	2	--	--	3	--	1	5
Outside of universe list	--	2	12	--	--	5	--	2	19
Total persons mentioned as influentials	4	11	38	3	4	19	6	9	44

[a] High=persons who received 5 or more nominations.

[b] Medium=persons who received from 2 to 4 nominations.

[c] Low=persons who received 1 nomination.

of their duties. The senior civil servants who were interviewed tend to place primary emphasis on the consultative aspects of their work, that is, specialized assistance in the formulation of policy, rather than on the implementation of policy. While the attitudinal data on role orientations suggests the evaluation that administrators place on their past behavior, as well as their expectations of future behavior, it does not tell whether their activities have actually conformed to these perceptions, or are likely to in the future.

The analysis of the sociometric data on interaction between administrators and legislators reveals the frequency and general pattern of contact between members of these two groups. Administrators claim to have frequent contact with elected deputies in carrying out their duties. In contrast, federal legislators appear to maintain a broad variety of contacts in their work, most of which are either with individuals and groups holding positions below the federal level or with top leaders in the party and other mass organizations. We do not know, however, how this pattern of interaction affects the relationship between administrators and legislators. Do such contacts, for example, enhance administrative influence in the formulation of policy, or perhaps provide an opportunity for legislative control over the state bureaucracy? The data on influence offers a somewhat more conclusive picture. When federal administrators and legislators were asked to name the people most influential in their field, they tended to choose a relatively small number of professional political activists in the League of Communists and the Federal Assembly. Again, however, we cannot tell from the data if, or in what way, this reputed influence affects the day-to-day tasks carried out by both administrative officials and parliamentary deputies.

The analysis of the survey interview data would lead one to conclude that administrative functionaries are primarily professional staff consultants who, although interacting frequently with legislators in the Assembly, exercise very minimal influence in the formulation of political decisions. Allen Barton, for example, in a preliminary analysis of data on the attitudes and values of the same administrative officials treated in this study, concludes that "the federal administrators tend to be the servants of those in power, rather than interest groups in their own rights, and do not express distinctive interests or values related to their position."[21] To what extent is this an accurate description of the political role of Yugoslav federal administrators? While the findings from our analysis would generally seem to give some support to Barton's view, it differs

substantially from the view frequently encountered among p
ticipants in the Yugoslav legislative process, namely, tha
professional civil servants exercise a strong influence on
the shape and substance of decisions made in the Federal A
sembly. The following quotation by the president of the C
mittee for the Federal Budget in the Chamber of Nationalit
is typical in this respect:

> It is difficult to overlook the reality that
> a single apparatus such as the Federal Ad-
> ministration of over 8,000 workers is a so-
> cial force which generates a tendency to
> preserve its position in the creation of
> legislative and economic policy. This was
> evident from its program of work during de-
> bates in committees in the Federal Assembly
> concerning the federal budget last year.
> Namely, one saw that the administrative or-
> gans established a program of work which the
> Assembly later adopted, as its program of
> work, rather than the opposite situation.
> The fact is that the administration
> which is primarily authorized to execute
> laws and other regulations, formulates and
> also initiates the majority of laws and pro-
> posals. It is true that they formulate them
> according to directions, and within the
> boundaries of their authority. However, by
> their nature, they cannot fail to use their
> professional supremacy for the promotion of
> their views and solutions.[22]

The view expressed above suggests a considerably grea
er role of Yugoslav civil servants in the policy-making pr
cess than the survey interview data indicated. Moreover,
this view does not belong to the general body of official
pronouncements and pro forma criticisms about the dangers
and evils of "bureaucracy" and "technocracy" in the construction of socialism; rather, it is characteristic of di
cussions among informed political functionaries, legal and
constitutional specialists on the parliamentary system, an
political scientists concerning the influence of the state
administration in the federal legislative process.[23] Accordingly, in order to obtain a more complete picture of t
political role of the state bureaucracy, it is necessary to
go beyond the analysis of the survey data and, at least
briefly, examine some additional evidence concerning administrative involvement in the policy-making process obtaine
by means of more "traditional" research techniques.

TECHNICAL EXPERTISE AND POLITICAL INFLUENCE

As suggested earlier in this study, federal administrators spend a great deal of their time providing "professional assistance" to the members of the Federal Assembly. This involves a variety of tasks including drafting proposals of laws, preparing the Assembly's "Program of Work," submitting reports and information to committees of the Assembly, and consultation about various aspects of administrative and legislative affairs. Some of this assistance is provided by the appointed functionaries and staff services of the Federal Assembly. The major portion of such activity, however, is carried out by senior officials in the federal administration and the administrative agencies of the Federal Executive Council. One of the most important bodies involved in this work is the Secretariat for Legislation and Organization (after 1971 the Secretariat for Legislation and Legal Affairs), which is the administrative arm of the Federal Executive Council for the preparation of legislative proposals.

Despite efforts to upgrade the Federal Assembly and make it the "highest organ of state authority," the executive and administrative agencies have continued to exercise almost exclusive control over the initiation of federal legislation. For example, out of 1,015 legislative proposals submitted to the Federal Assembly between 1963 and 1968, 84 percent were initiated by the Federal Executive Council and the Federal Administration, 15 percent by chambers and committees of the Assembly, and approximately 1 percent by individual deputies.[24] This situation, not unlike the role of executive and administrative agencies in other political systems, provides the senior civil servants with an important source of leverage for advancing their own political values and opinions. As one leading student of Yugoslav public administration, who served as head of the important Legislative Legal Commission of the Federal Assembly from 1967 to 1971, observed:

> It is impossible to construct a new parliamentary system alongside the continuing domination of the administration. And its domination is still evident. It imposes and pushes its attitudes, and it creates policies. Of course, not on the biggest questions, but certainly on everyday ones. The administration needs to implement policy and not to create it. Its role of policy making is only in the implementation of laws. But that doesn't seem to be the case. We, in

> fact, don't have a real administration, but
> rather a professional service for creating
> and influencing policies, in the federation,
> republics, and communes.[25]   (Emphasis added.)

The dominant role played by executive and administrative agencies in the initiation of federal legislation stems primarily from its pivotal role as a source of expertise and information. As Table 6.6 illustrates, the federal administration enjoys an overwhelming advantage with respect to the amount of technical expertise at its disposal. More important than the absolute number of technically trained personnel in the federal administration is the fact that only a small percentage of the administrative functionaries and other political institutions possess the technical skills necessary to deal with the complex issues they increasingly must confront.

An important factor contributing to the monopoly of the federal administration as a source of technical expertise in the policy-making process has been the failure or disinclination of the Federal Assembly to utilize sufficiently the services of various experts and specialized groups outside of the administration. There is no doubt that such "free floating" specialized resources that are relatively independent of political influence are now available in Yugoslavia. Up to now, however, they have played a rather insignificant role in the policy-making process.[26] The need for tapping such alternative sources of expertise has been particularly acute, given the rapid turnover of legislators in Yugoslav representative assemblies. Serving primarily as short-term amateur politicians who face mandatory rotation out of their elected positions after two terms, the majority of Yugoslav legislators, even more than their counterparts in foreign representative bodies, generally do not have either the time or the motivation to become well acquainted with the complex technical issues presented to them by the executive and administrative agencies.* This situation naturally leads most deputies to solicit, and rely heavily upon, specialized advice from professional civil servants. In this regard, it is important to note that those parliamentary deputies who are best qualified to deal competently with administrative

---

*There are, of course, important exceptions. In each session of the Federal Assembly there have been a few so-called free-lance federal legislators who have subjected the executive and administrative officials to extensive criticism and interrogation.

TABLE 6.6

The Distribution of University-Trained Employees in Federal Political and
Administrative Institutions by Type of Higher Education Received

Type of Higher Education	Institutional Sector				
	Federal Administration	Federal Executive Council (Cabinet)	Federal Assembly	Party and Mass Sociopolitical Organizations[a]	Total by Field of Education
Agriculture	4.9 / 92.4	1.6 / 2.5	1.7 / 2.5	1.2 / 2.5	100.0 (n-79)
Technical (engineering)	7.1 / 95.5	1.0 / 0.1	1.0 / 0.1	1.6 / 2.7	100.0 (N-110)
Economics	24.7 / 81.3	16.6 / 4.5	26.7 / 6.9	17.7 / 7.4	100.0 (N-449)
Law	39.1 / 73.0	78.3 / 11.9	51.7 / 7.6	32.3 / 7.6	100.0 (N-792)
Philosophy	11.8 / 71.1	1.6 / 1.0	12.1 / 5.8	29.0 / 22.3	100.0 (N-242)
Other[b]	10.9 / 81.7	-- / --	4.3 / 2.6	16.7[b] / 15.7	100.0 (N-197)
Two or more	1.5 / 75.0	1.0 / 3.6	2.6 / 10.7	1.6 / 10.7	100.0 (N-28)
Total university-trained employees	100.0 (N-1475) / 77.8	100.0 (N-120) / 6.3	100.0 (N-116) / 6.1	100.0 (N-186) / 9.8	100.0 (N-1897)

[a] The professional apparatus of the Central Committee of the Yugoslav League of Communists, Central Council and Central Committee of the Yugoslav League of Trade Unions, Federal Conference of the Socialist Alliance (SSRNJ), Central Committee of the Yugoslav Youth League, the Central Committee of the Yugoslav League of War Veterans, and the Conference for the Social Activity of Yugoslav Women.

[b] Degrees received from Higher Party and Political Schools are probably highly represented in this category.

Source: Pregled broja i strukture kadrova u saveznim organima, organizacijama, i ustanovama [A Survey of the Number and Structure of Cadre in Federal Organs, Organizations, and Institutions] (Beograd, Savezno Izvrsno Vece, Uprava za personalne poslove, 1967), pp. 43-44, 55-56.

officials concerning complex policy issues have been concentrated in the functionally specialized chambers of the Federal Assembly (the so-called Chambers of the Working Communities, the Economic Chamber, the Social-Health Chamber, etc.), which have had the least amount of formal authority to exercise political control over the state administration. Moreover, the functionally specialized chambers have had the highest rate of membership turnover, thereby preventing technically qualified legislators from developing an intimate familiarity with various policy questions (see Table 6.7 for data on the professionalization of federal legislators).

In contrast, the "political chambers" (Federal Chamber and Chamber of Nationalities) of the Federal Assembly, having primary responsibility for the control of federal administrative officials (for example, the power of appointment and dismissal), have been composed almost entirely of older career politicians, who, though considerably experienced in legislative assemblies at different levels of the federal system, have either nontechnical educational backgrounds, or in many cases, no higher education at all. In short, those parliamentary representatives with the most expertise to comprehend, scrutinize, or challenge the provisions of programs initiated by the state bureaucracy have the least "political weight" in the legislative process.[27] Despite the overall improvement in the educational qualifications of federal deputies, and the effort by the Assembly to develop its own specialized staff as an alternative source of expertise and information, almost all technical information used as a basis for legislative decisions has continued to come directly from senior administrative officials or to be channeled through administrative agencies. The influence of administrative officials is most apparent in the various committees and commissions of the Federal Assembly, which in recent years have assumed an important role in legislative affairs. One Yugoslav political scientist has even suggested that independent specialists from outside the administration be invited to meetings of these committees specifically in order to check the influence of civil servants in policy making:

> This method would ensure that the influence
> of the administration on the decision of
> deputies would occur within tolerable pro-
> portions. The administration would use its
> specialized knowledge and offer the legisla-
> tors its opinions and attitudes. Specialists
> from outside the administration, from work-
> ing organizations and institutions, would

The Political Institutionalization of the Yugoslav Federal Assembly:
Some Empirical Indicators

	January 1953–December 1957	January 1958–63	1963–67/68
I. Parliamentary activity			
A. Sessions of the Federal Assembly	214	140 (April 1963)	376 (October 1968)
B. Legislative output:			
1. Laws, decisions, and other acts adopted by the Federal Assembly	254 (15.6)	435 (28.6)	993 (55.2)
2. Decisions and regulations adopted by the government (Federal Executive Council)	1,373 (84.4)	1,085 (71.4)	805 (44.8)
Total	1,627 (100.0)	1,520 (100.0) (December 1963)	1,798 (100.0) (December 1968)
C. Parliamentary control			
1. Questions posed by federal deputies to the executive and administration	59	243 (April 1963)	498 (December 1967)

	1953	1958	1963	1965	1967	1969
II. Parliamentary composition						
A. Educational background of federal deputies						
1. Elementary school or less	46.1	38.0	9.1	7.3	4.3	2.6
2. Secondary and vocational schools	30.3	31.8	24.6	22.1	20.6	15.1
3. Higher schools/university faculties	23.6	30.2	66.3	70.6	75.0	82.3
4. Total	100.0	100.0	100.0	100.0	100.0	100.0
	(554)	(587)	(670)	(670)	(670)	(670)
B. Professionalization: percent of federal deputies who previously served in federal, republican, and provincial assemblies						
1. Political chamber(s)[a]	66.0	59.8	71.0	78.4	82.6	83.3/69.2[c]
2. Functional chamber(s)[b]	10.0	18.1	21.7	19.4	21.7	36.7
Total Assembly	45.4	43.3	35.7	36.1	39.0	53.4

Notes to Table 6.7

[a]Political Chamber(s): 1953-68, the Federal Chamber including the Chamber of Nationalities; 1969-73, the Chamber of Nationalities and the Sociopolitical Chamber.

[b]Functional Chamber(s): 1953-63, the Chamber of Producers; 1963-73, the Economic Chamber, Educational-Cultural Chamber, and (until 1969) the Organizational-Political Chamber.

[c]The data on the professionalization of deputies in the "political chambers" of the Assembly is divided between the Chamber of Nationalities (83.3 percent) and the Sociopolitical Chamber (69.2 percent). 1969 was the first year the Chamber of Nationalities had a separate identity as a branch of the Assembly. The Sociopolitical Chamber had succeeded the Federal Chamber as the popularly elected house in the Federal Assembly.

Sources: Dokumentacija Savezne skupstina [Documentation of the Federal Assembly] (1953-68); Savezna Narodna Skupstina [The Federal People's Assembly] (Belgrade: "Kultura," 1955); D. Tozi and D. Petrovic, "Politicki odnosi i sastav skupstina drustveno-politickih zajednica" ["The Political Relations and Composition of Assemblies of Sociopolitical Communities"], Socijalizam, no. 11 (1969), p. 1594; Statisticki bilten: Predstavnicka tela drustveno-politickih zajednica: izbori i sastav [Representative Bodies of Sociopolitical Communities: Election and Composition] (Belgrade: Savezni zavod za statistiku, 1964, 1965, 1967, 1969, Nos. 266, 372, 491, 590).

then be in a position to show the legislators when the administration attempts to
chart its own course. From personal experience I have seen that the administration
often uses its great competence so that the
legislators very often, although personally
not agreeing, accept the judgments and suggestions of the administration, because they
don't have sufficient counterarguments
against the views which the administration
explains are necessary.[28] (Emphasis added.)

POLITICIZED BUREAUCRATS OR SERVANTS OF POWER?

The previous discussion represents a preliminary effort
to explore the role of Yugoslav federal administrators in
the policy-making process. Our initial findings are tentative and at points are somewhat contradictory. The survey
data reveals that administrative officials, although claiming
to have a close working relationship with political decision
makers, regard themselves as playing an essentially instrumental role in the legislative process and that they are
perceived similarly by elected deputies serving in the Federal Assembly. There is also considerable evidence, however,
that administrators are deeply involved in the formulation
of political decisions, precisely as a consequence of their
"instrumental" role.

The fact that both administrators and legislators present a considerably more idealized picture of bureaucratic
activity in the political system than other evidence would
tend to indicate is neither surprising nor difficult to understand, particularly when they are responding to a survey
questionnaire prepared by an international team of social
scientists. This is certainly not to suggest that the attitudes expressed by higher administrative officials concerning their activities should be ignored, but only that additional research is needed to probe adequately the question
of bureaucratic influence in the decision-making process.
As Wallace Sayre aptly observed:

What is the role of the bureaucracy? The
formal and official answer in most countries
is that the bureaucracy is an agent of the
decision-makers, not in itself one of the
decision-makers but rather their instrument,
not an autonomous brain in their own right
but rather the neutral executor of plans

made by others. This formal theory of the
bureaucracy is of course a myth. It is a
myth which serves several purposes, but it
does not help in a realistic description of
the decision-making process. The fact is
that in all countries the bureaucracy is one
of the important actors in the making of
governmental decisions; in some systems the
bureaucrats are the leading actors, and in
most systems their power as decision-makers
would seem to be increasing.[29]

One major question not raised in this study is the extent to which higher administrative officials have a clearly
defined "mentality," or "ideology" and in what ways, if any,
their attitudes differ from those of elected parliamentary
representatives. Thus, it will remain impossible to obtain
an adequate understanding of the political influence of administrators as a group unless one can determine whether or
not such officials share a distinctive outlook on specific
issues that set them apart from other actors in the political process; in what ways they have actually sought to advance their interests; and how successful they have been.
Generally, it is far easier to find evidence of involvement
by senior civil servants in the formulation of legislative
policies than to explain precisely what effect such activity
has had on the specific decisions that are adopted. These
and many other related questions can and will be explored
further by carefully interrelating the different kinds of
research data discussed above. A more conclusive picture
of the relationship between bureaucracy and modernization in
Yugoslavia must await answers to such questions.

NOTES

1. H. H. Gerth and C. Wright Mills, From Max Weber:
Essays in Sociology (New York: Oxford University Press,
1958), p. 232; Max Weber, The Theory of Social and Economic
Organization, trans. Talcott Parsons and A. M. Henderson
(New York: The Free Press, 1964), p. 338.
    2. On the concept of modernization see, inter alia,
C. E. Black, The Dynamics of Modernization: A Study in Com-
parative History (New York: Harper and Row, 1966); Manfred
Halpern, "The Revolution of Modernization in National and
International Society," in Revolution, ed. Carl J. Friedrich
(New York: Atherton Press, 1966), pp. 178-214; David E.
Apter, The Politics of Modernization (Chicago: University

of Chicago Press, 1965). For a critical survey of the literature on modernization, including a useful bibliography on the subject, see Dean C. Tipps, "Modernization Theory and the Comparative Study of Societies: A Critical Perspective," Comparative Studies in History and Society 15, no. 2 (March 1973): 199-226.

3. For some representative studies treating the relationship of administrative elites to the process of socioeconomic modernization and political change, see John A. Armstrong, "Old Regime Administrative Elites: Prelude to Modernization in France, Prussia and Russia," International Review of Administrative Sciences 38, no. 1 (1972): 21-40; and by the same author The European Administrative Elite (Princeton, N.J.: Princeton University Press, 1973); Bernard S. Silberman, Ministers of Modernization (Tucson: University of Arizona Press, 1964); Leslie L. Roos, Jr. and Noralou P. Roos, Managers of Modernization (Cambridge, Mass.: Harvard University Press, 1971); Hahn Been-Lee, "The Role of the Higher Civil Service under Rapid Social and Political Change," in Development Administration in Asia, ed. Edward W. Weidner (Durham, N.C.: Duke University Press, 1970), pp. 107-31; Seymour Martin Lipset, "Bureaucracy and Social Change," in Reader in Bureaucracy, ed. Robert Merton et al. (New York: The Free Press, 1952), pp. 221-32.

4. Carl Beck, "Bureaucracy and Political Development in Eastern Europe," in Bureaucracy and Political Development, ed. Joseph La Palombara (Princeton, N.J.: Princeton University Press, 1963), pp. 281-82, and, in the same volume, Merle Fainsod, "Bureaucracy and Modernization: The Russian and Soviet Case," pp. 233-67. On the political role and influence of the state bureaucracy in various communist systems, see also the articles by A. Doak Barnett, Carl Beck, Ezra F. Vogel, and Joseph S. Berliner in Frontiers of Development Administration, ed. Fred W. Riggs (Durham, N.C.: Duke University Press, 1970), pp. 415-36, 437-55, 556-68, 569-600; Paul Hollander, "Politicized Bureaucracy: The Soviet Case," Newsletter on Comparative Studies of Communism 4, no. 3 (May 1971): 12-22.

5. Carl Beck has recently argued that the role of the state bureaucracy in the political process of East European countries is likely to increase in the near future, and "that members of the state bureaucracy will tend toward advocacy roles in regard to innovative proposals." In Beck's view, however, "the available evidence suggests that the state bureaucracy has not played a very significant or innovative part in Eastern European political developments. When members of the state bureaucracy were involved and took an innovative position they did so as advocates rather than

as initiators." "Unfortunately," he adds, "we do not have available to us any surveys of the perspectives of state bureaucrats. A body of case studies identifying and categorizing participants in the decision-making process is also not available. Almost all studies of politics in Eastern Europe focus on policy outputs rather than on policy-making processes." "Bureaucratic Conservatism and Innovation in Eastern Europe," Comparative Political Studies 1, no. 2 (July 1968): 282, 291, and footnote 6. For the utility of the "Western model of modern bureaucracy" for the study of administrative behavior in a community policy, see Jerry F. Hough, "The Bureaucratic Model and the Nature of the Soviet System," Journal of Comparative Administration 5, no. 2 (August 1973): 134-67.

6. Leon Gerskovic, Drzavna Uprava [State Administration] (Belgrade: Savez Udruzenja Pravnika Jogoslavije, 1956), p. 15. For a discussion of the change in the relationship between the party and governmental institutions in Yugoslavia, see Paul Shoup, "Problems of Party Reform in Yugoslavia," American Slavic and East European Review 18, no. 3 (October 1959): 334-50; George Zaninovich, "Yugoslav Party Evolution: Moving Beyond Institutionalization," in Authoritarian Politics in Modern Society: The Dynamics of Established One-Party Systems, ed. Samuel P. Huntington and Clement H. Moore (New York: Basic Books, 1970), pp. 484-508; Winston M. Fisk, "The Constitutionalism Movement in Yugoslavia: A Preliminary Survey," Slavic Review, June 1971, pp. 277-98. A good summary of the Yugoslav view of these developments is Najdan Pasic, "Self-management as an Integral Political System," in Yugoslav Workers' Self-Management, ed. M. J. Broekmeyer (Dordrecht, Holland: D. Reidel Publishing Co., 1970), pp. 1-29.

7. Fred W. Riggs, "Bureaucratic Politics in Comparative Perspective," Journal of Comparative Administration 1, no. 1 (May 1969): 31 (italics in the original).

8. See Aleksander Stojanovic, Uloga funkcionera i upravnih strucnjaka u razvoja javne uprave [The Role of Functionaries and Administrative Specialists in the Development of the Public Administration] (Belgrade: Savez Udruzenja Pravnika Jugoslavija, 1965). An excellent analysis of party control over the state administration before 1952 based on official sources is Branko Petronavic, Politicka i ekonomska osnova narodna vlasti u Jugoslaviji za vreme obnove [The Political and Economic Basis of National Authority in Yugoslavia During the Period of Reconstruction] (Belgrade: Institut za Savremenu Istoriju, 1969), pp. 256-78.

9. For a more detailed analysis of Yugoslav parliamentary development, see Lenard J. Cohen, "Conflict Management and Institution-Building in Socialist Yugoslavia: The Role of the Parliamentary System," in Legislatures in Plural Societies: The Search for Cohesion in National Development, ed. Albert F. Eldridge (Beverly Hills, Calif.: Sage Publications, 1974).

10. For a discussion of the impact that representative bodies have on the modernization of societies, see Allan Kornberg, Samuel M. Hines, Jr., and Joel Smith, "Legislatures and the Modernization of Societies," Comparative Political Studies 5, no. 4 (January 1973): 471-91.

11. A complete discussion of the methodological procedures and techniques employed by the International Study of Opinion-Makers can be found in Dragomir Pantic, "Some Practical Problems of Compiling the Universe and Its Characteristics," in Working Papers of the International Study of Opinion-Makers, Vol. I, ed. Bogdan Denitch (mimeo.; New York: BASR, Columbia University, September 1968), and Bogdan Denitch, "Elite Interviewing and Social Structure: An Example from Yugoslavia," in Opinion-Making Elites in Yugoslavia, ed. Allen H. Barton, Bogdan Denitch, and Charles Kadushin (New York: Praeger, 1973), pp. 3-23.

12. Ferrel Heady, Public Administration: A Comparative Perspective (Englewood Cliffs, N.J.: Prentice-Hall, 1966), p. 98.

13. The concept of "role" or "role-orientation" as used here refers to "that organized sector of an actor's orientation which constitutes and defines his participation in an interactive process. It involves a set of complementary expectations concerning his own actions and those of others with whom he interacts. Both the actor and those with whom he interacts possess these expectations." Talcott Parsons and Edward Shils, eds., Toward a General Theory of Action (New York: Harper and Row, 1962), p. 23. We will be concerned with the role-orientations of Yugoslav federal administrators that relate to their responsibilities in the legislative process.

14. Normativna delatnost drustveno-politickih zajednica: prirucnik za kadrove u drzavnim organima i strucnim sluzbama posebno opstinskim [The Legislative Activity of Sociopolitical Communities: A Handbook for Cadre in State Organs and Specialized Services particularly in Communes] (Belgrade: Republicki Zavod za Javnu Upravu, 1967), pp. 148-49.

15. See, for example, Raymond F. Hopkins, Political Roles in a New State: Tanzania's First Decade (New Haven, Conn.: Yale University Press, 1971), especially Chapter 4,

"The Role of the Administrator," pp. 108-39; Richard L. Harris, "The Effects of Political Change on the Role Set of the Senior Bureaucrats in Ghana and Nigeria," Administrativ Science Quarterly 13, no. 3 (December 1968): 386-401; Rober D. Putnam, "The Political Attitudes of Senior Civil Servant in Western Europe: A Preliminary Report," British Journal of Political Science 3, Part 3 (July 1973): 257-90; Jerry L. Weaver, "Role Expectations of Latin American Bureaucrats Journal of Comparative Administration 4, no. 2 (August 1972 133-66.

16. For a discussion of the difference between "polic counsel" and "program formulation" as alternative bases for administrative influence in the policy-making process, see Fritz Moorstein Marx, "The Higher Civil Service as an Actic Group in Western Political Development," in LaPalombara, op cit., pp. 77-83. See also Hahn-Been Lee, The Role of the Higher Civil Service Under Rapid Social and Political Chanc (Bloomington, Ind.: Comparative Administration Group, Amer ican Society for Public Administration, 1966), pp. 2-11.

17. Ljubomir Mijatovic, "Predstavnicki organi i uprav ["Representative Organs and the Administration"], Nedeljne informativne novosti, December 24, 1967, p. 4.

18. For the use of data on interaction to explain administrative-legislative relations, see Victor A. Olorunsola, "Patterns of Interaction between Bureaucratic and Political Leaders: A Case Study," Journal of Developing Areas 3 (October 1968): 51-68; Norman C. Thomas, "Bureaucratic-Congressional Interaction and the Politics of Education," Journal of Comparative Administration 2, no. 1 (1970): 52-80.

19. Charles Kadushin and Peter Abrams, "Social Structure of Yugoslav Opinion-Makers," in Barton et al., op. cit., p. 164.

20. In reporting to the Federal Assembly on parliamen tary development between 1963 and 1967, its president, Edvard Kardelj, emphasized that

> deputies increasingly developed into indepen-
> dent and responsible factors in Assembly work
> at all stages. . . . But I must again repeat:
> this role of deputies would be unthinkable if
> they did not at the same time rely on the so-
> cial role of the League of Communists as the
> most important factor at the present level of
> the development of socialist social rela-
> tions. . . . Naturally the Federal Assembly
> reached its decisions independently, but
> these decisions would not have been arrived

at in a democratic way, would not have reflected the real needs of society and have
been successfully implemented had it not
been for the mobilizing and integrating activity of the League of Communists, the Socialist Alliance, trade unions, and other
factors of socialist consciousness. For
the entire structure and method of work of
the Assembly has been devised so that its
successful action necessarily required maximum reliance on these factors.

Edvard Kardelj, Neka pitanja daljeg razvoja skupstinskog i
politickog sistema [Some Questions of the Further Development of the Parliamentary and Political Systems] (Belgrade:
Sekretarijat za informativnu sluzbu Savezne Skupstine, 1967),
Biblioteka Savezne Skupstine, Sveska 4, Kolo IV, pp. 22-23.
    21. Allen H. Barton, "Determinants of Leadership Atti-
tudes in a Socialist Society," in Barton, et al., op. cit.,
p. 237.
    22. Marin Cetinic, "Uvid i kontrola koristenja i
raspolaganja drustvenim sredstvima," in Simpozijum Savezne
Skupstine: Sistem finansiranja i poreski sistem, Referati
["The Inspection and Control of the Use and Disposition of
Social Resources," in A Symposium of the Federal Assembly:
The Financing System and Tax System, Papers] (Belgrade:
Kultura, 1970), p. 92.
    23. See, for example, Slavko Miloslavevski and Milan
Nedkov, Uloga i Polozaj Drzavne Uprave u Nasem Samoupravnom
Drustvu [The Role and Position of our State Administration
in our Self-managing Society] (Belgrade: Jugoslavenski
Savez Udruzenja za Upravne Nauke, Praksu, 1970); Veljko
Mratovic, "Uloga organa drzavne uprave u ostvarivanju
funkcija skupstina drustveno-polititickih zajednica" [The
Role of Organs of State Administration in the Realization
of the Functions of the Assemblies of Sociopolitical Communities"], Nasa Zakonitost 25, no. 1 (Sijecanj, 1971): 7-15;
and Branislav Markovic, "Uprava i zakonodavni proces fed-
eracija" ["The Administration and the Federal Legislative
Process"], in Karakter i funkcije federacije u procesu kon-
stituisanja samoupravnog drustva [The Character and Functions of the Federation in the Process of Establishing a
Self-Managing Society], ed. Ljubisa Stankov (Belgrade: Institut za politicke studije, VSPN, 1968), Politicke Sveske
IV/I, pp. 323-30.
    24. Dokumentacija Savezne Skupstine [Documentation of
the Federal Assembly] (Belgrade, February 1969), Prilog 4.

25. <u>Borba</u>, December 17, 1967, p. 4. Yugoslav studies
of political decision making on the republican and local
levels have also revealed the dominant position of administrative agencies in initiating laws and policies. For example, in the entire six-year period from 1963 to 1969 only
one deputy in the Serbian Assembly initiated a legislative
proposal. Miodrag Zecevic, <u>Skupstina SR Srbije u Periodu</u>
<u>1963-1969. Godine</u> [The Assembly of the Socialist Republic
of Serbia in the Period 1963-1969] (Belgrade: Institut za
Politicke Studije Fakulteta Politickih Nauka, 1972), pp.
301-09. See also Angel Klisinski, <u>Uloga Organa Uprave,</u>
<u>odnoso strucnih sluzba radnih organizacija u normativnoj</u>
<u>delatnosti skupstine drustveno-politickih zajednica odnoso</u>
<u>organa upravljanja radnih organizacija</u> [The Role of Adminis-
trative Organs with reference to the Specialized Services of
Working Organizations in the Legislative Activity of the As-
semblies of Sociopolitical Communities and the Management
Organs of Working Organizations] (Belgrade: Jugoslovenske
Savez Udruzenja za Upravne Nauke i Praksu, 1969); <u>Zena-</u>
<u>odbornik i zastupnika</u> [Women--Councillor and Deputy] (Zagreb
Konferencija za drustvena aktivnost zena Hrvatska, 1969);
Niko Tos, <u>Pregled skupnih podatkov iz raziskave poslanska</u>
<u>aktivnost</u> [A Survey of Data Collected from Research on the
Activity of Deputies] (Ljubljana: Visoka sola za sociologij
politicne vede in novinarstvo-Centar za raziskovanje javnog
mnenja, 1968), p. 36.
       26. Writing in 1969 the prominent Yugoslav economist
Branko Horvat, a former government advisor on planning, ob-
served,

> As things presently stand, the federal gov-
> ernment, the Federal Assembly, the trade
> unions, the Central Committee, and the Eco-
> nomic Chamber [Privedna Komora] do not have
> a single long-term arrangement with any
> scientific organization in the country for
> the investigation of fundamental problems
> within the jurisdiction of these leading
> bodies and social organizations. Moreover,
> up to now all suggestions and initiatives
> of scientific organizations in this sense
> have been unsuccessful.

"Integriranost jugoslovenske privrede i samoupravne
dogovoranje" ["The Integration of the Yugoslav Economy
and Self-Managing Agreements"] in <u>Ekonomist</u> 22, no. 2
(1969): 389-90. While admitting that many leading economic specialists have been given posts in the Federal

Administration, Horvat has argued, nevertheless, that these men "are in positions which require from them a specific conduct and discipline, and second when somebody is an official, he has no possibility for dealing with research. . . . scientific workers engaged in administration are not the same as science in administration." (Emphasis added.) Privredni Pregled, April 21, 1969, p. 3.

27. Professor Eugun Pusic has pointed to the weak position of deputies in the functionally specialized Chamber of Producers on the communal level when dealing with officials from the "administrative apparatus." Samoupravljanje: Prilozi teoriji i prakticni problemi [Self-Management: Contributions to Theory and Practical Problems] (Zagreb, "Narodne Novine," 1968), pp. 218 and 224.

28. Dr. Hamdija Cemerlic in Mesto i uloga odbora i komisija predstavnickih tela [The Position and Role of Committees and Commissions of Representative Bodies], ed. Borislav T. Blagojevic (Belgrade: Saveza udruzenja pravnika Jugoslavija, 1969), p. 237.

29. Wallace S. Sayre, "Bureaucracies: Some Contrasts in Systems," in Readings in Comparative Public Administration, ed. Nimrod Raphaeli (Boston: Allyn and Bacon, 1967), pp. 347-48.

III

EASTERN EUROPE AND THE SOVIET UNION: INTERACTION AND INFLUENCES

INTRODUCTION: THE INTERNATIONAL DIMENSION OF MODERNIZATION

Charles Gati

The modernization phenomenon normally belongs to the domain of comparativists and theorists--as the previous four case studies demonstrate. There the focus of analysis has to do with internal sources, processes, institutions, and relationships, with the resulting data and conclusions leading to explicit or implicit generalizations about modernization. In its internal emphasis, then, these case studies are rather typical of the literature dealing with other countries or regions of the world.

The following three chapters explore the international dimension of modernization rather than the internal; here the focus of analysis shifts to external influences, the impact of the outside world, as well as interaction within Eastern Europe. It would not be accurate to suggest that this is a "neglected" focus in modernization studies, for at least since the late 1950s a good number of books and articles have appeared on the Soviet impact on the Third World, the relevance of the Soviet model for the developing countries, and especially on the applicability of the Soviet industrialization experience for other industrializing societies.

At first glance, it may seem somewhat surprising, then, that Soviet-Eastern European relations are so infrequently analyzed from this perspective. Yet the reason for it is obvious enough: Since the Soviet Union originally imposed its pattern of modernization on Eastern Europe, the relevance of that pattern for Eastern Europe became an academic question. Whether or not it was relevant, it was imitated; whether or not it was applicable, it was adopted. It seemed even more far-fetched to consider the impact of Eastern Europe on the Soviet Union: If Eastern Europe had been compelled to copy the Soviet model, what could the Soviet Union learn from the Eastern European experiences in modernization?

As the following studies convincingly show, there is far more need for scholarly inquiry here than has been assumed so far. True, methodological problems abound: What do we mean by impact or influence? Can we identify a particular policy or trend with a particular external input? Can we assume that that particular policy would not have been conceived or implemented had it not been for that external input? And there is, always, the troubling problem of how to "measure" external, or for that matter internal, input. Such methodological difficulties aside, we are faced with important substantive matters, of which one stands out more than any other: Was the Soviet model of modernization helpful or detrimental to development in Eastern Europe?

This question is very much at the heart of Vernon V. Aspaturian's perceptive and elegant study. By employing an explicitly comparative methodology, he demonstrates that the Soviet impact has been far more "mixed" than Soviet analysts claim, even though in most aspects of modernization it has been neither detrimental nor negligible. What is equally interesting, however, is that in the more recent period it became clear that the Soviet model was being transplanted into the realities of the East European countries in different ways: Both the form and substance of adoption have varied from country to country and so has the extent to which the various facets of the Soviet modernization experience have been accepted and imitated. Under the circumstances, it has become a theoretical as well as practical possibility that the Soviet Union would seek to learn from East European experiences and that the several East European countries would look to each other as well. In their thorough chapters, Zvi Gitelman and Roger E. Kanet show the emerging mutuality of interest in and curiosity about each other's often divergent approaches to modernization and development.

Modernization-interaction thus constitutes an interesting as well as controversial aspect of the international relations of the communist world. Gitelman may be correct in suggesting that "in some ways Eastern Europe may serve as a stimulus to the adoption of more conservative, rather than more liberal, ideas in the Soviet Union" at the present time and that the first socialist state (and a powerful one at that) "is unlikely to look very diligently to the experience of lesser powers, especially if they happen to be client states, for inspiration and for models." In the longer run, however, should the Soviet Union run into additional difficulties on the road to modernity--difficulties it could not solve by the infusion of Western capital and the very selective adoption of Western experiences and techniques--it may become more willing to consider and learn from other modes of socialist modernization, including those of its junior partners in Eastern Europe.

7

THE SOVIET IMPACT ON DEVELOPMENT AND MODERNIZATION IN EASTERN EUROPE

Vernon V. Aspaturian

The impact of the Soviet experience and the Soviet Union on modernization in Eastern Europe has been both continuous and pervasive but also uneven and flexible (within certain limits); it has varied in degree and intensity from one country to another and probably reflects varying degrees of durability and performance as well, that is, the extent to which the Soviet influence has been effectively socialized and assimilated into the political culture. The Soviet model of modernization, whether in its ascriptive, normative, or emulative dimensions, is evident in all three broad areas of modernization in Eastern Europe: political, social, and economic, but the evidence establishing a causal relationship between the Soviet presence and the concrete manifestations of modernization in individual countries varies considerably not only from one country to another but between broad areas of modernization. In general, one can conclude that the Soviet impact in the area of political modernization has been the most conspicuously evident, while the connection between the Soviet presence and economic modernization, in terms of indicators, would be the most difficult to establish. It would be implausible to assume that the particular types of political institutions, processes, and structures that exist in Eastern Europe would have developed spontaneously had there been no Soviet influence, but it is quite another matter to assume that neither the rates nor levels of social and economic development would have taken place within a different political context. The specific institutions, structures, and priorities in economic modernization, however, must be included in the political sector, and these are more clearly derivative from the Soviet experience.

To put it another way, it would be virtually puerile
insist that Poland's Marxist-Leninist norms and processes
political development and modernization do not derive dire
ly from the Soviet impact, but it would be much more diffi
cult to establish that Bulgaria's relatively rapid industr
alization since 1948 or the rise in the literacy rate in
Romania from 77 percent in 1948 to 89 percent in 1956 are
equally due to the Soviet impact. There are many, of cour
who argue that modernization and development are inexorabl
processes and that Eastern Europe's time had come in the
postwar period and would have transpired with or without t
Soviet impact; considerable statistical data can be muster
to impart strong plausibility to this argument. There are
even those who contend that the modernization and economic
development of the Soviet Union itself owes little to the
Soviet impact, that Russia was on the brink of modernizati
before World War I, and that both rates and levels of grow
would probably be approximately the same had there been no
Soviet system.[1] These authors, of course, concede that th
Soviet impact has contributed a particular political and s
cial matrix that has affected the style and form, and perhaps even the direction and mix, of modernization and deve
opment, but they tend to concede little else.

Thus, in assessing the Soviet impact upon the modernization of Eastern Europe, one must, at the outset, accept
one of two assumptions: (1) Modernization and development
are inexorable and deterministic processes that are destin
to take place at some point in time and space; or (2) Mode
ization and development are essentially voluntaristic and
tional processes and take place only when the will and cap
bility exist, either internally or externally. If one accepts the first assumption, then any evaluation of the Sov
impact on modernization in Eastern Europe is bound to be re
stricted to trivial and marginal aspects of development, ur
less we assume that in some cases the rejection of the de-
cisiveness or importance of the Soviet system as a moderni
ing agency reflects not so much the affirmation of a deterministic theory of modernization as it does a polemical argument designed to demonstrate the irrelevance of the Sovie
experience on modernization in either Russia or Eastern
Europe. This argument, polemical though its implications
may be, derives considerable support from the fact that whe
the Soviet experience was transferred to existing modernize
and industrial states in Eastern Europe, most notably Czech
slovakia, the modernization and developmental processes wer
arrested, distorted, and even reversed. Indeed, one can
easily demonstrate the dysfunctionality of the Soviet experience insofar as modernization and development are con-

cerned, not only in terms of its applicability to countries at different points in the modernization process, but also in specific sectors of activity as well. But, if the Soviet experience can arrest, distort, and even reverse the modernization process, this serves to strengthen the voluntaristic assumption rather than the deterministic, unless one simultaneously accepts the inevitability of decline and decay at a certain point in the developmental process as well, in which case decline and decay must be viewed as stages in the developmental process.*

Thus, while manifestations of political modernization in Eastern Europe can be more persuasively ascribed to the Soviet impact, the impact of the Soviet experience on economic modernization is more nebulous, and the connection between social modernization and the Soviet influence falls somewhere in between, depending upon whether it is essentially sociopolitical in character--social structure of society and social composition of structures, for example--or socioeconomic in nature--population growth, urbanization, or male-female composition of the labor force, for example.

Aside from the differential and evidentiary nature of the Soviet impact on the three broad aspects of modernization, this variation in assessment is applicable to individual countries of Eastern Europe as well. Thus, the evidence is more persuasive that the modernization and development of Bulgaria have been more affected by the Soviet impact than have Poland's, for example. To a certain extent, the Soviet impact on the developmental process in Czechoslovakia is more evident than in the case of Romania. The direction of the impact, however, in the cases of Czechoslovakia and Bulgaria, has been in divergent directions. The reason why the Soviet influence can be more persuasively developed in these two cases is that the Soviet process of modernization was more applicable to Bulgaria than to Poland and the consequences seem dramatic enough to ascribe them to outside influences; in the case of Czechoslovakia the Soviet pattern was the least applicable and hence the conspicuously dys-

---

*The concept of decay, decline, or degeneration in development is, of course, a central theme in Oswald Spengler's Decline of the West and Arnold Toynbee's monumental A Study of History. Although Spengler and Toynbee were dealing with larger concepts called "cultures" or "civilizations," they were in fact dealing with the phenomenon of development, but without the prepackaged input of inevitable progress. Most developmental and modernization theories seem, a priori, to reject the possibility of decline or decay.

functional consequences of Czechoslovakia's development can
be more persuasively attributed to the Soviet influence tha
can those of Romania.

This raises the important question of how the Soviet
impact is to be measured, whether it be positive or negativ
in terms of modernization and development, and even, in son
cases, ascertained as a discernible impact or influence at
all. Or, to put the question more bluntly: How are we to
distinguish those aspects of modernization and development
that are derivative from the Soviet impact from those that
would have taken place in any event? Since some modernization would have taken place regardless of the Soviet impact
a variation of this question becomes the incremental contri
bution of the Soviet impact on the modernization of Eastern
Europe, that is, how much of an effect did the Soviet experience have, over and above that which would have happene
in the absence of the Soviet impact, assuming, of course,
that the Soviet experience did have an impact. All kinds o
methodological problems are involved in answering these que
tions and no pretense is being made in this study that thes
have been solved, or even all identified for that matter.
Since we are dealing with the development of Eastern Europe
within a historical context, we can only second-guess the
alternatives of history that remain concealed, and it would
be fatuous to maintain that one could deal with the situation methodologically simply by designing a model that woul
remove the Soviet variable. In the absence of a Soviet impact, how are we to assess the impact or influence of other
external influences, for example, and what difference would
this have made? A whole range of literally endless and un-
ending questions beg to be answered, including the ricochet
and spillover impact of the Soviet Union on modernization
and development on a global scale. To what extent, for example, was the challenge of the Soviet model of modernization instrumental in shaping and defining the response of
other countries, movements, political and social forces? T
what degree did it affect the U.S. response and reaction to
the whole issue of modernization and development as it applied to noncommunist states, to what degree was U.S. interest in modernization and development stimulated by the Soviet challenge, and finally, how did all this affect modernization in Eastern Europe? More importantly, how does it
affect the validity of comparing modernization of East European countries with noncommunist countries when the modernization and development of those countries were indirectly
affected by the Soviet challenge by impelling them to devise
alternative patterns of modernization?

These questions are critically relevant because this
analysis will employ the device of using three noncommunist

European countries as a sort of control group in assessing
the Soviet impact on Eastern Europe. These countries are
Austria, Finland, and Greece, all of whose development has
been indirectly affected by the Soviet challenge and presence. In the case of Greece, for example, to what extent
did the communist promise and threat of modernization stimulate the massive U.S. input into the development of Greece
in order to create a viable alternative modernization process?

In this analysis these questions will be approached in
a rather direct and uncomplicated manner. Statistical data
will be employed essentially for illustrative and descriptive purposes, designed to raise questions for which there
can be only a range of possible answers rather than develop
hypotheses and propositions to be verified or disconfirmed.
The statistical information will present a range of data designed to show the comparative rates and levels of modernization of the countries of Eastern Europe to one another, to
the Soviet Union, and to a group of selected noncommunist
countries on an individual or aggregate basis. In general,
I have tried to use Austria, Finland, and Greece as the principal noncommunist control group, since they are territori-
ally proximate to Eastern Europe and represent a range of
modernization and development that matches the spread in the
East European countries. Greece is thus employed to discern
the Soviet impact on Yugoslavia, Romania, and Bulgaria,
since before the advent of communist rule the four countries
were at approximately the same level of development. Similarly, Austria is employed as a control to assess the Soviet
contribution to the modernization of East Germany and Czechoslovakia and, in some instances, Hungary. Finland is a less
satisfactory control country for Poland and Hungary. Wherever possible, I have tried to employ comparable data, including prewar or precommunist data, but the availability of
the data is uneven, as is its reliability and phasing. Unfortunately, not all countries employ the same categories,
issue the data in the same year, or employ equally reliable
methods of gathering and reporting. Much of the statistical
data is full of booby traps and this is readily acknowledged
and will be noted in particular instances. (See introductory note to the Appendix at the back of this book.)

Yugoslavia poses a special problem, because its aggregate statistical data expresses the average or mean of component national republics that reflect the entire range of
modernization and developmental levels in Eastern Europe.
Slovenia, for example, falls into a range similar to that
for Czechoslovakia and Austria; Croatia falls into the same
range as Hungary; Serbia and Montenegro are comparable to
Poland in some respects and to Romania, Bulgaria, and Greece

in others; while Bosnia-Herzegovina, Macedonia, and the Kosovo region of Serbia fall into the lower end of the same range and in some respects are comparable only to Albania and perhaps Turkey, although the latter is not covered in this paper. Except for one table (Table A.1)* dealing with vital statistics, the Yugoslav data remains aggregated, but in this one table sufficient information is provided to establish both the range of developmental variation within Yugoslavia and general comparability of individual republics with the countries of Eastern Europe.

The statistical data at first blush appears to reinfor strongly the impression that the precommunist legacy of the individual countries concerned remains a powerful factor in accounting for the variations in modernization. This problem can only be recognized in this study and it represents one of the special statistical booby traps in the aggregate data that serves to homogenize and conceal important variations within countries. The statistical indicators of modernization and development in the social and economic areas of Eastern Europe do not reveal any broad, general departur from that in Austria, Finland, and Greece, either in rates or levels of growth and development. There are important, and in some cases surprising, exceptions, both with respect to certain aspects of modernization as well as individual countries. This would suggest, as some scholars maintain, that the Soviet impact was nil or in many cases harmful and not much more than marginal in any positive dimension. Developments in Eastern Europe cover both the Stalinist and the post-Stalinist phases and current levels represent an averaging out of both phases of influence. It is important in this connection to note that during the Stalinist phase the East European countries were simultaneously plundered and exploited as well as developed (that is, developed to enhance their value to the Soviet Union) and thus were subjected to considerable damage and dislocation, but it is nevertheless also true that rapid development in certain areas and countries has taken place in any event and one could maintain that the Soviet mold of modernization enabled the countries of Eastern Europe to be developed and modernized at a pace no slower, and in some cases more rapid, thar neighboring noncommunist countries while being exploited. With the relaxation of the Soviet grip, perhaps the modernized societies developed under the direction of the Soviet Union may, in the future, demonstrate more rapid and higher

_____

*Tables identified with the letter A are to be found in the Appendix at the back of the book.

levels of development than neighboring noncommunist countries since they will no longer be sharing their output and resources with the Soviet Union. There is already some fragmentary evidence that this is in fact the case, although the data here is not sufficient to demonstrate this possibility conclusively.

This raises the further interesting question as to how the Soviet impact can be disaggregated into its various components in order to evaluate the performance of East European communist states as independent, autonomous states in which the institutions, structures, and outputs of the modernization process are controlled locally as opposed to communist systems, subordinate in part or in toto to a larger and more powerful communist state that not only exercises political and social control but also devours a substantial share of the output.

Communist Yugoslavia does not constitute an adequate model to employ in this regard since she renounced Soviet control in 1948 before she was either modernized or exploited by the Soviet Union. Had Czechoslovakia under Dubcek succeeded in establishing Czech internal autonomy and control, the future development of Czechoslovakia might have provided a reference point for disaggregating the Soviet impact, but then had the "Prague Spring" succeeded, Czechoslovakia may have eventually abandoned the communist system in favor of another. Romania, to some degree, may serve as a control country in this regard in view of Ceausescu's ability so far to defy the Soviet Union on certain aspects of internal development.

Before we can measure the Soviet impact, we must, of course, first define what is to be measured, and this is by no means a simple matter. The Soviet impact as defined in this analysis is a complex aggregate of influences, contributions, and effects that have shaped the nature, process, and direction of political, social, and economic development and existence in the countries of Eastern Europe. The Soviet impact can be disaggregated into four discrete components, two of them direct in their effects and two derivative and indirect: (1) the impact of the Soviet experience as a modernized society to be emulated or imposed; (2) the impact of Soviet policies in Eastern Europe, whether conceived as developmental in design or for purposes extraneous to modernization; (3) the impact of local communist systems as subsidiary, but separate, influences on development; and (4) the impact of local communist policies, whether calculated for developmental or nondevelopmental purposes, especially after de-Stalinization and the evolution of limited autonomy.

Examples of the first type of impact would be the creation of institutions and processes modeled on the Soviet sy-
tem and the attempted transplantation of the Soviet developmental process to Eastern Europe. Illustrations of the second type of impact would be economic and political policies
designed to serve Soviet political, security, and foreign
policy interests, rather than to promote modernization and
development. Examples of the third type of impact would be
innovations, modifications, and adaptations that developed
as the Stalinization process was arrested and then partiall
reversed. Illustrative of the fourth type of impact would
be the effects of local communist policies on social and
economic priorities as opposed to those imposed externally.

All four components have operated coexistentially and
continue to produce their effects independently and in interaction with one another. All effects and influences subsumed under these four categories will be considered as
products of the Soviet impact on modernization and development in Eastern Europe.

MEASURING THE SOVIET IMPACT

The advent of Soviet power in Eastern Europe after
World War II quickly suppressed whatever individuality the
countries of Eastern Europe possessed before the war, as the
entire region was subjected to uniform patterns of social
convulsions set into motion by the Soviet Union and its local instruments, the Communist Parties and their collabora-
tors in individual countries. The old social and political
order was demolished, as the social and economic foundations
of power that supported the existing ruling and dominant
classes were destroyed through expropriation and confisca-
tion. The former political structures and institutions were
leveled or thoroughly renovated in accordance with the Lenin
ist maxim that the "bureaucratic-state machine" of the old
order had to be pulverized in order to facilitate the rule
of the new ruling class, the proletariat and its advanced
vanguard, the Communist Party (or its equivalent). The old
ruling and dominant classes were subjected to severe repres-
sion and in many instances to incarceration, physical destruction, or expulsion. A new temporary, transitional social order was manipulated into existence as the social
structural pyramid was steeply flattened with the decapita-
tion of its apex. Urban workers and peasants, particularly
of the poor and landless variety, were quickly drawn into
the political process, not as participants but as subjects
of involvement and manipulation, that is, via the communist
version of social mobilization.

To compress and summarize quickly a complicated and ruthless process that was completed in a matter of a few years, the advent of Soviet power first demolished the old social order and political structures, then swept away the spontaneous social eruptions that followed in its wake (that is, the emergence of a large, small and medium land-holding--not owning as it turned out--class that temporarily took over the land in the sweeping land reform programs) in order to prepare the groundwork for laying the foundations of socialism, building socialism, and then achieving socialism. Most of the countries of Eastern Europe are still viewed as being in the "building socialism" phase of communist modernization, although Czechoslovakia, Romania, and Yugoslavia have officially graduated themselves to the "socialist" stage. In the case of Czechoslovakia, which possessed both the industrial base and developed bourgeois-democratic institutions before the war, this step was plausibly warranted, but in the instances of both Romania and Yugoslavia (as was the case with the Soviet Union in 1936), their "socialism" is purely of the ascriptive or declaratory variety.

After 1948, with the transformation of the "peoples democracies" into second-class versions of the "dictatorship of the proletariat" (the "Soviet" form is the first-class version), all of the countries of Eastern Europe, except Yugoslavia which left the Soviet orbit in that year, were subjected to an intensified process of socioeconomic development to accelerate their transformation into microcosms of the Soviet system. Progress, that is, modernization, was measured in terms of how rapidly and faithfully the countries of Eastern Europe were reproducing the institutions, structures, and processes of the Soviet Union. Even Yugoslavia continues to retain some of the early pre-1948 vestiges of Soviet-style institutions and structures, which have been considerably modified during the past two decades. The Yugoslav multinational federation was modeled after that of the Soviet Union, and Marshal Tito's charismatic leadership is still an anachronistic residue from the Stalinist era when leadership in the East European countries was framed within the context of what was later condemned as the "cult of personality." Enver Hoxha of Albania represents still another variant of the Stalinist leadership style. All of the other countries, in certain respects, imitated the gyrations of the Soviet leadership that followed after Stalin's death, although after 1956 the imitative behavior of these countries was considerably modified and has eroded in various directions.[2]

The death of Stalin introduced a brief period of confusion reflecting that which was taking place in Moscow. But with the denunciation of Stalin in 1956, the legitimacy of many institutions, structures, and processes that had been "de rigueur" for the East European states up to that point were seriously eroded and many Soviet-style institutions and structures were arrested in their development, modified to suit local conveniences without provoking Moscow, and in some instances dismantled (the collective farms in Poland, for example).

Since 1956 the arrested or modified Soviet-style institutions and structures have, in many cases, developed along their own paths in accordance with the "many roads to socialism" doctrine. In some countries, institutions originally designed as temporary or transitional devices were made more or less a permanent part of the social and political landscape. Peasant cooperatives did not in all cases become transformed into state or collective farms, while the residual manifestations of pre-1948 noncommunist parties did not wither away or become merged into the hegemonic Marxist-Leninist Party, but remain as political appendixes, which, like the human counterpart, do no good and little harm but serve as a constant source of potential infection.

Thus, while the advent of Soviet power in Eastern Europe did in fact open up new paths of development, it simultaneously foreclosed alternative options. There is little conclusive evidence to assume, however, that the state of development that characterized most East European countries before the war was not a sufficient base for further development and modernization along lines other than those imposed by the Soviet Union. Most of these countries had a modernized middle class, relatively adequate levels of literacy, a core of professional and technical personnel, a substantial number of workers, other urban dwellers, and landowning peasants who were politically articulate and active to embark on further development. Even the land-owning aristocracy was by no means entirely addicted to anachronistic patterns of rural life, and self-interest could have dictated the modernization and mechanization of agriculture. To be sure, many of these social groups would have resisted socialist paths of development, but it is plausible to assume that at least in some instances, rates and levels of economic growth, social progress in the form of increased opportunities for education, upgraded public health and social services, and broadened political participation would have taken place comparable to those that have been achieved. Of course, the aggregate average or median indicators, which might have been the same, would have masked a different distribution of wealth, consumption, production, income, education, social services, etc. The political system would obviously be different in most instances and would probably reflect a variety of institutions and structures instead of a regional uniformity. Highs and lows would undoubtedly be more conspicuously reflected and the social-structural pyramid would have been steeper, with a much greater disparity in wealth and income between the top and the bottom; there would probably be more wealthy people than exist now and far more poorer people, but the overall aggregate means might well have been approximate to those currently existing.

In this connection, it might be useful to compare the social dimensions of development of the East European countries with that of Greece, Austria, and Finland, using data for three social indicators (literacy, infant mortality, and births) for which there exists relatively comparable data for both the prewar period and 1970. By viewing the development of these countries in a longitudinal frame, we might perhaps arrive at some reasonable judgment concerning the possible rates and levels of development the communist countries might have achieved without the benefit of the Soviet experience and impact. Greece, Austria, and Finland currently represent three distinct levels of development that correspond approximately to the range that exists in Eastern Europe today and before the war. This data is reproduced in Table 7.1.

Before the war, Finland had the lowest rate of infant mortality (73.9 infant deaths before the age of one per 1,000 live births). All of the other countries, including Austria, with 100.2, had rates over 100, with Romania having the highest rate at 179.3, more than twice that of Finland. In 1970, Finland still demonstrates the lowest rate (12.5), but with all states exhibiting substantial improvement. Among the communist states, East Germany and Czechoslovakia showed the lowest rates, and the others, except for Yugoslavia (55.2) and Albania (86.8) exhibited rates of less than 50 per 1,000 live births in 1970. Greece demonstrated an impressive rate of 29.3 in 1970, lower than that of Poland, Hungary, and Romania, although it should be noted that Greece possessed a lower rate than these three countries before the war. On the other hand, Czechoslovakia and Bulgaria, with their lower rates in 1970, registered more impressive progress than Greece. Yugoslavia demonstrated the poorest record in this regard, but it should be mentioned that the Yugoslav data represents a mean aggregate figure that conceals widely different levels of subsystem development. When the Yugoslav figure is disaggregated, we find that it ranged widely in 1970 from 23.1 per 1,000 in Slovenia to 92.4 for the Kosovo district of Serbia, thus placing Slovenia lower than Austria and slightly above Czechoslovakia (see Table A.1).

TABLE 7.1

Comparative Rates of Infant Mortality, Birth, and Literacy, Prewar and 1970

| Country | Infant Mortality before First Year (per 1,000 live births) | | Birth Rates (per 1,000 population) | | Literacy: Both Sexes, 10 Years and Older[c] | | |
	1930-34[a]	1970[b]	1938[a]	1970[b]	Prewar	Postwar	Percent Average Annual Increase
USSR	—	24.4	—	—	—	—	—
Czechoslovakia	128.5	22.1	16.7	15.8	95.7 (1930)	97.5 (1950)	—
East Germany	—	18.8	—	—	—	98.5 (1950)	—
Poland	139.6	33.1	24.3	16.8	76.9 (1931)	95.0 (1960)	.62
Hungary	156.7	35.9	19.9	14.7	94.0 (1941)	97.0 (1960)	—
Romania	179.3	49.4	29.6	21.1	76.9 (1948)	89.0 (1956)	1.50
Bulgaria	144.1	27.3	22.8	16.3	68.6 (1934)	90.2 (1965)	.70
Yugoslavia	154.9	55.2	26.7	17.8	54.8 (1931)	77.0 (1961)	.73
Albania	—	86.8	34.2	35.3	—	60.0 (1955)	—
Austria	100.2	25.9	13.9	15.2	97.8 (1937)	98.5 (1950)	—
Finland	73.9	12.5	21.0	13.7	98.1 (1930)	98.5 (1950)	—
Greece	118.9	29.3	26.1	16.3	59.2 (1928)	80.4 (1961)	.64

Sources: [a]Adapted from data in Paul F. Myers, "Demographic Trends in Eastern Europe," in Economic Developments in Countries of Eastern Europe, U.S. Congress, Joint Economic Committee (Washington, D.C., 1970), p. 71; [b]United Nations Statistical Yearbook, 1971; [c]Unesco Statistical Yearbook, 1949-50, 1955, and 1970.

When we examine the data for births, we find similar patterns with respect to birth control and population regulation. Albania alone of the countries under survey registered in 1970 (35.3 per 1,000 population) approximately the same relatively high birth rate as before the war (34.2). The other countries in 1970 ranged between 13.7 per 1,000 in Finland and 21.1 in Romania, down from a wider prewar range of between 13.9 in Austria and 29.6 in Romania. Romania's relatively high rate in 1970, up from 14.3 in 1966, reflects a deliberate official policy inaugurated in 1966 to increase the rate of population growth. In 1965 Romania experienced a disastrous 1,115,000 abortions (four abortions per live birth), and an alarmed regime rescinded the liberal abortion law in 1966 in order to promote the birth rate, which indeed did register a substantial increase by 1970. The birth rate per se, because of changing attitudes toward population growth, cannot be used as a reliable indicator of social modernization, but birth regulation, that is, the ability to consciously raise the birth rate after lowering it, does reflect a measure of social control associated with modernization. In the absence of liberal abortion laws, birth regulation is difficult to enact, particularly in the direction of raising the birth rate, as Mussolini discovered when in desperation he even turned off home electricity in an effort to increase the type of activity that normally results in more pregnancies. Romania has demonstrated, however, that by liberalizing and tightening abortion laws, a certain measure of birth regulation can be exercised.

Literacy rates, like infant mortality, represent a more reliable indicator of modernization because, like infant mortality, regulating the literacy rate is unidirectional official policy, designed to increase the rate. The prewar and postwar data on literacy presented in Table 7.1 suffer from a number of deficiencies with a corresponding lessening of its comparability value. Aside from the divergent and constantly changing criteria employed in measuring or registering literacy rates from one country to the next as well as within the same country from one census to the other, the data presented is seriously out of phase in some respects. For countries like Austria, Hungary, Finland, and Czechoslovakia, which had achieved virtual universal literacy before the war, this poses no problem, but for the others it does. Thus, the available "prewar" reference year varies from 1928 (Greece) to 1948 (Romania), a span of two decades.

Whatever it may be worth, the data suggests only a small incremental contribution as a result of the Soviet impact and a far from dramatic one, except for Bulgaria. By 1965 (the latest year for any country in the table), all of the states, communist and noncommunist, except for Albania (60 percent), Yugoslavia (77 percent in 1961), and Greece (80.4 percent in 1961), had achieved 90 percent literacy or above. The prewar range was 54.8 in Yugoslavia in 1931 to 98.1 in Finland, and Yugoslavia, except for Albania, trailed behind all other countries during the latest period recorded on the table, followed by Greece (80.4 in 1961). When we disaggregate the Yugoslav data again, we find a spread of between 67.5 percent for Bosnia-Herzegovina to 98.2 for Slovenia, which reaffirms the wide disparity in development within Yugoslavia.

When we turn to the average annual rate of increase in literacy for the earliest and latest years recorded on the table, we find a variation from .62 percent per year for Poland to 1.50 for Romania, bearing in mind that the Romanian data covers only the eight years from 1948 to 1956 and hence are not really comparable to the others. If we exclude Romania, the range is considerably contracted to from .62 percent per year in Poland to .73 in Yugoslavia, and thus very little can conclusively be attributed to the communist pattern of social modernization. Since virtually all children of primary school age (6-13 years) in all of the countries under discussion (including Albania) were enrolled in school in 1969 (enrollments ranged from 94 percent of all children in the primary age group in Yugoslavia to 109 percent for Greece), it is only a matter of time before all countries in Eastern Europe achieve universal literacy.

The data would thus seem to contradict the widespread impression that communist systems are more urgently concerned with education and that therefore literacy is accelerated at a faster pace in these countries than in others with comparable initial levels of literacy. Without passing any conclusive judgment, the contradiction between the data and the impression may derive from either one of two reasons or both: (1) educational progress plays a prominent role in communist propaganda, with its constant reiteration of progress before and after the advent of communist regimes, and therefore the impression of more rapid progress in communist countries is due to superior advertising techniques; and (2) educational development has indeed been more rapid in communist countries, but the data masks the fact that since virtually all members of the overthrown social classes were literate, population deficits resulting from their death or departure from the country lowered the literate proportion of the population and the communist data thus reflects a compensatory factor to make up for this loss without impairing relative overall increases in literacy. If this latter factor is indeed true, then the impression of more rapid educational development in communist countries is correct in that more people were educated at a faster pace than elsewhere. Thus, as may be possibly the case in economic development, the communist pattern of modernization must make sufficient progress to make up for the dislocations and losses connected with the communist seizure of power as well as maintain a creditable overall performance.

THE IDEOLOGICAL PARAMETERS OF MODERNIZATION
IN EASTERN EUROPE

All of the communist countries of Eastern Europe, including Yugoslavia and Albania, have developed since World War II within a common set of ideological parameters, which continue to exist, in spite of the individual variations that have manifested themselves to distinguish them from one another as well as from the Soviet Union. These parameters or system boundaries are defined and held in place, not only because of their partial internalization and socialization by the countries of Eastern Europe, but because of the existence of an external stabilizer and monitor, that is, the Soviet Union. While this broad generalization may not apply with equal force to all of the countries under discussion, especially Yugoslavia and Albania, it is nevertheless a historical fact that the ideosocial systems of all these countries were originally inspired by the Soviet Union, which became the common model to emulate, and their systems persist largely because of the omnipresence of Soviet power. The Soviet Union continues to function as an external stabilizer and monitor that polices the system boundaries and keeps the options and choices each country makes within certain narrow limits. Since 1956, considerable latitude has been allowed for idiosyncratic development within these boundaries, but whenever the boundaries themselves are threatened, Soviet power either intervenes or threatens to intervene to stabilize or regularize development within prescribed limits. To be sure, the definition of the boundaries can change, but these changes must be made or allowed by Soviet power, as was the case in 1956 when collectivized agriculture was transformed from a mandatory norm into an optional one, at least on a temporary basis. It is true that these system boundary changes resulted from pressures and demands from within the countries of Eastern Europe, but before the changes could be enacted, they had to meet with the approval of the Soviet Union.

The role of the Soviet Union as external stabilizer and monitor in Eastern Europe was formalized into the so-called Brezhnev Doctrine in 1968, whereby the Soviet Union unilaterally invested itself with the right to intervene to arrest and reverse any deviation from permissible patterns of behavior that might be inspired by either internal or external sources.[3] The decisive character of the Soviet Union's role as boundary policeman is verified by the fact that whenever the internal situation in the Soviet Union has been destabilized by domestic factional conflicts and the Soviet leaders are perceived as either unable or unwilling to exercise the monitor function, individual countries of Eastern Europe have attempted to free themselves from the system fetters imposed upon them and break out of the developmental mold in which they have been pressed. This was the case with Hungary and Poland in 1956 and Czechoslovakia in 1968.

The communist conception of modernization dictates that development must take place purposefully and systematically in the direction of a communist society as progressively and pragmatically defined by Moscow. The paths that each country selects may vary as may the pace and tempo of development, but they must all arrive at an approximately identical nirvana. To ensure this, the political order in each country must be under the exclusive direction of an internal stabilizer and monitor, the local Communist or Marxist-Leninist Party, which may masquerade under a variety of names. No matter what the name, this party exercises its functions in accordance with an explicit set of ideological beliefs and values called Marxism-Leninism, which is the ruling ideology and tolerates no competitors as a source of norms, values, and purposes.

The process of establishing system boundaries and parameters of permissible development will be called in this chapter, for want of a better concept, "ideological modernization." Although the term is deficient in many respects, it does have the virtue of corresponding with the communist perception of Marxism-Leninism as the most progressive, advanced, scientific, and modern ideology. Ideological modernization, because it is defined in terms of values and beliefs, is not subject to precise comparability since it is not subject to quantification or measurement, and it should not be confused with political socialization, since the latter refers not to the choice of ideology but the manner in which citizens are imbued with it and this, of course, is subject to indirect measurement.

Ideological modernization thus establishes these basic value norms and goals directing political, social, and economic modernization:

1. The superiority of the interests and values of the proletarian class, which are to be ultimately universalized as the interests of all society through the abolition of all

other social classes and their assimilation to the proletariat. In the interests of proletarian universalism, national, religious, and other distinctions that can create competing identities, even after the abolition of classes, are also to be erased.

2. The superiority of urban life over rural life as exemplified in the ideological goal of erasing the distinction between the two, that is, the conversion of rural life into a variant of urban existence. Just as society is to have a single identity--the proletariat, the latter is to have a single mode of existence--urbanization.

3. The superiority of physical labor over nonmanual labor, since physical labor is considered to be the source of all wealth and value. Soviet ideology reveals a basic ambivalence with respect to this norm since the goal of eliminating the distinction between manual and mental life by transforming all work into a combination of both physical and intellectual work is actually being accomplished by increasing the number of mental workers in all communist countries and creates, at least temporarily, a new ruling social stratum. The goal, nevertheless, is to endow all people with the capability to perform a wide variety of both physical and mental labor.

4. The elimination of scarcity to fulfill the communist goal of "from each according to his ability, to each according to his needs," that is, to infuse society with the higher ethic of distributive justice and free man from the tyranny of his natural environment from which he wrests his basic wants and needs.

5. The primacy of ideological values and norms (justice, equity, equality, etc.) over pragmatic norms (functionality, efficiency, rationality, etc.). The latter must always be subordinate to the former; functionality, efficiency, or rationality cannot be pursued for their own sake, particularly if they tend to conflict with or erode ideolgical goals and values.

6. To eliminate the exploitation of man by man, that is, to sunder the connection between power and ownership of the means of production by destroying the institution of private property and transferring it to the permanent ownership of the state and society from which it cannot be alienated.

These norms, of course, are as often honored in the breach as in practice, and are more operative than operational, but they have nevertheless continued to prevail and have imparted a powerful and pervasive egalitarian ethos into the entire developmental process. Temporary inequalities persist and are even sometimes encouraged in order to maximize the possibility of fulfilling specific goals during certain phases in the developmental process, but they are always subject to control. Egalitarianism thus emerges as an important overall criterion of modernization in communist countries. In some of the countries, for example, Czechoslovakia, the egalitarian ethic has been applied with a vindictive, ruthless simplicity that has proven to be chronically dysfunctional, as Stalin discovered in the early 1930s in Russia when he authorized the revival of limited, structured inequality in order to reduce inefficiency. In practice, the drive toward equality has resulted, nevertheless, in narrowing disparities of income and rewards in communist societies, with floors and ceilings rigidly defined and enforced.

Egalitarianism in communist systems, it must be emphasized, is limited largely to the social services and economic realm, whereas status and power inequalities have been correspondingly aggravated. This results from the system of property relations established in communist countries whose status and power consequences have often been deemphasized or overlooked by Western observers who have traditionally examined its effects in terms of its impact on the social structure and the distribution of income and wealth. Ostensibly, the nationalization of the means of production simultaneously serves ascriptively to abolish "exploitation" and to equalize everybody's relationship to the "means of production," in that all citizens are simultaneously nonowners of these means (in the private sense) and owners (in the social-public sense). The abolition of private ownership in the means of production does deconcentrate the private accumulation of property and wealth, but it simultaneously creates the conditions for the concentration of power and status in fewer hands.

In communist countries, unlike all previous sociopolitical systems, the venerable and durable linkage between the accumulation of property and wealth on the one hand and the acquisition of power and status on the other has been effectively sundered. Contrary to widespread misconception, the nationalization of the means of production in communist countries was not simply the extinction of capitalism as a system, but the abolition of private ownership of property and wealth as a source or social foundation of power and status. Capitalism was simply the latest, most refined, and most conspicuous manifestation of the dependence of power and status upon privately accumulated property and wealth.

Power and status have thus been liberated from dependence upon accumulated property and wealth in communist systems, but property remains an object of power, and its acquisition, distribution, and use is regulated by those who have power and it continues as an instrument of power. Power and status in communist societies depend upon the acquisition and possession of skills and thus reflect functions in the social system. As a consequence, property, wealth, and income are more evenly distributed, but the distribution of power and status remains steeply hierarchical. Restrictions are placed on the availability and accessibility of property and ceilings are imposed upon its accumulation. Similarly, stringent controls are exercised over its transferability, disposal, and use. No matter how much power and status may be accumulated by individuals, this power and status cannot be employed to amass huge accumulations of property and wealth and the incomes and accumulated wealth of the most powerful remain relatively modest. Conversely, large incomes and relatively large accumulations of property have very little correlation with power, although they do correlate more with status. (This discussion should not be interpreted to mean that property ownership and wealth were the sole sources of power and status in noncommunist societies. Power and social status in all social systems have diverse social and economic sources, but property (mainly productive land) was a principal source of power under feudalism and in the ancient slave-owning societies (along with slaves and serfs) alongside inherited status, and it became the principal source of power in capitalist social systems. Skills, abilities, and talents of various sorts have been subsidiary sources of power and status in all social systems, but under communist systems the latter became the sole social sources of power, particularly organizational, coercive, and other functional skills and abilities. Both heredity, which carried over into capitalism as a continuing, but subsidiary, source of power, and property have been abolished as power sources in communist systems.)[4]

Not only power, but leisure as well, has been separated from wealth and income in communist societies, and as in the case of property, leisure is legally restricted in amount and kind. No matter how large or legal an accumulation of wealth may be, it cannot be used to support a life of leisure, and income self-sufficiency cannot constitute a justification to be released from the obligation of performing socially useful labor. These restrictions are most stringently enforced in the Soviet system, with its antiparasite laws, the constitutional obligation to work, and the constitutional imperative that "who does not work . . . neither shall he eat." But similar impositions are operative in varying degrees in all communist countries.

As a consequence of property relations existing in communist countries, there is little correspondence between the
sociopolitical (power and status) and socioeconomic (income
and wealth) pyramidal structures in these societies. The
socioeconomic pyramids in all communist societies have been
flattened with ceilings lowered and floors elevated, whereas
the sociopolitical structure has assumed the contours of a
steeply inclined obelisk that is superimposed upon, but independent of, the socioeconomic pyramid, as shown in Figure
7.1. Whereas income inequalities are subject to periodic
manipulation and leveling and will tend to be less conspicuous, power and status inequalities are likely to retain
their tenacity since differential roles and functions in
communist societies, which they reflect, are likely to persist indefinitely.

FIGURE 7.1

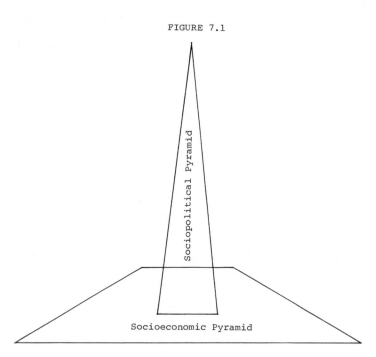

Thus, while the modernization process in communist coun
tries tends in the direction of an egalitarian social and
economic order, by enhancing capabilities through education
and regulating income, the accumulation of wealth, and consumption, it also tends to produce a highly unequal distribution of political power in which the overwhelming majority

has little or no political power at all. Ultimately, the
power and social pyramids are to become congruent as the
power pyramid is progressively flattened to coincide with
the social pyramid, which is also subject to further flatten-
ing as well.

These flattened social and steep power structures were
established throughout Eastern Europe by the simple device
of expropriating and confiscating all the means of production, communication, transportation, construction, financial
institutions, and natural resources, thus demolishing any
possible concentrations of power based upon the accumulation
of property or wealth. Thus, one of the most important communist goals in the modernization process, that is, "building socialism," was the nationalization of private property.
Originally, in conformity with the Soviet pattern, the collectivization of agriculture was designed to do in the countryside what nationalization of industry accomplished in the
cities: to deprive the peasantry of an independent economic
foundation of power from which to contend with the regime.

The process of nationalization has been a characteristic of all the countries of Eastern Europe, but only Bulgaria, Romania, and Albania have approximated the Soviet
model where virtually no private sector exists at all. Nevertheless, impressive strides have been made in all East
European countries in reducing the private sector. Yugoslavia still allows a considerable degree of private ownership even in the cities, provided that it is on a small
scale. Table 7.2 provides a comparison of the distribution
of civilian employment in industry and agriculture according
to social sectors (private, state socialist, cooperative--
including collectives--and semistate). In 1967 East Germany
showed the largest private sector in industry (12 percent),
with another 12 percent in the semistate sector. Poland
followed with 5 percent, but no less than 85 percent of her
agriculture was still in private hands, thus making Poland
the most retrogressive of the socialist states. Along this
continuum, Czechoslovakia was the most advanced socialist
state with no private sector at all in industry and only 13
percent in agriculture. Bulgaria was a close second and
close to perfection in agriculture with only 5 percent in
the private sector, which has since been all but obliterated.
Although collectivization of agriculture is a permissible socialist form of agricultural organization, state farms represent a higher form in that they approach the norms of
urban life. Czechoslovakia scored highest in this regard
as well as in 1967 with 33 percent of its farmers employed
in the state sector.

The ideological parameters that shape and contain a society determine in large measure the allocation of resources

TABLE 7.2

Civilian Employment by Social Sector in Eastern Europe, 1967

Country	Industry								Agriculture and Forestry					
	Private		State Socialist		Cooperative		Semistate		Private		State Socialist		Cooperative	
	1950	1967	1950	1967	1950	1967	1950	1967	1950	1967	1950	1967	1950	1967
Czechoslovakia	17.5	.0	78.0	95.0	4.5	5.0	0.0	0.0	88.0	13.0	11.0	33.0	1.0	51.0
East Germany	36.0	12.0	63.0	71.0	1.0	5.0	0.0	12.0	87.0	2.0	11.0	17.0	2.0	81.0
Poland	8.5	5.0	83.0	83.0	8.5	12.0	0.0	0.0	91.0	85.0	9.0	14.0	0.0	1.0
Hungary	18.0	3.5	80.0	84.5	2.0	12.0	0.0	0.0	89.0	21.0	8.0	18.0	3.0	62.0
Romania	17.5	2.0	70.0	84.5	12.5	13.5	0.0	0.0	95.0	10.0	3.5	6.5	1.0	83.5
Bulgaria	2.5	0.7	78.5	88.0	29.0	11.3	0.0	0.0	82.0	5.0	2.0	18.0	16.0	77.0

Source: Adapted from data in Andrew Elias, "Magnitude and Distribution of the Labor Force in Eastern Europe," in Economic Developments in Countries of Eastern Europe, U.S. Congress, Joint Economic Committee (Washington, D.C., 1970), pp. 180-96.

and the establishment of priorities. To measure the degree
to which communist countries resemble or differ from comparable noncommunist states in the allocation of resources and
the arrangement of priorities we have chosen three important
public services (defense, public health, and education) for
examination, since the three are usually in competition for
both money and skilled personnel. Table 7.3, which provides
comparative data in terms of total and per capita expenditures in 1970 for these three services, suggests that communist countries, while retaining a healthy regard for defense,
tend to allot higher priority for education and public
health than noncommunist countries, although admittedly the
data is far from conclusive. What it does show is that
while Austria and Finland lead all countries in expenditures
for education and public health and correspondingly are lowest in per capita expenditures for national defense, this
latter figure may reflect their nonaligned or neutral status,
which in turn allows for greater expenditures for education
and health. All of the other countries belong to alliance
systems and hence carry a higher military burden, the Soviet
Union scoring, as would be expected, highest in this regard
but also registering exceptionally high marks for education
and health. Greece, whose military burden is comparable to
Hungary's, spends considerably less for health and education
and indeed scores lower than any other country including
Albania. Among communist countries, Yugoslavia and Romania
spend the least on health and education, while Czechoslovakia and East Germany score highest among the East European
states in these two spheres as well as in the military realm.
     When we examine the data more closely and compare 1970
data with 1961 data (see Table A.2), we discover that Greece
and Yugoslavia were even further behind the other states,
communist and noncommunist, in 1961 than in 1970, which may,
of course, also reflect the international tensions of that
period. Between 1961 and 1970, Greece more than doubled her
expenditures for education while Yugoslavia nearly quintupled
hers, thus suggesting that both countries recognized their
delinquency in this connection. Their rates of increase for
defense were lower but nevertheless relatively high. Greece
and Yugoslavia, it will be recalled, lagged behind the others
in levels of literacy in 1970. Our tentative conclusion is
that the relatively higher levels of expenditures for public
health and education can be attributed to the Soviet experience and influence.

TABLE 7.3

Gross National Product and Expenditures for Armed Forces,
Education, and Health, 1970
(current dollars)

Country	Population (millions)	GNP (millions)	Expenditures (millions)			Per Capita (dollars)			
			Military	Education	Health	GNP	Military	Education	Health
USSR	242.2	497,000	65,000	38,500	16,800	2,047	268.0	159	69
Czechoslovakia	14.5	30,500	1,660	1,093	980	2,103	114.5	75	68
East Germany	17.1	32,300	2,200	1,408	820	1,889	128.6	82	48
Poland	32.5	39,400	2,250	1,683	1,520	1,212	69.2	52	47
Hungary	10.3	14,300	560	513	290	1,388	54.4	50	28
Romania	20.3	22,300	610	682	460	1,099	30.1	34	23
Bulgaria	8.5	9,800	310	366	180	1,153	36.5	43	21
Yugoslavia	20.5	19,000	667	585	559	927	32.5	29	27
Albania	2.2	800	95	118	30	364	43.2	54	14
Austria	7.4	14,300	165	660	687	1,932	22.3	89	93
Finland	4.7	10,200	140	688	437	2,170	29.8	146	93
Greece	8.9	9,500	474	188	109	1,067	53.3	21	12

Source: World Military Expenditures, 1971, U.S. Arms Control and Disarmament Agency
(Washington, D.C., 1972).

228

POLITICAL DEVELOPMENT

The political development of Eastern Europe since the war perhaps owes more to the Soviet impact than any other aspect of modernization and can be traced directly to the Soviet experience. Otherwise, one must accept the absurd premise that all of these countries adopted virtually identical state forms of political organization in a rare outburst of coincidental spontaneity. All of the countries were eventually designated "Peoples Republics" and "Peoples Democracies," and with the exception of Yugoslavia, all were transformed into "Dictatorships of the Proletariat" at about the same time. There is little doubt and no precise documentation is required to demonstrate that the political systems are all cut from the same bolt of Soviet cloth although they may differ in pattern and style.

The rigid application of the usual criteria and indexes of "political modernization" to these political systems tends to produce bizarre results in the form of overfulfillment of some of the norms of modernization established by Western scholars, thus reflecting a Stakhanovite impulse acquired from the Soviet Union. If we use the traditional criteria of "political modernization" as meeting the tests of rationalization of authority, national and social integration (socialization), differentiation of functions, roles, and structures, the expansion of participation (if manipulation and involvement are defined as participation), and the systematic reordering of priorities to meet the demands of larger numbers of people through the ever-widening distribution of wealth and services, then the East European systems qualify in a superficial sense.

Instead of wrestling with elusive criteria of political modernization in order to adapt them to the communist political systems, it might be more useful to examine some of the processes, structures, and institutions of rationalization, socialization, integration, participation, and distribution to determine the degree to which they are derived from the Soviet experience.

In all communist states, power rests exclusively in the hands of a Marxist-Leninist party, which may call itself a "communist" party or some type of "workers" party.[5] This party acts as the mobilizing agent, establishing norms, goals, and purposes, monitoring their execution and checking on their faithful fulfillment. In Poland, Czechoslovakia, East Germany, and, to a much lesser extent, Bulgaria, residues of a multiparty system exist whereby remnants of other parties are allowed to function in order to facilitate the involvement and socialization of the masses. These parties are dominated by the Marxist-Leninist Party in one form or another and are pressed into a "national front" (various names in individual countries) that offers a single slate of candidates for elective office, except for Poland which allows a limited number of multiple candidates to local bodies and even the national parliaments.[6] Each "party" is designated a fixed number of nominees, but as Table 7.4 demonstrates, the Communist Party in all cases except East Germany (a divided national state and hence a special category) retains an absolute majority of the seats in parliament, ranging from 55.4 percent in Poland to 77.1 percent in Czechoslovakia.

Albania, Hungary, Romania, and Yugoslavia allow only a single Marxist-Leninist party to function as a party (called a League in Yugoslavia). Yugoslavia and Hungary, like Poland, allow a limited number of multiple-candidate elections to take place. These countries also employ the device of a national front to mobilize and involve the non-Party mass organizations in the electoral process, and they are alloted a certain proportion of nominations, including non-Party candidates. Except for Yugoslavia and Hungary, as noted earlier, a single slate of candidates is the rule. This pattern closely resembles the electoral mode in the Soviet Union where about 25-30 percent of the seats are filled by "non-Party Bolsheviks." The proportion of female candidates varies widely, from 3.80 percent in Poland to 35.25 percent in East Germany in the most recent elections. In this connection, Austria's performance exceeds Poland's, while Finland's matches that of Romania.

Table A.3 provides data (incomplete) on mass organizations in Eastern Europe, which are institutions designed to expand the involvement of the people in the political process. As can be seen from the table, these organizations have large, in some cases mandatory, memberships and are designed to impart to the citizenry a sense of participation in the political process while simultaneously being excluded from the Marxist-Leninist Party, which remains a self-selective, although no longer an elite, political organization that provides the only real avenues to power in the system.

Table 7.5 provides data on the electorate, electoral participation, and the size of Marxist-Leninist Parties in Eastern Europe. Electoral participation provides the most comic evidence of the communist overfulfillment of what might be called "modernization" norms. Nearly 100 percent participation in elections is exhibited by all communist countries except Yugoslavia (87.9 percent), with nearly 100 percent voting for official candidates. This suggests not

Distribution of Deputies in National Parliaments by Party Nominations

Country	Year	Communist Party (percent)	Other Front Parties (number)	Other Parties and Non-Party	Total	Districts Contested	Number of Women[a]	Percent Women
USSR	1970	1,096 (72.2)	--	421	1,517	0	463	30.50
Czechoslovakia	1971	270 (77.1)	80 (4)	0	350	0	--	--
East Germany	1971	127 (25.0)	208 (4)	165[b]	500	0	153	35.25
Poland	1972	255 (55.4)	156 (2)	49	460	c	62	3.80
Hungary	1971	--	--	--	349	49	69	19.77
Romania	1969	465 (100)	--	--	465	0	67	14.40
Bulgaria	1971	266 (66.5)	121 (2)	13	400	0	70	17.50
Yugoslavia	1969	--	--	--	620[d]	49[e]	49	7.90
Albania	1970	264 (100)	--	--	264	0	--	--
Austria	1970	--	--	--	183	--	8	4.37
Finland	1968	--	--	--	198	--	28	14.14
Greece		--	--	--	300	--	--	--

[a]The Political System of the Socialist Countries, Supplement to the World Marxist Review, August 1970, p. 17.

[b]Includes deputies from non-Party mass organizations representing youth, trade unions, women, and intellectuals.

[c]In 1969, 622 candidates stood for 460 seats.

[d]Includes all six chambers of the Federal Assembly.

[e]For the 120 seats in the Socio-Political Chamber.

Sources: Keesings Contemporary Archives; World Strength of the Communist Party Organizations, Bureau of Intelligence and Research, U.S. Department of State (Washington, D.C., 1973).

TABLE 7.5

Electorate and Elections

Country	Year	Population (in millions)	Electorate	Percent Voting	Percent Voting for	Communist Party 1971	Percent of Total Population	Percent of Electorate
USSR	1970	242.8	153,237,112	99.96	99.74	14,524,000	6.0	9.46
Czechoslovakia	1971	14.5	10,300,000	99.45	99.81	1,200,000*	8.4	11.65
East Germany	1971	17.1	11,401,090	98.48	99.85	1,909,859	11.0	16.75
Poland	1969	32.5	20,600,000	97.61	99.22	2,270,000	7.0	11.01
Hungary	1971	10.3	7,589,600	98.70	99.10	693,000	6.4	9.13
Romania	1969	20.3	12,500,000	99.96	99.75	2,089,085	10.0	16.72
Bulgaria	1971	8.5	6,168,931	99.85	99.90	699,476	8.0	11.33
Yugoslavia	1969	20.5	11,148,150	87.90	--	1,049,334	10.0	9.41
Albania	1970	2.2	1,097,123	100.00	99.99	86,985	4.6	7.92
Austria	1971	7.4	4,557,103	92.49	--	--	--	--
Finland	1972	4.7	3,179,000	81.10	--	--	--	--
Greece	1964	8.9	5,800,000 (est.)	80.00 (4,600,000)				

*1,699,677 in January 1968.

Sources: Data compiled and calculated from official sources and national press, supplemented with data from Keesings Contemporary Archives for the relevant years, and from World Strength of the Communist Party Organizations, Bureau of Intelligence and Research, U.S. Department of State (Washington,

participation but mobilization, manipulation, and mandatory
behavior, which is involvement but hardly participation.
Greece (1964 elections) and Finland report 80 percent or
more participation, while Austria registers a high 92.49
percent of the electorate participating, which suggests that
single-party systems are not the only way to ensure a high
level of voter participation.

When we move to the Communist Parties, however, to assess the real state of participation in political activity,
Table 7.5 shows that party membership is restricted to from
4.6 percent of the population in Albania to 11 percent in
East Germany. If we use the electorate as the base of comparison, we find that party membership ranges from 7.92 percent in Albania to nearly 17 percent in Romania and East
Germany. The mode appears to be about 10 percent of the
electorate for all countries.

An examination of the social composition of Marxist-
Leninist Parties will provide additional clues to the state
of participation by revealing the relative access that different social groups have to party membership. Table 7.6
provides us with data on social structures of communist societies as compared with the social composition of Communist
Parties. Unfortunately, industrial and office workers are
collapsed into a single category for social structure and
the data is not strictly comparable. An examination of the
social composition of the Party betrays close resemblances
to the social composition of the Soviet Party. The workers
constitute in no case an absolute majority, although in East
Germany, Hungary, Romania, and Bulgaria they constitute a
plurality. In Czechoslovakia, the most advanced communist
state, the intelligentsia and office workers make up nearly
58 percent of the Party. Romania and Bulgaria reflect relatively high proportions of peasants in the Party (26.4 and
29.8 percent, respectively). Thus, in almost all East European countries, the peasantry is provided relatively little
access to political participation, while the intelligentsia
and office workers are overrepresented in all countries, including those in which "workers" constitute a plurality of
Party membership.

Bearing in mind that the Communist Parties are restricted political parties operating largely in a single-
party atmosphere, it might be useful to compare the social
distribution of political participation as reflected in prewar party membership in some countries of Eastern Europe
(before the advent of authoritarian regimes). Using relatively early data as a guide (derived from R. V. Burks),
Table 7.7 shows the breakdown of party membership by social
composition.

TABLE 7.6

Social Structure and Social Composition of Marxist-Leninist
Parties in Eastern Europe, 1969-70

Country	Social Composition of Population			Social Composition of Marxist-Leninist Parties			
	Industrial and Office Workers	Peasants in Co-ops and Collective Farms	Other	Workers	Intelligentsia and Office Workers	Peasants	Other
USSR	77.7	22.3	0.03	39.3	45.1*	15.6	
Czechoslovakia	87.9	9.4	2.7	36.0	57.6*	6.4	
East Germany	82.7	13.5	3.8	47.1	28.1	5.8	19.0
Poland	66.8	3.5	27.7	40.2	42.8	11.4	5.8
Hungary	71.1	25.9	3.0	42.7*	38.1		19.2
Romania	52.3	40.7	7.0	43.6	22.8	26.4	7.2
Bulgaria	59.2	39.2	1.6	38.2	25.6	29.8	6.4
Yugoslavia	40.1		59.9	31.1	68.9	--	--
Albania	37.9	43.4	18.7	35.2	35.8	29.0	--

*1971.

Source: The Political System of the Socialist Countries, Supplement to the World Marxist Review, August 1970, p. 4.

TABLE 7.7

Social Composition of All Prewar Parties
in Eastern Europe

Country	Year	Workers	Peasants	Middle Class	Other
Czechoslovakia	1927	53.4	14.6	18.5	13.5
Poland	1932	42.3	33.8	23.9	0
Bulgaria	1919	39.0	40.5	5.5	15.0
Greece	1932	42.6	54.4	3.0	0

Source: R. V. Burks, The Dynamics of Communism in Eastern Europe (Princeton, N.J.: Princeton University Press, 1961), p. 35.

The results are striking. In none of the cases for which data has been assembled was the participation of workers in party activity proportionately greater in communist countries than in the prewar bourgeois party system. For Poland, the workers' proportion of party membership in 1932 was 42.3 percent as compared to 40.2 percent for the Marxist-Leninist Party in 1969-70; for Czechoslovakia, it was 53.4 percent in the prewar period as opposed to 36.0 percent in 1969-70; for Bulgaria in 1919 the respective figures are 39.0 percent and 38.2 percent. Greece fell within the same range in 1932. Other social groups, which no longer exist, were also represented, but in no instance did the middle classes in those years dominate party political activity as did their counterparts in 1969-70. This suggests that even in these countries, workers and peasants were quite active politically within the context of a multiparty system and that communist regimes instead of expanding political participation for "excluded" groups may instead restrict their participation and provide more mobilization, manipulation, and involvement.

Since the prewar data reflects multiparty systems, it should not be interpreted that prewar social composition was evenly reflected in all parties, but rather it should be recalled that certain social groups and classes had a tendency to cluster in different parties. Workers, peasants, and the middle class, as well as various national minorities, had their own parties and the aggregate data subsumes this. When we move from the social composition of parties to that of national parliaments in communist countries (Table 7.8), we find that except in the case of East Germany the intelligentsia and office workers tend to dominate and constitute

TABLE 7.8

Social Composition of National Parliaments in Eastern Europe

Country	Year	Deputies	Intelligentsia and Office Workers		Workers		Peasants	
			Number	Percent	Number	Percent	Number	Percent
USSR	1970	1,517	845	55.7	481	31.7	282	18.6
East Germany	1967	500	169	33.8	287	57.4	44	8.8
Poland	1969	460	311	67.6	79	17.2	70	15.2
Hungary	1967	349	171	49.0	126	36.1	52	14.9
Romania	1969	465	297	63.9	92	19.8	76	16.3
Bulgaria	1966	416	315	75.7	50	12.0	51	12.3
Yugoslavia	1969	620*	615	99.2	4	0.6	1	.02

*Total for the five chambers of the Federal Assembly.

Source: The Political System of the Socialist Countries, Supplement to the World Marxist Review, August 1970, p. 11.

an absolute majority in all instances except in East Germany
and Hungary. In some cases, the presence of this class is
more than double for the total of workers and peasants combined (Poland, Bulgaria, and Yugoslavia). Burks provides
some prewar data on the social composition of prewar candidates for parliament that can provide us with some basis of
comparison. This data (Table 7.9) shows that the middle
class provided more candidates than any other in communist,
socialist, and other parties (44.6 percent to 50.4 percent),
but that the social mix was otherwise different. Socialist
and communist parties offered most of the candidates of
working-class status (22.5 percent and 29.4 percent) with
about 20 percent of their candidates selected from the peasantry. The other parties, including those that were peasant-
oriented, supplied only 7.5 percent of all candidates of
working-class status with over 80 percent made up of roughly
equal parts of peasants and middle-class people.

TABLE 7.9

Social Composition of Parliamentary Candidates
in Eastern Europe
(in percentages)

[N = 9,943]

Party	Workers	Peasants	Middle Class	Other
Communist	29.4	21.4	44.8	4.4
Socialist	22.5	19.0	50.4	8.1
Other parties	7.5	40.3	44.6	7.6

Source: R. V. Burks, The Dynamics of Communism in
Eastern Europe (Princeton, N.J.: Princeton University
Press, 1961), p. 35.

Thus, the communist argument that their political system provides greater opportunity for worker and peasant access to elective positions is not correct, but represents an
exaggeration rather than an untruth. What communist political systems do is restrict the competition from other social
groups in favor of the new propertyless intelligentsia and
office-worker class rather than for the working and peasant
classes as such. No account is taken here of the differential opportunities for social mobility that exist in communist regimes, that is, children of worker and peasant origin
are likely to have greater opportunities for upward mobility

than under previous regimes, but here too the issue becomes extremely complex because of the radically different social systems and the different avenues for upward mobility that exist in communist states as opposed to those that provide such avenues via the accumulation of property and wealth.

In summary, we can say that the Soviet experience has indeed left its imprint on political development in Eastern Europe. The single-party system, the massive official bureaucracies, the absence of competing centers of political power, the substitution of mobilization and manipulation for spontaneity and participation in the political process, the reduction of avenues to power but broadening the single one that is permitted, the concentration of power in the hands of an elite while denying it elsewhere, the proliferation of mass organizations, all operating under the direction of the Communist Party, are only a few of the political beliefs of modernization of the Soviet variety imposed upon Eastern Europe.

SOCIAL MODERNIZATION

As we move away from political development in Eastern Europe toward social and economic modernization and the evidence indicators of modernization become increasingly more measurable, it becomes progressively more difficult to attribute modernization in Eastern Europe to the Soviet impact. As noted earlier in this chapter, Marx designated capitalism as the stage historically responsible for the industrialization and modernization of society and hence inevitable in the life of any society. Hence, insofar as the basic industrialization and modernization of Eastern Europe is concerned, the Soviet experience in a sense becomes irrelevant since even Soviet theorists must concede that capitalism could perform the same function. The Soviet pattern of modernization, however, combined two historical functions: (1) the industrialization and modernization functions historically assigned to capitalism; and (2) the infusion of an egalitarian ethos into development as distributive justice is prepackaged into the infrastructure of the industrialization and modernization process instead of being imposed upon a fully developed, industrialized, and capitalist society.

Thus, the process of constructing socialism in immature capitalist societies in which the industrialization and modernization process was incomplete is bound to produce effects similar to industrialization and modernization in noncommunist states and it should not be surprising that both communists and noncommunists share many objective indicators of modernization in common. Both emphasize rates and levels of industrialization, urbanization, and mechanization as indicators of modernization. Similarly, the development, expansion, and equalization of human capabilities and opportunities (education, science, technology, and training) and the expansion of public welfare and services (health, recreation, leisure, social security, job security, etc.) are considered to be evidences of modernization. The expansion of communication and transportation facilities, raising the standard of living, improving the amenities of life, including housing, are also indicators employed by both communists and noncommunists to measure modernization.

Because of different parametric restrictions and constraints, however, social and economic modernization in Eastern Europe cannot proceed in a spontaneous and unregulated manner, but must be developed within a specific context of priorities and possibilities. The Soviet pattern of modernization, which constituted the original inspiration and model of modernization for Eastern Europe, tends to reflect the following structure of priorities. Higher priority is assigned to defense than to basic public welfare and services, both of which are favored over personal consumption; industrialization is favored over agricultural development, the cities have higher priority than rural constituencies; heavy industry is favored over light industry and the consumer goods industries; quantity production has higher priority than quality; reliable routine is favored over uncertain and risky innovation; centralized planning and management are preferred to local administration. Priorities are determined neither by profit nor public demand but by needs as defined by the modernizing elite. Efficiency is subordinated to social values, as defined above, and public demand has little relevance to production.

These are basic tendencies of the Soviet pattern of modernization and they are reflected unevenly in the individual countries of Eastern Europe, with Bulgaria conforming most faithfully and Yugoslavia exhibiting the greatest departure. All of the countries of Eastern Europe have adapted, accommodated, and even circumvented these tendencies to the degree that they are tolerated by the Soviet Union. This structure of priorities in the modernization process seriously affects the social differentiation and stratification in Eastern European society, determines the direction and proliferation of roles, functions, structures, and institutions, which in turn generate interests and attitudes to be defended, promoted, and propagated, as the modernization process then tends to satisfy the needs and demands of its own creations and becomes more an instrument for the self-perpetuation of these structures than further development.

Functionality of structures and institutions in communist countries increasingly becomes defined in terms of system maintenance rather than system development. As long as structures and institutions operate within the context of the priorities enumerated above in a manner that does not conflict with the basic parameters of the system, even though they do not perform these functions with efficiency, or effectiveness, they are more tolerated than if they resort to options and possibilities that may be more efficient or effective but are incompatible with the parametric imperatives of socialism. Empirical and pragmatic behavior that might discover solutions to problems outside permissible bounds are discouraged and prohibited, no matter how effective they may be in a narrow functional sense; permissible innovations and reforms are those that improve functionality while strengthening the parameters of the system or at the very least are not incompatible with them. Even increased productivity, which enjoys a high priority in communist countries, is subordinated to higher parametric imperatives and cannot be improved through the employment of forbidden incentive or efficiency mechanisms. While ideological incentives have highest priority, material incentives can be employed within certain limits; the profit mechanism can be employed under carefully controlled conditions, although a greater latitude for both material incentives and profit formulas exists in Eastern Europe than in the Soviet Union. The employment of management and administrative devices is similarly restricted; local control and autonomous management of structures and enterprises and workers councils are similarly circumscribed, although here again a wider latitude of application exists in Eastern Europe than in the Soviet Union. Solutions involving the possible restoration of private ownership of the means of production, which tend to create wide disparities in income and the accumulation of wealth or result in unemployment, are the most stringently controlled and are barely tolerated in the Soviet Union but are still relatively widespread in Eastern Europe, particularly in agriculture, retailing, services, handicrafts, and some small-scale enterprises. In many Eastern European countries, "cooperatives" are essentially ideological fig leaves disguising forbidden economic behavior.

Yugoslavia betrays the greatest deviation from the Soviet norm and has developed to the point where even Marshal Tito has become alarmed. Although relaxation of restraints has improved the quality of Yugoslav life and enhanced her economic efficiency, it has introduced a distortion of priorities (within the communist context), eroded the power and influence of the Communist League, fostered localism and self-interest, encouraged nationalism in the Republics, developed serious inequalities in income, wealth, and standards of living, created unemployment (whose deleterious consequences have been postponed by the export of surplus labor to West Germany), and has in general arrested the drive toward social equality.

In the Soviet view, empirical and pragmatic approaches to efficiency, effectiveness, and functionality, while accelerating the modernization process, may result in the dreaded "restoration of capitalism." And as noted previously, no matter how modernized and industrialized capitalism may be, it represents a retrograde phase in the developmental process, and thus modernization must take place only within the context of developing a socialist society. A Soviet journalist in reporting on recent developments in Yugoslavia emphasized the dangers to socialism posed by the spontaneous, unregulated, and pragmatic approach to modernization as it eroded and undermined the influence, guiding role, and power of the Communist Party, which has the dual responsibility "both for the fulfillment of the program in the production section and for the fate of socialism":

> Communists and workers in the Central Committee of the League of Communists of Slovenia told me [that] the party organizations' influence at industrial enterprises was inadequate. . . . The director and the administration were absolute masters there. Often they had complete control over matters of production, capital investment and the distribution of income. "Smart dealers" of this type gained strength and concentrated power in their hands, while wresting the reins of control from the working class. . . .
> In industrially developed Slovenia . . . under the protection of anarcho-syndicalism [Workers Councils], which encouraged technocratic aspirations and gave a free hand to their proponents, the unregulated market began to take over, a tendency toward the formation of private and group ownership became stronger and public capital flowed into private pockets. Social differentiation in society took on significant proportions. Groups of people appeared who had grown rich on earned income; the nature of economic policy, particularly the investment policy became distorted.[7]

When we turn to a comparative examination of the data
on social and economic modernization, we find that the prog
ress of modernization in the communist countries of Eastern
Europe does not markedly differ from that in noncommunist
countries. Where conspicuous departures exist, they reflec
the parametric priorities discussed above and are most evident in indexes referring to personal consumption, where in
dicators in noncommunist countries are generally higher.
Table A.4 provides us with basic population data, including
population growth. In all of the countries under discussio
population growth reflects that which is normally associate
with modernization, that is, relatively stable population d
velopment. Except for Albania (3 percent), the average annual population growth between 1963 and 1970 was about 1 pe
cent or less (ranging from 0.1 in East Germany to 1.1 in
Romania and Yugoslavia). East Germany's extremely low rate
reflects emigration while Yugoslavia's figure is the usual
aggregate mean that reveals the usual spread when disaggregated (see Table A.1). Table A.4 also shows the changing
patterns of ethnic distribution in the countries of Eastern
Europe as a result of boundary changes and population movements after World War II. All of the countries of Eastern
Europe are now more ethnically homogeneous than before the
war and this serves to facilitate socialization and foster
national integration. Poland and Czechoslovakia show the
greatest changes in this dimension and are among the most
ethnically homogeneous currently, whereas before the war
they were the least.

Table 7.10 provides us with data on vital statistics a
reported in 1970. Comparative birth and infant mortality
rates have been previously discussed and need not detain us
here (Tables A.5 and A.6 provide additional data). When we
examine the data for life expectancy, we find a remarkable
degree of uniformity within narrow limits, which may reflec
the differential years for which the data was reported. Hi
average life expectancy is an important indicator of social
modernization and reflects both the state of public health
and nutrition as well as emotional and psychological stability. The range for male life expectancy reported in Table
7.10 is 64.9 years for Albania to 68.8 for Bulgaria while
for female life expectancy it is from 67 in Albania to 73.6
in Czechoslovakia and East Germany. There is no discernibl
difference between communist and noncommunist countries.
Life expectancy in Greece (67.5 for males, 70.7 for females
is lower than Bulgaria's, but higher than Yugoslavia, Albania, and Romania. Furthermore, the Greek data reflects
an earlier reporting period and this could account for some
of the difference.

Vital Statistics, 1970

| Country | Year | Rate per Thousand | | | | | | Life Expectancy | | |
		Marriages	Divorces	Crude Birth Rate	Crude Death Rate	Infant Mortality	Natural Increase	Year	Male	Female
USSR	1970	9.7	2.6	17.4	8.2	24.4	9.2	67-68	70.0	70.0
Czechoslovakia	1970	8.7	1.7	15.8	11.4	22.1	4.4	1966	67.3	73.6
East Germany	1970	7.7	1.6	13.9	14.1	18.8	-0.2	65-66	68.7	73.6
Poland	1970	8.6	1.1	16.8	8.2	33.2	8.6	65-66	66.8	72.8
Hungary	1970	9.4	2.2	14.7	11.7	35.9	3.0	1964	67.0	71.8
Romania	1970	7.2	0.4	21.1	9.5	49.4	11.6	64-67	66.4	70.5
Bulgaria	1970	8.6	1.2	16.3	9.1	27.3	7.2	65-67	68.8	72.6
Yugoslavia	1970	9.1	1.0	17.8	9.0	55.2	8.8	66-67	67.7	68.99
Albania	1969	7.4	0.7	35.3	7.5	86.8	27.8	65-66	64.9	67.0
Austria	1970	7.1	1.4	15.2	13.4	25.9	1.8	1970	66.3	73.5
Finland	1970	8.6	1.3	13.7	9.5	12.5	4.2	61-65	65.4	72.6
Greece	1970	7.6	0.4	16.3	8.3	29.3	8.0	60-62	67.5	70.7

Source: United Nations Demographic Yearbook, 1971.

When we examine the impact of modernization on marriage and divorce, the data for marriages reveals no surprises or marked deviations from one country to another (ranging from 7.1 marriages per 1,000 in Austria to 9.4 for Hungary), but the data for divorces does reflect a distinct unevenness. Since communist modernization emphasizes sex equality, which manifests itself in relaxed divorce and abortion laws, communist countries show a slightly higher rate of divorce than noncommunist countries, with Hungary showing the highest (2.2 per 1,000) and Romania and Greece exhibiting the lowest (0.4 per 1,000). Romania and Greece are also among the lowest in the number of marriages, while Hungary exhibited the highest marriage rate. Just as a higher rate of marriage correlates with a high rate of divorce, high death rates seem to correlate with higher life expectancies and the age structure that develops as a consequence.

Table A.7 provides additional data on births in conjunction with abortions and pregnancies. If a high rate of abortion is an indicator of modernization, then the communist countries of Eastern Europe are exceptionally modernized in this dimension. The five countries for which we have relatively complete data exhibit high rates of abortion since the relaxation of abortion laws. Romania was the most "modernized" in this connection until the abortion law was rescinded in 1967. What the data seems to show, however, is that communist countries use abortion as a substitute for birth control and family planning, which reflects the absence of effective birth control devices and hence a lag in modernization.[8]

Table A.8, providing data on medical facilities and personnel, does reveal some surprises. Given the communist emphasis on the expansion of public health, we would expect remarkable progress in this realm, and in general this is true. Greece lags behind all communist states except Yugoslavia and Albania in the number of hospital beds, but she compares favorably in the total number of doctors and dentists. Finland, Austria, East Germany, and Czechoslovakia show the highest number of hospital beds per population. The data for medical personnel is somewhat mixed, with the number of nurses particularly low in Greece and out of phase with the number of doctors and dentists. Greece's departure from comparable communist states would seem to reflect the differences in parametric priorities that exist between communist and noncommunist countries, and the availability of medical services varies considerably as a consequence. Medical facilities in Greece reflect an entrepreneurial society in which medical treatment varies in accordance with ability to pay, whereas in communist states it is a free public service.

and is developed accordingly. Thus while Greece may have the same rate of doctors and dentists per population, they may, in fact, serve far fewer people, as the data on hospitals and nurses would seem to reflect.

Table A.9 provides data on urbanization in six communist countries of Eastern Europe. Bulgaria shows the highest rate of urbanization (it started with the lowest base in 1946), and in 1965-67 only Romania and Bulgaria were still less than 50 percent urbanized. Poland has also demonstrated considerable progress in urbanization, but East Germany and Czechoslovakia remain the most urbanized of the communist states.

Tables A.10 and A.11 provide us with data on the amenities of life, particularly housing and transportation. In terms of average aggregate data, the communist states do not show any marked difference from noncommunist states at comparable stages of modernization. Greece (compared to Romania and Bulgaria) is somewhat superior in the areas of inside piped water, flush toilets, and fixed baths or showers, but falls behind Bulgaria (still ahead of Romania) in home electricity. Again, the aggregate data masks different social distributions, with the higher Greek rates reflecting the existence of a relatively prosperous middle and upper class, while the facilities in communist countries are apt to be more evenly distributed. Austria shows superiority in almost all aspects of housing when compared with the more industrialized communist states. The data would seem to suggest that communist states give higher priority to electrification, piped water, flush toilets, and fixed baths and showers in that order, which seems to coincide precisely with the unstructured development in the noncommunist states.

Table A.11 on transportation does reveal important differences between communist and noncommunist states. Communist countries still rely primarily on rail transport for freight traffic, whereas the trend in Western Europe is toward truck traffic. Insofar as personal transportation is concerned, the communist states are still in the motor-scooter or motorcycle stage as compared to West Germany. Automobiles for personal use have a low priority in communist countries and this reflects the low priority of personal and material consumption that generally prevails.

Table 7.11 provides education data for the years 1960 and 1969. The data does not conclusively demonstrate the superiority of communist concern for education. Greece compares favorably with communist states generally at all three levels of education. Yugoslavia, Bulgaria, and Albania show higher proportions of students in institutions of higher learning than the other countries; with the exception of

TABLE 7.11

School Enrollment, 1960 and 1969
(percentage enrolled of corresponding
population group in each country;
female enrollments in parentheses)

Country	Primary (6-14)	Secondary (10-19)	Higher (20-24)
	1960		
USSR	104 (--)	60 (--)	11.03 (9.54)
Czechoslovakia	98 (98)	36 (34)	10.94 (7.51)
East Germany	109 (--)*	71 (--)*	9.24 (4.82)
Poland	108 (107)	39 (42)	7.46 (5.25)
Hungary	101 (99)	47 (29)	4.29 (3.17)
Romania	97 (94)	42 (37)	4.53 (3.00)
Bulgaria	93 (92)	59 (--)	10.54 (8.54)
Yugoslavia	94 (89)*	34 (27)	8.60 (5.06)
Albania	93 (84)	20 (11)	4.52 (1.52)
Austria	85 (81)		8.01 (3.78)
Finland	--	54 (57)	7.38 (6.93)
Greece	109 (107)	39 (30)	3.98 (2.04)
	1969		
USSR	105 (--)	67 (--)	26.52 (--)
Czechoslovakia	96 (97)	37 (43)	11.02 (8.43)
East Germany	118 (--)	66 (--)	13.04 (8.89)
Poland	104 (102)	46 (54)	12.14 (10.36)
Hungary	100 (99)	61 (52)	6.76 (6.09)
Romania	107 (107)	62 (53)	10.14 (8.77)
Bulgaria	101 (100)	66 (--)	14.20 (14.00)
Yugoslavia	94 (89)	45 (41)	14.61 (11.79)
Albania	105 (101)	30 (24)	14.02 (9.22)
Austria	106 (105)	84 (79)	11.09 (6.53)
Finland	98 (95)	72 (76)	12.99 (12.85)
Greece	109 (107)	60 (52)	10.98 (7.18)

*1965.

Source: Unesco Statistical Yearbook, 1971 (Paris: Unesco Statistical Office, 1972).

Yugoslavia and Albania, all countries showed 60 percent or more of the relevant age group enrolled in institutions of secondary education and with more than 10 percent in institutions of higher learning, except for Hungary (6.76 percent). Comparative data on literacy was previously discussed (see Table 7.1). Table A.12 provides information on scientific and technical manpower.

Communist countries boast of the great strides made in the production of books, the circulation of newspapers, and the expansion of communications media. Table A.13 provides us with some comparative data, but statistical data on book production is relatively meaningless by itself. Communist states do exhibit an inflated number of book titles published annually and newspaper circulation is remarkably high, but since books and newspapers, along with radio receivers and television sets, are vehicles of propaganda as well as information and culture, it is difficult to disaggregate the functions where communist countries are concerned. One marginal clue is the comparative distribution of telephones, which have little propaganda value but considerable value for interpersonal communication and are instruments of communication that enable the citizen to initiate communication. Table A.14 provides us with the number of telephones in use and it is at once obvious that the manufacture of telephones has a relatively low priority in communist states. Only Czechoslovakia (13.8) and East Germany (12.3) for example, have more telephones per 100 people in use than Greece (10 per 100), while Austria and Finland report 19.3 and 24.9 per 100, respectively. The number of radio receivers and television sets in communist countries is impressive and Greece falls behind all countries in this category except for Albania. The television age has apparently not arrived in either Albania or Greece.

ECONOMIC DEVELOPMENT

Among the proudest accomplishments of the Soviet mode of modernization is rapid industrialization, and progress in this connection has been remarkably fast, particularly for those states like Bulgaria that were primarily agricultural. The results for Czechoslovakia and East Germany have been mixed, but on balance probably detrimental as compared to alternative patterns that may have been adopted. Table A.15 summarizes economic growth rates for the communist countries since the war and is broken down into the Stalinist and post-Stalinest periods. Rates were most rapid during the Stalinist period, when the economic base was smaller and heavy industry was emphasized. Since the Stalinist period growth

rates have slowed down and in Czechoslovakia they approached
the vanishing point.

Table A.16 provides us with data on growth rates of industrial output and indexes of industrial growth, including
fragmentary data for Austria and Greece. Other Western countries are included to provide a broader basis for comparison.
Communist countries failed to demonstrate any clear-cut superiority over noncommunist states in industrial output and
the picture was still a mixed one in 1969. Western countries show greater fluctuation in growth from year to year
than do communist states as would be expected. When we turn
to the index ratings, they show that all communist states
except East Germany registered higher rates of industrial
growth than Austria or Greece, with the former showing the
lowest rate. Bulgaria's rate of industrial growth was
double that of Greece, while Romania's was 50 percent more.
Bulgaria demonstrates the most impressive rate of all countries, and in all cases, heavy industry exhibited a substantially higher rate of growth than other industry and achieve
almost twice the rate in Bulgaria.

When we examine the data for the gross national product
provided in Table 7.12, Greece, surprisingly, shows the most
impressive growth of any country, registering an average annual rate of change of 10.1 percent between 1961 and 1970.
Bulgaria and Romania followed in that order. Table A.16 pro
vides data for indexes of total GNP for communist countries
for the period 1937-68, while Table A.17 provides indexes
and growth rates of GNP per capita. On a per capita basis
(the data is contained in Table 7.3), the GNP per capita in
1970 for Greece was $1,067 and was approximately the same
for Romania ($1,099) and Bulgaria ($1,153), and higher than
Yugoslavia's ($927) and Albania's ($364), so no distortion
is concealed by rate and index data.

In terms of labor productivity, the communist record is
less impressive (Table A.18). Using West Germany's labor
productivity in 1967 as a base of 100, Austria's performance
(47) was superior to that of Hungary (35); France (81),
Italy (67), and Belgium (87) were superior to Czechoslovakia
(54) and East Germany (62).

Communist performance in agriculture up to 1968 was
relatively dismal and continues to betray the effects of the
low priority agriculture receives in communist countries.
Table A.19, on indexes of agricultural output in the postwar
period as compared to prewar, shows an inferior overall performance as compared to Western Europe.

The dysfunctionality of the socialist system for agricultural production is even more graphically displayed by
the differential performance of those communist states with

248

TABLE 7.12

Gross National Product, 1961-70
(in millions of dollars)

Country	1961	1963	1965	1968	1970	Percent Change 1961-70	Average Annual Rate of Change
USSR	247,000	268,000	318,000	413,000	497,000	101.2	8.1
Czechoslovakia	17,100	17,400	19,500	25,300	30,500	78.4	6.6
East Germany	18,700	20,200	22,400	27,400	32,300	72.7	6.3
Poland	20,400	21,900	25,000	33,100	39,400	93.1	7.6
Hungary	7,600	8,500	9,300	11,900	14,300	88.2	7.3
Romania	10,000	11,400	13,300	17,900	22,300	123.0	9.3
Bulgaria	4,300	5,000	5,800	7,800	9,800	127.9	9.6
Yugoslavia	11,300	12,000	14,800	16,500	19,000	68.1	5.9
Albania	500	600	600	800	800	60.0	5.4
Austria	6,800	7,800	9,300	11,400	14,300	110.3	8.6
Finland	5,500	6,400	8,100	8,000	10,200	85.4	7.1
Greece	4,000	4,700	3,900	7,600	9,500	137.5	10.1

Source: World Military Expenditures, 1971.

private agriculture as compared to those with socialist agri
culture. The index for the former is 175.7 compared to 139.
for the latter. Communist countries with a large private ag
ricultural sector thus approach the West European index of
186.4. This difference in performance emerges as even more
remarkable when we examine the relative mechanization of agriculture in communist countries as measured in terms of
tractors per 1,000 hectares and 1,000 workers. Although the
communist countries with socialized agriculture have more
than twice as many tractors per hectare and per worker than
those with private agriculture, the performance of the forme
is substantially poorer, thus suggesting that mechanization
of agriculture by itself is not a sufficient substitute for
human incentive in agricultural productivity (see Table A.20
    While the Soviet impact on agricultural productivity ha
been deleterious, Table A.21 shows that food prices have remained remarkably stable between 1953 and 1970, except in
Yugoslavia, where inflation has been rampant. The number of
calories consumed per day is high and exceeds 3,000, except
for Albania (2,370). Communist citizens, however, are apt
to consume less food of animal origin than noncommunist, although their protein intake (except for Albania) matches tha
of noncommunist countries. In the number and character of
calories consumed, little difference exists between communis
and noncommunist states.
    The advent of communist systems in Eastern Europe has
seriously affected the size and the male-sex distribution of
the economically active population and the distribution of
the labor force among manufacturing, agriculture, and services. Table A.22 shows that communist countries are apt to
have a higher proportion of the economically active population drawn from the female side than noncommunist states.
In the 1960s the percentage of females who were economically
active ranged from 32.8 percent in Hungary to 48.1 percent
in Romania. Greece, with 27.8 percent, had the lowest ratio
of women engaged in economic activity. Modernization on the
whole has had only a surface impact on increasing either the
proportions of the total population who are economically active or on the ratio of women who are economically involved.
    Table 7.13, however, shows that while proportions of
the economically active population may remain the same, the
distribution of the labor force has been radically altered.
Modernization tends to increase the number of people working
in manufacturing at the expense of agriculture and then the
proportion of workers in manufacturing is eroded in favor of
the service sector. In the 1960s the service sector in communist countries was not as highly developed as that in noncommunist countries at comparable stages of modernization.

TABLE 7.13

Distribution of the Labor Force by Economic Sectors
(percent of Labor Force)

Country	Prewar			1950s			1960s		
	Manufac-turing	Agricul-ture	Services	Manufac-turing	Agricul-ture	Services	Manufac-turing	Agricul-ture	Services
USSR							36.9(1959)	38.7	14.6
Czechoslovakia	34.2(1930)	38.3('30)	7.3('30)	28.3('50)	38.0('50)	10.7('50)	33.2('61)	24.9	16.1
Poland	16.9(1931)	64.9('31)	2.2('31)	18.7('50)	57.1('50)	10.1('50)	23.3('60)	47.7	12.7
Hungary	23.1(1930)	53.0('30)	6.1('30)	--	--	--	24.3('60)	38.4	10.4
Romania	7.2(1930)	78.1('34)	5.5('30)	14.2('56)	69.6('56)	6.8('56)	19.4('66)	57.2	9.3
Bulgaria	7.7(1934)	79.9('34)	4.9('34)	15.9('56)	64.1('56)	9.8('56)	23.3('65)	44.4	11.4
Yugoslavia	11.0(1930)	78.7('30)	4.7('31)	10.6('53)	66.7('53)	6.9('53)	11.9('61)	56.9	8.7
Austria	32.7(1934)	36.6('34)	4.6('34)	40.2('51)	31.6('51)	10.0('51)	28.6('61)	22.8	18.3
Finland	16.2(1940)	57.4('40)	5.1('40)	20.6('50)	46.9('50)	11.4('50)	21.6('60)	35.5	14.8
Greece	--	--	--	15.8('51)	48.1('51)	13.6('51)	13.4('61)	53.9	12.1

Source: Yearbook of Labor Statistics, various years (Geneva: International Labor Organization).

The proportion of the labor force in the service sector for Greece (12.1) exceeded that for Bulgaria (11.4), Yugoslavia (8.7), Romania (9.3), and Hungary (10.4). Austria possessed the largest service sector (18.3) as compared to 16.1 for Czechoslovakia and 14.8 for Finland. Greece, however, had a smaller manufacturing sector (13.4) than either Romania (19.4) or Bulgaria (23.3), but higher than Yugoslavia (11.9) It should be noted, however, that the data for Greece was four to five years older than that for Romania and Bulgaria.

POSTINDUSTRIAL MODERNIZATION

The communist states of Eastern Europe, after more than two decades of development and modernization under Soviet tutelage, stand at a new threshold of development. Whether they could or could not have achieved comparable rates and levels of modernization within an alternative pattern can neither be proven nor disproven, and while their progress has been remarkable, their record of performance exceeds that of comparable and neighboring countries only in selected areas and is deficient in others. The modernization of the Central Asian Soviet Republics, in contrast, does exhibit dramatic progress as compared with adjacent countries of the Middle East and South Asia.

This differential character of the Soviet impact stems from the fact that the Soviet pattern of development is primarily a surrogate or alternative process of industrialization, whose model was the advanced capitalist states of the West, the basic industrialization of which had been completed by the time of the Russian Revolution and thus could be conceptualized and adapted for Soviet purposes. Postindustrial modernization, on the other hand, is largely a post-World War II phenomenon and remains incompleted and thus cannot be so easily conceptualized and employed as a model. Hence, modernization beyond the phase of industrialization confronts the communist regimes in both Eastern Europe and the Soviet Union with perplexing dilemmas: What should be selected from abroad as a model and be adapted, and what modernizing innovations should be generated from within?

To some degree communist elites remain victims of the original Marxist perception of developed capitalism as the highest phase of industrialization, whose innovative and developmental potential was blocked by its inner contradictions and hence was exhausted. The industrial order that capitalism had constructed was to be rescued from its constrictive fetters and employed in the cause of social justice. Socialism and communism, to the degree they can be identified in the writings of Marx and Engels, appear to be little more than the intensified horizontal development of capitalism as it existed in the 1880s, but whose productivity would be distributed equitably to benefit all humanity instead of the ruling class.

Socialism and communism, for Marx and Engels, were thus more precisely phases in the development of social justice than modes of production. The Soviet pattern of development continues to reflect this, which explains why innovation in modes of production is in short supply in the Soviet Union and Eastern Europe. The communist regimes must either concede that capitalism has continued to demonstrate vertical growth and innovative, productive vitality and has not reached its full maturation, and thus still must be mined as a developmental model, or they must continue to reject it as essentially the intensification of horizontal growth in its final stages of decay and degeneration. Concretely, communist elites must decide whether to adapt the postindustrial capitalist phase, including high consumption norms, to their own societies or create alternative forms of postindustrial modernization.

This dilemma also serves to explain their indignation and outrage at so-called theories of convergence, since at best this reflects a Western concession that while communist norms of distributive justice may be superior to those of capitalism, capitalist norms of production remain superior to those in the Soviet Union and that convergence would represent a fusion of the two.

The real test for Eastern Europe as modernized polities still lies in the future. Are they better equipped than Greece, Finland, Austria, and other comparable states to press forward with development, or must they parasitically await further development in the Soviet Union, which in turn must decide either to further imitate the modernization norms of the West or develop its own?

As far as China is concerned, Mao has already rendered his decision that the process of convergence between the Soviet Union and capitalism is already taking place. Mao has rejected the Soviet model as essentially a distorted and inferior version of capitalist bureaucratic modernization and apparently is searching for an alternative path of development by reexamining Chinese civilization as a possible source of innovation.

1. See, for example, Cyril E. Black, "Soviet Society: A Comparative View," in Prospects for Soviet Society, ed. Allen A. Kassof (New York: Praeger, 1968), pp. 14-53.
2. For the definitive treatment of this period, see Zbigniew Brzezinski, The Soviet Bloc, rev. and enlarged ed. (Cambridge, Mass.: Harvard University Press, 1967).
3. The monitor function of the Soviet Union was clearly defined by Brezhnev himself shortly after the invasion and occupation of Czechoslovakia:

> We emphatically oppose interference into the affairs of any states, violations of their sovereignty. At the same time the establishment and defense of the sovereignty of states, which have embarked upon the road of building socialism, is of particular significance for us, communists. . . . The CPSU have always advocated that each socialist country determine the specific forms of its development along the road of socialism with consideration for its specific national conditions. However, it is known, comrades, that there also are common laws governing socialist construction, a deviation from which might lead to a deviation from socialism as such. And when the internal and external forces hostile to socialism seek to revert the development of any socialist country toward the restoration of the capitalist order, when a threat to the cause of socialism in that country, a threat to the security of the socialist community, as a whole, emerges, this is no longer only a problem of the people of that country but also a common problem, concern for all socialist states.

Pravda, November 13, 1968.
4. For further explanation of this point, see Vernon V. Aspaturian, "Social Structure and Political Power in the Soviet System," in The Soviet Political System, ed. Richard Cornell (Englewood Cliffs, N.J.: Prentice-Hall, 1970), pp. 118-32.
5. For a number of political and historical reasons, the Marxist-Leninist parties in East European countries bear a variety of names. Only in Bulgaria, Czechoslovakia, and Romania is it explicitly designated a Communist Party. In Yugoslavia, it is officially a League of Communists. In three countries, the party name reflects the fact that it is

a fusion of communist and socialist parties. Thus, in Hungary, Poland, and the German Democratic Republic, the parties are named, respectively, the Hungarian Socialist Workers Party, the Polish United Workers Party, and the Socialist Unity Party. In Albania the party is called the Albanian Workers Party. The Marxist-Leninist party, while dominant in all countries, is technically the only permissible party in Albania, Hungary, Romania, and, of course, the USSR. Technically, no party at all exists in Yugoslavia, with the single massive Socialist Alliance of Working People functioning as the only electoral political organization. In the other countries, residual or vestigial forms of "bourgeois" and "peasant" parties continue to function and are in electoral alliance with the Marxist-Leninist party within an overall front organization (see below).

6. Every East European country retains a front organization that, like the residual multiparty system in some countries, is a carryover from the antifascist fronts organized during the war and converted into electoral organizations during the immediate postwar period to serve as a cover for the establishment of Soviet and communist control. In some East European countries, the front organization still reflects its original "national" or "patriotic" cover in its name, whereas in others this symbolism has been dropped in favor of "ideological" symbolism. Thus, in Czechoslovakia and East Germany, the fronts are called National Fronts; in Poland, the National Unity Front; in Bulgaria, the Fatherland Front; and in Hungary, the Patriotic Peoples Front. The name of the front in Romania was recently changed from the Front of National Unity to the Front of Socialist Unity; in Yugoslavia it is the Socialist Alliance of Working People, changed recently from the Patriotic Front of Yugoslavia; whereas in Albania it is called the Democratic Front. Organizationally, the fronts function differently in individual countries. In Yugoslavia the front is a mass organization with individual membership; in Albania and Hungary they are mass movements without the institution of membership; in Poland, Czechoslovakia, and East Germany they are primarily collective affiliations of political parties; in Romania and Bulgaria they are collective affiliations of social organizations (trade unions, youth organizations, farmers organizations, etc.). No front exists in the USSR, but something called the "bloc of Communists and non-Party Communists" is a continuous ad hoc front that materializes during election campaigns.

7. _Pravda_, February 9, 1973.

8. See Robert J. McIntyre, "The Effects of Liberalized Abortion Laws in Eastern Europe," in The Politics of Population, ed. Richard Clinton and Kenneth Godwin (New York: Heath, 1972).

8

THE IMPACT ON THE
SOVIET UNION OF THE
EAST EUROPEAN EXPERIENCE
IN MODERNIZATION
Zvi Gitelman

Soviet leaders have long held out the experience of the USSR in industrializing, spreading literacy, radically reshaping social structures, revolutionizing values and habits and mobilizing the population for political ends as a successful model to be emulated by other revolutionary and nation-building elites. Soviet patterns of modernization have been presented as not only desirable but even inevitable. Nowhere has the Soviet precedent been as relevant as in East Central Europe, and the influence of the Soviet experience on modernization in East Central Europe has been widely acknowledged by the Soviets, by Eastern Europeans, and by other students and observers of East Central Europe. Nevertheless, the pattern of modernization in East Central Europe has not been uniform and, hence, it has not strictly followed the Soviet pattern in any single case. The Soviet modernization model was applied, not always and not everywhere in the same way, to East Central Europe about 20 years after its initiation in the USSR. Of course, modernization in East Central Europe did not begin with the communist era, and so the precommunist modernization experiences of each country had a profound impact on the rate and type of development that ensued under the sponsorship of communist regimes. Paul Shoup has shown that, in contrast to the USSR, rural living standards in Eastern Europe rose faster than urban ones, that the turmoil accompanying the industrialization collectivization drives in East Central Europe was less sever

---

*The author would like to thank Professor Morris Bornstein, Ms. Sharon Wolchik, and Aleksander Zmurkiewcz for their helpful suggestions and assistance.

than that which had accompanied the Soviet drive of the 1930s, and that in some significant ways Soviet society after World War II was less developed than East Central European societies.[1]

If modernization in the East European countries had not been merely a replication of Soviet experience, and if in some ways parts of East Central Europe modernized even before the USSR did, we may be led to assume that various East Central European experiences may have had some impact on the USSR itself. Because of the close ties between East Central Europe and the USSR, processes and consequences of modernization in East Central Europe may have affected the Soviet Union. It is difficult to establish with any certainty what are the consequences of modernization in general--scholars have not agreed upon what modernization itself is--and it is especially difficult to determine whether what appear to be the consequences of certain aspects of modernization in one country will have the same form and substance in another country.[2] Without trying to trace out the consequences of modernization in each East Central European country and attempting to assess their impact on the USSR, we can view broadly the entire political, social, economic, and cultural history of East Central Europe in the past 25 years as an extended experience of modernization and try to assess what impact, if any, the East Central European experience in the last quarter century has had on the Soviet Union.

EAST EUROPEAN EXPERIENCES AS MODELS FOR THE USSR

Eastern Europe has often been viewed as a corridor through which Western influences penetrate into Russia and the Soviet Union. R. V. Burks has suggested that "Eastern Europe itself has long been recognized as a kind of ideological antechamber to the USSR. What is permitted in Eastern Europe becomes politically available, so to speak, inside the Soviet Union."[3] Elsewhere, I have tried to show that the relationship between Eastern Europe and the USSR as regards innovation and liberalization is considerably more complicated and that in some ways Eastern Europe may serve as a stimulus to the adoption of more conservative, rather than more liberal, ideas in the Soviet Union. Since the Soviet leadership would find it difficult to deny the socialist legitimacy of what is allowed in Eastern Europe, it may feel constrained to block innovation and reform in Eastern Europe in order to avoid pressures from domestic sources to allow similar changes in the USSR. Conversely, it may reject innovations in the USSR that it might otherwise have accepted were it not for the fact that adoption in the USSR might stimulate Eastern Europeans to make similar innovations. This can be destabilizing for the East Central European regimes that operate in the context of less-well-socialized and less-politically reliable populations. Furthermore, the process of innovation or idea diffusion from Eastern Europe to the USSR is an intricate one, with the nature of the innovation, its sponsor in Eastern Europe its Soviet "linkage agent," and other factors determining the ultimate fate of an idea or reform generated in Eastern Europe and brought to the attention of the Soviet Union.[4]

By and large, I would suggest, the actual East Central European experience in modernization has had little impact on the Soviet Union in the sense that the Soviets have seen little of relevance to their own system in the problems encountered by Eastern Europeans and in attempted solutions. As I shall argue later, it is not the experience as such but the fact itself of East Central European modernization that has had an influence on Soviet ideology, foreign policy, behavior within the communist camp, and perhaps even in some sense on Soviet domestic policy as well.

There are several reasons for the irrelevance, or in some cases marginal relevance, of the East Central European modernization experiences to the Soviet Union. Shoup states that "Eastern Europe is, if anything, a model for the development of the Soviet Union," but he himself shows that once the USSR embarked on collectivization, "parallel problems and parallel responses to modernization in Eastern Europe and the Soviet Union" ended.[5] The point is that by the time the East European states began to modernize in ways acceptable and relevant to the USSR, the latter had already established its own pattern of modernization and Stalin had elevated it to the status of a universal law of development, so it was not easily amended or revised. The chronological primacy of the Soviet Union also involved its assertion of ideological primacy. As Vernon Aspaturian remarks, "There is . . . something absolute and irrevocable about chronological primacy. . . . As the first party-state, the Soviet Union will continue to be the inspiration, direct or indirect, of all future Communist states, just as it survives as the common genealogical ancestor of all existing party-states."[6] The long and lonely existence of the USSR as the only socialist state in the world before World War II and its ability to survive foreign and domestic threats to its existence have not unnaturally reinforced Soviet belief in the viability of the system and its ideological primacy. Domestic and international success over the long term have convinced the Soviet leaders that they have little to learn

from other socialist systems.[7] When confronted by the same
crisis of de-Stalinization, the Soviet system remained on an
even keel, whereas some of the East European regimes nearly
went under and had to be bailed out by the USSR. The Soviet
system has survived a collectivization campaign more traumatic and destabilizing than that experienced by those East
Central European countries that have collectivized (and some
of them proved too weak to even make the attempt). The Soviet system survived war and occupation, economic crisis,
and purges of gargantuan dimensions. Today,

> there is more "slack" in the Soviet system
> than in many of the East European ones be-
> cause a longer and more effective sociali-
> zation process, undoubted Soviet power and
> prestige resulting from impressive domestic
> and foreign achievements, and the isolation
> of the population from external influences
> have provided the USSR with a greater reser-
> voir of legitimacy than most other socialist
> countries in Europe.[8]

Even if the Soviet Union saw the East Central European
countries on a par with it, which it does not, learning from
the experience of others is not a process easily engaged in.
The literature on the diffusion of innovations is replete
with examples of how resistant individuals and institutions
are to learning from the examples of others. These examples
need not be detailed here,[9] and it is sufficient to emphasize that a state that sees itself as a superpower--and is
far larger geographically and more powerful politically,
economically, and militarily--is unlikely to look very diligently to the experience of lesser powers, especially if
they happen to be client states, for inspiration and for
models.

Finally, East European experiences have not served as
models for the Soviets to emulate because there are important objective differences between the USSR and the East
European countries. Aside from the chronological differences in development, there are differences in size, both of
territory and of population, that make certain East European
models nontransferable to the USSR. It is one thing to implement a major economic reform in a small country such as
Hungary with a different type of economy and different kind
of economic bureaucracy; it is something else to try to design and implement a similar reform for the USSR. The
Czechoslovak political culture establishes a subjective environment for politics quite different from that created by

Russian and Soviet culture. The kinds of concerns and priorities that engage the attention of a superpower are dramatically different from those that occupy the leaders of Romania or Bulgaria. A multiethnic and vast state may have to deal with political and cultural problems in quite another way from an ethnically homogeneous, smaller country. The modernization of some of the East European economies has brought them to the point where they find it necessary to trade with the West if they are to sustain their growth rates, whereas the Soviet Union has been less pressured to do likewise, and foreign trade is a far less important factor in the Soviet economy than in the Polish, Czechoslovak, Hungarian, or other East European economies.

In sum, the problems of modernization and its consequences are somewhat different in most of the East European countries from what they are in the USSR. For this reason, among others, Eastern Europe cannot serve as a model for the Soviet Union. For subjective reasons, the USSR does not see itself as learning from Eastern Europe; for objective reasons it can do so only in limited ways. East European innovations are sometimes adopted in the USSR and do serve as inputs to internal Soviet policy debates, but these lead to incremental and limited, not systemic and large-scale, changes in the USSR. In fact, at various times the USSR has reduced the flow of influence from other socialist countries by placing them outside the socialist camp and thus rendering them illegitimate as sources of reform (Yugoslavia); it has actively intervened to reverse innovative trends in East Central Europe, trends that threatened to spill over into the USSR itself (Hungary, Poland, Czechoslovakia); and it has severely criticized reformist groups and individuals in East Central Europe, thereby signalling its unwillingness to import their ideas. The USSR has served as a model for Eastern Europe, especially during the initial stages of modernization, but there is little reason to believe that in later periods the roles of Eastern Europe and the USSR have been--or, indeed, will be--reversed.

BEING AND BECOMING MODERNIZED: THE IMPACT ON THE USSR

If the process of becoming modernized in East Central Europe has had relatively little impact on the USSR, the fact of being modernized has made more of a difference. The Soviet Union has not looked to the East Central European modernization experiences for models and instructive lessons that might apply to its own situation, but the existence of a socialist East Central Europe and the fact that this area has undergone a series of intensive modernization experiences under a socialist aegis have made a difference to Soviet domestic politics as well.

The modernization of a bloc of countries associated with the USSR could have redounded to the latter's benefit in many ways. In actual fact, the Soviet Union made certain choices about the kinds of modernization it would tolerate in East Central Europe, which limited the benefits it gained, though they remain impressive. Economic, cultural, political, and military modernization of East Central Europe would have increased the overall strength and prestige of what had become the socialist camp as it became increasingly drawn into a confrontation with the "capitalist camp." A modernized East Central Europe could have served as a source of technology, innovations, and institutional reforms for the Soviet Union. The achievement of economic self-sufficiency in East Central Europe would have freed the USSR from the need to aid these economies, which it would have to do for client states especially since economic difficulties would soon become political ones. The achievement of political stability in East Central Europe would reduce the need for a Soviet military presence and would at the same time allow the Eastern Europeans to make a real contribution to the perceived defense needs of the USSR vis-à-vis the West. Successful modernization in East Central Europe would reconfirm the correctness and efficacy of Marxist-Leninist ideology and of Stalinist development strategies. Furthermore, East Central Europe, which in the interwar period had many of the characteristics common to what came to be recognized after 1945 as the underdeveloped countries, could serve as a relevant model of rapid, successful development for the emerging states of Africa and Asia and could therefore aid in the dissemination of the socialist revolution the world over. The more developed socialist countries, and Czechoslovakia in particular, could even serve as developmental models for some of the Central and West European states that were emerging from the chaos of World War II and were seeking ways of rehabilitating themselves economically and restructuring themselves politically.

Only some of these benefits were reaped by the USSR. This was partly due to the fact that Stalin made some choices that precluded the realization of some of the benefits and partly to Soviet disinterest in achieving other potential benefits. Stalin had explained to the Yugoslavs that "this war is not as in the past; whoever occupies a territory also imposes on it his own social system. Everyone imposes his own system as far as his army can reach. It cannot be otherwise."[10] As the Yugoslavs were to find out, Stalin meant this literally and expected the East Central European states to emulate the Soviet model without trying to search for modernization strategies that might have been more efficient in their particular national settings. When confronted with a choice between strict Soviet control and allowing the Eastern Europeans to strike out on their own in attempts to find better means than those provided by the Soviet model for economic and political development, Stalin consistently opted for Soviet control. Indeed, his successors have done the same, though they have been less insistent on emulating the lesser details of the Soviet model. As the Czechoslovaks learned in 1968, the present Soviet leadership is more interested in adherence to the Soviet version of socialism, whatever its political and economic shortcomings when applied elsewhere, than in the development of a successful but non-Soviet variant of socialism. For Stalin, control was even more important than for his heirs. "The crucial operative aim for Stalin was <u>control</u>. . . . The operative aim, implicit in all that Stalin did, was to get control by every available means, the principal one being police terror."[11] Paul Shoup has pointed out that there were really two interpretations of the concept of "Peoples' Democracy," one advanced before 1948 and the other announced after that date. The earlier

> view suggested that conditions in Eastern
> Europe precluded simple imitation of Soviet
> development, [whereas] by comparison, the
> post-1948 "narrow" interpretation of Peoples'
> Democracy left the satellites with little
> room for independent development. . . . So-
> viet socialism could be duplicated in each
> Communist state. . . . The pattern of devel-
> opment which was to lead to a world Communist
> state was therefore unique. It was not inte-
> grative so much as it was reproductive.[12]

If control had a higher priority than development, and if modernization was to be promoted only as long as it could be controlled by the Soviet Union, it follows that some of the potential benefits mentioned earlier could not be realized. Eastern Europe could not easily become a source of technological innovation, institutional reform, and political dynamism for the USSR since these would imply experimentation and departures from the relevant Soviet precedents. Forcing East European systems into Soviet molds also meant that economic self-sufficiency and political stability could not be achieved easily, for the Soviet forms proved to be constricting and distorting. Political instability and economic crisis in East Germany, Poland, Hungary, and Czechoslovakia forced the USSR to intervene with economic, political, and sometimes military means. This meant not only that Eastern Europe was not playing a useful role in the Soviet confrontation with the West, but that it was imposing an absolute burden on the USSR, which had to bail it out of its difficulties. But rather than allow the East European regimes to seek their own solutions to their own problems, even if this might involve a search for alternatives to Soviet models, the Soviets have preferred to maintain control and sacrifice possible, though by no means guaranteed, success.

The priority given to control was complemented by the limited aspirations that Stalin had for East Central Europe in terms of the role it would play in the world historical process, at least in the short run. That is, the Soviet Union did not benefit from East European modernization in some of the ways that it might have because it was not really interested in those benefits. For Stalin the importance of East Central Europe lay in the added security that a buffer zone, controlled by the USSR, would provide. Stalin, never one to be overly concerned with the world revolution and content to build socialism in one country for a rather long time, was not interested in the "demonstration effect" East Central Europe might have on developing countries. Therefore, he was not so much concerned with the successful and rapid modernization of these countries as he was in establishing the kind of control over them that would secure their role as a vital part of the Soviet defense perimeter. In an interview with a _Pravda_ correspondent in 1946, Stalin maintained that the USSR's war losses justified the attempts to insure that the East Central European countries "should have governments whose relations to the USSR are loyal" since the Germans had struck at the USSR through those countries and were able to do so "owing to the fact that these countries had governments hostile to the Soviet Union."[13] The only way the USSR could be sure that a revanchist Germany or a hostile West could not easily march through East Central Europe on the way to attacking the Soviet heartland was to have the USSR exercise total control over these countries. The kind of friendly relations a Benes government (in Czechoslovakia) was prepared to have with the USSR was insufficient; direct and total control would be necessary. East Central Europe would provide a land buffer against invasion, would move Soviet air defenses forward, and would allow the Soviets to mount a credible threat against Western

Europe, a move seen as the only possible deterrent to an American nuclear attack at a time when the Soviets had not yet developed a nuclear capability.

As it turned out, Eastern Europe was used by the Soviets as a functional equivalent of the Marshall Plan: The economic exploitation of East Central Europe contributed substantially to the Soviet recovery effort. The presence of controllable allies in international organizations such as the United Nations and various international commissions strengthened the Soviet position in international affairs, and the Eastern Europeans were made to contribute to Soviet foreign policy efforts, whether in the form of Polish and Czechoslovak armaments supplied to the Korean front or the later use of Czechoslovakia as a Soviet stalking horse in Africa and the Middle East. But the primary use of East Central Europe in Stalin's eyes was to strengthen the USSR's defensive, antiimperialist posture in the immediate postwar era.

A secondary, and related, function performed simply by the existence of socialist states in East Central Europe was to confirm Soviet ideology and the Soviet scheme for modernization. This theme runs through some Soviet statements about East Central Europe during the Stalin era and it becomes even more prominent later on. The advent of socialism in East Central Europe confirmed and reinforced the validity of the process by which socialism is achieved, a process first undergone in the Soviet Union. The key elements in this process are said to be: (1) the leading role of the working class that, in order to be successful, must be led by a Marxist-Leninist party; (2) the stubborn resistance of the capitalist class; and (3) the necessity for the dictatorship of the proletariat to fight not only against internal enemies but also against "world reaction" in order to secure the internal conditions favorable to the transition to socialism.[14] Furthermore, "the superiority of socialism over capitalism was now revealed in the framework of the entire world socialist system."[15] More specifically, the East European experience in industrialization, following the pattern of successful industrialization in the USSR, is said to prove that there are basic laws (zakonomernosti) of industrialization that hold true in different national contexts.[16]

In the post-Stalinist period a new theme has emerged regarding the historical relevance of East Central Europe's transformation into a socialist camp. Until 1953, when the two-camp concept of the world predominated, Zhdanov and Stalin had stressed that Yugoslavia (until 1948), Poland, Czechoslovakia, Albania, Bulgaria, Romania, and Hungary (and to some extent Finland) helped make up the "antifascist, antiimperialist camp." After the mid-1950s the accent was placed on the "world socialist system" rather than on the "antiimperialist camp." This implied a shift from the view of East Central Europe as playing a primarily defensive, somewhat passive role to one that saw the East European countries as full-fledged socialist systems playing a positive, active role in international relations. In fact, a new importance was attributed to the association of the USSR and Eastern Europe. "The formation of a world socialist system changed not only the structure of the contemporary world, but introduced basic changes in the system of international relations. . . . Alongside the capitalist system a new world appeared, a new system of governments with their own social, economic, and political structures."[17] The Soviets began to speak of "international relations of a new type" and some went so far as to claim that "the world system of socialist states serves as a model of the future united world economic system, and its very existence deepens the crisis of bourgeois ideology, making the imperialists less sure of themselves and more fearful of what the future held in store for them."[18]

Stalin had not attributed such historical importance to the formation of a socialist bloc, nor was there much talk during his rule of "international relations of a new type," at least not in the sense that his successors understood that notion. He did admonish the Yugoslavs that Soviet ambassadors were not the same as ambassadors from nonsocialist countries, and he clearly behaved as if the relations between the USSR and its East European associates were very different from those prevailing among capitalist states or between capitalist and socialist ones. But he treated intersocialist relations in effect as the relations that exist between an imperial center and its satrapies. Since 1955, Soviet leaders have attempted to redefine international socialist relations, moving from "consensus" to "cooperation" in the sense in which I. L. Horowitz uses those terms.[19] But the Soviet leadership has been hesitant and inconsistent in moving away from Stalinist notions of how the socialist camp is to be organized, and it has reverted back to them when it felt it necessary to do so, as in the invasion of Czechoslovakia. While Stalin's successors have paid lip service to the legitimacy of "multiple paths to socialism," they have appointed themselves the sole judges of what constitutes socialism and what is deviation from it. The USSR has not committed itself to a fundamental and consistently applied shift from consensual to cooperative relations with the other East European states, and this has caused uncertainty and instability in those relations. The Soviet-East Central

European relationship is becoming increasingly differentiated and is still in a state of flux. The doctrinal basis
of these relations is adjusted to meet the pragmatic needs
of the Soviet leadership, and so there is no clear guide to
the operative principles governing the relationship between
the USSR and its European allies.

EXPECTATIONS AND REALITIES

Has East Central Europe played the role expected of it
by Stalin and by his successors? In some ways East Central
Europe's existence as a socialist bloc has met Soviet expectations and in others it has disappointed them. Stalin's
vision of East Central Europe as a protective guard around
the USSR seems to have been fulfilled, though there is no
evidence that the West planned a military attack on the USSR
at any time after World War II. Nevertheless, judging by
reactions in the United States and in East Central Europe,
the ability of the Soviets to take up forward positions in
Europe was a credible military posture, and it has always
helped shape Western policy toward the USSR. The East European armies themselves, however, were clearly far less important both in Soviet strategy and in Western assessments
of the balance of power in Europe and in the world.
    Both Soviet and local armed forces in Eastern Europe
perform a dual role: They are part of the socialist bloc
defense system but they also perform internal security and
policing functions. They have not been tested in the first
role but they have been called upon to perform the second,
and they have done so with mixed results. The Hungarian and
Polish armies proved unreliable in 1956; the command of the
Czechoslovak army had to be purged in 1968-69, though the
rank and file proved passively loyal to the Warsaw Pact; the
Bulgarians experienced an attempted military coup d'état in
1965; and the equivalent of three divisions of the East German army frontier guards defected to the West before 1961.[20]
With the Bulgarian exception--and that incident seems to
have involved a relatively small number of officers--these
armies have not presented challenges to civilian (that is,
Party) control in "normal" times and, with the exception of
the Romanians, they have participated in the Warsaw Pact in
a manner that has not seemed to arouse Soviet displeasure.
Nevertheless, Thomas Wolfe suggested in 1964 that the Soviets
"may entertain some doubts" about the reliability of the East
European armed forces and they are therefore likely to plan
on meeting requirements for a European war primarily from
their own resources.[21] Polish, German, Hungarian, and

Bulgarian forces did participate in the invasion of Czecho-slovakia, but that participation was largely symbolic and these forces were withdrawn very quickly in any case. The military significance of the East Central European forces may be somewhat increased if the Mutual and Balanced Force Reduction (MBFR) negotiations result in a reduction of the Soviet military presence in East Central Europe, but this would not involve a major readjustment of Soviet strategy.

As was mentioned earlier, the Soviets have asserted that the spread of socialism to East Central Europe and the modernization of the region confirm the fundamental wisdom of Soviet ideology and modernization patterns. Nish Jamgotch has pushed this point to its extreme when he asserts that

> as an ideologically oriented great power and the first Marxist-Leninist state, the USSR must ultimately depend upon its political transplants abroad. . . . Reduced to its simplest terms, the practical interrelation-ship means . . . Soviet dependence upon system-member behavior as at least partial but last-resort confirmation for Marxist-Leninist writ, and . . . the preference by "true" allies for contemporary Soviet for-mulas . . . as necessary prerequisites for much-desired costly modernization and indus-trialization, supported by the Soviet Union's ample and impressive resources.[22]

The Soviet system has not really lost internal strength and stability as a result of problems encountered by the social-ist regimes, though Soviet dissidents and observers else-where have been impressed by the obvious shortcomings of Soviet-type modernization strategies and political-economic models as applied in East Central Europe, and they have questioned the universal validity and the fundamental sound-ness of Soviet doctrine. The Soviet system has not risen or fallen with the ones in East Central Europe, but the gener-alizability of the system has been called into question.

Just as importantly, if not more so, the mixed record of modernization in East Central Europe has deprived the so-cialist systems there of the chance to serve as models for modernization in the Third World. It is significant that, with the possible exception of Cuba, no developing country has sought to emulate in toto the modernization strategy the USSR established and that was emulated in East Central Eu-rope. Perhaps the forces of nationalism are too great for this to happen spontaneously, or perhaps Third World leaders have decided that the results of the East European experience are so mixed as to indicate that only selective and partial borrowings from their experiences are in order. It may also be that Third World elites perceive the objective domestic and international situations of the East European countries, as well as their economic and political cultural settings, as significantly different from their own, thus making it impossible to follow consistently East Central European or Soviet precedents. In 1968, the Czechoslovaks hinted that they were developing a variant of socialism suited particularly to developed economies and polities, but the Soviets crushed the notion that a non-Soviet variant model could be legitimate in East Central Europe or beyond.

So the modernization of East Central Europe has served neither to alter significantly the Soviet model of modernization itself nor has it enhanced the appeal of Soviet-type modernization outside East Central Europe. This is not to say that modernization, by anyone's definition, has not been achieved in East Central Europe; it has been achieved to a greater or lesser extent by the various countries. East Germany and Bulgaria have been particularly successful in combining economic growth with political stability (East Germany after 1961); Poland and Czechoslovakia have had rather poor records of economic development and spotty records of political development; whatever successes Yugoslavia and Albania have enjoyed, they have gained despite, rather than because of, the USSR; Hungary's record until 1956 was a disastrous one, but since then the Hungarians have combined impressive economic growth with political stability, if not dynamism. Perhaps of all the countries in Eastern Europe, Romania would be the Soviet-type system most appealing to the Third World. It combines relatively high growth rates in what was one of the most backward countries in the area, the ability to introduce industry into a hitherto agrarian state, success in maintaining authoritarian rule over an extended period of time, and, uniquely, the ability to accomplish all this while remaining relatively free of foreign domination and colonial-type rule. Still, as far as can be seen at present, the Romanian internal modernization strategy has not had much impact on the Third World.

The claims (or hopes) of having developed a substantially new type of international relations, which would serve as a prototype of all future international relations, have not been substantiated. The Soviet leadership has not been able to break decisively with Stalinist modes of inter-socialist relations, though it has moved a good distance away from them. International relations among the socialist states in Europe have been marked by many of the same phenomena that characterize nonsocialist international relations: economic disputes, military invasions, differences over foreign policies, charges of interference in another country's internal affairs, seeking allies outside the nominal alliance, ruptures in relations and reconciliations. Even leaving aside the tempestuous history of Sino-Soviet relations, it is clear, as Zbigniew Brzezinski pointed out, that ideologically allied states may often have sharper conflicts with each other than countries that do not have a common ideology, since ideology and doctrine themselves become points of dispute and add a dimension to disputes around other kinds of issues.[23] As long as the real nature of relations among socialist states remains undefined in any stable way--and that definition must come about by practice rather than in theory--it will remain impossible to accept the notion that intersocialist relations are radically different from international relations in general. William Zimmerman has suggested that the Soviet-East European area be viewed as a "hierarchical regional system" and that other such systems exist (as, for example, in the Western Hemisphere) with similar kinds of behavior--what Zimmerman calls "the politics of system boundaries"--exhibited within them.[24] Clearly, the Soviet Union has benefited greatly by virtue of its position as a regional hegemony, but, as Zimmerman shows, lesser units in the system can also derive benefits from the arrangement and can even in some sense "exploit" the hegemony that must accede to certain pressures placed on it by putative clients in order to preserve the overall relationship. In any case, that kind of relationship is not unique to socialist countries and it falls short of the characteristics attributed to the "new type of international relations" that is said to prevail in the socialist camp.

There is general agreement that the Soviets took full advantage of Eastern Europe's economic assets in the late 1940s and early 1950s in order to reconstruct their economy and that this involved an exploitation of the Eastern Europeans who benefited little, if anything, in the short run from their association with the USSR. Eastern Europe is still important to the USSR as a source of supplies and machinery and as a market for Soviet exports. The Soviets and the Eastern Europeans trade more with each other than they do with any other group of countries. But the economic relationships between the USSR and Eastern Europe have moved to the point where it is impossible to speak of Soviet exploitation of the region. In fact, the question may be _kto-kogo_, who is exploiting whom? When the Hungarian, Polish, and Czechoslovak economies got into serious trouble, the

USSR came to their rescue with large amounts of credits, loans, and other forms of aid. From 1955 to 1965 the Soviet Union delivered approximately $1.3 billion of aid to East European countries, with Bulgaria, Poland, Romania, and Hungary the chief recipients.[25] In 1957, shortly after the Hungarian revolution, the USSR provided large amounts of outright aid and a long-term loan to the struggling Kadar regime, in addition to deferring "for a long period" Hungarian debts to the USSR and freeing the Hungarians from paying nearly a billion dollars to the USSR in connection with German property transferred to Hungary and the Soviet share of the former joint holding companies.[26] Following the invasion of Czechoslovakia in 1968, the USSR seems to have assisted the Czechoslovak economy in significant ways so that political discontent could be assuaged by consumer satisfaction.[27] Similarly, the Gierek regime in Poland received emergency aid in early 1971 to help satisfy the economic demands of the disgruntled working class.[28]

This is the price the USSR has had to pay to maintain the economic and political viability of its client states, much as it has had to subsidize the Cuban economy in order to keep the Cubans alive and in the fold. Members of Comecon are insulated from world market prices and can market goods within Eastern Europe that would probably not be marketable in Western Europe or North America. Moreover, the Soviet Union must supply Eastern Europe with raw materials such as crude oil that would bring substantially higher prices on the lucrative world market.[29] As the exchange between Horst Menderhausen and Franklyn Holzman illustrates, the economists cannot agree on whether Eastern Europe is indeed "exploiting" the USSR, but the fact that this is an open question means that the East European-Soviet economic relationship is not unequivocally to the advantage of the Soviet Union.[30] If the East European economies continue to run into trouble and the USSR is called upon to bail them out, the USSR will find Eastern Europe a growing burden rather than an economic advantage.

Politically, Eastern Europe has been a mixed blessing to the USSR. The existence of socialist systems in the area has increased the size, and hence the prestige and quantitative power, of the socialist camp led by the Soviet Union, but the political instability of the area, which results partially from the consequences of its modernization, has imposed on the USSR the role of policeman, intervening to maintain and restore law and order as the Soviets define it. Soviet interventions of this type have demonstrated to the world that East European regimes have encountered profound political problems and that they have not been able to solve them with their own resources. When they have attempted to do so by searching for alternatives to the Soviet model, the Soviet leadership has ruled such attempts inadmissable and has been willing to lose international prestige and pay political and economic costs in order to maintain control and conformity. The Soviet model was transplanted to the East European countries, but in some instances the transplant has been partially rejected by the body politic and several operations have been required to restore the patient to reasonably good health and to allow minimal functioning of the system.

The Bolshevik preference for consciousness over spontaneity has been translated into an insistence on control at the price of economic and political success. Just as the Soviet regime has consistently emphasized controlled rather than spontaneous activity at home (as in the case of youth in Tashkent who were doing civic good on their own but not under the aegis of the Komsomol and so came under suspicion), so has it consistently opted for control, by local parties and by the USSR, rather than the free and possibly beneficial--even by Soviet standards--search for alternatives. The benefits of control are obvious: a standardization of communist strategies of modernization, reliability of the East European states in international affairs, close political, military, and economic cooperation. The security and economic benefits of the Soviet Union derives from Eastern Europe are not clear cut. Opting for control has cost the USSR a source of innovation in many fields and has precluded the possibility that Eastern Europe would serve as a developmental model for other countries, whether underdeveloped, developing, or developed.

But even if the costs of association with Eastern Europe along present lines become very high in economic and political terms, the costs of dissociation might well be higher. The Soviets would stand to lose not only clients and reliable allies but prestige, ideological self-confidence, and standing in the world communist movement. As Alexander Dallin said 15 years ago, "Moscow must hold on to the satellite sphere even if it hurts. Even if Soviet economic and military expenditures there exceed the material benefits, Moscow must stand fast."[31] While the Hungarian declaration of neutrality in 1956 presented the USSR with an intolerable movement away from the socialist camp, the Czechoslovaks presented them with a more ambiguous situation in 1968. But the Soviet leadership, after much hesitation, ultimately chose the reassertion of control over permitting an experiment that might have strengthened socialism in Czechoslovakia and beyond, but at the same time might have weakened the appeal and the claims of Soviet socialism outside the USSR and even within it. The Soviet Union has consistently placed a higher priority on its role as a regional hegemony than on its self-asserted role as the leader of a historical movement that transcends national and regional boundaries. The primary function of Eastern Europe in the Soviet vision of the world is defined in regional an immediate terms rather than in global and long-range ones.

NOTES

1. Paul Shoup, "Eastern Europe and the Soviet Union: Convergence and Divergence in Historical Perspective," in Soviet Society and Politics in the 1970s, ed. Henry W. Morton and Rudolf L. Tokes (New York: Free Press, 1974), pp. 340-68.

2. For a penetrating critique of attempts to apply developmental notions to communist politics, see William Taubman, "The Change to Change in Communist Systems: Modernization, Post-Modernization and Soviet Politics," paper presented to the American Political Science Association Annual Meeting, September 1972.

3. Richard V. Burks, "Technological Innovation and Political Change in Communist Eastern Europe," RAND Memorandum RM-6051-PR. (Santa Monica, Calif., 1969), p. 59.

4. For an elaboration of this, see Zvi Gitelman, The Diffusion of Political Innovation: From Eastern Europe to the Soviet Union, Comparative Politics Series, Vol. III, no. 27 (Beverly Hills, Calif.: Sage Publications, 1972).

5. Shoup, op. cit., p. 20.

6. Vernon V. Aspaturian, The Soviet Union in the World Communist System (Stanford, Calif.: Hoover Institution Press, 1966), p. 84.

7. See Gitelman, op. cit., pp. 26-27.

8. Ibid., p. 23.

9. For an elaboration, see ibid., pp. 12-18.

10. Milovan Djilas, Conversations With Stalin (New York: Harcourt, Brace, 1962), p. 114.

11. Robert C. Tucker, "The Psychology of Soviet Foreign Policy," in Soviet Conduct in World Affairs, ed. Alexander Dallin (New York: Columbia University Press, 1960), pp. 230-31. See also W. W. Rostow, The Dynamics of Soviet Society (New York: Norton, 1952), pp. 148-52.

12. Paul Shoup, "Communism, Nationalism and the Growth of the Communist Community of Nations After World War II," American Political Science Review 56, no. 3 (September 1962): 890 and 892.

13. "Otvet Korrespondentu 'Pravdy,'" Pravda, March 14, 1946. Cited from Robert McNeal, ed., I. V. Stalin, Sochineniia (Stanford, Calif.: Hoover Institution, 1967), vol. III (XVI).

14. See Sh. P. Sanakoev, Mirovaia sistema sotsializma (Moscow, 1968), p. 44.

15. M. E. Airapetian and G. A. Deborin, Etapy Vneshnei Politiki SSSR (Moscow, 1958), p. 44.

16. Institut Ekonomiki, Academiia Nauk SSSR, Sotsialisticheskaia industrializatsiia stran narodnoi demokratii (Moscow, 1960), p. 8.

17. Sanakoev, op. cit., p. 68.

18. Ibid., pp. 68-69.

19. For an elaboration, see Gitelman, op. cit., p. 9, and Kenneth Jowitt, "The Romanian Communist Party and The World Socialist System: A Re-definition of Unity," World Politics 23, no. 1 (October 1970).

20. The latter figure is based on Raymond Garthoff, Soviet Military Policy (New York: Praeger, 1966), p. 153.

21. Thomas W. Wolfe, Soviet Strategy at the Crossroads (Cambridge, Mass.: Harvard University Press, 1964), p. 216.

22. Nish Jamgotch, Jr., Soviet-East European Dialogue: International Relations of a New Type? (Stanford, Calif.: Hoover Institution Press, 1968), pp. 108-11.

23. Zbigniew Brzezinski, "Deviation Control: A Study in the Dynamics of Doctrinal Conflict," American Political Science Review 56, no. 1 (March 1962): 6.

24. William Zimmerman, "Hierarchical Regional Systems and the Politics of System Boundaries," International Organization 26, no. 1 (Winter 1972).

25. Calculated from Marshall I. Goldman, Soviet Foreign Aid (New York: Praeger, 1967), p. 28.

26. See New York Times, January 3, March 29, December 19, and December 25, 1957.

27. See New York Times, September 11, November 21, and December 23, 1968; February 8, October 21, and October 29, 1969.

28. Radio Free Europe, "Soviet Reactions to Polish Situation-I," February 1, 1971; Neue Zurcher Zeitung, February 28, 1971; and New York Times, February 16, 1971.

29. See Felix Kessler, "Will Success Spoil . . .?," Wall Street Journal, February 22, 1973.

30. See Horst Menderhausen, "Terms of Trade between the Soviet Union and Smaller Communist Countries, 1955-1957," Review of Economics and Statistics 41, no. 2 (1959); "The Terms of Soviet-Satellite Trade: A Broadened Analysis," Review of Economics and Statistics 42, no. 2 (1960); "Mutual Price Discrimination in Soviet Bloc Trade," Review of Eco-

nomics and Statistics 44, no. 4 (1962); and Franklyn Holzma
"Soviet Foreign Trade Pricing and the Question of Discrimir
tion: A 'Customs Union' Approach," Review of Economics and
Statistics 44, no. 2 (1962); and "Soviet Bloc Mutual Price
Discrimination," Review of Economics and Statistics 44, no.
4 (1962). See also Jan Michal, "Czechoslovakia's Foreign
Trade," Slavic Review 27, no. 2 (1968); Laszlo Zsoldos, The
Economic Integration of Hungary into The Soviet Bloc (Colum
bus: Ohio University Press, 1963); John Hardt, "East European Economic Development: Two Decades of Interrelationshi
and Interactions with The Soviet Union," Economic Developme
in Countries of Eastern Europe, U.S. Congress, Joint Econom
Committee (Washington, D.C., 1970), pp. 5-40.

31. Alexander Dallin, "The Soviet Stake in Eastern Eu
rope," Annals of the American Academy of Political and Social Science 317 (May 1958): 145.

CHAPTER

9

**MODERNIZING
INTERACTION WITHIN
EASTERN EUROPE**
Roger E. Kanet

During the past quarter century the communist countries
of Eastern Europe have undergone a process of major socioeconomic change that can well be referred to as modernization. At the end of World War II, with the exception of the
Czech lands and the area that became the German Democratic
Republic, the countries that came under communist control
were composed largely of agricultural societies that had not
yet entered the stage of "modern" industrialization and urbanization. For example, in 1950, 54 percent of the population of Poland was engaged in agriculture and 40 percent of
the national income was derived from agricultural activities.
Twenty years later the corresponding figures were 37 percent
and 13 percent (see Tables 9.1 and 9.2).

By 1970 all of the countries of Eastern Europe had made
significant gains on all of the indexes usually employed to
measure modernization, including education, industrialization, urbanization, medical care, etc. (See Tables 9.3-9.5;
see also the tables in Chapter 7.) In the following pages
an attempt will be made to examine the interrelationship of
the processes of modernization among the East European countries, with special emphasis on the impact that political
and economic innovations in one country have on the process
of innovation elsewhere. The title of the chapter is based

The author wishes to express his appreciation to the
Research Institute on Communist Affairs and the Russian In-
stitute of Columbia University, and in particular to Jane
Leftwich, for assistance in preparing this chapter. In ad-
dition, he is indebted to the American Council of Learned
Societies for financial support.

TABLE 9.1

Distribution of Labor Force in Eastern Europe by Economic Sector, 1950, 1960, and 1970
(in percent of total labor force)

	Bulgaria	Czechoslovakia	East Germany	Hungary	Poland	Romania
1950						
Manufacturing and construction	11.4	36.3	43.7	23.3	26.2	14.2
Agriculture and forestry	79.5	38.6	27.3	50.6	54.0	74.3
Transport	1.8	5.2	6.0	4.2	4.4	2.4
Trade	2.3	8.6	8.3	5.5	5.3	2.5
Services	5.0	11.3	14.4	16.4	8.6	6.4
1960						
Manufacturing and construction	27.1	45.6	48.3	34.0	32.2	20.0
Agriculture and forestry	55.5	25.9	17.3	38.9	44.2	65.6
Transport	4.1	6.1	7.1	6.2	5.3	3.1
Trade	4.1	8.2	11.6	6.6	6.0	3.4
Services	9.2	14.2	15.3	14.3	10.2	7.6
1970						
Manufacturing and construction	38.8	46.2	49.8	43.7	35.0	30.8
Agriculture and forestry	35.8	18.3	13.0	26.2	37.3	49.3
Transport	5.7	6.8	7.2	6.8	5.7	4.8
Trade	6.1	9.6	10.9	8.1	5.8	4.3
Services	13.4	19.1	18.8	15.2	11.9	10.2

Source: SEV, Sekretariat, Statisticheskii Ezhegodnik Stran-Chelnov Soveta
Vzaimopomoshchi 1971 (Moscow: SEV, 1971), pp. 377-80.

on several assumptions that should be made explicit at the very outset: (1) it assumes that communist sociopolitical systems have not been static but, rather, that they have been involved in a process of socioeconomic change that can be called modernization; and (2) it assumes that developments within one East European country can have and have had an impact on developments within other countries.

During the last decade increasing numbers of students of the communist political systems have argued that the original models employed in the analysis of the Soviet Union and Eastern Europe--in particular the model of totalitarianism-- have hindered rather than assisted our understanding of the underlying social, economic, and political processes at work in the area, at least since the death of Stalin. In place of the totalitarian model, they have offered a variety of alternative approaches to the study of communist politics, ranging from the application of models of political development that view the communist political system as a variant form of modernization to the argument that the communist system can best be understood as a form of bureaucratic politics.[1] These efforts have often, however, suffered from the failure of their authors to provide precise definitions of the major terms they employ or from the assumption that terms defined largely in the context of Western political systems can, with minor modifications, be adapted to the analysis of communist political systems. Some efforts at a more careful delineation of terms for their use in the context of Eastern Europe have resulted in rather tortured exercises in semantics.[2]

John Kautsky was one of the first Western scholars to argue that communism could be best viewed as a form of developmental politics (as a method of achieving modernization) and that the tripartite division of political systems, usually employed by American scholars, into "developed," "developing or underdeveloped," and "communist," had obscured many of the similarities between communist and "developing" countries.[3] Kautsky's work, however, deals primarily with the period of power seizure and consolidation by leftist modernizing intellectuals and provides little detail for later periods. In addition, his substantive studies concern the countries of Asia and Africa and not Eastern Europe.[4] A few other scholars have attempted to apply a developmental approach to the analysis of East European countries with varying degrees of success.[5]

The present examination of the "modernizing impact" of individual East European countries on other countries in the area will attempt to initiate an analysis of a topic that, to date, has yet to receive any systematic treatment. Although

TABLE 9.2

Structure of the East European National Incomes,
1950, 1960, and 1970

Country	Industry			Construction			Agricultur	
	1950	1960	1970	1950	1960	1970	1950	1960
Bulgaria	36.8	45.6	49.1	6.6	7.1	8.7	42.1	31.5
Czecho-slovakia	62.5	63.4	62.1	8.7	10.7	11.4	16.2	14.7
East Germany	47.0	56.4	60.9	6.1	7.0	8.2	28.4[a]	16.4
Hungary	48.6	60.1	43.6	6.8	10.4	12.0	24.9	22.5
Poland	37.1	47.0	57.5	7.9	9.3	9.8	40.1	23.3
Romania	43.4	42.1	60.1	6.2	8.9	10.8	27.3	34.8

[a]Agriculture includes forestry.

[b]Figure for 1955.

many writers on East European politics have noted (usually
in a very general and passing way) the impact of a particular event or development--such as the Polish "liberalization" of 1956-57--on political developments elsewhere, no
one has made an effort to examine the general process of
"modernizing interaction" within Eastern Europe.[6] As shall
become clear below, there are a number of very valid reason
for this, not the least of which is the difficulty in obtaining the type of "hard" data necessary to deal with the
topic.

MODERNIZATION, POLITICAL DEVELOPMENT,
AND INNOVATION

I have to this point been using the terms "modernization," "political development," and "innovation" without
having defined them. Anyone familiar with the literature o
economic and political development is well aware that these
terms are used with a great variety of meanings. For the
purpose of our analysis we shall borrow from Cyril Black th
definition of modernization as "the dynamic form that the
age-old process of innovation has assumed as a result of th
explosive proliferation of knowledge in recent centuries."[7]
More specifically, the modernization process is the rapid

278

| Transport | | | Trade, etc. | | | Other | | |
1950	1960	1970	1950	1960	1970	1950	1960	1970
2.0	4.2	6.9	8.1	8.7	9.9	4.4	2.9	2.8
2.8	3.0	3.8	7.8	6.0	9.2	7.8	6.0	9.2
7.1	5.5	5.1	10.1	13.0	12.6	10.1	13.0	12.6
4.2	4.9	5.8	14.9	2.1	14.4	0.6	--	6.0
5.2[b]	5.9	6.3	7.5[b]	9.1	8.5	6.6[b]	5.4	4.8
5.8	5.2	6.4	11.6	6.2	1.1	5.7	2.8	1.5

Source: SEV, Sekretariat, Statisticheskii Ezhegodnik
Stran-Chelnov Soveta Vzaimopomoshchi 1971 (Moscow: SEV, 1971),
pp. 46-47.

political, economic, social, and intellectual change that
has resulted from the impact of industrialization and involves a great variety of interrelated changes within a society. (The concept does imply an end state that will be
realized, namely the "modern" society that is characterized
by a high level of industrialization, urbanization, etc.)
While modernization refers to a broad process of change
that affects an entire social system, political development
refers to the process by which a polity adapts to new demands placed upon it by a changing environment--whether the
demands come from the internal or external, social or material environment.[8] Most Western writers on political development have included at least four types of change in
their definitions of political development:

1. rationalization: the movement from particularism,
diffuseness, and ascription as criteria for success to universalism, specificity, and achievement. In other words, as
societies develop politically they select leaders and administrative personnel according to standardized criteria of
ability and achievement, rather than accidents of birth.
Also, as tasks become more complex, new specialized organizations and "jobs" are created to deal with them in a regu-
larized manner.

2. national integration: the development of a sense
of loyalty and commitment to the political system on the
part of its members.
3. participation: the bringing in of new groups which
have been formed by the demands of specialization, into some
form of meaningful sharing in the making and execution of
policy. This assumes the development of pluralism and com-
petitiveness within a social system.
4. distribution: the sharing of the newly produced
"wealth" of a society with a larger proportion of its members.[9]

TABLE 9.3

Birth Rates, Infant Mortality, and Doctors
in Eastern Europe, 1950 and 1970

Country	Birth Rates (per 1,000 population)		Infant Mortality before First Year (per 1,000 live births)		Doctors (per 10,000 population)	
	1950	1970	1950	1970	1950	1970
Bulgaria	25.2	16.3	94.5	27.3	9.2	22.2
Czecho- slovakia	23.3	15.9	77.7	22.1	10.1	22.9
East Germany	16.5	13.9	72.2	18.8	11.3	20.3
Hungary	20.9	14.7	85.7	35.9	10.3	22.0
Poland	30.7	16.6	111.2	36.6	4.6	19.3
Romania	26.2	21.1	116.7	49.4	9.5	14.7

Source: SEV, Sekretariat, Statisticheskii Ezhegodnik
Stran-Chelnov Soveta Vzaimopomoshchi 1971 (Moscow: SEV,
1971), pp. 8, 413.

In 1965 Samuel Huntington argued that this whole approach, which views political development largely in terms
of increased differentiation and democratization, is heavily
biased toward the Western democratic type of development and
assumes a unilinear movement toward more and more "development."[10] He provided an alternative view of political development as "the institutionalization of political organizations and procedures, . . . [which] focuses attention on
the reciprocal interaction between the on-going social processes of modernization, on the one hand, and the strength,
stability, or weakness of political structures, traditional,

transitional, or modern, on the other."[11] For Huntington, political development was the process by which a polity adapts, and institutionalizes that adaptation, to changing economic and social conditions.[12]

TABLE 9.4

Urban Populations in Eastern Europe,
1950, 1960, and 1970
(percent of total)

Country	1950	1960	1970
Bulgaria	27	38	53
Czechoslovakia	52	57	62
East Germany	71	72	74
Hungary	38	42	46
Poland	37	48	52
Romania	25	32	41

Source: SEV, Sekretariat, Statisticheskii Ezhegodnik Stran-Chelnov Soveta Vzaimopomoshchi 1971 (Moscow: SEV, 1971), p. 10.

TABLE 9.5

National Economies in Eastern Europe, 1955-70
(1952 = 100)

Country	1955	1960	1965	1970
Bulgaria	117	153	222	339
Czechoslovakia	116	140	169	207
East Germany	108	121	146	173
Hungary	121	142	179	222
Poland	112	131	156	198
Romania	125	161	223	338

Source: SEV, Sekretariat, Statisticheskii Ezhegodnik Stranchlenov Soveta Ekonomicheskoi Vzaimopomoskehi 1971 (Moscow: SEV, 1971), pp. 21-28.

Huntington's approach added to the list of characteris
tics of political development that of institutionalization,
for, according to him,

> political modernization involves the ration-
> alization of authority, the differentiation
> of structures, and the expansion of politi-
> cal participation . . . [and] involves the
> extension of political consciousness to new
> social groups and the mobilization of these
> groups into politics. Political development
> involves the creation of political institu-
> tions sufficiently adaptable, complex, auton-
> omous, and coherent to absorb and to order
> the participation of these new groups and to
> promote the social and economic change in
> the society.[13] (Emphasis added.)

Important in Huntington's conception of development is the
balance between the development of new environmental demands
placed on the political system and the creation of institutions that will be able to deal adequately with these new
demands.

Without becoming bogged down in debate on the merits of
the various approaches to a definition of political development in Eastern Europe, we shall view political development
as the process of adapting the political system created in
the Stalinist era to the demands of changes occurring within
the social and economic system, including the creation of
institutions capable of regularizing the change.[14] Finally,
I shall use the term "innovation" to mean the purposive creation and implementation of a policy or program that is institutionalized and is acknowledged to have a significant
impact on the entire economic, social, or political system.[1]

MODERNIZATION IN EASTERN EUROPE

Although we are most interested in examining the process of modernizing interaction among the nations of Eastern
Europe since 1953, it is important to understand the general
social, economic, and political environment in which this
interaction has occurred. In 1953, as a result of the imposition of the Stalinist model of forced industrialization
and centralized administration, the economic and political
systems of the East European countries were almost identical

to one another.* The period from 1945 to 1953 had been one
in which Soviet experience and institutions were forced on
the Eastern Europeans without any real consideration for local conditions, level of prior economic development, or historical tradition.[16] Even when the first move toward "liberalization" occurred during the New Course period immediately after Stalin's death, the process was initiated in Moscow
and imposed on the communist leaders in Eastern Europe.

The entire first decade of postwar Eastern Europe saw a
form of rapid socioeconomic change imposed on the societies
in which traditional elites were dispossessed and replaced
by a new group of leaders intent upon creating new, industrialized societies. The result of this process, which was
initiated by the Soviet Union, was the establishment of the
foundations of industrialized societies. However, since
this had been carried out without regard to the entire political and economic environment, the process of industrialization and collectivization, in almost dialectical fashion,
contained within itself the seeds of change.

Forced industrialization, without regard for human and
material cost, had resulted in the creation of serious economic dislocations in most of the East European countries by
1953. In addition, the emphasis placed on the expansion of
heavy industrial production had led to continued shortages
in foodstuffs, consumer goods, and housing. Also, in contrast to the ideological images of socialism and the promises made by the Communist parties during the period of
Stalinist takeover of power, the standard of living for the
vast majority of the population had not improved and in most
cases had actually decreased. A situation of rising expectations not matched by the performance of the socioeconomic
system intensified the opposition to the communist regimes
that existed in most of the countries. The challenges to
the Stalinist system that emerged soon after the Soviet dic-
tator's death--for example, the riots that broke out in East

---

*The fact that some of the political systems were fed-
eral, while others were unitary; that collectivization of
agriculture had gone further in some countries than in
others; that residual multiparty systems existed in several
of the countries does not really deny this claim, since in
all of Eastern Europe, with the exception of Yugoslavia, the
Communist Party leadership had acquired a virtually total
monopoly on decision making and the Soviet governmental system had been established.

Germany and in Czechoslovakia--gave rise to attempts to reform the entire Stalinist system, including the relationships between the East European countries and the USSR.[17]
Throughout the late 1950s, increasing authority, but still
within prescribed limitations, was granted by the Soviet
leadership to the Eastern Europeans to determine their own
domestic priorities and to deal with local problems in ways
best suited to local conditions.

Two developments in particular have resulted in a degree of differentiation within the domestic policies of the
East European countries that would have been unthinkable
only 20 years ago: (1) the reduction in direct Soviet intervention in the governance of Eastern Europe, and (2) the
very successes of the drive to modernization that have resulted in the emergence of specialist elites, the increased
complexity of the economic system, the creation of a more
educated and urban population, and other developments usually associated with modernization. These factors have con-
verged to exert pressures for the adaptation of the political (as well as the economic) system to the new realities.

Most Western commentators have argued that, of the
major tasks that any political system must perform if it is
to remain viable, the ones that the communists have performed least well relate to the functions of legitimation of
the political system, or the development of widespread popular support for both the political system and its goals.[18]
In fact, an examination of most of the economic and political innovations introduced in Eastern Europe since the mid-
1950s (as well as those discussed but not implemented) indicates that they are related in some way to the question of
popular participation and consumer satisfaction as a means
to reduce popular hostility to the political system (and to
the regime) and to create the foundations of positive loyalty.[19]

In the following pages we shall describe briefly a number of efforts at economic and political innovation that
have been discussed or implemented in Eastern Europe and
shall attempt to indicate how they are related to the process of modernization, defined broadly, and to political development, viewed as the institutionalization of procedures
to cope more effectively with social and economic change
(which has been partially the result of past governmental
policies), as well as the development of methods to expand
the system of elite selection and expanded participation in
decision making.

Economic Reform

The most widespread and persistent efforts at innovation within Eastern Europe over the past 20 years have dealt

with the economies of the Comecon countries. Stalin had left a legacy of centrally controlled economies based on planning and a strong emphasis on investment, especially in heavy industry. Already by 1953 it had become clear that this system, although it had largely succeeded in providing the foundations for industrialization, was not readily adaptable to the demands of an increasingly complex economy. Since the mid-1950s, and with even greater urgency since the mid-1960s, the Eastern Europeans have been discussing and experimenting with a number of forms of economic reform. All of the early attempts at economic reform included a retreat from Stalinist capital-investment policy. The New Course introduced in Hungary in 1953 by Imre Nagy, for example, included (1) price reductions and wage increases, (2) an amelioration of the demands for agricultural deliveries made on peasants and a reduction of emphasis on forced collectivization, and (3) a significant reduction in the use of terror and greater tolerance of religious deviation.[20]

Soon, however, discussions of much more sweeping economic reform began, including the reduction of the role of central planning and a corresponding increase in the authority of enterprises to make decisions concerning purchases, investments, etc. These discussions have continued until the present and in several countries, most notably in Hungary, the decentralization of economic decision making has moved quite rapidly.[21]

The major purpose of the economic reforms discussed and introduced in the countries of Eastern Europe has been to overcome the inefficiencies of the economic system that was created in the first years of forced industrialization. Economic reform is supposed to help solve the problems of "stagnation" that resulted from the overconcentration of decision-making power and the overemphasis on investments in heavy industry. It is related to the desire to increase the capacity of the economic system to provide adequate material goods for the use of its members. In addition, since most of the reforms initiated in Eastern Europe call for some type of decentralization of economic decision making, they can be viewed as an attempt to broaden the decision-making procedures within the societies.

Political Reform

Efforts to adapt the political systems of several of the countries to the changing realities of both the domestic and international political situation have been closely related to the rather widespread efforts aimed at reforming the economic systems of East European communist countries.[22] In the mid-1950s, for example, the use of terror and coercion was reduced significantly as a regular means of ensuring the allegiance of the populace to government policy. More specific political reforms have included electoral reforms in Hungary and Poland that, in theory at least, are to grant citizens greater influence in the selection of political representatives. Local government administration has been changed in several countries--most recently in Poland--in order to make it more responsive to local needs.

All of these modifications can be seen as attempts on the part of the political elite to make the political system respond more effectively to the new demands placed upon it and to expand the popular base, and legitimacy, of the system itself.

INNOVATION INTERACTION IN EASTERN EUROPE

Adam Bromke has stated that "all changes in the communist world tend to reinforce themselves. Reforms in one communist country generate pressures for similar changes in the others."[23] Unfortunately the data available on the interrelationship and mutual influence for specific examples of political and economic innovation is extremely sparse--both in Western sources and in the more general East European sources--and makes the analysis of the topic extremely difficult (not to speak of the difficulty of any attempt to "prove" the contention that interaction is a crucial or even important input into the process of political and economic innovation in Eastern Europe).[24] The best that can be hoped for at present is to indicate that (1) innovation occurred in one country, (2) decision makers in a second country were aware of the innovation, and (3) innovations occurred in the second country that were similar to the original ones.

The Influence of Economic Reforms

As we have already noted, economic reform has been a major concern of most of the East European countries since the mid-1950s and has been emphasized even more during the last ten years. In discussing the reforms that were being carried out simultaneously throughout the Comecon countries, a Hungarian economist has stated:

> This is no accident, and is not the result
> of the subjective resolution and agreements
> of the socialist countries. Certainly the
> members of the Comecon exchanged and are

still exchanging their views concerning the
economic mechanism, by the recognition of
the necessity and preparation of the reforms
may be led back to results of economic scientific research which was generated in the atmosphere after the 20th Congress of the Soviet Communist Party.[25]

An examination of the reforms introduced in Hungary and
Czechoslovakia (since 1969 largely rescinded) and those proposed by some economists in Poland indicates that they are
very similar to reforms advocated in the years immediately
following the 1956 Soviet Party Congress that gave official
approbation to the idea of "different roads to socialism"
and, thus, seemed to open the way for changes in both the
political and economic systems of Eastern Europe that would
be more in line with local conditions and problems.

Although modest efforts at some type of economic reform
were attempted from 1952 to 1955,[26] the main thrust for reform came only after 1956. The first major theoretical discussion of economic reform, as well as the first reform program recommended for implementation (outside of Yugoslavia)
occurred in Poland. Andrzej Brzeski argues rather conclusively that "the theoretical rudiments of current economic
reforms had been laid, years ago, in Poland. Hardly a notion had been overlooked that has since passed into the
stock-in-trade of the diverse schools of reform monger-
ing. . . ." An incomplete list of proposals considered by
the Polish economists at that time includes:

Pricing: market-determined; selectively controlled according to sector, by levels or
limits; based on marginal cost; related to
the world market.
Profit criteria: absolute; incremental;
in relation to cost or assets.
Cost accounting: full depreciation; interest charges; rent.
Finances: retained profits; discretion-
ary bank loans; money and capital markets.
Planning: aggregate through banks and
treasury; selective for sectors; limited to
few indicators for firms; indicative; long-
term only.
Enterprise: fully autonomous; self-
financing; demand and profit oriented.[27]

The major elements of the discussion on economic reform, in
spite of the differences in recommended solutions, centered

on economic decentralization, the revival of consumption priorities, and a type of economic nationalism. As we shall see, the first two have been crucial elements of the reforms introduced in Hungary and planned for Czechoslovakia in 1968

As many Western commentators have pointed out in the past, the Yugoslav example has played a major role in influencing thinking on reform in Eastern Europe. During 1955 and 1956, for example, the Yugoslav model exercised significant attraction for those elsewhere in Eastern Europe who were attempting to eliminate both the economic and political inheritances of Stalinism. Throughout the period of economi debates in Poland in 1956-57, Polish economic periodicals published a large number of analytical studies of the Yugoslav economic system and one can assume that these articles played a role in influencing Polish views of economic reform.[28]

Besides the more technical discussions about decentralization of the economy, some Poles advocated the development of workers councils and independent labor unions as remedies against excessive bureaucratic control of the economy.[29] In 1956, ranking party officials actually went to Yugoslavia to examine the operation of workers councils in that country. On their return they were at least tolerant enough of this development to grant official approval to what the workers had already established in Poland.[30] In 1957, an economic council of experts, rather than of Party bureaucrats, was formed to prepare recommendations for the overhaul of the economic system. Their "Theses on Directions for Change in the Economic Model" called for decentralization, reliance on prices, and indicative planning.[31]

Although the recommendations of the economic council were not implemented and the movement toward reform in Poland floundered, the entire discussion of economic reform in 1956-57 has continued to exert an influence on developments over the past 15 years. In 1970, for example, Jan Glowczyk, the editor of the Polish economic journal Zycia Gospodarcze, attacked Stefan Kurowski for advocating the introduction of a market system, including competition, in Poland and noted that Kurowski was merely representing the ideas that he and others had advocated in 1956.[32] Several years earlier, W. Brus, one of the economists associated with the reform movement in Poland, noted that "ten years ago, when basically analogical changes [to those being implemented in the mid-1960s] were promoted in a particularly advanced fashion in Poland, the attitudes were sharply different and in a majority of the socialist countries a strongly critical evaluation was in evidence."[33]

The evidence seems to indicate quite clearly that these Polish economic discussions of the 1950s had a direct influence on developments in Hungary and Czechoslovakia. The parallels are very clear and, as Brzeski argues, the more recent reformers in the latter two countries "could have hardly remained oblivious to the debates in Po Prostu, Zycie Gospodarcze, and other 'fraternal' journals which in 1956 and 1957 were virtually black-market items in the communist capitals of Europe."[34] Speaking of a more recent example, the impact of Yugoslav and Polish ideas on the reform movement in Czechoslovakia, a Yugoslav philosopher has stated that

> it is clear that Sik's [the Czechoslovak
> economist associated most closely with the
> proposed reforms] ideas were influenced not
> only by Polish and Yugoslav ideas on the de-
> centralization of economic management and by
> the development of a market-tested economy
> within a socialist framework, but also by the
> deep economic and political crises in which
> Czechoslovakia found itself in the '60's.[35]

Some possible confirmation of the influence of the Yugoslav model on Czechoslovak developments might be found in the fact that during the mid-1960s, delegations were sent from Czechoslovakia to Yugoslavia to study the organization of the latter's economy and especially the role of the workers councils.[36]

Besides the question of the influence of Yugoslav and Polish reformers on later developments in Eastern Europe, there are several additional examples of the impact of economic innovations on other countries. According to a Hungarian economist, Hungarian initiatives in introducing specific innovations in the economic system--for example, a system of profit sharing in 1957, a price reform and the introduction of a technical development fund in industry in 1959, and a levy on fixed and working capital in 1964--have been adopted in other countries as well.

> These measures, mentioned by way of example,
> had an effect on the methods of [the eco-
> nomic] mechanism used in the friendly coun-
> tries as well. The interest in profit--
> though in somewhat different forms--has
> gained ground and the new system of finan-
> cing of technical development has been in-
> troduced in similar forms in almost all
> Comecon countries and the application of
> the levy on fixed and working capital can
> be considered as generally accepted.[37]

In many respects the changes implemented in the Hungarian economy since 1968 are similar to those advocated by the Poles in 1957—decentralization of decision making and an increase in the role of enterprises; the introduction of a price system "where the relative prices of products and services are roughly proportionate to the amounts of socially necessary labor embodied in them."[38] However, there is also evidence of direct Yugoslav influence on the Hungarian economic reforms. Yugoslav reports of Kadar's visit to Tito in 1966 indicated that the planned Hungarian reforms were one of the topics discussed. For example, the chief architects of the Yugoslav economic reforms were present at all of the meetings between the two leaders. Borba, in an article published on June 4, 1966, stated that Tito and Kadar had had the opportunity "to exchange views to a greater extent, concerning some specific problems in socialist construction in the two countries, such as economic reform. . . ."[39]

Workers Councils and Labor Unions

Closely related to the problem of economic reform in Eastern Europe has been the issue of the development and role of workers councils and labor unions as means of reducing the centralized bureaucratic control of the economy. It has often been noted that one of the most attractive aspects of the Yugoslav model elsewhere in Eastern Europe has been the introduction of workers' influence in the process of economic decision making through workers councils and, more recently, the labor unions. In fact, Tito himself has claimed, in a visit to Poland in 1972, that "the changes which we, especially of late, have introduced into our political and economic system have led to a further deepening of direct socialist democracy, [and] we have made our own contribution to the treasury of Marxism-Leninism by constructing the self-managing socialist society. . . ."[40]

During recent years the powers of the workers councils in Yugoslavia have been expanded significantly and the labor unions are increasingly active in defending the interests of workers, rather than in functioning as "transmission belts" in the traditional Soviet manner.[41] Elsewhere in Eastern Europe efforts have been made on several occasions to expand the role of workers in enterprise management. In both Hungary and Poland in 1956, workers councils were created by the workers themselves, not as in Yugoslavia on the initiative of the political leadership. The Soviet invasion of Hungary and the gradual "counterreform" measures introduced in Poland after 1957 eliminated these organs of workers self-management.[42]

An interesting example of the influence of the Yugoslav model of workers councils--and of the entire Yugoslav economic system--can be found in a 1963 article in the Bulgarian journal Novo Vreme in which A. Miloshevski called for the adoption of the Yugoslav economic model, including co-management of enterprises by workers councils and profit-sharing schemes.[43] The recent creation of general assemblies of workers and economic committees in Bulgarian enterprises as "collective organs of economic management of enterprises" is far from the model in Yugoslavia, however, since the director of the economic unit must be the chairman of the committee and the director is also appointed from above, not elected by the economic committee as in Yugoslavia.[44]

Recent developments in Hungary, where labor unions have been granted the authority to veto the actions of enterprise managers, thereby automatically taking an issue to an arbitration board, seem to be modeled in part on the changes that occurred earlier in Yugoslavia, although, to date, they are far more restricted.[45]

The Impact of Political Innovation

Besides the changes that have occurred within the economic system in Eastern Europe there have also been innovations and discussions of innovation in the political system proper that appear to have had influence beyond the borders of the original innovating country.[46] Many commentators on the revolutionary upheaval in Hungary in 1956 have pointed to the influence of Yugoslavia on developments there throughout 1956 (in addition to the significance of the 20th Soviet Party Congress and Khrushchev's Secret Speech) and have argued that the successful defiance of the Soviet Union by Poland encouraged those in Hungary who were seeking a revision of the existing political system and in the relationship of Hungary to the Soviet Union. In fact, the first outbreak of violence in Budapest on October 23 was triggered by a demonstration of approximately 100,000 people (in front of the statue of a Polish supporter of the 1848-49 Hungarian Revolution) to support the Polish reform movement. Twelve years later the student rebellion in Poland was apparently inspired, in part, by the progress of reforms in neighboring Czechoslovakia. Among the slogans of the students was a call for the replacement of Gomulka with a "Polish Dubcek."[47]

Other interesting examples of this type of influence of political events in one country on developments elsewhere--what Brzezinski has called "noninstitutionalized revisionism"--were the cases of Wolfgang Harich in 1956 and the impact of the 1970 Polish riots elsewhere in Eastern Europe. Harich was an East German philosopher who advocated major revision of the political and economic system in East Germany, including internal democracy, an end to collectivization, the increase of consumer goods production, freedom of thought and religion, etc. According to Harich, "personal discussions with Polish, Hungarian, and Yugoslav comrades have confirmed us in our conclusions."[48] In 1971, soon after the riots in Poland that were inspired by a gradual worsening of the standard of living and precipitated by a price rise in early December 1970, Gustav Husak of Czechoslovakia stated that the problems of the economy would be solved, "but not at the expense of the working man, at the cost of threatening his standard of living."[49] A similar reaction was evidenced in Romania where Ceausescu began speaking, virtually for the first time in his career as head of the Party, of a concern for the standard of living, the food supply, etc. In a period of 30 working days at the beginning of 1971, he visited 45 industrial and agricultural units. Finally, at the February 10-11 Plenum of the Central Committee of the Romanian Communist Party the trade unions were reorganized in order to make them more effective in representing the interests of the workers--five months earlier, at a meeting of the Central Committee of the Central Council of Trade Unions, virtually no mention of workers' problems and workers' democracy had been made.[50]

Additional institutionalized examples of political innovation in one country affecting developments in a second country are somewhat more difficult to find. There has been first of all, the general process of liberalization that characterized the mid- and late-1950s--largely at Soviet initiative--throughout all of Eastern Europe. (The influence of developments in both Yugoslavia and Poland were closely linked to the entire process of economic reform, which has already been discussed.) More specifically, there was the reduction of terror and a turn to more reliance on the norms of socialist legality. Recently two important forms of political innovation have been carried out in several of the East European countries: an expansion of the role of elected governmental organs and the reorganization of local administration. There is some evidence that developments in one country have at least been taken into consideration when changes were contemplated in a second country.

In 1957, major efforts were made in Poland to expand the role of the parliament in the decision-making process. Although the role of the Sejm (Polish parliament) was expanded from what had existed prior to 1959--legislation by decree was virtually abolished, debates on the economic plan and the bidget began to occur, and parliamentary control over administration was broadened--this expansion of parliamentary activity did not change the essential nature of the political system. The Communist Party continued to retain its commanding position within the system.[51]

Although one of the major developments in Czechoslovakia in 1968 was the revival of the parliament as a major force in Czechoslovak politics, there is little evidence that this development was influenced by prior attempts elsewhere in Eastern Europe at parliamentary reform. Rather, the prewar experience with parliamentary government seems to have been a far more important influence.

Since the late 1960s, Hungary has been gradually modifying its political system to expand the role of parliament and to provide for a broader input in the nomination and election processes. By 1970 the Hungarian parliament was playing a more important role in the determination, or at least approval, of national policy, although it still continued to be bypassed regularly on important matters (for example, most of the decrees concerning the establishment of the New Economic Mechanism were not passed by parliament).[52]

Although, aside from Yugoslavia, no other East European country has yet followed the example of Hungary in expanding the authority of representative organs, the discussions in Poland following the upheavals of December 1970 did indicate an interest in the political reforms being instituted in Hungary. For example, the commentator Z. Szeliga wrote in Polityka on May 8, 1971: "Personally, I am convinced that in the entire development of socialist democracy--not only in Hungary--the changed voting system of the Hungarian Republic inaugurates a new, important era."[53] The editor of Radio Warsaw stated on May 15, 1971 that "the consistent and creative efforts of the Hungarian Party in perfecting the system of socialist rule by the people are being followed in Poland with interest."[54]

Ever since the mid-1950s, efforts have been made in most East European countries to improve the functioning of local administrative organs. One characteristic of most of these efforts has been the attempt to expand the authority of local government and a decentralization of the system of administration in order to make administrators more responsive to local needs. In most of the East European countries in the 1960s there was a tendency to replace the very small administrative unit (the single village) with a larger basic unit comprising ten or more villages and to grant them more fiscal and administrative authority. Most recently, effective on January 1, 1973, the Poles instituted what is probably the most radical reform in local administration when

they reestablished a system of division between the executive and representative authorities in rural local administration.[55] As in the 1971 reform of local councils in Hungary, the Polish local councils will have increased functions, including the authority to make decisions on development and investment funds.[56]

SOME CONCLUDING REMARKS

The data that I have been able to muster is, at very
best, sketchy and inconclusive. The information presented
is far from adequate either to prove or disprove the hypothesis that "modernizing interaction" in Eastern Europe is
important (or even exists), even given the very minimal goal
of establishing that innovation in one country was known by
the leaders of a second country who, in turn, introduced
similar innovation.

Several points do emerge from this examination, however
even though they are by no means original. First, the pre-
ponderant role of the Soviet Union in the area is emphasized
by the data. The first attempts to innovate within Eastern
Europe during the period of the New Course were initiated or
instructions from Moscow. Only after the approval by
Khrushchev of "separate roads to socialism" and the 20th
CPSU Congress in 1956 did the East Europeans begin to innovate on their own. This attempt, however, was short-lived,
partly as the result of Soviet intervention in Hungary and
increasing pressures against revisionism, partly as the result of internal East European opposition.

Once again in the 1960s the movement toward reform and
innovation, this time primarily in the economic field, was
touched off by a Soviet initiative--in the form of the publication of the economic reform proposals of Liberman in
September 1962.[57] In the late 1960s, when the Czechoslovaks
ignored the warnings voiced with increasing insistence in
Moscow concerning the dangers that their rapid moves toward
reform were risking, the Soviets intervened militarily to
bring Czechoslovakia back to its "proper" course and announced the doctrine of limited sovereignty of communist
states, according to which the ultimate decision on political and economic innovation was to be made in Moscow.

Even the Hungarian reforms since the late 1960s, which
have gone further than any other reform movement in a communist country, with the major exception of Yugoslavia, have
been carried out with a constant eye on Soviet reactions and
a reiteration of the claim that Hungary, unlike Yugoslavia
or Czechoslovakia, is not really innovating and is definitel

not attempting to present an alternative model of socialist development that it wishes to export to other countries.[58]

In concluding his study of the impact of political innovation in Eastern Europe on the Soviet Union, Gitelman has maintained that it is likely that the East European states will continue to have to innovate in order to "strengthen their own internal legitimacy, efficiency, and stability, but at the same time having to satisfy their external audience as well."[59] This statement appears to be borne out by the events of the last two decades. What is most important is that any East European leadership that considers the introduction of political and economic change must continually take into consideration the possible reaction of the Soviet Union, as well as the possible reaction of other East European countries that are affected by the changes. (In 1968, the leaderships of both Poland and East Germany saw in the reforms initiated in Czechoslovakia a potential threat to their own stability. Both countries were among the most vocal critics of the Czechoslovak reforms during the spring and summer of 1968.)

Returning to the question of the interrelationship of political (and economic) innovation in Eastern Europe, it appears clear that, although the specific examples of "modernization interaction" may not be conclusive, the experience of one communist country does have an impact on the others. During the course of the last decade several institutional developments, especially in the economic realm, have ensured the continued interaction of specialists in a variety of fields in attempts to work out solutions to problems in the specialized commissions of the Council for Mutual Economic Assistance. Also, the citations and examples listed in this chapter do indicate that developments in other countries are studied for their possible relevance elsewhere--either as potential future problems or possible solutions to existing problems.

What is needed, in order to develop a more complete picture of the interrelationship of political and economic innovations in Eastern Europe, is a much more careful survey of the specialist literature and the possibility of interviewing middle-level and upper-level decision makers and administrators--at least in areas that are not sensitive politically--concerning the possible impact that events elsewhere in Eastern Europe have had on their past decisions.

Finally, a better understanding of the role of "modernizing interaction" requires more information concerning the relative importance in decision making of domestic factors, as well as a variety of possible external influences--both those from within the communist country and those from

outside. (It should be noted that there is substantial evidence that many of the East European innovators have been
looking beyond the boundaries of Eastern Europe for possible
models for future reform. This was especially true of
Czechoslovakia in 1968, when some of the more radical reformers suggested that Sweden might represent a viable alternative model to the traditional politicoeconomic model
of Czechoslovakia.) In collecting this information, it
should not be forgotten that it has become standard procedure in communist countries for advocates of a particular
policy to point to examples in other "fraternal" countries
in support of their position--or in opposition to the position of their domestic opponents.[60] This, obviously, makes
more difficult a determination of the question of the real
influence of innovation in other communist countries.

NOTES

1. See, for example, the articles by Alfred Meyer, H.
Gordon Skilling, John H. Kautsky, and Robert C. Tucker reprinted in Communist Studies and the Social Sciences, ed.
Frederic J. Fleron, Jr. (Chicago: Rand-McNally, 1969).
2. See, for example, Kenneth Jowitt, "The Concepts of
Liberalization, Integration and Rationalization in the Context of East European Development," Studies in Comparative
Communism 4 (1971): 78-91. Jowitt's definition of "liberalization," based on the work of Ralf Dahrendorf, divides
the term into the two categories of "problematic liberalization" characterized by the absence of constraint and the opportunity for self-realization and "assertoric liberalization," which also provides for assistance to the individual
in achieving self-fulfillment. This permits Jowitt to note
that the Novotny period in Czechoslovakia can be called one
of "assertoric liberalization." (p. 86) It is extremely
questionable whether this type of terminological sophistica-
tion is likely to facilitate our greater understanding of
developments within the countries of Eastern Europe.
3. See John Kautsky, "Communism and the Comparative
Study of Development," in Fleron, op. cit., pp. 198-203,
and, especially, his Communism and the Politics of Development (New York: John Wiley, 1968) and The Political Consequences of Modernization (New York: John Wiley, 1972).
4. An argument similar to that of Kautsky can be found
in Adam Ulam's The Unfinished Revolution (New York: Random
House, 1960).
5. Some especially interesting applications of a developmental approach are Kenneth Jowitt's Revolutionary

Breakthroughs and National Development: The Case of Rumania, 1944-1965 (Berkeley: University of California Press, 1971); William R. Kintner and Wolfgang Klaiber, "The Dynamics of Communist Political Development," in their Eastern Europe and European Security (New York: Dunellen, 1971), pp. 45-190. Another study that takes a developmental approach is Dennis Pirages's Modernization and Political-Tension Management: A Socialist Society in Perspective: A Case Study of Poland (New York: Praeger, 1972). In addition, Charles Gati's "Modernization and Communist Power in Hungary," East European Quarterly 5 (1971): 325-59, uses the modernization model in its analysis (see Chapter 3 of this volume).

6. Several studies of related interest have been published in recent years. Andrzej Brzeski has examined the role of "Poland as a Catalyst of Change in the Communist Economic System," The Polish Review 16, no. 2 (1971), here cited from reprint no. 385 of the Slavic and East European Series of the Center for Slavic and East European Studies at Berkeley. Leon Smolinski has written about East European Influences on Soviet Economic Thought and Reforms, Working Paper No. 6 (Bloomington: Indiana University, International Development Research Center, September 1971). Finally, Zvi Gitelman has published a monograph entitled The Diffusion of Political Innovation: From Eastern Europe to the Soviet Union, Comparative Politics Series, Vol. III, no. 27 (Beverly Hills, Calif.: Sage Publications, 1972).

7. Cyril E. Black, The Dynamics of Modernization: A Study of Comparative History (New York: Harper and Row, 1966), p. 7.

8. See Leonard Binder, "The Crises of Political Development," in Crises and Sequences in Political Development, ed. Leonard Binder et al. (Princeton, N.J.: Princeton University Press, 1971), p. 16.

9. See, for example, Gabriel Almond and G. Bingham Powell, Jr., Comparative Politics: A Developmental Approach (Boston: Little, Brown, 1966), pp. 35-37; and Binder, "The Crises of Political Development," op. cit., pp. 52-67. By far the best brief summary of the major assumptions and characteristics of the literature on political development can be found in Samuel P. Huntington, "The Change to Change: Modernization, Development and Politics," Comparative Politics 2 (1971): 283-322. An earlier survey appears in Ann Ruth Willner, "The Underdeveloped Study of Political Development," World Politics 16 (1964): 468-82.

10. Samuel P. Huntington, "Political Development and Political Decay," World Politics 17 (1965): 388-90. In an unpublished paper on the application of modernization concepts to the analysis of the Soviet Union, Arthur Jay

Klinghoffer explicitly argues that modernization is a unilinear process. See his "A Developmental Approach to Soviet
Politics," p. 3.

11. Huntington, "Political Development," op. cit., p.
393.

12. Huntington measured institutionalization on four
scales: (1) adaptability-rigidity, (2) complexity-simplici-
(3) autonomy-subordination, and (4) coherence (unity)-
disunity. The more adaptable, complex, autonomous, and uni-
fied political structures are, the more institutionalized
they are. Ibid., pp. 394-403.

13. Samuel P. Huntington, Political Order in Changing
Societies (New Haven, Conn.: Yale University Press, 1968),
pp. 93, 266. In a more recent article Huntington has summarized the major criticisms that have been brought against
modernization theory and against the concept of political
development. The concepts of modernization and political
development are not clearly defined. In addition, in spite
of numerous efforts of scholars to eliminate the value implications of the concepts, they still tend to be ethnocen-
tric--that is, to view both modernization and political development largely in "Western" terms. Finally, the distinction between "modern" and "traditional" societies ignores
the fact that most "modern" societies tend to retain much of
the traditional pattern of behavior, while many "traditional"
societies contain elements that are usually associated with
a "modern" society. See Huntington, "The Change to Change,"
op. cit. For a perceptive critique of attempts to analyze
modernization in communist countries, see the article by
John Michael Montias entitled "Modernization in Communist
Countries: Some Questions of Methodology," Studies in Comparative Communism 5 (1972): 413-22.

14. See Zvi Gitelman, "Beyond Leninism: Political Development in Eastern Europe," Newsletter on Comparative
Studies of Communism 5, no. 3 (1972): 20, 43. Gitelman has
argued that the communist systems lack the institutions for
regular "change-making" and "change-absorption" and that,
although they have been very successful in political modernization, they "have been thus far unsuccessful in political
development."

15. This definition is slightly modified from that
used by Gitelman, The Diffusion of Political Innovation, op.
cit., p. 11. See also Lawrence A. Brown, "Innovation Diffusion in a Developing Economy: A Mesoscale View," Economic
Development and Social Change 21 (1973): 274-92.

16. Since this procedure has been well documented in
numerous scholarly studies, I will not dwell upon the process of Stalinization in Eastern Europe. See, for example,

Zbigniew Brzezinski, The Soviet Bloc, rev. ed. (Cambridge, Mass.: Harvard University Press, 1967), pp. 41-154; Hugh Seton-Watson, The East European Revolution (New York: Praeger, 1951).

17. Until 1953 this relationship probably can be best viewed as an imperial one with the Soviet Union acting as the coordinating center. See Gitelman, "Diffusion of Political Innovation," op. cit., pp. 7-8; Ghita Ionescu, The Break-up of the Soviet Empire in Eastern Europe (Baltimore: Penguin, 1965), pp. 7-8. Still the best treatment of the methods employed by the Soviets to maintain their control in the area is Brzezinski, The Soviet Bloc, op. cit., esp. pp. 105-38.

18. See, for example, Richard V. Burks, "Technology and Political Change in Eastern Europe," in Change in Communist Systems, ed. Chalmers Johnson (Stanford, Calif.: Stanford University Press, 1970), pp. 266-68.

19. Burks notes three major approaches to the problem of legitimation: (1) appeals to national sentiment, (2) attempts to democratize the single-party system of government, and (3) efforts to raise the standard of living. Ibid.

20. See Brzezinski, The Soviet Bloc, op. cit., p. 163. These changes largely paralleled changes earlier advocated by Malenkov in the Soviet Union.

21. See Michael Gamarnikow, Economic Reforms in Eastern Europe (Detroit: Wayne State University Press, 1968); J. Wilczynski, Socialist Economic Development and Reforms (New York: Praeger, 1972).

22. Kintner and Klaiber have discovered, based on case studies of three Eastern European countries, that economic and political development are not as closely related as is sometimes assumed. In East Germany and Bulgaria, for example, moderate economic reforms have not been accompanied by increased independence of parliamentary organs or of labor unions. Kintner and Klaiber, op. cit., pp. 74-75, 138-39.

23. Adam Bromke, "Poland's Role in the Loosening of the Communist Bloc," in Eastern Europe in Transition, ed. Kurt London (New York: Praeger, 1966), p. 67.

24. One possible source of some of the information that would be required for a more conclusive study of modernizing interaction may be the very specialized journals published by the East European countries. For example, during 1972, while reforms in rural local government in Poland were being discussed, the Polish weekly Rada Narodowa published a series of articles on rural government in the other communist countries, including recently implemented reforms in Hungary.

25. Dr. J. Wilesek, "Reforms of the Economic Mechanism in the Socialist Countries," Magyar Nemzet, March 3, 1968, in Radio Free Europe Research (hereafter referred to as RFER) Hungarian Press Survey, no. 1921 (April 1, 1968).

26. See Wilczynski, op. cit., pp. 47ff.

27. Brzeski, op. cit., pp. 8-9. See the excellent summary of the three major approaches to reform taken in Poland in this period in John Michael Montias, Central Planning in Poland (New Haven, Conn.: Yale University Press, 1962), pp. 272ff. According to Montias there were (1) the "value men" who argued for a complete market approach with planning used only to prod the economy; (2) a more moderate group, led by Wlodzierierz Brus who wished to use major investments as a means of planning, but to lessen the controls of the administration and grant wide-ranging powers to workers councils; and (3) those who opposed the use of the market mechanism.

28. See Gamarnikow, op. cit., p. 25.

29. Brzeski, op. cit., pp. 9-10.

30. Montias, Central Planning in Poland, op. cit., pp. 270, 307.

31. Brzeski, op. cit., pp. 10-11.

32. See Jan Glowczyk, "The Limits of Reform or a Reform without Limits," Zycie Gospodarcze, September 7, 1970, in RFER, Polish Press Survey, no. 2247 (October 8, 1970); and Stefan Kurowski, "The Limits of Reform of Planning and Economic Management," Gospodarka Planowa, April 1970, in RFER, Polish Press Survey, no. 2147 (October 8, 1970). In 1956 Kurowski was associated with the most radical group of reformers, the "value men." See Montias, Central Planning in Poland, op. cit., p. 272.

33. W. Brus, "Some Remarks on the Changes in the System of Planning and Management," Gospodarka Planowa, no. 11 (November 1966), p. 11, cited in Gamarnikow, op. cit., p. 26

34. Brzeski, op. cit., p. 6. According to the Hungarian economist Gyorgy Ranki, the Polish model of economic reform greatly influenced the discussions on the economic changes that occurred in Hungary after 1960. In addition, in the late 1960s all of the works of Ota Sik were translated into Hungarian. Comments by Ranki made at the workshop conference on "Eastern Europe: The Impact of Modernization on Political Development," New York, March 23-24, 1973. (See Chapter 10 of this volume.)

35. Vranick Predrag, History of Marxism (Zagreb: Naprijed, 1971, in Serbian), excerpted and translated in Slobodan Stankovic, "Yugoslav Marxist Philosopher Critical of the Soviet Bloc Communism. Part III: Tragedy of Czechoslovakia's Occupation," RFER, Communist Area, Yugoslavia, no. 1139 (September 23, 1971). Since 1969 Ota Sik has been

accused of having attempted to return the economy of Czechoslovakia to "the liberalistic period, and hence to take
over--in essence--the Yugoslav model." Jan Vecer, Radio
Prague, October 21, 1969, cited in Harry Trend, "The Return
to Economic 'Normalcy' in Czechoslovakia," RFER, Czechoslovakia, no. 11 (April 9, 1970).

36. John P. Windmuller, "Czechoslovakia and the Communist Union Model," British Journal of Industrial Relations 9,
no. 1 (1971): 46.

37. Wilesek, op. cit., pp. 3-4.

38. Istvan Friss, "Principal Features of the New Sys-
tem of Planning, Management, and Economic Control in Hungary," in Reform of the Economic Mechanism in Hungary, ed.
Istvan Friss (Budapest: Akademiai Kiado, 1971), pp. 12-17.
See also the excellent study of the reforms in Hungary by
William F. Robinson, "The Pattern of Reform in Hungary:
Part I: On the Road to Reform," RFER, Hungary, no. 16 (July
27, 1970) and "The Patterns of Reform in Hungary: Part II:
The Reform in Operation," RFER, Hungary, no. 17 (July 27,
1970). The Hungarians decided not to follow the Czechoslovak
example of introducing economic reform piecemeal, but rather
to introduce broad reforms simultaneously.

39. Cited in Slobodan Stankovic, "Yugoslavs Say Kadar
Discussed Economic Reforms with Tito," RFER, Communist Area,
Yugoslavia, June 6, 1966. Even in Bulgaria there have been
statements to the effect that commodity-money relations have
been underestimated in the communist countries and "the
theory that under socialism commodity-money relations are a
foreign element is not true." N. Popov, "On the Character
of the Economic Reforms in the Socialist Countries," Novo
Vreme, no. 10 (1968), in RFER, Bulgarian Press Survey, no.
688 (November 8, 1968).

40. Tito's speech of June 20, 1972 is reported in
Trybuna Ludu, June 21, 1972 and cited in RFER, Eastern Europe, Situation Report, Poland, no. 26 (June 29, 1972). For
an interesting analysis of workers' self-management see Egon
Neuberger and Estelle James, "The Yugoslav Self-Managed Enterprise: A Systematic Approach," in Plan and Market: Economic Reform in Eastern Europe, ed. Morris Bornstein (New
Haven, Conn.: Yale University Press, 1973), pp. 245-84.

41. See Zdenko Antic, "Socio-Political Influence of
Yugoslav Trade Unions Growing," RFER, Communist Area, Yugoslavia, no. 0544 (April 6, 1970), and "Yugoslav Party Theo-
reticians Discuss New Role of Trade Unions," RFER, Communist
Area, Yugoslavia, no. 0959 (March 30, 1971).

42. Bogdan Denitch has noted that both of these attempts, as well as the council movement in Czechoslovakia in
1968, represented very different approaches to the question

of self-management. See his "Notes on the Relevance of
Yugoslav Self-Management," Politics and Society (Summer
1973), pp. 473-89.

43. A. Miloshevski, "On the Question of Strengthenin
Economic Incentives in Our Country," Novo Vreme (November
1963), cited in Gamarnikow, op. cit., p. 55.

44. See R. T., "New Regulations for Economic Committees in Enterprises," RFER, Bulgaria, no. 12 (March 26, 19

45. See K. K., "The Trade Union Veto: A Lesson in D
terrence and Timidity," RFER, Hungary, no. 21 (August 10,
1970); Robinson, "Pattern of Reform in Hungary, Part II,"
op. cit., pp. 88-89.

46. In the late 1950s, in response to innovations in
troduced in the Soviet Union in line with Khrushchev's cal
for governmental authority gradually to be turned over to
voluntary organizations, Poland and other East European co
tries expanded the role of voluntary organizations. See A
Bromke, Poland's Politics: Idealism or Realism? (Cambridg
Mass.: Harvard University Press, 1967), p. 170.

47. See Adam Bromke, Eastern Europe on the Threshold
of the 1970's, Occasional Paper No. 7 (Ottawa: School of
International Affairs, Carleton University, 1970), p. 2.
Peter Potichnyj and Greg Hodnett have demonstrated that the
reforms in Czechoslovakia found willing supporters among
Ukranian "nationalists" in 1968. See Peter J. Potichnyj a
Greg Hodnett, The Ukraine and the Czechoslovak Crisis, Occa
sional Paper No. 6 (Canberra: Australian National Univers
Department of Political Science and Research School of Soc
Sciences, 1970), esp. pp. 100ff.

48. Cited in David Childs, East Germany (New York:
Praeger, 1969), p. 37. See also Brzezinski, Soviet Bloc,
op. cit., pp. 312-13.

49. Cited in Robert W. Dean, "Husak Speech Reflects
Polish Events," RFER, Czechoslovakia, no. 18 (February 22,
1971). The original speech was reported on Radio Prague on
February 17, 1971. This is an example of what might well b
called negative influence.

50. See Robert R. King, "Rumanian Reaction to the
Polish Events," RFER, Rumania, no. 6 (February 25, 1971).
Another example of noninstitutionalized influence on the ad
vocates of liberalization can be found in an article by O.
Machatka, published in Literarni Listy in 1968. Speaking o
Imre Nagy, Machatka said that "the Hungarian politician and
scholar Imre Nagy, who anticipated present events by his re
proach to the Stalinists--'you have forgotten man, you have
forgotten social relations with their moral and ethical pro
lems. . . .' Even in our country his ideas, which anticipated so many future events and which are probably much les
terrifying today, should not remain unknown." O. Machatka,

"Another Anniversary," <u>Literarni Listy</u>, no. 16 (June 13, 1968), in <u>RFER, Czechoslovak Press Survey</u>, no. 2090 (June 21, 1968).

51. See Bromke, <u>Poland's Politics</u>, op. cit., pp. 166-68. In 1971 <u>Tygodnik Democratyczny</u>, the organ of the Polish Democratic Party, published a number of articles by Democratic Party deputies to the Sejm who called for the strengthening of the role of representative organizations on all levels as a "basic condition for the development of democracy." See "So that the Sejm might be a <u>Sejm</u> (How to Increase the Role of the Polish Parliament as a Legislative Body)," <u>Tygodnik Demokratyczny</u>, April 11, 1971, in <u>RFER, Polish</u> Press Survey, no. 2298 (May 6, 1971).

52. Robinson, "Pattern of Reform in Hungary: Part II," op. cit., pp. 67-68. See also, Kintner and Klaiber, op. cit., pp. 102-10.

53. Z. Szeliga, "The Hungarian Elections," <u>Polityka</u>, May 8, 1971, in <u>RFER, Polish Press Survey</u>, no. 2303 (May 21, 1971).

54. <u>RFER, Situation Report, Poland</u>, no. 30 (May 21, 1971).

55. See Suzanne Lotarski, "Reform of Rural Administration: A Test of Managerial Solutions," <u>Canadian Slavonic Papers</u> 15 (1973): 108-22; <u>RFER, Situation Report, Poland</u>, no. 37 (October 5, 1972); Marek, "Reform of Poland's Rural Administration," <u>RFER, Poland</u>, no. 27 (November 3, 1972).

56. See Friss, "Principal Features of the New System," op. cit., p. 39.

57. See J. F. Brown, <u>Bulgaria under Communist Rule</u> (New York: Praeger, 1970), p. 161; Windmuller, "Czechoslovakia and the Communist Union Model," op. cit., p. 37.

58. See Gitelman, <u>The Diffusion of Political Innovation</u>, op. cit., pp. 46-49.

59. Ibid., p. 53.

60. For examples of this in the Soviet Union, see Gitelman, <u>The Diffusion of Political Innovation</u>, op. cit., pp. 28-33.

The third and final session of the conference on modernization in Eastern Europe has proved the most complex and the most difficult to define and coordinate. These papers are also the hardest to summarize. Case studies of Hungary, Romania, and other socialist countries--the subject of the first session (Part II in this book)--are relatively clearcut affairs: National boundaries are still there, perhaps more firmly than ever, hence each nation can be dealt with separately, as an integral unit. Mutual influences between Eastern Europe and the Soviet Union--the topic of the second session (Part III)--is also comparatively easy to discuss and to understand. But any study of tradition and change presents many pitfalls, and no matter how stimulating the debate, one is usually left with the uneasy feeling that apples are being compared with pears. No one disputes for an instant that modernity "does make a difference," and that in the last few decades the East European societies have changed drastically. But the divergent professional interests of the speakers and the contributors to this Part make comparisons and a final synthesis extremely difficult.

The economic historian, Gyorgy Ranki, manifested his fascination with the rapid development from agrarian to industrial economies since 1945. The sociologist Jan Szczepanski, whose comments were not submitted in writing for this volume, turned to the political roles of the various social strata in Eastern Europe and maintained that only very recently has the working class begun to exercise effective political control in some of the socialist countries. Ivan Volgyes, political scientist, presented a general scheme on the relationship between modernization and political development. Another political scientist, Barbara Jancar, approached the problem from a very different perspective: She questioned the interaction of political dissent and modernization in present-day society. She was curious to know how modernity will affect society in the future, rather than what modernization did to Eastern Europe in the past. William E. Griffith, in his comment on these studies, suggested that none of them deal with the most modern political theories, or at least do not favor them. He therefore propounded his own theories.

However, one answer to the problem of contemporary Eastern Europe was involuntarily provided by the participants

themselves. Reinforcing the widespread view that politica
frontiers are still a major factor in Eastern Europe, and
that each nation continues to be bound by its historical
peculiarities, Gyorgy Ranki constructed most of his very
original theories on the Hungarian experience; Ivan Volgye
drew on his extensive knowledge of Hungarian political developments since World War II; Jan Szczepanski consistently
referred to Polish events, and Barbara Jancar to developments in Czechoslovakia. If such outstanding scholars, al
perfectly capable and usually willing to engage in comparative studies, could not completely transcend their special
affinities, then it is clear that the subject of this session was too ambitious. One nevertheless must agree with
Gyorgy Ranki that Hungarian considerations are in many way
typical of Poland and of the other East Central European
countries. It is also true that Professor Ranki carefully
divorced his treatment of East Central Europe from that of
the Balkan countries.

Ultimately, it was the outstanding qualifications of
the participants that saved the day. Gyorgy Ranki is the
deputy-director of the Institute of History in Hungary. He
is a participant in Hungarian political life as well as an
observer; his prolific scholarly production is the wonder
of his friends and of his few opponents. The author or coauthor of at least a dozen monographs on economic history
and on the history of World War II, Ranki has produced hundreds of articles and commentaries in the last two decades.
He is also a frequent guest of the Hungarian radio and tele
vision. Jan Szczepanski is a scholar and a statesman in hi
native Poland; his studies on Polish society have changed
our views on the socialist world; his political activity
might change Poland. Ivan Volgyes, Hungarian-born but
American-educated, reflects that particular background in
his contribution (and especially in his oral presentation),
coupling his easy-going, often humorous style with substantial social-science content. Barbara Jancar is an American
with scholarly ties to Eastern Europe. Her work deals with
one of the most burning issues in the socialist bloc: Is
there a place a hope, a future for political dissent, for
the development of a pluralistic society in a monolithic
system? Finally, William E. Griffith, another American wit
only professional ties to Eastern Europe, once exercised a
remarkable political influence on the socialist countries
and is now influencing all of us with his very erudite,
witty, and imaginative views.

The chapters presented here speak for themselves. Wha
one comes away with is a series of questions provoked by
their excellence. Since traditions, habits, and historical

prejudices are still very much alive in Eastern Europe,
alive despite all the social mobility, equalization, and
industrialization--for this is Ranki's main thesis--are
these remnants of a reactionary past likely to disappear
gradually, or will they lead to a new, rigid, hierarchical
society? In other words, do conservative tendencies form
part of a "still" phenomenon, or do they belong to the realm
of "again and already"? Will the Polish working class expand its now tenuous control over the Party and the government, or is the workers' political and economic power merely
temporary and transitional? Will modernization allow the
political opposition to increase its activity, as Barbara
Jancar believes to be the case? Will the mass media really
provide the opposition with the means of both domestic and
foreign contact? Will the new quality of political expertise, now no longer the prerogative of the few but increasingly shared throughout society, truly make a difference and
reinforce the opposition? Or will Eastern Europe become an
increasingly fixed, dull, unimaginative, and eternally semi-
developed area? This writer, never able to quash his pessimism, tends to believe the latter. But then, predictions
are the privilege of political scientists, not of this historian.

10

HAS MODERNITY
MADE A DIFFERENCE?
Gyorgy Ranki

Has East European society changed? Frankly, I find that question moot if not irrelevant. Changes are so clear that nobody could or would deny them. Indeed, it would be easy to prove, with masses of relevant data, how much the East European social structure has changed. But if we put the question another way, I think we can approach the problem more closely. The real questions are:
1. What were the main features of East European society before the war and what are they now, that is, what are the characteristics and directions of change?
2. How much of the old social structure or its social, cultural, and ideological remnants have survived?
3. Are the East European societies becoming typical modern industrial societies, or do they have special features as a result of industrialization taking place under socialist conditions?

THE INTERWAR YEARS

Although the East European countries before World War II could not be regarded as classical underdeveloped countries comparable to the Asian and African nations now, they were certainly underdeveloped by comparison with Western countries. From a historical perspective they all lagged behind Western Europe and North America. With the exception of Czechoslovakia, the economic development and social struc ture of the more industrialized East European countries-- Poland and Hungary--and the mostly agrarian Balkan countries significantly differed from those of their Western neighbors

Poland and Hungary, though dissimilar in many respects, had essentially hierarchical societies with many remnants of feudalism. The predominance of a rural economy (51 percent of Hungary's population was engaged in agriculture on the eve of World War II; the figure for Poland was somewhat higher) was the key to the fundamental characteristics of the society. One of the most important features of this rural society was the survival of the gentleman-peasant or master-serf relationship, the division of society into two worlds. Although there were many other, newer conflicts, which were sometimes expressed more vehemently than this old one, the peasant-lord conflict ought to be treated as the most important feature of these societies.

Of course, the economic base of this social conflict was the survival of the large estate with the accompanying disproportionate division of land and wealth between the aristocracy and the peasantry. But it would be very one-sided to disregard the other social consequences of such feudal, hierarchical societies, some of which were more difficult to destroy after the abolishment of large estates and the redistribution of land. One such consequence was the low level of urbanization and the relatively small role of industry and commerce. But even more important was the consequent formation of the middle classes. As is well known, in both Poland and Hungary a relatively large share of the middle classes, intellectuals, clerks, and state officials came from the landed gentry and displayed the feudal hierarchy of values deeply engrained in the traditions of gentry culture: aristocratic discrimination, orientation toward the past, and lofty scorn for hard work.

Between the two world wars the intelligentsia became more powerful and began to fulfill a function characteristic of intellectuals in those countries where the social structure was not crystallized and the class system was indistinct. The economically poor middle class, as opposed to the nouveau riche bourgeoisie with low social prestige, represented the cultural tradition of the country as well as some promise of advancement for those elements of the peasantry able to rise above their class origins. The high prestige of white-collar jobs--with the exception of business--was testified to by the growing social prestige of the middle classes and the increasing importance of education as a mark of social superiority opening the road to social advancements.

Let us now turn to the Balkans, to the more characteristically agrarian countries. If in the case of Hungary and Poland the feudal values of the bourgeoisie strengthened the gentry middle classes and intelligentsia, in the case of the Balkans the weakness of the native bourgeoisie gave special status to the newly created middle classes and intelligentsia. Generally, in the Balkan countries society was less hierarchical--Romania was somewhere in between the two type --more democratic, but more underdeveloped and traditional as well. In these countries we find an overwhelming majority of the peasantry living in a self-sufficient economy based on family enterprises. Even between the two world wars, their traditional mentality was solidly entrenched and nourished by a system of social relations almost unchanged for many generations.

In these poorly industrialized countries, the industrial proletariat, along with the bourgeoisie, held much less economic influence than in Poland or Hungary. Only about 10 percent of the population could be classified as industrial workers usually in handicraft or textile industries, with few skilled workers a low cultural and economic level, and the majority recently recruited from the peasantry. Although all calculations show that urban workers enjoyed a relatively high living standard compared with the peasantry or the large numbers of landless agrarian proletariat, their situation was bad enough to create a great deal of social tension in the towns. According to one estimate, monthly consumption for a Romanian worker's family of four in 1940 was

74 kg. bread	28 eggs
28 kg. potatoes	15 kg. beans
3 kg. sugar	8 kg. fat
11 kg. meat	

Overpopulation in the rural areas placed a heavy burden on wages in the city. During the interwar years unemployment in the cities was high and the slow pace of industrialization created a demand mostly for the kind of manpower that was available very cheaply and in large quantities in the countryside. In Croatia in 1935, 53 percent of the workers were really low-paid peasants; 73 percent of those in the building trades and 60 percent in the textile industry were peasants who had recently come to the cities. The low level of organization among the workers, a consequence not only of their low cultural and political level, but of political oppression as well, made it possible to keep the urban proletariat in very difficult social circumstances.

It is really unnecessary to go into detail concerning living standards in these countries. As typical agricultural countries, they were strongly hit by the economic depression and the upheaval in the international division of labor between the wars. They were the prime deliverers of agricultural goods for the Western powers until after World War I, when this role was taken over by the United States. Despite the unsatisfactory diet of the majority of the population in these countries, tremendous quantities of unsold grain, meat, and vegetables were stocked awaiting export.

A Hungarian populist writer gave an astonishing picture of the diet in a typical Hungarian village, and Hungary was probably richer than the Balkan countries where the staple diet for most of the year consisted of bread, cheese, and onions with paprika sprinkled on everything. Overwork and insufficient food, high infant mortality, poor public health facilities--Hungary was rightly called the country of 3 million beggars.[2]

One of the fundamental problems of East European society in the interwar period was relative overpopulation. According to some estimates made by W. Moore and published by the League of Nations, 30-50 percent more people than needed were employed in agriculture.[3] In Poland, Romania, Yugoslavia, Bulgaria, and Hungary there were nearly 15 million peasants virtually unemployed. In every respect industrialization was badly needed--to satisfy increasing domestic demands, to ease overpopulation in the villages, and to raise the purchasing power of the urban and rural proletariat. The main obstacles to industrialization were lack of capital, lack of markets, and the economic nationalism that precluded common efforts and cooperation. Conflicts of interest between the bourgeoisie and the landowners were a special feature of the industrially more developed countries. Industrialization was not only an economic issue, it was strongly connected with social issues.

Industrialization also affected the educational levels of the East European countries. A marked advance must be acknowledged between the two world wars. The illiteracy rate was lowered or almost abolished, the number of elementary schools was increased, and the secondary school system was expanded. Nevertheless, we cannot disregard the fundamental conditions of cultural backwardness and social inequality inherited by the school system.

Hungary was probably the country with the highest education level. Illiteracy was almost nonexistent (about 5 percent); the elementary education system actually improved between the two world wars and secondary education was on a relatively high level. But even in Hungary, where 92 percent of the school-age population received some education, about 35 percent of those entering the first class never finished elementary school, and the number of high school students fell from 10 percent to 5 percent of the school-age population. In addition, as is well known, the Hungarian educational system was socially restrictive so that sons or daughters of peasants or workers rarely could afford higher education.

But in Romania at the same time, 38 percent of the population was illiterate (and in Yugoslavia the figure was 44 percent). Only 58 percent of the pupils who were legally required to enter elementary schools completed the course, and only about 5 percent of those who received elementary education went on to secondary schools. Education was limited to the urban middle and upper classes. Although the agricultural population was about 80 percent of the total population, only 1 percent of the peasant youth went beyond elementary-level education. The proportion of urban to rural students in secondary schools was 8.3 to 1. The rural population was deprived of secondary education principally because there were no secondary schools in rural areas and, even if a peasant was willing to send a child to a secondary school, he could hardly afford it. The same material limitations affected working-class youth as well.[4]

To summarize: during the interwar years even in the Western countries the standard of living suffered. But in the West new cultural and recreational habits became commonplace with the introduction of the radio and motion pictures for example, and new services--such as regular visits to hairdressers--made their appearance. In Eastern Europe such elements hardly existed, and for the most part life was truly miserable.

SOCIALIST TRANSFORMATION IN THE POSTWAR WORLD

Postwar social changes emerged as a result of economic growth and the socialist transformation of society. However complex the political (domestic and international) components of the Communist parties' emergence in these countries it was undeniable that the communists appeared after World War II as a dynamic force capable of organizing efforts to set the countries moving along the path of industrial and economic development and creating a new social system more favorable to the masses. Central economic planning based on government ownership of the basic means of production promised to provide the most important tools for this task. Agrarian reform, nationalization, the disappearance of the rural proletariat, and the introduction of unprecedented social mobility literally turned the traditional social structure upside down.

To make any judgment on changes in a society you must take into account all the elements--economic, social, political, technical, cultural, health, and demographic--that have a role in the formation of the new society. Although there are as yet no comprehensive studies on contemporary East European society, disregarding even one of these factors involves a great risk of oversimplification. However, I will present only some of the changes I consider most

important. It must be remembered that even the most profound changes reflect continuity with the past, and in
Eastern Europe tradition is still alive and frequently revived.

The most important changes could be grouped along the
following lines: (1) modification of the social structure
in connection with structural changes in the economy; (2)
demographic changes; (3) structural social changes, social
mobility; and role of cultural factors. Of course, the most
marked social transformation took place in connection with
economic growth, affecting factors like the numbers and
salaries of wage earners (especially the new socioeconomic
role of women) and their distribution among the different
branches of the economy.

If we look at Hungary, for example, we find that the
number of people employed rose from 4.4 million in 1949 to
5.9 million in 1968; their proportion of the total population was 48 percent in 1949 and 58 percent in 1968. In
spite of the increasing numbers and proportion of old people
on pensions, the ratio of dependents to earners decreased
from 100:120 in 1949 to 100:144 in 1960. The preponderance
of the agricultural sector, which had hardly changed since
the turn of the century, has rapidly decreased since 1949.
Nearly 1 million people left agriculture and in 1970 only
25-30 percent, as opposed to 50 percent, earned their living from agriculture. With almost half of the population
employed in industry (after the war it was about 25 percent)
and agriculture organized in state farms or cooperatives,
the character of employment has changed as well. Among the
active population, 76 percent was employed in comparison
with 46 percent in 1949. (Members of cooperatives are not
counted.)[5]

Comparable figures could be presented along the same
lines from the other East European countries as well. If
there is any difference, it is only the larger proportion of
agricultural population in less-developed Poland. As to the
Balkans, Romania, Bulgaria, and Yugoslavia have still got 50
percent of their population in agriculture, a 25 percent
drop from the prewar period. In these countries the shift
is going on at about the same rate as in Hungary. (Of
course, the difference between having 25-30 percent and 50
percent of the population in agriculture is significant, especially considering the conservative nature of the peasant
population.)

Property, as the traditional Marxist view has always
stressed it, is one factor in the conservative makeup of the
peasantry, but one should also consider (1) one-dimensional
social mobility (mass exodus altered the age structure, and

agriculture became an occupation for old people); (2) cultural backwardness (lack of education or ideological heritage); and (3) economic backwardness. But even if we do consider all these factors, we cannot doubt that, as a consequence of economic growth, East European societies are more or less uniformly changing, indeed have already changed into modern, industrial societies.

Of the demographic changes that have taken place in the course of the past 25 years, perhaps the most important is the modification in the age structure. Partly as a consequence of improvements in living, health, and welfare conditions, partly a result of the fall in the birth rate, the East European population has become older. In Hungary, in 1900, 8 percent of the population was over 60; in 1941 it was 11 percent; in the early 1970s, it is 16 percent. This means that now roughly 1.3 million pensioners live in Hungary, which, even with pension rates as low as they are, represents a tremendous burden for a modernizing economy.

People are getting married earlier than before and divorcing more often. The birth rate was about 20 before the war, 23 in 1954 13 in 1962, and 15 in 1968. This represents a 3.9 rate of natural increase. But in spite of the rather sharp and often emotional discussion going on concering the low birth rate, an argument based more on sentiment and nationalism than on rationality, we must not forget one of the most typical socioeconomic changes in Hungarian society, namely the change in the activities of women. In Hungary, and the other East European countries, the proportion of female wage earners (between 20 and 55 years of age) grew from 30 to 40 percent. (In Western countries the percentage has been falling: unmarried women work more, marry less.) The mass employment of women has been made easier by the shift of rate between manual and nonmanual work and by the rapid rise in the women's educational level and qualifications. It is well known that in the East European countries girls constitute the majority in secondary schools, and among university students their proportion is almost half.[6]

The third modification that could be looked upon as very important relates to structural social changes and social mobility. The marked change in means, processes, and consequences of social mobility is well known. Of course, in every country increased social mobility is a concomitant of modernizing a rigid social system and an underdeveloped, traditional economy.

The increased possibilities of social mobility were created during the past decades as an almost inherent consequence of economic and political changes. Economic

changes created a greater demand for intellectuals to serve
as directors in the economy, in social organization, and in
administration. The socialist assumption that for a modern
socialist economy it was not enough merely to expand the
number of educated people gave a tremendous impetus to social mobility. One had to change the old ruling class and
replace them in key positions with people born members of
the proletariat or the peasantry and devoted to the socialist aims of the Communist Party. In the early 1950s, enormous quantities of people from the lower classes climbed up,
took over leading positions, and almost completely changed
the ruling strata. From the strict viewpoint of economy
this was not always good.

Between 1945 and 1953, the former Hungarian ruling
classes, together with various groups of hangers-on and certain petite bourgeoise strata, lost their standing in the
social hierarchy. Approximately 350,000 to 400,000 families
lost their former positions and were obliged to seek new
places in society. While this broad change was taking place,
an opposite social movement set in resulting from the revolutionary transformation of Hungary and the new power relations that were established. Fresh elements from the working class and the peasantry rose in large numbers to fill
leadership positions at various levels of the government and
the economy, and many blue-collar workers moved into white-
collar occupations. Taken together with the changes of the
immediately preceding years, the members of these "rising"
groups, with their dependents, numbered close to a million
people. By the beginning of the 1960s, only 15 percent of
those in professional and managerial posts came from families in similar circumstances, while 40 percent were from
workers' families, and 26 percent were of peasant origin.[7]
Changes in social position involving on the one hand both
the extreme poles of society, and on the other hand the
movements of those who initially were on the middle, radically altered the social standing and circumstances of
nearly a quarter of the population at least.

However, upward mobility, at least in terms of its proportion, was a unique phenomenon during this period. The
expanding economy and the modernization of society offered
vast possibilities, and for several years the range of social mobility was very wide. The principal means of advancement, at least in the beginning, were political. De-
votion to the principle of socialism represented by the
Communist Party was the key factor. Later, though the previous approach was still maintained, the role of education
became more and more significant as a means of individual
advancement.

Although many new sociological studies make critical remarks on the problem of the Hungarian educational system, everybody agrees that the tendency to democratize education by making all levels available to an increasingly large proportion of the population has been genuine. The following table, giving the highest school level reached by percentages of the population over seven years old, is indicative of the trend:[8]

	1941	1949	1960	1970
No education	7.2	5.6	4.0	2.3
1-5 years of primary school	36.3	31.9	17.4	20.3
6-7 years of primary school	43.6	44.4	39.9	31.3
8 years of primary school	7.4	11.4	18.4	28.9
1-4 years of secondary school	2.2	2.2	3.3	4.5
Graduate of secondary school	2.2	3.3	5.1	8.4
Graduate of university	1.1	1.2	1.9	4.3
	100	100	100	100

Although the means of advancement are still available, it will become impossible to sustain the rapid social mobility rate of the revolutionary period. Due to the marked shift toward education and ability as the prime criteria for upward mobility, political merit and ideological virtues in themselves are no longer sufficient qualifications for upper-level jobs. A shift from the political-ideological to the technical-managerial elite was bound to--and has in fact --happened. (One important indication of this tendency is the tremendous increase in the number of persons with higher education among the so-called political-ideological elite.) As available data concerning East European societies shows, social stratification is becoming a function of education. This may be regarded, not so much in the present but for the future, as an important indication of social mobilization.

In the 1960s in Hungary over 44 percent of the secondary school students and 33 percent of all university students were children of industrial workers. By the beginning of the 1960s, 26 percent of those in professional or managerial positions came from peasant families. The contrast with statistics from before the war, when scarcely more than 1 percent of secondary school children and 1.5 percent of university students came from peasant or farm servant origins, is clear. Three decades later, 17 percent of the secondary school students and 11 percent of the university students came from peasant families.

Intergenerational changes are also extremely high. On the average, among 100 fathers employed in agriculture, only

41 will have sons remaining in the same social stratum; of
the remainder, 50 will have gone over to the nonagricultural
manual work stratum and 9 will have become nonmanual workers.
Among nonagricultural manual workers, 70 percent remain in
the original stratum and 24 percent go over to nonmanual
work; the remaining 6 percent become agricultural workers.
Among nonmanual workers, 68 percent remain in the same stratum, 30 percent go over to nonagricultural manual work, and
2 percent are employed in agriculture.

As a result of the intergenerational processes outlined above, the structure of the background of nonmanual
workers indicates maximum heterogeneity: Only 29 percent of
them are descended from parents who were nonmanual workers,
45 percent come from nonagricultural manual workers, and 26
percent from agricultural manual workers. By contrast, the
parents of 44 percent of nonagricultural manual workers belonged to the same strata, those of 52 percent were agricultural manual workers, and 4 percent were nonmanual workers.
In this respect, the stratum of the agricultural workers is
the most closed one, with a 90 percent proportion of homogeneity.

SOCIOLOGICAL ASPECTS OF SOCIALIST MODERNIZATION

While the rate of intergenerational change is ebbing,
generally it may be said that East European societies are
still very fluid and unsettled, especially in relation to
class status. There is still no firm classification for
this type of society because, even when industrialization
and modernization impose their logic on the social structure, the absence of privately owned means of production
continues to be the key factor shaping the general hierarchy
of this type of society. The classification of Branko
Horvat--underlining the horizontal differentiation in Yugoslav (East European) society as opposed to the vertical
stratification in capitalist society (where differences
among groups lead to conflicts of interest)--seems both
factually acceptable and persuasive. In his essay, Horvat
tries to distinguish six strata in Yugoslav society:

1. Government people, leading political figures, economic leaders, all of whom have high income, decision-making
responsibilities, and high status.
2. Intellectuals: technocrats, bureaucrats, humanist
intelligentsia, all of whom have relatively high income, the
possibility of making decisions or influencing those who
make decisions, and the highest social status.

3. White-collar workers, low income.

4. Blue-collar workers of varying skills, whose position is relatively advantageous (improved by special benefits and privileges, social services, better working conditions, and security), but whose income is comparatively low.

5. Artisans with high income and low social status. Self-renewal rate is very low; most of the children try to go over to other strata.

6. Peasants with fair income and low social status.[9]

While there is still not enough sociological evidence to prove decisively the correctness of such a stratification scheme, the assumptions underlying it are entirely justified; that is, differences in social prestige and reputation, financial status, and social power.

Of course, this stratification differs from those found in earlier writings about socialist societies, and it remains to be seen whether it is a passing phenomenon or one of longer duration. On the other hand, in spite of all the similarities with modern, capitalist, industrial societies, it would be a grievous error to conclude that East European societies are coping in the same ways and moving in the same direction. We must not disregard the fundamental principles deriving from the socialist origin of these societies.

Some Western theorists have maintained that two contradictory factors have affected the social structure of contemporary European communism--Marxist ideology and modern industrialism. I would like to challenge such views. Without denying that ideological rigidity has been a contradictory force in the past and sometimes can be so in the present, the pattern of Western industrial society as a guide for modernizing every country cannot be accepted. Nor can one regard certain measures taken in order to eliminate some negative social consequences of industrialization as contrary to the interests of modernization.

It is certainly true that developing countries tend to imitate the pattern of life in economically more advanced countries. Can the East European societies become more open to this possibility, especially through the development of the mass communications media? While technological progress creates a whole series of almost identical problems, the question is whether these problems have to be solved by the same answers given in the same way. In other words, must the objectives of humanitarianism be subordinate to economic effectiveness, or is some kind of compromise between value-oriented and ratio-oriented societies possible? What is the relation between economic growth and social equality or social differentiation?[10] What differences are really necessary and can be justified in a long-range perspective?

What current phenomena of interest in East European societies represent a bad application of unduly fast economic growth on the Western pattern or unhealthy tendencies toward inequality as practiced in the West?

Now we may turn to the central question of whether East European society can be regarded as a modern society or not. Is the French proverb "plus ca change, plus c'est la meme chose" valid or not? If one regards just the main tendencies, it is easy to declare East European society modern, and this opinion would not be entirely false. But if one regards some intrastructural phenomena--cultural and social habits, for example--then one can maintain that East European societies have not entirely escaped their past. Traditional ways of living, habits, and prejudices are still very much alive.

A few years ago such problems were easily dismissed as trivial relics of capitalism that would be liquidated with progress. But in recent years social questions, either in traditional or in new terms, are appearing again. Speaking of change and tradition, we must stress the survival of many traditions (both good and bad) appearing quite incongruously under changed circumstances or reshaped by the force of post-World War II economic development in Eastern Europe.

Of the present social problems, some are the usual consequences of industrialization and urbanization processes, others result from the socialist system itself, and some, finally, are largely remnants of the past. I shall discuss those related to industrialization and urbanization first. Closely connected with the inadequacy of earlier social legislation--and indeed a natural reaction against it--was the frequent extension of social benefits beyond the limits of practical possibilities. This created new difficulties in certain areas. The achievement of universal free medical insurance, for example, gave rise to overcrowded conditions that often affected the quality of medical treatment adversely. This in turn led to the search for private treatment and the payment of extra fees in hopes of receiving superior treatment. Likewise, the unusually low age limits set for pension eligibility (60 for men, 55 for women), in disregard of existing material resources, led to very low pension payments that sometimes barely provided subsistence living standards. Because of socialist industrialization and pricing policies, consumption of clothing has grown very little in the past two decades. Clothing tends to be used a long time before it is replaced, and many people are still obliged to wear worn-out articles of clothing.

The improved starting opportunities, which were main factors in the socialist transformation, are decreasing very fast. The former basis of unequal social relations, private

property, or private ownership of the means of production
has actually disappeared, but new social differences and
tensions are created by the asymmetrical or uneven distribution of production within the socialist system. There are
two factors that have increased in social importance--knowl-
edge and decision-making power. The first is a result of
the demands of technical development; the second arises from
the more complicated and bureaucratic nature of social organization. One serious problem in the socialist countries
in the last few years has been the narrowing of chances for
higher education for children of workers and peasants due
to differences created by the emergence of the new middle
class and increased emphasis on effectiveness and ability
as criteria for advancement.

Looking at the secondary school population, we find
that in Budapest 69 percent of the gymnasium or high school
students and 52 percent of vocational school students are
children of intellectuals, managers, and white-collar workers. This is not bad in comparison with the international
level, but it indicates both a slowing down of social mobility and an increase in the distance between social strata.
Working-class students or, more properly, children of unskilled workers and peasants tend to have a higher failure
rate and a somewhat lower level of achievement. On the
other hand, the abolition of private property made education
more important in society, and in some sense a conflict
arose between the educational and social functions of school.

The former egalitarian approach, with the consequent
lack of impetus for improvement, creativity, and independence in economic activity, posed a serious problem for economic development. On the other hand, this was in part com-
pensated for by the well-known socialist principle of distribution according to work done. It became a privilege of
certain strata of society to receive desirable goods that
were in short supply, and, as a consequence of strong bureaucratization, the one-sided distribution of goods and
benefits became more important than income differences in
social and economic differentiation. Many studies have been
written about the preference given to executives and functionaries in the distribution of housing. A much larger
proportion of high-standard, inexpensive state housing, requiring no prior payment, is allocated to higher social
groups than to lower ones. Bureaucratization and shortages
of some supplies have created many other inequalities in income levels, availability of cars, holidays, building lots,
etc., which are leading to an increase in hierarchical differentiation as well.

One interesting feature of this phenomenon is that some
of the differences were created by the old economic mechanism

and the value-centric political system that emphasized loyalty to the new ideas and institutions, while some differences were created by the attempt to introduce a more rational economic mechanism.[11] The difficulty was that a number of social reforms (full employment, equal rights for women, education, and high standards of medical care) connected with a value system were relatively expensive and generally could be afforded only by more prosperious and efficient economies. To reach such a level the new system had to be strengthened with stepped-up technological growth and higher efficiency. In the long run this seemed to be the only way to maintain and develop a rational value system, but for the time being it created contradictions and raised doubts that such activity would lead to the abolishment of those special values that were features of modernization in socialist societies.

In Hungary, even the creation of a new middle class posed certain ideological and political problems, among them the relations between the middle class and the working class, their place in the given social and political system, the conflict between ideology and efficiency, and so on. But another aspect should be stressed, namely the value system of the middle class. It has become a special mixture of modern industrialized (Western), socialist, and very traditional Hungarian middle class or intellectual values. If one takes into consideration the influence of the gentry on the shaping of former intellectual traditions, and if one doesn't forget that among the new intellectuals coming up from the lower classes there are more from peasant than from worker backgrounds, then it is quite understandable that many traditional, patriarchal, rural-oriented, in some sense premodernization values (anticapitalist in both senses), became an organic part of the Weltanschauung of this stratum, causing considerable conflict. Social differences, some kind of hierarchical structure, are inherent in any given social and economic system, but there are many other social phenomena that are really more remnants of the past than consequences of the present system.

As demonstrated above, the marked peculiarities of Hungarian society in the past were the feudal, hierarchical structure on the one hand and the peasant society on the other. Class and status distinctions, which sometimes remain very strong, have nothing to do with the ideology of the present system and could be regarded almost entirely as remnants of former views and behavior. The survival of rural values and behavior patterns is also more a relic of the past than a consequence or demand of socialism.

Of course, some preconditions for differentiation are given in society. The urban, industrial population is already a majority of the total population, but this urban or worker society is very young. Not quite half of the new recruits in the labor force come from the working class itself; more than half come from other social strata. Of those from the working class, nearly 66 percent come from the younger generation, nearly 33 percent from the ranks of women who had not worked before, and about 10-15 percent from among the small craftsmen. The influx from the peasantry has been especially large, about 80 percent, while formerly self-employed persons, white-collar workers, and other elements make up the remaining 20 percent of industrial workers coming from nonworking-class origin. The incorporation of these elements has greatly swelled the ranks of the young Hungarian working class. (In the 1960s, half the workers came from peasant families.)

This new working class with moderate income levels preserved former habits, views, and consumption patterns, as reflected in the relatively large proportion of income spent on food, the relatively low expenditures on clothing (only half of what is spent on clothing in advanced industrial countries), and the even lower consumption of consumer durables (only one-third of what is spent on such items in the advanced countries). The same state of affairs is evident in the makeup of food consumption itself. Of the average daily intake (3,054 calories), 45 percent is provided by cereals and 17 percent by fats. A similar problem exists in the countryside where the traditional high-carbohydrate, low-protein diet is still prevalent. A survey showed that 30 percent of the country's population, including high-income groups, live on such food. Malnutrition is not a function of financial means, but rather a question of cultural standards.

It is very difficult to say what the main contributors to the very one-sided preference for nonmanual work are--the value system of the past or the present stress on education as the main route for upward mobility. A recent study of a Hungarian school showed that 80 percent of the students wished to be intellectuals or at least white-collar workers, and only 20 percent wished to undertake some kind of manual labor, including skilled work. The same preference is shown in another survey of parents: 51.2 percent wish to have their children in nonmanual work, 11.8 percent in either nonmanual or nonagricultural manual work, 32.8 percent in industrial manual work, and 3.2 percent in agricultural work. The picture in Budapest is even more dramatic, where the proportions are 70 percent parental preference for nonmanual labor, 8 percent for nonmanual or nonagricultural manual, and 22 percent for manual industrial work. Of the skilled workers, 62 percent in Budapest and 50 percent in the countryside would like to have their children employed in nonmanual work. Such preferences are especially amazing in view of the fact that only intellectuals in leading positions get better salaries than skilled workers, and, unlike the Western countries, in Hungary the proportion of average wages for white-collar and blue-collar workers favors the latter.

One of the most important consequences of postwar social transformation was the abolishment of the rigid class structure, the elimination of stiff barriers between classes. This was indicated by marriage statistics. For instance, among the nonmanual workers, the wives of managers and intellectuals came in relatively large proportions from the workers (32 percent) and peasants (13 percent). Likewise, 46 percent of the wives of white-collar workers were of worker origin, while 19 percent were peasants. However, if one examines present occupations as well as social background, the picture becomes quite different, particularly in the first category. Broadly speaking, recent trends testify to a new strengthening of differences between social strata or increased consciousness of these differences. From these statistics on Hungarian marriages, it can be stated that the consciousness of belonging to a social stratum is still a psychologically significant motivating factor. In more than two-thirds of all marriages, husbands and wives belonged to identical social strata. Sociological research in the countryside has also discovered that former differences among smallholders, large farmers, and servants in the villages could be traced down to the members of the cooperatives and workers on state farms in our day.

This means, then, that traditions are still shockingly powerful in the countryside, and the old social distinctions survive in very different ways. Broadly speaking, in spite of widening income differences in the last few years, many differences between social strata are more connected with traditional consciousness than with any direct material basis.

CONCLUSIONS

In conclusion, Hungarian, or indeed East European, society has completely changed during the last 20-25 years, more rapidly than was the case in Western societies where the modernization process took place gradually. Instead of closed feudal or peasant societies, the more open and mobile society of the present has been shaped by economic growth and social transformation. The overall importance and generally positive balance of social changes, the new character of society, and the process of modernization are facts that cannot be underestimated.

However, traditions or remnants of the past are stronge than had been expected. In a well-known article, a famous Hungarian economist described the Hungarian economy--particularly referring to some problems not shown in the main indicators--as a quasi-developed economy. Such conceptualization, controversial as it may be, is applicable to the society as well. That is, in spite of the radical transformation that has taken place, not enough has been achieved. The past is still too much in the present as is evident, for instance, in the relatively low standard of living. Creating a modern and socialist society is still a task for the future connected not only with economic growth but with positively correlating a rising standard of living and social reforms with economic efficiency.

NOTES

1. The most useful history remains Hugh Seton-Watson's Eastern Europe Between the Wars, 1918-1941 (New York: Harper & Row, 1967).

2. Some of the best descriptions of the Hungarian countryside before the war are found in the works of the so-called populist writers or village explorers. See, especially, Geza Feja, Viharsarok [Stormy corner] (Budapest, 1937); Gyula Illyes, Pusztak nepe [People of the Puszta] (Budapest, 1936); Zoltan Szabo, Tardi helyzet [The situation at Tard] (Budapest 1936). For a brief evaluation, see Charles Gati's chapter in this volume.

3. Wilbert Ellis Moore, Economic Demography of Eastern and Southern Europe (New York: Columbia University Press, 1946).

4. Iosif I. Gabrea, Scoala Romaneasca: Structura, si politica Ei 1921-1932 [The Romanian school: its structure and politics, 1921-1932] (Bucharest, n.d.).

5. Sandor Orban, Ket agrarforradalom Magyarorszagon [Two agrarian revolutions in Hungary] (Budapest, 1972).

6. For more details, see Ivan T. Berend and Gyorgy Ranki, Economic Development in East-Central Europe in the 19th and 20th Centuries (New York: Columbia University Press, 1974).

7. Szuzsa Ferge, Tarsadalmunk retegezodese [The stratification of our society] (Budapest, 1968).

8. Ibid.

9. See Branko Horvat's excellent study, <u>An Essay on Yugoslav Society</u> (White Plains, New York: International Arts & Sciences Press, 1969).

10. Ibid., p. 144.

11. Cf. Jozsef Bognar, "Economic Reform, Development and Stability in the Hungarian Economy," <u>New Hungarian Quarterly</u> 13, no. 46 (Summer 1972): 29-43.

11

THE IMPACT OF
MODERNIZATION ON
POLITICAL DEVELOPMENT
Ivan Volgyes

The purpose of this chapter is to draw some tentative conclusions regarding the general impact of the last two decades of modernization on the political development of Eastern Europe as a whole--to synthesize complex political events into what might be regarded as a tentative schema of political development in the communist systems of Eastern Europe.*

At the outset it should be made clear that no common level of political development can be observed in these states since the end of World War II. Indeed, one of the most important tasks that political scientists face is to continue to emphasize that, in Eastern Europe, political development cannot be treated as a general phenomenon equally applicable to all of these states at any given time. The political development in these states, however, does seem to contain some common elements of rule enforcement and of popular involvement in rule making. These elements have appeared a number of times during different eras in many of the countries, but there is a noticeable time lag in the appearance of these phenomena.

Even though the time lag may be considerable, one can observe a pattern in the changes that have occurred since 1945 and from this pattern can deduce the existence of a common framework of political development in Eastern Europe.

---

*Yugoslavia and East Germany have been excluded from the geographical area included in this chapter for the obvious reasons that their development has been conditioned by political and economic considerations not applicable to the other communist party-states of Europe.

To begin with, political development appears to possess strong correlation with the level of modernization reached by the individual countries and is attendant with the processes of modernization. Political development seems to occur in three distinct phases in all of these countries: mobilization, stagnation, and reform. Some of the states of Eastern Europe still are plodding along in the first phase. In others the second stage has been attained, while in others the third phase of political development may be witnessed. A tentative time table is contained in Table 11.1.

TABLE 11.1

Phases of Political Development in Eastern Europe

Country	Phase I	Phase II	Phase III
Albania	1945-73		
Bulgaria	1945-73		
Czechoslovakia	1945-68	1968-	
Hungary	1945-56	1956-68	1968-
Poland	1945-56	1956-70	1970-
Romania	1945-73		

FIRST PHASE: MOBILIZATION

The first phase, political mobilization, obviously occurs with the first phase of economic modernization. The goal of the latter may best be defined in broad terms as bringing a backward society into the economic mainstream of the modern world through an all-out national effort. The first phase of communist rule in Eastern Europe was undertaken by copying the economic and political models of change in the USSR. The goals of economic modernization were clear: the nationalization of existing industries, the creation of heavy industry, the opening up of new power sources, urbanization, the abolition of agriculture as the major source of social activity, the collectivization of agriculture, and the forced creation of new sources of labor supply from a backward peasantry. These efforts succeeded in abolishing the organic life of the villages and small communities and atomized members of the society, thereby limiting the possibilities for open insurrection. Even though some of these elements of economic modernization had existed in some East European states, for example, Czechoslovakia, the general

process of economic modernization was repeated in every one
of these countries.

During this first phase, stringent dictatorial methods
were utilized to effect what might be called the "political
modernization" of society. The masses were forced to enter
into the political arena, but their activities were carefully controlled by the Party. Their participation in politics was limited to serving support functions, but that participation was required and rigidly enforced. They were
forced to march in countless demonstrations, with their
presence insured by vigilant Party secretaries calling the
roll. They were forced to sign up for "peace bonds," giving
10 percent of their incomes to the state. They were forced
to collect signatures for the abolition of the American
atomic bombs or to applaud enthusiastically the explosion
of the first Soviet atomic bomb. They had to participate
in seminars after long hours of work and to study Stalin's
Kratkii kurs, day in and day out. They were required to
work in _agit-prop_ teams to mobilize the entire population
for some timely cause. And, above all, the first stage of
political development was characterized by the adoration of
a beloved leader, the all-knowing, wise father of mankind,
be he known by whatever name.

The first phase, all-out mobilization, brought about
successes in the economic sphere. The changes in the life
of the states of Eastern Europe were significant; by and
large most of these states were transformed from industrially backward, agrarian countries to partially industrialized or at least industrializing states. It cannot be
denied that even in previously industrialized states like
Czechoslovakia factories were built and the high percentage
of people employed in agriculture decreased; but this progress in the economic sphere was accompanied with enforced
political mobilization that led the most advanced, most
modernized countries down the path to revolution. The con-
flagrations in Hungary and Poland in 1956 and the Prague
Spring of 1968 were due in no small measure to the raised
political consciousness of the citizenry and to the development of cognitive dissonance, created by the continually
changing political line. All of the requirements to learn,
to relearn, reexamine, alter, and accept the Party dictates
had some very obvious results. Specifically, the masses began to express their own political concerns, while the system did not have the flexibility to deal with independent
demand articulation. The revolutions clearly signaled a
need for new institutions, for greater _real_ popular involvement, for less Party control, for increased freedom, and for
more credibility--expressing familiar demands similar to the
Party's own, albeit empty, slogans advanced during the previous decade.

It became clear, however, that these slogans would not and could not be implemented within the framework of the communist systems that existed during the mobilization phase. Party rule could not, of course, coexist with real democracy; an independent state could not exist within the Soviet orbit; and the applied rule of the working class could not be reconciled with the imposed rule of an elite. Consequently, none of the revolutions resulted in immediate political change.

SECOND PHASE: STAGNATION

The second phase of political development, for want of a more precise term, could be described as an era of stagnation. The revolts that had tried to implement changes failed, and in their aftermaths new rulers came to power. The principal concern of this postrevolutionary leadership was to find new ways to stabilize their rule and to further the economic modernization necessary for the continuation of the system and their own power. Each of these postrevolutionary regimes--specifically the Polish, Czech, and Hungarian regimes--had four general goals: to get the state apparat functioning again; to insure their own survival as leaders; to move the state along on its path toward economic progress; and to achieve legitimacy for their own rule.

In the countries that have experienced this second phase, the leaders have generally been successful in insuring their own survival and they have been able to restore order and get the state functioning again. The new regimes, however have failed to improve significantly on the economic development of the state and they have been unable to gain a sense of legitimacy in the eyes of the people.

The reasons for the lack of serious economic progress are perhaps inherent in the system of production the leaders inherited from their predecessors, and the very nature of the communist system inhibits significant improvement in the postrevolutionary mobilization phase. The familiar causes of failure--the lack of hard currency, the lack of innovative management, the low level of technology, the small amounts invested in research and development, the inherent economic exploitation by the USSR, the closed international economic structures--are well known. What does need to be pointed out, however, is that at this stage the political system appears to inhibit further economic development. To implement the status-quo-maintaining phase-two goals, the Party needs disciplined managers for industry. These managers must be selected on the basis of their loyalty to the

Party and not for their managerial ability. Production on any basis--even minimal, lagging, closely regulated, centralized, poor-quality production--is preferable to no production, strikes, and opposition to Party rule. Obedience to Party orders, the necessary condition for the survival of Party rule, is not, however, a quality that fosters independent thinking, decision making, creativity, and initiative. Consequently, the economic growth rate during the period of stagnation remains minimal, ranging roughly between 2 and 4 percent, but the Party retains power and continues to "call the tune."

Even more significantly, the fourth goal of the Party--to foster an acceptable sense of legitimacy of its rule among the citizenry--clearly meets with failure. The new regimes inherit triple stigmata: they are associated with the forces that struck down a national revolt; they are associated with the continuation of an unpopular, disliked rule; and they are blamed for every failure of the system, including bad harvests due to inclement weather and unfortunate mine accidents. While in the West one may blame bad management, bad administrative practices of a particular party, or inclement weather for unfortunate failings, in the communist society every accident, fault, or failure is blamed on the system. During the second phase, the population, with its raised level of political consciousness, continues to see and verbalize the cognitive dissonance caused by the demanded acts of fealty, and the recognition of the regimes' failures add significantly to stresses and tensions that develop during this stage.

These failures result in a buildup of tensions and an increase in demand articulation that become noticeable toward the end of the second phase. The stagnation in the economic sphere brings an actual decrease in standards of living, a virtually ruined agriculture, low morale, and a further degeneration of the national spirit. Eventually the leaders face the possible threat of renewed insurrection against the regime. (The most notable example of this phenomenon was the Gdansk riots of 1970.) Haltingly and in exasperation, the holders of power slowly attempt to come to grips with the real problems facing the state. It is at this juncture when they first realize that serious changes are indeed mandatory if they are to retain their rule.

It becomes obvious that some of the economic benefits promised by the system have to materialize. The people, bone-weary with building socialism, need to see that something has been built. Slogans simply won't suffice anymore, and the regimes realize, sooner or later, that they have to perform miracles of some kind to provide at least an illu-

sion of progress. Gomulka, in Poland, served as an example
of a leader who failed to realize the danger potential of
these increasing tensions, while Kadar and Gierek, in Hungary and Poland, have provided the kind of innovative leadership necessary for political survival. But the changes in
the economic sphere cannot be accomplished as long as the
sullen masses pose even a theoretically possible threat to
the leading elite of the Party. The only acceptable change
that can be accomplished is reform from above and not revolution from below. Hence, toward the end of the stagnation
phase the leaders begin to consider policies unprecedented
for a communist state. Contrary to the practices prevalent
in the mobilization phase, the regime now begins the depoliticization of everyday life and tries to disengage people from political activity.

There are many signs of the depoliticization of everyday life. Instead of demanding absolute, active allegiance
from the citizenry, the rulers demand only a lack of activity against the state. Kadar summed up the policy suc-
cinctly with his famous phrase: "He who is not against us
is with us." Participation in marches and demonstrations is
no longer compulsory, although social pressures and the
ghost of the fear of the past remain strong reinforcers of
participation. Political seminars and political meetings
dwindle in number, and the Party, in practice, requests its
population to "leave the driving to us." Once depoliticization is at least partially accomplished, the Party starts to
alleviate the tensions and release the pressures by beginning to implement a comprehensive set of economic and political reforms that issue in the third phase of development.

THIRD PHASE: THE REFORM ERA

The third phase, the era of reform, presents us perhaps
with the most difficult relationship between economic and
political development in which the relationships between economic change and political change are intricately intertwined and are constantly altered. During this phase, sometimes it is the needs of the economic subsystem that force
the alteration of the method of rule, in other instances the
needs of the political subsystem force the alteration of the
economic substructure of the country. Since to date only
Hungary and Poland have entered this phase, and since these
states are at different levels of reform, it is rather difficult to establish a clear model of political and economic
development for this stage. Nonetheless, by examining the
changes undertaken by these states we may see the emergence

of a model for the type of rule to be practiced during thi
stage.

The entry into the era of reform, as mentioned above,
is preceded by limited successes in the program of modernization that have taken place during the two previous phase
of rule. The states now possess significant industries,
some of which have growth potential; collectivization and
mechanization have made some inroads into agrarian backward
ness; urbanization has created a pool of available skilled
labor; and the country is not dependent on agriculture as a
major source of social activity.

In the economic sphere, however, significant problems
still exist. The emphasis on heavy industry created factories based on labor intensive production, low wages, low
material costs, and producing for a monopoly market, where
the products, regardless of their poor quality, are pur-
chased for want of better available items. These industries, however, become more and more unprofitable as labor
costs rise, as material costs increase, and as competition
crowds them out of domestic and foreign markets. The state
is thus forced either to abolish them or to continue paying
significant price supports for their products, allocating
scarce state financial resources for nonproductive activities.

At the beginning of this phase, the economic managemen
of the country is in the hands of inherited "yes-men" who
were needed in the second stage to insure political control
These managers, however, cannot be counted upon to understand or implement needed economic innovation. Finally, th
Party is still isolated and regarded as an illegitimate
holder of rule, and the citizenry compares its lot with tha
of the people living in the Western industrialized states.
Consequently, the reforms that the poststagnation era regimes undertake have a primarily political purpose: the
legitimation of Party rule through provision of a better
standard of living. The changes, which are undertaken in
order to insure the retention of Party rule, occur both in
the economic and the political spheres.

As the experiences of Hungary and post-Gomulka Poland
illustrate, the reforms generally occur in six different
areas:

1. The universal emphasis on heavy industry is abolished as light industrial production and some consumer-
oriented production begin to be recognized as the most important industrial sectors. Some unprofitable heavy industrial production is abolished even at the cost of minimal
social dislocation.

2. Serious specialization of production is undertaken to assure the greatest efficiency for state investments. The traditionally lucrative industries of the past are re-emphasized again, and new branches of industry that concentrate on such diverse production as plastics and the chemical industry begin to receive preference in budget allocation.

3. Some elements of the market economy are introduced, such as differentiated prices, profitability, and competition for various types of goods and services.

4. A decentralization in planning and enforcement activities replaces the highly centralized system of the past. Managers are given greater freedom to decide what to produce and what to sell, including the right of hiring and firing practically at will.

5. Technology and capital from advanced countries is imported without a great deal of avowed attention to political considerations. The possibility of increased production rather than the origins of the technological advances is the major concern.

6. Imports, particularly from the West, are significantly increased, and managers are given large measures of freedom in concluding independent agreements with Western firms. These changes bring an influx of consumer goods and force the domestic production to upgrade itself. In addition, enterprises begin producing competitive goods for foreign markets without significant state interference.

To some extent, the leaders who implement these reforms may be said to have pulled rabbits out of their political hats. The population is struck with a sudden illusion of progress. Cars, pullovers from Italy, nylon shirts, cosmetics, and paper products suddenly become available in an admittedly striking contrast to the situation of the past. Agriculture begins to prosper, more food products reach the market, a trickle of foreign capital comes in, and the weary, deprived population breathes a collective sigh of relief. The regime thus finally gets its mandate of legitimacy because "things are getting noticeably better."

These reforms in the economic sphere, however, also demand political change and create significant revision in the political sphere. The power of the huge economic bureacracy is reduced. Party interference into production techniques and processes has to decrease. Managers are no longer expected to be "yes-men," carrying out party policy, but efficient technocrats, managers, and specialists whose prime aim is profit. The decentralization allows independent decision making for people who were hitherto used to

following orders. The increased need for technology and th
freer export-import system enlarges contacts with Western
firms, thereby eroding the previously emphasizing ideological claims to total communist supremacy over the West. And
finally, the Party's role in the economic production of the
state assumes secondary importance, an unprecedented development in the evolution of communist systems.

Depoliticization continues. Some electoral reforms ar
undertaken: multiple candidacies for parliamentary and
council seats are restored, and the nomination processes ar
opened up to include greater personal competition for legis
lative power. Greater individual freedoms are allowed: th
power of the political police is reduced, travel to the Wes
becomes easier, and literary liberalization takes place.

Furthermore, within the Party elite the process of
interest-group articulation and demand aggregation gives
rise to the emergence of leaders who are associated with
different interests. In short, a pluralization of function
can be observed. The need for continuing economic progress
clashes with the need for the maintenance of rigid Party
rule. In order to maintain that rule, the Party leadership
must act very cautiously and with precise timing. In spite
of functional pluralization during this phase of development, the Party must retain the powers of ultimate decision
making and must make certain that the reforms do not exceed
the carefully delineated parameters of acceptability: They
cannot be accompanied by the emergence of real opposition-
Party politics or the pluralization of decision making, nor
may the reforms push the state to assume a posture that may
be perceived as hostile by the USSR.

Alienated and separated from the depoliticized masses,
the Party governs the nation and continues its economic reform activities from above. But the people now seem to accord the much-desired legitimacy to the ruling Party. They
accept the legitimacy of the Party because the reforms of
the third stage of development seem to accord them more benefits than they have known in the past few decades.

As Barrington Moore stated, during periods of great social transformation "to maintain and transmit a value system, human beings are punched, bullied, sent to jail, throwr
into concentration camps, cajoled, bribed, made into heroes,
encouraged to read newspapers, stood up against a wall and
shot, and sometimes even taught sociology."[1] In the third
phase of reform, after the mobilization and the stagnation
phase, the people are no longer punched or bullied, cajoled,
incarcerated, and shot. What is interesting to observe,
however is that in this third phase the Party does not even
wish to teach sociology to the people. All it hopes to

accomplish is to create a world where the Party is left free to rule and where the people accord their rulers a sense of legitimacy because the Party offers material advancement and because the Party leaves them alone. Accordingly, it appears that the reforms result in the successful maintenance of Party rule and in an adequate standard of living. These two achievements represent an important accomplishment for these East European communist regimes and point to significant within-the-system political change.

NOTE

1. Barrington Moore, Jr., <u>Social Origins of Dictatorship and Democracy</u> (Boston: Beacon Press, 1966), p. 486.

**MODERNITY AND THE
CHARACTER OF DISSENT**
Barbara Wolfe Jancar

In 1960 Paul Zinner stated at the annual Political Science Association meeting that Eastern Europe was no longer "a focal point of popular unrest and strife between subjugated peoples and their political masters, nor was it a locus of ideological and power struggles. . . ."[1] These comments were made after the Soviet invasion of Hungary had seemingly silenced the dissent movements that had begun in 1953 and came to a head in 1956. Since 1960 Eastern Europe has witnessed the Prague Spring, the Polish labor strikes of December 1970, and the 1971 nationality crisis in Yugoslavia. Far from having been quelled, dissent in the communist world seems more vigorous today than ever before. Dissent has shown itself capable of changing leaderships, modifying political and economic systems, and even, as was the case with Czechoslovakia, completely transforming the political and social environment. And while violence may temporarily drive it underground, it seems to have a tenacious capacity to resurface at the forefront of any new political crisis.

This chapter is concerned with tradition and change in the character of dissent in Eastern Europe and the Soviet Union. The question is, "Has modernity made a difference in the nature and practice of dissent under communism?" Given the fact that some form of opposition has always existed in the area under noncommunist and modernizing communist regime alike, what new factors can modernization be said to have introduced into the traditional dissent equation? Although a great deal of dissent material emanating from the Soviet Union and Eastern Europe has been published, to the best of my knowledge there has been little inquiry into a possible relationship between modernization and opposition in the communist absolute monopoly system. This chapter attempts a preliminary investigation.

At the outset, some definitions would seem necessary. Zev Katz's definition of dissent as applied to communist polities seems a useful one and will be operative here. In his view, active dissent as practiced in communist countries has both an objective and subjective aspect. On the one hand, it is an overt politically related act that rejects official goals or means. On the other hand, in order to be considered a bona fide dissent, the overt act must be characterized by the authorities as politically related and therefore a challenge to existing norms.[2] For example, demands for freedom of the press are acts of dissent precisely because the ruling group has decided a free press is contrary to "socialist" community. Dissent can be manifested either from within the Party framework or some other officially approved institution or from outside all regime-sanctioned channels. Beyond the active opposition, there is the vast amorphous arena of passive dissent, identified with the population at large--disaffected workers, ethnic groups, religious and cultural affinities--from which the active dissent draws its sustenance and support.

Modernity is less easy to define. The simplest definition would be the application of the scientific mentality to production.[3] But this focuses primarily on economic development. A more inclusive definition would have to take in social and cultural development as well: an increase in economic capacity through the application of science to production, with a concomitant differentiation in the social structure and the generalization of cultural values.[4] A critical question regarding modernization is whether economic development promotes a pluralistic social order that in turn gives rise to demands for a competitive political system. Robert Dahl has argued that it does.[5] Alexander Eckstein goes even further in suggesting that the totalitarian features of communist systems per force have to be modified by the process of economic growth because modernization demands structural differentiation and consensus, not terror, as the norm of predictable social interaction.[6] Elsewhere, I have described what I consider the main impediment to economic growth in communist societies, namely, the subservience of the economy to the maintenance of the power of the ruling group. This "second function" of control has historically been at the expense of the economy's primary function of efficient economic development.[7] It is not within the scope of this chapter to decide whether economic growth can indeed occur without accompanying social and political pluralization, as George Fischer has argued it can in his theory of monist societies.[8] Suffice it to say that in the world as we know it, technology appears to be at its highest level of development primarily in countries having pluralistic economic, social, and political systems. Although little research has been done on defining the relationship between economic growth and political and social institutions, for the purposes of this chapter I would like to accept the proposition that whether or not a necessary and sufficient relation between competitive political pluralism and a high level of economic development can be demonstrated,[9] modernization does bring with it definite tendencies toward social pluralization. The hypothesis of this chapter is that the pluralistic tendencies inherent in the modernization process have affected the traditional character of political dissent in communist systems in three major ways: in its permanency, its *modus operandi*, and its goals

All authoritarian regimes have known opposition, and communist systems are no exception to the general rule. But I believe we have to distinguish between the sporadic and spontaneous outbreaks of dissent typical of preindustrial authoritarian society (such as a peasant uprising) or the violent but unsynchronized protests of a developing communist society (such as the Kronstadt Revolt) and the highly orchestrated event that was the Prague Spring. It is the contention here that modernization has made it possible for opposition in communist systems to achieve permanent organization and purpose in its efforts to influence preferred value accumulation and distribution. Whether the communist regimes give dissent institutional legitimacy or not, opposition exists and will continue to exist either as factions within the formal institutional structures or informal groupings without.

THE PERMANENCY OF DISSENT

An advanced economy requires certain basics for its successful operation. Among the most important should be mentioned literacy, increased educational opportunities, skilled workers, managers, and professionals, and the development of bureaucracies and other organizations. These fundamental requirements necessitate the learning and distribution of political skills to large numbers of individuals, such as managerial and organizational expertise, communication skills, knowledge, status, and prestige. As the economy becomes more complex, the number of organizations proliferates and the number of individuals with sufficient skills and social access to maneuver and succeed in society increases. Organizations and institutions develop their vested interests and compete with each other for autonomy and a fair share of the distribution of available resources and labor.[10]

The impact of this process on the permanency of the opposition in the communist systems may be described as three-
fold: in the first place, it has promoted a permanent
cleavage in the ruling group. Economic and social differentiation requires entrance of an ever-expanding number into
the new class, from which the leadership is recruited. Because of the economy's need to perform the second function
of maintaining the ruling group in power, the competition
between vested economic interests inevitably involves a political power struggle.[11] De-Stalinization was the recognition by the Soviet leaders that fundamental tension existed
between the ongoing development of the Soviet economy and
centralized, coercive political control. From then on, all
the communist leaderships have been roughly divided over
whether to push forward economic growth through liberalization at the expense of political power or whether to continue on a modified Stalinist course. Typically, those who
have been in the seat of power, such as Novotny, Gomulka
after 1956, Brezhnev, and even Tito, have opted for the continuation of centralized political control at the expense of
the economy. Those who have been vying for power, such as
Gomulka in 1956, Dubcek and Smrkovsky, Khrushchev in 1953,
have preferred more rational economic growth. This division
between political power and economic development is a permanent one. Modernization has no predetermined model. More
important, technological advance is predicated upon free access to information in order to arrive at as accurate an
evaluation of a given situation as possible, and on the basis of that information rapid decision making that will secure optimal adaptation to a continually changing environment.

A further type of leadership division is that between
the elites of the various constituent groups of the economic
and social order. In all communist societies, the scientific and cultural intelligentsia were the first to recognize the importance of free information and to demand the
guarantees of civil rights. On their part, the technocratic
elites (managers and professionals) have pressured for economic rationalization that would depoliticize the economy
and allocate managerial responsibility, while the Party and
state bureaucratic elites have consistently opposed such reform. It should be noted that this type of dissent followed
the demands for free expression and developed after the Stalinist economic model proved incapable of solving the problems of industrialized society. In their turn, the elites
of the different demand sectors have also been divided over
economic goals and methods, the producer demand and military
sectors being generally aligned against the agricultural,
consumer, and public service interests.[12] As with the first

division between liberals, or revisionists, and neo-Stalinists, the cleavage between the members of the top echelons of the economic and social groupings is permanent. It is rooted in the centralized control structure of the communist system where decisions regarding resource allocation are made only at the leadership level, at the convergence of an increasing number of input demands that vie with the economy's capacity to meet them. Thus the ruling group functions by factionalism and compromise. When no consensus can be reached, the ruling group either falls apart, as it did in Hungary in 1956 and in Czechoslovakia in 1968 (to a limited extent), or one faction gains the ascendant with full authority to "purge" the dissenters. This process gives birth to the phenomenon of political swings toward more centralized control or greater liberalization.

A second impact of modernization upon the permanency of dissent in communist systems is that economic differentiation has now fused with traditional interest conflicts, such as nationality and religion, thereby fostering mutual reinforcement. The influence of modernization upon the nationality problem in Czechoslovakia and Yugoslavia is particularly evident. In each case, there has been a polarization of economic interests along national lines, with an economically advanced ethnic group evincing greater reform tendencies than its less fortunate neighbor. While Bohemia was industrialized under the former "bourgeois" regime, Slovakia's industrialization took place for the most part under communist direction. By 1966, their relative economic success encouraged the Slovaks to pressure for and win less domination by Prague, a greater share for Slovakia of the total national investment, and the assignment of priority to Slovak economic growth. The Slovaks' essentially negative reaction to official economic policies reinforced those elements in the Czech elite that had been demanding thoroughgoing economic reform. However, when the reform came, the Slovaks proved much less susceptible to the winds of the Prague Spring than did the more economically advanced Czechs

In Yugoslavia the marked economic imbalance between Croatia and Serbia has served to exacerbate the traditional Serb-Croat rivalry. The pre-1965 centralized economy policy attempted to rectify the situation by making the southern republics the foremost beneficiaries of federal and republican investment funds and subsidies. Croats protested what they termed the economic exploitation of Croatia by Belgrade An economic reform was instituted in 1965, but no agreement could be reached between the nationalities as to the nature of its decentralized structure, the Croats favoring more decentralization, the Serbs demanding greater control by Belgrade. The conflict over economic arrangements attained

such proportions in 1971 that Tito had to intervene personally to keep the federation together.[13]

In Poland, the marriage of interests was between religion and the economic and political reformers, as the latter
favored greater pluralization than did the more orthodox
Party leaders. Gomulka needed the support of the Catholics
to come to power in 1956, yet it was the church that became
increasingly critical of him, as his reformist measures collapsed. It is no coincidence that shortly after the December 1970 riots, the church should have published its terms
for full normalization of relations with the new Polish
leadership. Among the conditions were the right "to truth
of information and free expression of one's views and demands," and the right to "material conditions which insure
decent existence to families and the individual citizen."[14]
With this last condition, the church indicated it had sided
with the workers. The effect of the consolidation of economic with traditional dissent elements is not only to
broaden the basis of dissent but, more important, to achieve
the permanent identification of historic opposition trends
with the fundamental problems of modern society.

A final aspect of modernization as related to the permanency of dissent in communist systems is the fluidity of
opposition alignments. It cannot be assumed that certain
groups will always be in opposition, while other groups are
always going to be pro-regime. The blue-collar workers are
a case in point. It was in many respects a tragedy that the
Czech and Slovak working class came over to the cause of reform so late. Up to mid-summer 1968, the reformist coalition, if one can call it that, included the Slovaks and the
economic and technical elites, including the cultural intelligentsia. Supporting the more conservative line were the
hard core of the Party apparat and the blue-collar workers,
who feared a loss of pay and a reduction in their living
standards that had been one of the main contributions of
Stalinism.[15] During 1964 and 1965, as some reforms began to
be implemented, there were strikes against government direc-
tives. Even as late as March 1968, Novotny was able to make
a last effort to return to power by a direct appeal to working class solidarity. It was not until the breakdown of the
Revolutionary Trade Union Movement in the summer, when it
became clear that economic reform would permit the restoration of full trade-union activity, that the workers went
over to the side of the liberals.[16] This late but full-
scale mobilization of the Czech trade unions, in particular,
was decisive in keeping Dubcek in power as long as he was.

In Yugoslavia, the much-vaunted worker ownership of the
factories was a cause for worker hostility toward the intellectuals and reformers. The 1965 reforms in effect meant

that the profits made in the enterprises could not go back
into worker pockets but had to be allocated to investment.
Thus, the worker might have been theoretically the factory
owner, but in fact he was bringing home often less than hal.
his pay, while his "employee," the manager, was taking home
full pay. In Poland again, the December 1970 riots were in
direct response to reform proposals, which would institute a
worker incentive program to increase productivity. At stake
was the take-home pay of the average worker. In both countries in the 1950s the workers had been on the side of reforms and against official policies. In the 1970s the workers found themselves again in opposition, this time against
a set of reform proposals endorsed by the regime. The significance of the Polish riots may be said to lie in the fact
that the Polish worker had realized that reform or no reform
there was a basic antagonism of interest between the ruling
privileged elite and himself, and this antagonism had to
find political expression and a political solution.

The fluidity of dissent alignments is perpetuated by
the cleavages within the ruling group. The permanent tension between economic progress and the maintenance of political power means that, in their struggles for ascendancy,
the contestants must seek political support among the conflicting interests. If they adopt a too-Stalinist approach,
they will lose domestic standing and be forced to rely on
the Soviet Union. If they permit too much liberalism, they
run the risk of losing power completely. In the shifts between the two extremes, the liberal period is characterized
by the leadership's heavier courting of client groups, as
Gomulka did with the church, Gierek and Novotny with the
workers, and Dubcek with the Czechs and the intelligentsia.
However, success in modifying regime policy in the direction of their demands reinforces the constituent group's
power position and thus gives it quasi-permanent sanction.
The downfall of Gomulka after the 1970 riots proved to the
Polish workers the efficacy of their action, as did the
Slovak success in ending the Novotny regime.

The difference between Stalin's liquidation of the
kulaks and the Polish worker opposition of today cannot be
too much stressed. In the 1930s the peasant represented
traditional social and economic patterns. As such, his demands lay outside the modernization process. Thus, his future and the political future of members of the politburo
were essentially nondependent, distinct one from another.
Present communist leaders, however are dependent upon the
working class if they want to maintain economic development.
Similarly, they cannot risk the total alienation of the scientific and managerial elites who provide the innovation,

know-how, and managerial skills necessary to an advanced society. As a result, the ruling group is in a situation where they have to allow some dissent because terror is dysfunctional to economic progress, and they must cater to that dissent in order to stay in power. In this respect, it could be argued that the continuous power struggles within the ruling group tend to give legitimacy to the diversification of interests brought about by modernization without providing formal legal recognition.

INTERACTION BETWEEN THE REGIME AND ITS CRITICS

A second impact of modernization upon dissent in communist systems is in the mode of interaction between the regime and its critics. Perhaps the most significant development in this area is what appears to be the increasing ineffectiveness of political violence both as an opposition tactic and a regime response as modernization has progressed.[17] Violence initiated by dissenters begets violent reprisals on the part of the authorities, which have a certain intrinsic justification. What is more, the dissenters seem to have learned that violence on their part tends to be counterproductive. Regime retaliation is swift, overwhelming, and certain, thereby preventing any hope of success. More important, in societies where mass coercion has been the norm, there is more moral mileage and greater public sympathy to be gained by being the victim of violence rather than its perpetrator. As Amalrik wrote to Kuznetsov, the only way to have complete freedom is to be ready to submit to violence.[18] The cultivation of nonviolent methods—sit-ins, demonstrations, petitions, fasts, letter writing—is a relatively new feature of communist dissent movements that are outside the officially approved institutional structure. As regards movements from within the legal Party and government framework, the Prague Spring, in my opinion, is one of the prime examples of how carefully organized, planned opposition within the Party and government can lead to ultimate success in a communist system.

The adoption of nonviolence by the opposition intensifies the negative impact of violent retaliation by the regime, which is thereby deprived of any moral rationalization for its actions. In this sense, it could be argued that the Soviet invasion of Czechoslovakia was perhaps even less justifiable than the previous invasion of Hungary in 1956, precisely because there was no violent uprising in progress. On their part, the people of Czechoslovakia demonstrated the essential ineffectiveness of armed intervention by their

determined nonviolent stand against the Soviet tanks. To a
limited extent, their nonviolence brought results. The Soviets were unable to impose their original plan and had to
settle for a compromise. The Czechoslovak leaders were not
liquidated but returned to their country, and the proponents
of "socialism with a human face" were able to remain in
power for another half year.

If armed intervention by a foreign power has negative
consequences in the face of nonviolence, the impact of violent reprisals by the domestic ruling group is even more
dysfunctional. The fact that the Polish authorities fired
on their own workers in 1970 dramatized the distance between
the rulers and the ruled and intensified feelings of hostility that possibly will take years to remove. Faced with an
economic crisis, the Polish leadership could ill afford such
an action. (Gierek, in my opinion, fully realized the disastrous consequences of Gomulka's violent reaction against
the strikers. Hence, his decision to meet the workers' demand and to talk with them at their place of work.)

Indeed, it would seem as if modernization had made it
impossible for any ruling body to liquidate those opposing
its policies. First and foremost, the smooth functioning of
an advanced economy requires relatively predictable working
conditions for all strata of society. The arbitrary intimi-
dation of people into submission by terror means that fewer
are willing to take responsible jobs because of the enormous
risks involved. Forced labor is less efficient than willing
labor. During the early stages of industrialization, when
manual labor takes the place of technology, the firing or
liquidation of skilled personnel is relatively less important than in an advanced economy, where considerable time
must be invested in the training of managers and technical
specialists who cannot be immediately replaced. The damage
done to the Czechoslovak economy by the defection or purge
of the country's leading cadres may take a generation to re-
pair. The 1968 Polish purge of Jews and intellectuals had
similar implications.

Second, as David Apter has argued, high coercion results in low information.[19] Where low information exists,
governments tend to have poor communication with their client groups and reduced feedback as to the consequences of
actions taken. Hence, the ability to make effective choices
is impaired. The problem is to find the right balance between information and coercion. I suggest that the Party
leaders cannot run a permanent purge because during such
purges the process of modernization suffers more than at
other times, as the power struggle within the ruling group
intensifies the economy's "second function" of coercion and

control, subordinating it to the political requirements of the leadership.[20] It can even be questioned whether a highly industrialized society can afford any kind of purge because of the economic disruption and reduction of information produced. If the communist regimes were willing and able to borrow all technological innovation from the West, periodic purges might cause less upheaval. But borrowing can only take place at the loss of a certain amount of independence. Hence, the regimes' dilemma that the more advanced their economies, the less functional does violence become and the greater the need to tolerate dissent, which challenges their power position.

A second influence on the modus operandi of dissent is what Eugen Loebl has termed the social benefits of technology.[21] In preindustrial societies, dissent has a greater tendency to remain localized for several reasons: There is no rapid way for knowledge about it to spread; there are inherent difficulties in maintaining an organized dissent network over extended distances; and the absence of a generalized system of values tends to encourage and maintain a parochial perception of issues. Modernization with its mass transit and mass communications brings totally new conditions. While such limitations as the domestic passport and media censorship are attempts to keep regime monopoly of the distribution of the social benefits accruing from improved transportation and communications, no communist leadership is in a position to deny these totally to its population if economic development is to continue. In terms of its use by the opposition, the most profitable benefit is probably the mass media, since they furnish dissent with the means of both domestic and foreign contact. Mass communications would seem to serve two functions: information and publicity. During the Prague Spring there was little doubt that the liberals who captured control of the media saw their role primarily in terms of providing information. In the words of one Czech refugee, "Our problem, then, was to make real information acceptable to people who had never had any."[22] The same could be said of the Soviet samizdat. The stress here is on real or accurate information. For an opposition to establish its validity and acquire followers in communist systems, the first step would seem to be to create trust, where trust in the printed or spoken word did not exist. A prime factor in the creation of trust is accuracy of information, not only to actual and potential domestic followers, but also to the outside world.[23]

The dissemination of information thus serves as a link between leaders and followers and contributes to the mobilization and organization of the dissent movement. It is no coincidence that every recent dissent group in the communist countries has managed either to capture a legally existing mass medium or to start one of its own, whether it be the Polish Student, the Czech Literarni listy, or the Soviet Chronicle of Human Events. In Yugoslavia, each nationality has its own series of publications to support its cause. The ability of the mass media to mobilize and organize followers was nowhere so well demonstrated as in Czechoslovakia in August 1968. The resolution and determination promoted by the press and television during the first day of the invasion forged a united nation almost overnight. This unity was sustained until the free radio and television were forced off the air. The communications media's capacity for mobilization and organization is one of the principal reasons why no communist government can tolerate a free press.

The information function of the mass media extends beyond national boundaries. The sit-ins, demonstrations, petitions, self-immolations, and other methods used by opposition groups would seem to indicate that the dissenters in the communist countries have learned about nonviolence from the West and are adapting its tactics to their particular environment. Moreover, what happens in one country quickly spreads to another. In my recent review of samizdat literature, I was surprised to find such a high number of translations from Czech and Slovak writers of the Prague Spring, evidence that the Soviet dissidents were keeping well abreast of developments there.[24] In this respect, more research is necessary on the influence of the modus operandi of a dissent movement in one communist country upon opposition groups in another. Certainly, it could be hypothesized that successful methods in one area are very likely to be copied all over. The tragedy for the Czechs and Slovaks in 1968 was that they apparently thought they had improved on the Hungarian dissenters by refusing recourse to violence. Yet, the tanks came all the same. This was no doubt an important lesson for the Polish strikers of 1970.

The publicity function of mass communications is a correlate of the information function. Through the effective use of press and television, a dissent group can make its situation known both at home and abroad. As illiteracy drops, and radio and television sets become more common in the home, the opposition can count on an expanding domestic audience, not to mention the larger audience of the external world. Indeed, it would seem as if reaching the international audience has often been more crucial than contacting domestic viewers and readers, Czechoslovakia being the possible exception. To reach the wider audience, the dissenters have to overcome the handicap of censorship. One way is to capture control of some of the legal media as has been mainly the case in Eastern Europe. Another is to perform acts that themselves are sufficiently "newsworthy" to attract world attention. These would include such desperate deeds as the self-immolations of Jan Palach or Roman Kalanta in 1972, or the attempted suicide of Ilya Rips in Riga in 1968, as well as the extraordinary feat of the obtaining of 17,000 signatures on a petition to the United Nations by the Lithuanian Catholics in 1968. Again, there can be a concerted effort to arouse world opinion as the Soviet Jews have done, or the organized exploitation of letters and petitions as the Soviet Baptists have done. Eastern Europe seems less rich in instances of this kind, probably because the opposition has had greater access to the approved media. To the degree that an individual or group succeeds in attracting international attention through publicity, the examples of Solzhenitsyn and the Soviet Jews suggest that violent reprisals on the part of the authorities tend to be reduced. Thus, the support of the outside world through the intermediary of the world press has a sustaining and supportive influence upon dissenters within the communist countries, since it can contribute to the modification of regime policies vis-à-vis the dissenting groups.

A final factor of modernization relative to dissident behavior is the increase in organizational and political skills that accompany economic development. In my opinion, one of the reasons why the East European and Soviet peasantry has played so small a role in the opposition movements in modernized communist societies has been their lack of political and organizational skills. (The peasants were the last to organize and did so sporadically during the Prague Spring.) Robert Lane has found that a deprived group does not always seek to gain entrance into the political arena. On the contrary, he presents a strong case that an improvement in living standards and educational skills is necessary before any group attempts political participation no matter what the society.[25] I believe that the evidence shows that the most vocal dissent groups in both Eastern Europe and the Soviet Union have either (1) had experience in mass organization in a precommunist modernized society, or (2) have acquired the requisite skills through their communist education and training. Certainly, the first proposition seems intuitively substantiated by Eastern Europe's intellectuals, working class, and nationality groupings. If Amalrik's statistics can be believed, the second hypothesis would find verification in the high percentage of intellectuals in the Moscow Democratic Movement.[26] The recent demonstration of

the amazing organizing abilities of the Soviet dissident
Baptists and the Crimean Tartars suggests an additional hypothesis of a time lag between the acquisition of skills and
the assumption of political activism. Such a proposition
would seem to shed some light on the relative passivity of
both groups prior to the 1960s, although the former had been
consistently persecuted with but little respite throughout
Soviet rule, and the latter endured the loss of its homeland
in 1944.

Modernization means that political expertise is no
longer the prerogative of the few, but through mass education and the organized living pattern of urbanized modern
life it has been diffused throughout all society. Just as
the regime cannot totally control the social benefits of
technology if it wants some degree of availability of information, so it cannot control the effects of the generalized acquisition of political skills. In both cases, total
control necessitates a resort to violence and the vicious
circle continues, further crippling the progress of economic
development or reversing it to nondevelopment, as Otto Ulc
argues in Chapter 4 of this volume. Thus, the ruling
group's attempts to control these aspects of modernization
only impede the process in the long run.

THE GOALS OF THE OPPOSITION

Up to 1956, the goals of the opposition may be described primarily in terms of the overthrow of the Stalinist
political system. The fundamental concepts that had built
that system remained unquestioned. Thus, Milovan Djilas
could argue that the Soviets had not built socialism, but
had created a new property-owning class. And Yugoslavia
could propose a new type of common ownership, the worker
ownership of enterprises. According to Djilas, Stalinism
may even be useful as an ideological instrument in the first
stages of modernization, but it cannot be equated with socialism. What the Soviet Union produced was a perversion of
socialism.[27]

With de-Stalinization, the focus of dissent started to
change, although the significance of that change did not become fully obvious until 1956, and not all of the dissenters
made the adjustment.[28] Significantly, the shift in focus
came from within the Communist Party membership. After
1956, the all-engrossing question was how to account for
the atrocities that had been committed in the name of immutable historical progress. In order to answer this question,
the fundamental premises of socialism, such as the virtues

of public property ownership and the leading role of the
working class, had to be challenged. What produced alienation? How could true socialism be brought about? The problem was not simply that Stalinism had brought political dictatorship, but this dictatorship had proved catastrophic to
economic development. The great need was to transform the
system from within, to rationalize it so it could enter the
postindustrial era.

It would be misleading to present the new goal orientation of the various oppositions as uniform either cross-
nationally or intranationally. Not only, as has been mentioned earlier, did different opinion groups think differently, but within groups there were tendencies to develop
solutions along entirely divergent lines, witness the conservatism of the Leningrad "Veche" group, which questioned
progress and upheld the past, as compared with the Moscow
Democratic Movement. Opinions varied greatly among those in
favor of greater economic rationalization as to how this
could be best accomplished. Czech economist Radovan Ripka,
for example, was far more to the right of the more radical
Ota Sik. Still, it does not seem to me to be too great a
distortion of the truth to say that with de-Stalinization
the primary problem for the majority of East European and
Soviet dissenters became the investigation of the reality of
their particular society, and that the main thrust of their
dissent was toward change rather than tradition.

This attitude did not imply the simple restoration of
the political and civil rights of bourgeois society, although many considered them starting points. The ideas of
the Prague Spring provide some indication as to what dissenters in one country perceived as the main issues involved
in moving an industrialized communist country into the postindustrial society. Foremost among these was the question
of the relationship between the concentration of power exemplified in the Stalinist system and economic development.
In Ludvik Vaculik's words, power was "subject to its own un-
breakable laws of development," and economic production relations were not the prime determinants of a political superstructure.[29] To launch Czechoslovakia into the technological revolution the power monopoly had to be broken and a
model developed that would truly make possible the application of science to production.[30] A second problem was the
relation of the technocratic elites to the general population. Ripka argued that because science, not labor, had become the decisive factor in economic growth, the ruling
class of the industrialized state was the technical and professional personnel. It could never be the worker. He saw
the possibility of a new conflict between the professional

and democratic aspects implicit in the scientific revolution.[31] The third problem, democracy, included and went beyond the other two. Liberals like Ivan Svitak insisted that
democratization within the Party was not enough, since it
did not challenge the basis of communist rule. He saw the
press playing a major role in breaking down what he termed
the hierarchy of privilege.[32] Others thought the way to
achieve true socialism was to institute a competitive political system.[33] But most asked the same basic question: How
to solve the loss of the human dimension brought about by
industrialization, which affected both capitalist and socialist countries alike? How to put man back into the center of his social and political world?

Such thinking has not been confined to Czechoslovakia.
In Yugoslavia, Professor of Sociology Mihailo Markovic has
written that ownership is a useless concept with which to
study the sources of social inequality in "socialist" countries. In his words, it can serve as "a means of ideological mystification."[34] Leszek Kolakowski looks at the problem from another viewpoint. For him, the dethronement of
Stalinism meant that Marxism had lost its universality and
had become diluted with what he terms "alien" elements. The
old axioms of immutable historical laws, the inevitability
of socialism, and the nature of the superstructure were all
obsolete. When Stalinism proved itself incapable of solving
modern economic and social problems, the acceptance of a
total Marxist credo became intellectually impossible. In
his view, barring the miraculous, Marxism as a coherent
philosophical system was dead. The dilemma of Marxism in
Eastern Europe, as he sees it, is that

> neither the fundamental issues concerning the
> functioning of society nor the views of the
> public about such issues may be investigated
> or discussed . . . without exposing the power
> system to mortal danger. . . . The fact that
> no self-regulatory mechanisms or feedback in-
> formation systems are able to function within
> the framework of these societies is not a de-
> fect that is transitory or remediable. It is
> an innate feature of a system wherein social
> stratification is based . . . on a qualitative
> inequality of privilege. A monopoly of "power"
> cannot be partially removed.[35]

What the dissenters have definitely realized is that
unless one challenges the basic premises of the communist
system, there is no way to undermine its inexorable dicta-

torial logic and little possibility of attaining the post-industrial society.

The Soviet invasion ended the Czech experiment and we do not know what new societal model the Czechs and Slovaks might have produced. During the brief eight months, there had been a sincere effort to break down man's isolation from man. Loebl coined the term "anthropocracy," or the rule of man as opposed to democracy, or mass rule. Czechs and Slovaks alike had known the grim inhumanity of Stalinism and wanted to create a system where power was not the sole criterion, but where consideration for human beings would characterize social relations. Such thinking may be naive and highly simplistic. One looks in vain among the proponents of the Prague Spring for a full-blown discussion of such critical areas as bureaucratization and social mobility. Still, the ideas generated there find sympathetic echoes in dissent movements across the world. Common to all is the conviction that modernization in its best sense demands, in Harold Lasswell's terms, "widespread participation in all preferred values," not only wealth and power, but more importantly, in well-being, respect, and justice.[36]

In sum, modernization has brought about a radical change in goal orientation on the part of dissent movements in Eastern Europe and the Soviet Union. In those countries where the Stalinist model has lost its efficacy in securing economic advance, the conceptual dogmas of the nineteenth century have been abandoned and the meaning of socialism reformulated in terms of the twentieth century reality of technology and its impact on the human condition.

CONCLUSION

The question posed by this chapter was whether modernity has made a difference in the traditional constitution and behavior of dissent in communist systems. Although, as was stated initially, the foregoing analysis represents only an exploratory investigation of the relationship between modernization and dissent in communist societies, the answer it suggests is affirmative. Modernization has created conditions that institutionalize if they do not legitimize an ongoing process of alignment-realignment of the client groups of communist societies into opposition or regime-supporting clusters. Such a process, as summarized in the findings below, did not exist in the preindustrial or modernizing systems of Eastern Europe and the Soviet Union and seems only to have emerged with modernity:

1. Through its structural diversification of interests, modernization in communist systems has given permanent
form to the organization of dissent, formerly expressed
through traditional cultural and religious channels.
2. The necessity for a predictable social order, the
social benefits, and the generalization of political skills
generated by modern society requires communist regimes to be
increasingly tolerant of dissent as modernization progresses
3. The goals of dissent tend more and more toward rationalization of the system in terms of free access to information, flexible decision making, and adaptation to
change as the communist countries move into the postindustrial society.
4. The tension between the leadership's incapacity to
respond to the demands made by modernization and those demands is a fundamental feature of modern communist monopoly
systems and is characterized by periodicity, with crises occurring at the points of greatest economic imbalance.
5. The mix and intensity of dissent vary with the objective severity of the economic crisis at hand, and the
number and kinds of perceived ills identified by constituent
groups is in need of rectification.

NOTES

1. Paul Zinner, paper delivered before the American
Political Science Association, New York, September 1960.
(Mimeographed.)
2. Zev Katz, Soviet Dissenters and Social Structure
in the USSR (Cambridge, Mass.: M.I.T. Center for International Studies, December 1971), Part A.
3. Raymond Aron, The Industrial Society (New York:
Praeger, 1967), p. 55.
4. Among the many books that could be cited as dealing with the definition of modernization, I would like to
mention Robert K. Merton, Social Theory and Social Change
(New York: Free Press of Glencoe, 1957); Talcott Parsons,
The System of Modern Societies (Englewood Cliffs, New Jersey:
Prentice Hall, 1971); Crises and Sequences in Political Development, Leonard Binder et al., eds. (Princeton, New Jersey: Princeton University Press, 1971); Foundation for Research on Human Behavior, Comparative Theories of Social
Change (Ann Arbor, Michigan: Foundation for Research on
Human Behavior, 1966); and David E. Apter, The Politics of
Modernization (Chicago: University of Chicago Press, 1965).
5. Robert A. Dahl, Polyarchy: Participation and Opposition (New Haven, Conn.: Yale University Press, 1971),
Chapters 4 and 5.

6. Alexander Eckstein, "Economic Development and Political Change in Communist Systems," World Politics 22, no. 4 (July 1970): 475-95.

7. Barbara W. Jancar, Czechoslovakia and the Absolute Monopoly of Power: A Case Study of Political Power in a Communist Country (New York: Praeger, 1971), Chapter 2.

8. George Fischer, The Soviet System and Modern Society (New York: Atherton Press, 1968).

9. Dahl finds significant correspondence between what he terms hegemonies and low economic development, and a similar level of correspondence between competitive political regimes and high economic development. Dahl, op. cit., pp. 65-67.

10. Ibid., pp. 76-80.

11. This point was very well made by an individual signing himself as P. Razummy in an essay entitled "The Disposition of Political Forces in the CPSU" published by samizdat. See Arkhiv samizdata, No. 570, as compiled by Radio Liberty Research Department.

12. These are Vernon Aspaturian's categories as described in "The Soviet Military-Industrial Complex--Does It Exist?" Journal of International Affairs 26, no. 1 (January 1972): 3.

13. For a discussion of Czechoslovak and Yugoslav nationality rivalries, see Barbara W. Jancar, "The Case for a Loyal Opposition Under Communism," Orbis 12, no. 2 (Summer 1968): 415-40.

14. As cited from New York Times, January 2, 1971.

15. In 1964 and 1965, as a prelude to reform, 1,300 production units were closed. Rude pravo, March 24, 1966.

16. See the author's discussion of the shift in worker alignments in Jancar, Czechoslovakia, op. cit., pp. 184-88. In his analysis of public opinion surveys in Czechoslovakia in 1968-69, Jaroslav Piekalkiewicz finds that of all the socioeconomic groups the farmers tended to support Dubcek the most, but that the high-water mark of overall popular support for his regime was not reached until September 1968, after the Soviet invasion. Jaroslav A. Piekalkiewicz, Public Opinion Polling in Czechoslovakia, 1968-1969: Results and Analysis of Surveys Conducted During the Dubcek Era (New York: Praeger, 1972), pp. 252-73.

17. In Trends in World Politics (New York: Macmillan, 1965), Bruce M. Russett presents statistical evidence in support of this contention, that political violence and economic development may vary inversely. In his study, countries with a per capita income exceeding $800 exhibit a low level of violence, while those with per capita incomes under $90 tend to exhibit high levels of violence (p. 137).

18. As published in Khronika, no. 11 (December 12, 1969), AS 333, p. 38.
19. Apter, op. cit., pp. 237-40.
20. Jancar, Czechoslovakia, op. cit., pp. 31-34.
21. Eugen Loebl, Conversations with the Bewildered (Cambridge, Mass.: Schenkman, 1972), Chapter 6.
22. Pavel X, "From Prague to Paris, Reflections of a Czech Refugee," Encounter 22, no. 2 (February 1969): 4.
23. Western observers are particularly anxious to verify the truthfulness of dissent literature, witness Peter Reddaway's deliberate care to assure the reader of the accuracy of samizdat reports in his Uncensored Russia: Protest and Dissent in the Soviet Union (New York: American Heritage Press, 1972), pp. 35 ff.
24. See particularly Khronika, nos. 3, 5, 8, 9, 11 (AS nos. 055, 112, 229, 260, 333).
25. See Robert E. Lane, "The Fear of Equality," American Political Science Review 53, no. 2 (March 1959): 35-51
26. Reference here is made to Amalrik's breakdown by occupation of what he considers the core membership of the Moscow Democratic Movement. See Andrei Amalrik, Will the Soviet Union Survive Until 1984? (New York: Harper & Row, 1970), pp. 15-16.
27. See Milovan Djilas, The New Class (London: Thames and Hudson, 1958), pp. 37-60.
28. For example, the Medvedev brothers are unable to offer comprehensive explanation of Stalinism, precisely because they start from the orthodox communist premises. Roy Medvedev, "Pravda o sovremennosti," Posev, no. 1 (1970), pp. 39-45.
29. From Ludvik Vaculik's speech to the Fourth Congress of the Czechoslovak Writers' Union, as published in Czechoslovak Press Survey No. 1946, September 4, 1967, put out by the Radio Free Europe Research Department. (Mimeographed.)
30. Eugen Lobl, Uvahy o dusevnej praci a bohastvo naroda (Bratislava: Vydavatelstvo Slovenskej akademie vied, 1967), Chapters 1 and 2.
31. Radovan Ripka, Civilization at the Crossroads (Prague, 1967).
32. Ivan Svitak, "Banging One's Head Against a Wall," Student, April 10, 1965, as translated in Survey, no. 66 (July 1968), pp. 83-86.
33. Vaclav Havel located the logical opposition to the Communist Party in the noncommunist majority of the population. This majority was to be organized as an independent and equal political alternative. "On the Subject of Opposition," Literarni listy, April 4, 1968.

34. Mihailo Markovic, "The Power Structure in Yugoslav Society," _Student_, November 2, 1971, pp. 6-7.

35. Leszek Kolakowski, "The Fate of Marxism in Eastern Europe," _Slavic Review_ 29, no. 2 (June 1970): 175-81.

36. Harold Lasswell, "Toward a General Theory of Directed Value Accumulation and Institutional Development," in _Comparative Theories of Social Change_, pp. 12-53.

COMMENT: SOME
PROBLEMS OF ANALYSIS
William E. Griffith

East European studies in the United States are beginning to absorb some of the contemporary theories of modernization and political development but, I regret to say,
rather uncritically and without an analysis of them from the
viewpoint of the Mannheimian sociology of knowledge. I find
it strange, for example, that what I regard as the best recent article on theories of political development, Samuel
Huntington's "The Change to Change,"[1] was not mentioned in
any of the papers or discussions at the conference. It may
therefore be of some use if I very briefly summarized Huntington's views and tried to apply them to theories of political development in Eastern Europe.

As Huntington pointed out, modernization theories developed after World War II in the United States as a result
of reaction against the Spenglerian-Lasswellian pessimism of
the 1920s and the 1930s and because of the post-1945 American
nationalistic optimism, anticolonial enthusiasm, and enthusiasm for the Third World. These theories tended, if only un-
consciously, to be based on belief in progress, "social science," and the benevolent virtues of industrialism--in other
words, to follow in the tradition of Comte, Mill, and Marx,
that is, of positivism, British liberalism, and Marxism.

However, recent developments in the Third World have
produced considerable disillusionment about it and have
therefore brought these theories into question. This disillusionment was in my view expressed by an earlier article
of Huntington's, "Political Development and Political Decay,"[2] in which, drawing on some of Karl Deutsch's earlier
work, he pointed out that when socialization and mobilization become greater than institutionalization, political decay sets in. Huntington was thinking of Third World countries, but Poland in 1970 was in my view another such example.

There are other criticisms of the classical American
theories of political development that Huntington does not
make. For example, modernization, especially in the development of mass communications media, increases nationalism,
which can be as easily traditional (the Flemings, Irish, and
French Canadians) as modernizing. This is particularly true
if modernization brings an ethnic minority into a perceived
discriminatory position: Croatia vs. Serbia and Slovakia

vs. the Czech lands. Finally, economic development can reverse or slow down, thus leading to political disdevelopment and decay: Eastern Europe in the 1950s; Uruguay, Argentina, and Chile today. (Indeed, the best antidote for overly optimistic theories of political development is the southern part of Latin America.)

As to concepts: As Huntington points out, modernization is probably a valid concept but it is not necessarily inevitable, nor is industrialization necessarily coupled with democracy. Political development is probably not a useful concept, since (as Huntington points out) it is neither aggregative nor distinguishing but legitimatizing.

Several other points may be made with respect to various aspects of modernization. I shall begin with the intelligentsia. It is important to realize, as Polish sociologists have so often pointed out, that the intelligentsia in Eastern Europe was fundamentally ambivalent toward modernization. Moreover, as economic development proceeded, the intelligentsia normally split into the creative and technical intelligentsia, with important political consequences.

This splitting process, and the more general process of bureaucratic rationalization, can be interrupted or delayed by foreign pressures. I am struck, for example, in Poland and elsewhere in Eastern Europe, by the persistence, and sometimes the revival, of the historic aristocratic, hierarchical values and behavior patterns. Indeed, in some respects the Polish and Hungarian developments of 1956 and the Czechoslovak developments of 1968 can be viewed as the conscious attempt of the intelligentsia to recover power from communist apparatchiki of working-class origin--that is to say, their conscious revival of their humanistic, elitist, aristocratic role. As Peter Ludz has pointed out in a penetrating criticism of the Czech intelligentsia in 1968,[3] and as one might say of much of the Latin American intelligentsia, it tends to be utopian and romantic, opposed to and more generally irrelevant to bureaucratization and rationalization.

To return to Eastern Europe: As Andrew Janos has pointed out, while bureaucratization and rationalization were inevitable as modernization proceeded in Eastern Europe, its effects tended to be cyclical.[4] Bureaucratic modernization in the pre-1939 period proved to be too slow. This led to the development of mass radical parties: first, integral nationalist and often (as in Romania) mystical, then, because of the Soviets, communist. All these parties were usually led by marginal men, ideologically motivated, particularly in search for personal identity. Initially, except in Yugoslavia and Albania, they were antinational. Eastern Europe has seen great economic development and social mobility since World War II, the first less than the West, the second greater. Bureaucratization has been present in both, but in Eastern Europe as compared to the West it has been less rationalized and more politicized. Zygmunt Bauman in his article in Archives: European Journal of Sociology has given in my view the best definition of what he calls the problem of phases in socialism.[5] There seems to be a 20-year cycle in Eastern Europe that results in the revival of bureaucratism and of greater inequality status and privileges for the children of the elite--that is, against the egalitarian ideals of socialism. Furthermore, the "pre-industrial" peasants, who have just become workers, have developed, as Jan Szczepanski has pointed out, working-class consciousness.[6] Finally, elite stratification leads, as Bauman and Ludz have pointed out, to the development, to use Ludz's terms, of a political/strategic elite and various counterelites, generational and occupational: the younger generation (for example, Gierek, Nyers, and Tripalo) and a technocratic counterelite in favor of bureaucratic rationalization.[7] Indeed, the strategic elite, those who hold the summits of political power, is also increasingly in favor of bureaucratic rationalization especially as a replacement for utopian and egalitarian ideology. Thus the trend toward bureaucratization and rationalization is inevitable. This results in three opposing groups: (1) the old political elite that slows down rationalization in order to keep political privileges; (2) the workers, who fear economic rationalization, for it would lead to the end of overemployment, and who therefore can be mobilized against it by the old political elite; and (3) the humanistic intellectuals, who are against rationalization because they are against bureaucracy, mass culture, and consumerism. Only the technocratic counterelite is for it because it would lead via decentralization to their status autonomy vis-à-vis the political/strategic elite. Thus the political elite can mediate between the workers and the technocratic elite (see, for example, some of the writings of Andras Hegedus in Hungary).[8]

Democratization and pluralism coming from the intellectuals is reversible and threatens the status of the political elite, the technocrats, because it is so political, and the workers, all of whom are therefore mobilized against it. Decentralization insofar as it means tenured privileges by managers is inevitably also rejected by the other elites. Therefore one can best expect a gradual incremental change in the present system, with its essentials remaining, for it has become the least common denominator between the elites

and the masses. As Max Weber pointed out, charismatic leadership is a way of overcoming such strains, and one sees in
the case of Ceausescu an attempt to use this and more generally to use nationalism. Since nationalism in Eastern Europe, with the exception of Czechoslovakia, has been normally right rather than left, it has also been a useful weapon
against the leftist intellectuals and is easily compatible
with bureaucratization and the technological revolution.
Finally, one must remember the continuing threat of Western
Europe to this least common denominator, for it has greater
economic development and cultural pluralism and historic
ties with Eastern Europe. In other words, it is a more attractive model of modernization for most of the left and
most of the right.

To conclude: Any analysis of these phenomena will inevitably have a normative component. Modernization and political development theory, except such a revision of it as
Huntington has made, passively assumes Western liberal democratic values. Barrington Moore's <u>Social Origins of Dictatorship and Democracy</u> is an exception from a radical neo-
Marxist point of view,[9] but Stanley Rothman's devastating
review of it has in my view brought many of its conclusions
into question.[10] One's analytical conclusions about modernization in Eastern Europe therefore will partly reflect one's
own values--aristocratic, bureaucratic, democratic, or egali-
tarian--values that, in my neo-Kantian view, are not susceptible to rational or scientific proof.

NOTES

1. Samuel P. Huntington, "The Change to Change: Modernization, Development and Politics," <u>Comparative Politics</u>
2 (1971): 283-322.
2. Samuel P. Huntington, "Political Development and
Political Decay," <u>World Politics</u> 17 (1965): 386-430.
3. Peter Ludz, "The New Socialism: Philosophy in
Search of Reality," <u>Problems of Communism</u>, July-August,
September-October 1969, pp. 33-42.
4. Andrew Janos, "The One-Party State and Social
Mobilization: East Europe between the Wars," in <u>Authori-
tarian Politics and Modern Society: The Dynamics of Established One-Party Systems</u>, ed. Samuel P. Huntington and
Clement H. Moore (New York: Basic Books, 1970), pp. 204-36.
5. Zygmunt Bauman, "Social Dissent in the East European Political System," <u>Archives: European Journal of So-
ciology</u> 12, no. 1 (1971): 25-51.

6. Jan Szczepanski's comments were made at the March 23-24, 1973 conference at Columbia University, "Eastern Europe: The Impact of Modernization on Political Development."

7. Peter C. Ludz, ed., <u>The Changing Party Elite in East Germany</u> (Cambridge, Mass.: MIT Press, 1972).

8. See, for example, "Documents: Hegedus, His Views and His Critics," <u>Studies in Comparative Communism</u> 2 (April 1969): 121-52.

9. Barrington Moore, Jr., <u>Social Origins of Dictatorship and Democracy</u> (Boston: Beacon Press, 1966).

10. Stanley Rothman, "Barrington Moore and the Dialectics of Revolution: An Essay Review," <u>American Political Science Review</u> 64 (March 1970): 61-82.

APPENDIX: COMPARATIVE STATISTICAL DATA ON MODERNIZATION AND DEVELOPMENT IN EASTERN EUROPE

Compiled by Vernon V. Aspaturian

The following statistical tables were originally compiled to supplement Chapter 7 ("The Soviet Impact on Development and Modernization in Eastern Europe") and still support the textual analysis in that chapter. However, since the comparative data in these tables is of equal relevance to the theme of the volume as a whole, they have been collected together into a separate Appendix. The data covers a variety of selective political, social, and economic indicators drawn from various sources, most of which are ultimately based upon national official sources.

The tables are designed to illustrate comparative levels, rates, and directions of development and growth within a longitudinal context, that is, over time. Data is provided, wherever available, to cover both the prewar and postwar periods, and to document development before and after the advent of the Soviet presence in Eastern Europe. The data serves to illuminate three discrete perspectives of modernization and development and is designed (1) to compare the communist states of Eastern Europe with one another; (2) to compare modernization in Eastern Europe before and after the establishment of communist systems; and (3) to compare modernization and development in the communist states of Eastern Europe with that in comparable noncommunist states in the same geographical area.

The usual caution and reserve should be employed in interpreting the data. Since the data covers several decades of development, it was gathered under diverse conditions, circumstances, and auspices of varying and uneven degrees of consistency, reliability, and technical competence. The data is by no means automatically comparable, since even within a single country the criteria employed in defining categories have changed over time, and noncomparability is further magnified in transnational comparisons.

Wherever possible, in order to mitigate the distortions involved in statistical comparisons across countries, the data has been collected from statistical yearbooks issued by the United Nations and the League of Nations organs and agencies. All of this data ultimately derives from national official sources, but is subjected to a uniform set of qualifications and explications as exemplified in the fastidious documentation and multitudinous explanatory footnotes. Two other sources have been of considerable assistance in compiling the data and should be mentioned here. The first is the compendium of papers published by the Joint Economic Committee of the United States Congress, <u>Economic Developments in Countries of Eastern Europe</u> (Washington, D.C., 1970). The second is <u>World Military Expenditures 1971</u>, published by the U.S. Arms Control and Disarmament Agency (Washington, D.C., 1972).

TABLE A.1

Vital Statistical Data for Yugoslavia, by Republics

| Republic | 1961 | | 1969 | | | | | 1968 | |
	Population (thousands)	Literacy (percent)	Live Births per 1,000	Deaths per 1,000	Natural Increase per 1,000	Infant Mortality per 1,000	Pharmacists (total)	Physicians (total)
Yugoslavia	18,549	77.0	18.7	8.9	10.2	55.3	3,446	20,436
Slovenia	1,592	98.2	16.9	10.5	6.4	23.1	438	2,270
Croatia	4,160	87.9	14.7	9.9	4.8	36.5	1,098	4,865
Bosnia–Herzegovina	3,278	67.5	22.3	6.2	16.1	66.6	263	2,334
Montenegro	472	78.3	20.5	5.7	14.8	38.0	53	422
Macedonia	1,406	75.5	25.1	7.6	17.5	89.9	136	1,468
Serbia	7,642	78.1	18.2	8.7	9.5	57.4	1,460	9,077
Kosovo	--	--	37.6	9.3	29.6	92.4	--	--
Voivo	--	--	13.3	8.0	4.0	36.2	--	--
Serbia	--	--	15.4	8.7	6.7	44.0	--	--

Source: Statistical Pocketbook of Yugoslavia, 1970 (Belgrade: Federal Institute for Statistics, 1970).

365

TABLE A.2

Military and Educational Expenditures Compared, 1961 and 1970

Country	Military Expenditures				Educational Expenditures			
	1961	1970	Percent Change 1961-70	Average Annual Rate of Change	1961	1970	Percent Change 1961-70	Average Annual Rate of Change
	(millions of dollars)				(millions of dollars)			
USSR	39,000	65,000	66.7	5.9	15,500	38,500	148.4	10.6
Czecho-slovakia	960	1,660	72.9	6.3	520	1,093	110.2	8.6
East Germany	280	2,200	685.7	25.7	779	1,408	80.7	6.8
Poland	950	2,250	136.8	10.1	832	1,683	102.3	8.1
Hungary	170	560	229.4	14.1	273	513	87.9	7.3
Romania	310	610	98.8	7.8	313	682	117.9	9.0
Bulgaria	230	310	34.8	3.4	164	366	123.2	9.3
Yugoslavia	198	667	236.9	14.5	100	585	485.0	21.7
Albania	48	95	97.9	7.9	66	118	78.8	6.7
Austria	73	165	126.0	9.5	187	660	252.9	15.0
Finland	98	140	49.9	4.1	280	688	145.7	10.5
Greece	168	474	182.1	12.2	58	188	224.1	14.0

Source: World Military Expenditures, 1971, U.S. Arms Control and Disarmament Agency (Washington, D.C., 1972).

TABLE A.3

Mass Organizations in Eastern Europe, 1969-70

Country	Trade Unions	Youth Organizations	National Front	Women's Organizations	Agrarian Unions	Independent Cooperatives
USSR	86,000,000	27,000,000	--	--	--	--
Czechoslovakia	5,200,000	443,000[a]	--	--	--	--
East Germany	7,100,000	1,700,000	--	1,300,000	--	--
Poland	10,100,000	2,200,000[b]	--	--	2,600,000	--
Hungary	3,000,000	791,000	120,000	--	--	316,000
Romania	4,100,000	2,300,000	--	--	--	--
Bulgaria	2,417,000	1,100,000	--	--	120,000	--
Yugoslavia	3,220,000	2,085,000	8,126,000	--	--	--
Albania	400,000	210,000	--	284,000	--	--

[a] Student organization only.

[b] Includes 1 million in Rural Youth Organization.

Sources: The Political System of the Socialist Countries, Supplement to the World Marxist Review, August 1970; Keesings Contemporary Archives; World Strength of the Communist Party Organizations (1973), Bureau of Intelligence and Research, U.S. Department of State (Washington, D.C., 1973).

TABLE A.4

Population Growth, Density, and Ethnic Homogeneity

| | Population Growth and Density[a] | | | | Ethnic Homogeneity[b] | | | |
| | | | | | Prewar | | Postwar | |
Country	1963 (millions)	1970 (millions)	Annual Rate '63-'70	Density 1970	Majority Group	Minority Group	Majority Group	Minority Group
USSR	225,063	242,768	1.1	11	--	--	--	--
(Asian Part)	55,163	59,685	1.7	4	--	--	--	--
Czechoslovakia	13,952	14,467	0.5	113	69.7	30.3	93.9	6.1
East Germany	16,093	16,183	0.1	150	--	--	--	--
Poland	30,691	32,473	0.8	104	68.9	31.1	98.5	1.5
Hungary	10,068	10,309	0.3	111	92.9	7.1	98.2	1.8
Romania	18,813	20,253	1.1	85	77.9	22.1	85.7	14.3
Bulgaria	8,078	8,490	0.7	77	85.6	14.4	88.2	11.8
Yugoslavia	19,029	20,371	1.1	80	--	--	--	--
Albania	1,762	2,168	3.0	75	--	--	--	--
Austria	7,172	7,391	0.4	88	--	--	--	--
Finland	4,543	4,692	0.5	14	--	--	--	--
Greece	8,480	8,892	0.7	67	--	--	--	--

Sources: [a]United Nations Demographic Yearbook, 1971, Statistical Office of the United Nations (New York, 1972).

[b]Adapted from data in Paul F. Myers, "Demographic Trends in Eastern Europe," Economic Developments in Countries of Eastern Europe, 75

TABLE A.5

Infant Mortality, 1930-70

Country	Deaths under One Year per Thousand			
	1930-34	1951	1961	1970
USSR	--	--	32.0	24.4
Czechoslovakia	128.5	73.4	22.7	22.1
East Germany	--	59.9	33.7	18.8
Poland	139.6	107.8	54.8	33.1
Hungary	156.7	83.9	44.1	35.9
Romania	179.3	101.0	71.4	49.4
Bulgaria	144.1	101.0	37.8	27.3
Yugoslavia	154.9	140.0	82.0	55.2
Albania	--	121.2	79.5	86.8
Austria	100.2	61.3	32.7	25.9
Finland	73.9	35.4	20.8	12.5
Greece	118.9	44.4	40.1	29.3

Sources: United Nations Demographic Yearbook, 1961 and 1971; United Nations Statistical Yearbook, 1955 and 1964.

TABLE A.6

Birth Rates, 1938-70

Country	Birth Rates Per 1,000 Midyear Population					
	1938	1947	1954	1959	1966	1970
USSR	--	--	25.1[b]	24.9[c]	18.2	17.4
Czechoslovakia	16.7	24.2	20.6	16.0	15.6	15.8
East Germany	--	--	16.8[b]	17.2[c]	15.8	13.9
Poland	24.3	29.3[a]	29.1	24.9	16.7	16.8
Hungary	19.9	20.6	23.0	15.2	13.6	14.7
Romania	29.6	22.4	24.8	20.2	14.3	21.1
Bulgaria	22.8	24.0	20.2	17.6	14.9	16.3
Yugoslavia	26.7	28.1[a]	28.5	23.1	20.2	17.8
Albania	34.2	--	40.9[b]	43.4[c]	34.0	35.3
Austria	13.9	18.6	14.9	17.6	17.6	15.2
Finland	21.0	27.8	21.4	18.9	16.8	13.7
Greece	26.1	27.4	18.4[b]	18.9[c]	17.9	16.3

Sources: United Nations Statistical Yearbook, 1955, 1960, and 1967; United Nations Demographic Yearbook, 1971.

TABLE A.7

Abortions, Pregnancies, and Live Births in Eastern Europe, 1953-67

| | Abortions in Thousands | | | | | | Total Abor-tions and Live Births | | Total Abortions | | Live Births | | Total Abortions | | | |
| | Total | | Legal | | Other | | | | | | | | Per 100 Pregnancies | | Per 1,000 Women Aged 15-49 | |
Country	1953*	66-67	1953	66-67	1953	66-67	1953	66-67	1953	66-67	1953	66-67	1953	66-67	1953	66-67
Czecho-slovakia	30.6	121.2	1.5	96.4	29.1	24.8	23.6	23.6	2.4	8.5	21.2	15.1	10.1	36.0	9.6	35.1
East Germany	--	--	1.0	20.0	--	--	--	--	--	--	--	--	--	--	--	--
Poland	103.0	222.2	1.4	156.7	101.6	65.5	32.9	23.7	3.8	7.0	29.1	16.7	11.5	29.5	14.3	28.5
Hungary	42.7	222.4	2.8	187.5	39.9	34.9	26.0	36.3	4.5	21.8	21.6	14.6	17.1	59.9	16.9	85.5
Romania	112.0	1115.0	--	--	--	--	--	--	--	--	--	--	--	--	--	--
Bulgaria	17.4	119.5	1.1	101.4	16.3	18.1	23.2	29.4	2.4	14.5	20.9	14.9	10.2	49.3	8.9	56.8

*Except for Poland and Romania. The year for Poland is 1955, for Romania--on abortions--it is 1958.

Source: Adapted from data in Paul F. Myers, "Demographic Trends in Eastern Europe," Economic Development in Countries of Eastern Europe, pp. 91-99.

TABLE A.8

Medical Facilities and Personnel, 1969-70

	Hospitals		Beds		Health Personnel						
Country	Year	Total Number	Total Number	Population per Bed	Year	Physicians	Population per Physician	Dentists	Pharmacists	Nurses	Midwives
USSR	1969	24,429	2,567,300	94	1969	555,400	433	87,100	--	986,800	284,100
Czecho-slovakia	1969	411	147,906	97	1969	28,842	500	5,423	5,395	72,080	5,415
East Germany	1970	626	190,025	85	1970	27,255	594	7,349	2,885	--	12,171
Poland	1970	1,521	248,596	131	1970	49,283	659	13,611	12,298	102,838	12,171
Hungary	1969	--	83,600	123	1969	19,717	521	2,300	4,142	41,957	1,885
Romania	1970	--	168,115	120	1968	27,806	709	3,194	4,707	29,419	9,111
Bulgaria	1970	3,628	65,606	129	1970	15,819	537	--	2,382	25,265	5,839
Yugoslavia	1970	504	115,013	177	1970	20,369	1,000	3,001	3,616	--	4,891
Albania	1969	292	12,715	164	1967	1,157	1,694	144	221	3,608	1,037
Austria	1970	--	80,549	92	1970	13,682	540	1,822	2,627	18,672	1,322
Finland	1969	770	65,544	72	1970	4,795	978	2,695	4,600	25,771	2,454
Greece	1969	871	53,733	164	1969	13,711	644	3,935	--	7,755	3,300

Source: United Nations Statistical Yearbook, 1971.

TABLE A.9

Postwar Urbanization in Eastern Europe

Country	Urban Population (Percent of Total Population)					Percent Growth of Urban Population Since 1946-50
	1946	1948-50	1954-56	1963-67	1965-67	
Czechoslovakia	--	51	53	--	61	32
East Germany	68	--	72	--	73	1
Poland	32	--	42	--	51	118
Hungary	--	36	--	42	--	26
Romania	--	23	31	--	34	73
Bulgaria	25	--	34	--	46	120

Source: Adapted from data in Paul F. Myers, "Demographic Trends in Eastern Europe," Economic Developments in Countries of Eastern Europe, p. 84.

Housing and Facilities

Country	Year	Households		Dwellings			Facilities			
		Number	Average Size	Number	Average Size Room/per Dwelling	Average Density Person per/Room	Inside Piped Water	Flush Toilet	Fixed Bath or Shower	Electrical Lighting
USSR	1960	50,333,847	3.7	50,900,000	2.8	1.5	--	--	--	--
Czecho- slovakia	1961	4,397,579	3.1	5,819,873	2.7	1.3	49.1	39.5	33.3	97.3
East Germany	1961	6,638,247	2.5	5,507,000	2.6	1.2	65.7	32.7	22.1	--
Poland	1970	9,225,478	3.5	8,316,080	2.5	1.7	48.6	33.3	13.9	80.1
Hungary	1970	3,358,100	3.0	3,034,600	2.6	1.2	36.4	32.7	32.2	92.1
Romania	1966	5,954,555	3.2	5,380,299	2.6	1.4	12.2	12.2	9.6	48.6
Bulgaria	1965	2,526,635	3.2	2,079,853	3.2	1.2	28.2	11.8	8.7	94.8
Yugoslavia	1961	4,648,563	4.0	4,082,000	2.8	1.6	--	--	--	54.8
Albania	1960	279,805	5.8	--	--	--	--	--	--	--
Austria	1970	2,471,000	2.9	2,590,000	4.2	0.9	85.3	69.7	54.7	98.3
Finland	1960	1,315,434	3.3	1,211,200	2.7	1.3	47.1	35.4	14.6*	88.6
Greece	1961	2,142,968	3.8	2,260,831	2.6	1.5	28.7	14.6	10.5	53.2

*Excludes dwellings with Finnish sauna.

Source: United Nations Statistical Yearbook, 1971.

TABLE A.11

Commercial and Personal Transportation Facilities
in Eastern and Western Europe, 1955-67

Country	Percent of Total Traffic[a]		Automobiles[b] per 1,000 (stock)			Motorcycles or Motorscooters[b] per 1,000 (stock)		
	Rail	Truck	1955	1960	1967	1955	1960	1967
USSR	--	--	2	3	5	4	13	27
Czechoslovakia	88	2	10	18	36	33	56	94
East Germany	90	5	--	--	--	--	--	--
Poland	91	4	1	4	11	5	32	55
Hungary	75	12	12	3	14	17	24	46
Romania	87	7	--	--	--	--	--	--
Bulgaria	69	25	--	--	--	--	--	--
West Germany	42	22	33	76	171	47	34	7
Austria	54	39	--	--	--	--	--	--
Belgium	31	42	--	--	--	--	--	--
France	39	27	--	--	--	--	--	--
Italy	26	73	--	--	--	--	--	--

Sources: [a]Adapted from data in Economic Developments in Countries of Eastern Europe, Appendix A, p. 286.

[b]Adapted from data in Terence E. Byrne, "Levels of Consumption in Eastern Europe," in Economic Developments in Countries of Eastern Europe, p. 313.

Scientific and Technical Manpower and Distribution of Computers

| Country | Year | Scientific and Technical Manpower[a] | | | | Number of Computers and Origin[b] | | | |
| | | Total Number | | Total Number Engaged in Research | | Source of Origin | | | Total |
		Scientists and Engineers	Technicians	Scientists and Engineers	Technicians	USSR	Eastern Europe	External	
USSR	1970	6,042,000	8,914,000	927,709	--	80	50	135	265
Czecho-slovakia	1969	227,350	842,200	35,889	57,163	10	72	53	135
East Germany	--	--	--	--	--	7	103	30	140
Poland	1969	569,000	2,942,000	54,500	52,900	14	14	42	70
Hungary	1970	303,000	408,300	15,304	23,375	3	2	15	20
Romania	1969	--	--	18,711	8,392	2	1	24	27
Bulgaria	1969	130,088	270,143	19,990	8,933				
Yugoslavia	1969	183,787	644,177	14,453	10,279	0	0	120	120
Austria	66-67	--	--	2,568	1,938				
Finland	1969	--	--	3,602	3,179				
Greece	1969	124,400	138,670	1,032	785				

Sources: [a]United Nations Statistical Yearbook, 1971.

[b]Adapted from data in Robert L. LeBoeuf, "Production and Use of Computers in the Countries of Eastern Europe," in Economic Developments in Countries of Eastern Europe, p. 331.

TABLE A.13

Book Production and Communications Media, 1950 and 1970

Country	Book Production (titles in 1,000s)		Daily Newspapers				Radio Receivers		TV Receivers per 1,000 Population	
			1952	1949		1970	1950	1970		
	1950	1970	Number	Circulation per 1,000	Number	Circulation per 1,000	Per 1,000 Population	Per 1,000 Population	1960	1970
USSR	43,060	78,899	40	158	639	336	61	390	22	143
Czecho-slovakia	4,990	9,041	13	193[c]	28	252	195	267	58	214
East Germany	2,142	5,234	37	--	40	445[d]	190	347	60	282
Poland	5,218	10,038	22	125	43	209	59	173	14	129
Hungary	4,219	5,238	21	109	27	214	66	245	10	171
Romania	5,290[a]	7,681	30	--	55	169	19	152	3	73
Bulgaria	2,155	3,799	nd	--	12	193	31	270	5	121
Yugoslavia	4,371	8,119	16	80	24	85	21	163	1.4	88
Albania	125	502[b]	2[a]	--	3	52	7	74	0	1.2[e]
Austria	2,903	4,781	35	254[c]	33	268[e]	190	273	98	192
Finland	1,891	5,595	64	278	67	--	180	375	169	221
Greece	1,068	2,027	68	102	110	79	22	113[b]	0	10[e]

[a] 1959.
[b] 1965.
[c] 1950.
[d] 1968.
[e] 1969.

Source: UNESCO Statistical Yearbook, 1951 and 1971 (Paris

376

TABLE A.14

Telephones in Use, 1966 and 1970

Country	In Use		Per 100	
	1966	1970	1966	1970
USSR	7,872,000	11,000,000	3.4	5.0
Czechoslovakia	1,583,000	2,003,000	11.1	13.8
East Germany	1,724,000	2,089,000	10.8	12.3
Poland	1,411,000	1,867,000	4.5	5.7
Hungary	597,000	824,000	5.9	8.0
Romania	510,000	639,000	2.7	3.2
Bulgaria	306,000	473,000	3.7	5.5
Yugoslavia	452,000	736,000	2.3	3.6
Austria	1,087,000	1,427,000	15.0	19.3
Finland	892,000	1,181,000	19.2	24.9
Greece	579,000	1,045,000	6.7	10.0

Source: United Nations Statistical Yearbook, 1971.

TABLE A.15

Economic Growth Rates in Eastern Europe, 1928-65
(average annual rates)

Country	Stalinist Periods			Post-Stalinist Periods		
	1928-37	1950-58	1950-55	1958-64	1956-60	1960-65
USSR	4.8-11.9	7.1	--	5.3	--	--
Czecho-slovakia	--	--	8.0	--	7.1	1.8
East Germany	--	--	11.4	--	7.0	3.5
Poland	--	--	8.6	--	6.6	5.9
Hungary	--	--	6.3	--	6.5	4.7
Romania	--	--	13.9	--	7.0	8.7
Bulgaria	--	--	12.2	--	9.7	6.5

Source: Adapted from data in John P. Hardt, "East European Economic Development," in Economic Developments in Countries of Eastern Europe, p. 9.

TABLE A.16

Rates and Indexes of Industrial Growth in Eastern and Western Europe, 1950-69

| Country | Rates of Growth of Industrial Output[a] | | | Indexes of Industrial Growth (1955=100)[b] | | | | |
| | 1950-60 | 1960-68 | 1969 | Rate of Growth in All Industry | | | | Rate of Heavy Industry to All Industry |
				Prewar	1950	1960	1967	
Czechoslovakia	8.0	4.4	5.0	60	77	157	213	1.23
East Germany	9.1	3.7	7.0	95	58	140	177	1.23
Poland	8.2	6.8	6.0	60	62	147	230	1.39
Hungary	9.8	6.9	8.3	43	61	132	205	1.19
Romania	9.8	11.5	10.8	43	63	161	342	1.46
Bulgaria	12.7	11.9	11.6	24	60	200	444	1.89
Yugoslavia	9.2	7.9	8.0	--	--	--	--	--
Austria	--	4.2	9.8	44	64	133	174	--
Belgium	--	4.8	11.7	--	--	--	--	--
Greece	--	--	--	63	63	131	220	--
West Germany	--	4.9	13.5	--	--	--	--	--
Portugal	--	5.1	9.6	--	--	--	--	--

Sources: [a]Adapted from data in Laszlo Cziriak, "Industrial Structure, Growth, and Productivity in Eastern Europe," in Economic Developments in Countries of Eastern Europe, p. 437.
[b]Adapted from data in Edwin H. Snell, "Economic Efficiency in Eastern Europe," in Economic Developments in Countries of Eastern Europe, pp. 243-44.

TABLE A.17

Indexes and Growth Rates of GNP per Capita in Eastern Europe, 1950-67 (1955 = 100)

| Country | Indexes | | | Annual Percentage Increase | | | |
	Prewar	1950	1967	1950-55	1960-67	1950-67	1965-67
Czechoslovakia	73.5	89.3	154.1	2.3	2.4	3.3	4.5
East Germany	--	69.3	163.4	7.6	3.0	5.2	3.2
Poland	62.4	87.8	148.2	2.6	3.6	3.1	4.8
Hungary	86.5	80.8	158.5	4.4	4.2	4.0	5.0
Romania	--	74.8	171.4	6.0	5.7	5.0	6.6
Bulgaria	74.7	76.8	203.8	5.4	6.0	5.9	6.6
Yugoslavia	--	86.8	176.3	2.9	3.9	4.3	2.4

Source: Adapted from data in Alton, Economic Developments in Countries of Eastern Europe, p. 47.

TABLE A.18

Labor Productivity in Eastern and Western Europe, 1950-67

	Output per Worker in Industry		
	1938 = 100		West Germany = 100
Country	1950	1965	1967
Czechoslovakia	110	184	54
East Germany	57	132	62
Poland	183	331	50
Hungary	99	138	35
France	107	209	81
Austria	90	188	47
Italy	123	242	67
West Germany	94	182	100
Belgium	109	192	87

Source: Adapted from data in Edwin M. Snell, "Economic Efficiency in Eastern Europe," in Economic Development in Countries of Eastern Europe, pp. 266-67.

TABLE A.19

Indexes of Growth of Agricultural Output
in Eastern Europe, 1948-68
(1934-38 = 100)

Country	1948-50	1960-62	1968
Czechoslovakia	82.7	108.3	132.8
East Germany	72.9	97.7	121.5
Poland	99.4	141.9	184.2
Hungary	80.6	113.0	139.5
Romania	65.6	123.5	156.2
Bulgaria	82.5	136.4	169.0
Yugoslavia	86.0	129.4	155.6
Countries with socialist agriculture	74.6	111.9	139.1
Countries with private agriculture	95.2	138.2	175.7
Total Western Europe	102.9	155.0	186.4

Source: Adapted from data in Gregor Lazarcik, "Growth of Output, Expenses, and Gross and Net Product in East European Agriculture," in Economic Developments in Countries of Eastern Europe, pp. 476-77.

TABLE A.20

Number of Tractors per 1,000 Hectares of Agricultural Land and per 1,000 Agricultural
Workers in Eastern Europe, Prewar–1968

Country	Prewar		1948-52		1958-62		1968	
	Per 1,000 Hectares	Per 1,000 Workers	Per 1,000 Hectares	Per 1,000 Workers	Per 1,000 Hectares	Per 1,000 Workers	Per 1,000 Hectares	Per 1,000 Workers
Czechoslovakia	.73	2.34	3.7	13.7	13.2	63.9	28.1	167.0
East Germany	1.12	4.61	2.4	8.4	12.9	63.5	26.9	151.4
Poland	.01	.03	1.3	3.8	4.0	12.6	10.3	33.0
Hungary	.99	3.59	2.0	7.3	5.4	21.8	9.7	49.3
Romania	.26	.58	.9	1.8	3.1	6.4	6.5	16.5
Bulgaria	.28	.56	1.6	3.3	6.9	16.3	15.0	52.4
Yugoslavia	.15	.36	.5	1.2	2.3	7.2	3.4	12.4
Countries with socialized agriculture	.61	1.63	1.9	5.1	7.3	21.6	15.2	55.3
Countries with private agriculture	.06	.15	1.0	2.6	3.3	10.3	7.3	24.7
Total Eastern Europe	.34	.88	1.5	4.0	5.5	16.5	11.6	40.8
Total Western Europe	1.28	5.91	5.4	26.5	18.9	116.9	33.1	265.7

Source: Adapted from data in Gregor Lazarcik, "Growth of Output, Expenses, and Gross and Net
Product in East European Agriculture," in Economic Developments in Countries of Eastern Europe, p. 513.

TABLE A.21

Consumer Price Index and Calories Consumed, 1953 and 1970
(1963 = 100)

Country	All Items		Food		Calories Consumed per Day			
							Percent Animal Origin	Protein Grams
	1953	1970	1953	1970	Year	Total		
USSR	104	98	95	100	64-66	3,180	21	92
Czechoslovakia	115	102	116	100	64-66	3,030	27	83
East Germany	99	99	99	100	64-65	3,040	37	76
Poland	96	109	90	111	64-66	3,140	30	93
Hungary	100	102	100	101	1969	3,180	35	97
Romania	99	103	97	108	64-66	3,010	18	87
Bulgaria	124	103	111	107	64-66	3,070	13	91
Yugoslavia	56	248	50	248	1968	3,130	20	91
Albania	--	--	--	--	64-66	2,370	14	71
Austria	93	128	91	114	69-70	2,950	36	87
Finland	67	115	66	116	69-70	2,960	44	91
Greece	97	118	96	120	1967	2,900	20	99

Source: United Nations Statistical Yearbook, 1971.

TABLE A.22

Economically Active Population
(in percentages)

Country	Prewar (1928-34)*			Postwar (1950s)*			Recent (1960s)*		
	Male	Female	Total (percent of population)	Male	Female	Total (percent of population)	Male	Female	Total (percent of population)
USSR	63.0	51.6	57.5	--	--	--	54.8	41.5	47.5
Czechoslovakia	65.5	30.5	47.5	59.5	35.4	47.1	52.7	42.9	47.7
East Germany	--	--	--	62.3	33.1	46.1	60.1	39.8	49.1
Poland	58.5	36.3	47.0	59.4	42.4	50.4	55.1	40.1	47.3
Hungary	66.7	22.4	44.1	66.7	25.2	45.1	63.9	32.8	47.8
Romania	64.8	52.2	58.4	67.2	52.7	59.7	60.7	48.1	54.2
Bulgaria	62.2	41.2	56.5	63.3	45.7	54.5	58.1	45.7	51.9
Yugoslavia	63.0	30.4	46.5	63.0	30.7	46.3	59.6	31.1	45.0
Albania	--	--	--	60.6	45.7	53.3	53.1	36.3	47.6
Austria	64.7	30.5	46.9	63.7	35.0	48.3	61.0	36.0	47.6
Finland	61.2	46.8	50.7	61.9	38.4	49.2	56.0	39.2	47.3
Greece	64.1	29.1	44.2	62.6	13.1	37.2	59.7	27.8	43.4

*Various years for various countries during the general time period.

Source: Yearbook of Labor Statistics, 1939-40, 1951, 1957, 1962, 1965, and 1971 (Geneva, International Labor Organization).

Union of Soviet Socialist
  Republics (USSR), v, 6,
  8-16, 24, 25, 27, 29-30,
  34, 35-36, 43, 44-46, 47,
  51, 74, 77-80, 84, 93-94,
  102, 104, 113-14, 162,
  203-04, 283-84, 287, 290-
  91, 294-95, 307, 329, 330,
  336, 341, 345, 347-50, 353
United Kingdom, 27
United States, 15, 27, 34-35,
  36, 94, 208-09, 266, 312
Uruguay, 359

Vaculik, Ludvik, 351
Volgyes, Ivan, 307-08

Warsaw Pact, 266-67
Weber, Max, 160-61, 361

Weiner, Myron, 26
Wolfe, Thomas, 266

Yugoslavia, 18, 27-29, 35,
  44, 45-47, 48-49, 160-99
  209-11, 213, 215, 218,
  219, 227-32, 237, 239-42
  242, 244, 245, 247, 248,
  250, 252, 260, 264-65,
  268, 287-88, 289-92, 294
  313, 315, 319, 338, 342,
  343, 348, 352, 360

Zaninovich, M. George, 29
Zhdanov, Andrei, 264-65
Zimmerman, William, 269
Zinner, Paul, 338

CHARLES GATI, the editor of this volume, is Professor of Political Science and Director of the Program in Comparative Communist Studies at Union College and Visiting Professor of Political Science at Columbia University. He is editor and coauthor of Caging the Bear: Containment and the Cold War, and has written on Eastern European politics and Soviet foreign policy in scholarly periodicals and books.

VERNON V. ASPATURIAN is Evan Pugh Professor of Political Science and Director of the Slavic and Soviet Area Studies Center at Pennsylvania State University. He is the author of Process and Power in Soviet Foreign Policy, The Soviet Union in the World Communist System, The Union Republics in Soviet Diplomacy, coauthor of Foreign Policy in World Politics and Modern Political Systems: Europe, and has published in scholarly periodicals and books.

CYRIL E. BLACK is Professor of History and Director of the Center of International Studies at Princeton University. He is the author of The Dynamics of Modernization, editor and coeditor of numerous books on Russian history, contemporary Eastern Europe, and various aspects of world politics, and has written extensively in scholarly periodicals and books.

LENARD J. COHEN is Assistant Professor of Political Science at Simon Fraser University (Barnaby, Canada). He is coeditor of Communism in Comparative Perspective and has published on the Yugoslav parliamentary system in scholarly periodicals and books.

ISTVAN DEAK is Professor of History and Director of the Institute on East Central Europe at Columbia University. He is the author of Weimar Germany's Left-Wing Intellectuals, coeditor of Eastern Europe in the 1970s (Praeger, 1972) and Everyman in Europe: Essays in Social History, and has published on nineteenth- and twentieth-century Eastern and Central European history in scholarly periodicals and books.

TROND GILBERG is Assistant Professor of Political Science at Pennsylvania State University. He is the author of

<u>Modernization in Romania Since World War II</u> (Praeger, 1974), <u>The Soviet Communist Party and Scandinavian Communism: The Norwegian Case</u>, and has written on Eastern European politics in scholarly periodicals and books.

ZVI GITELMAN is Assistant Professor of Political Science at the University of Michigan. He is the author of <u>Jewish Nationality and Soviet Politics: The Jewish Sections of the CPSU, 1917-1930</u>, and has published on Eastern European and Soviet politics in scholarly periodicals and books.

WILLIAM E. GRIFFITH is Professor of Political Science at the Massachusetts Institute of Technology, Adjunct Professor of Political Science at the Fletcher School of Law and Diplomacy, and Visiting Professor of Political Science at Columbia University. He is the author of <u>Albania and the Sino-Soviet Rift</u>, editor of <u>Communism in Europe</u> (2 vols.), and has written extensively in scholarly periodicals and books.

BARBARA WOLFE JANCAR is Visiting Associate Professor of Political Science at Union College and Executive Director of the consulting firm, International Science Exchange. She is the author of <u>Czechoslovakia and the Absolute Monopoly of Power</u> (Praeger, 1971) and has published in scholarly periodicals and books.

ROGER E. KANET is Associate Professor of Political Science at the University of Illinois. He is the editor of <u>The Behavioral Revolution and Communist Studies</u> and <u>The Soviet Union and the Developing Nations</u>, coeditor of <u>On the Road to Communism</u>, compiler of <u>Soviet and East European Foreign Policy: A Bibliography of English and Russian Language Publications</u>, and has published in scholarly periodicals and books.

GYORGY RANKI is Professor of History at the University of Debrecen (Hungary) and Deputy Director of the Institute of History of the Hungarian Academy of Sciences in Budapest. He is the coauthor of <u>Economic Development in East Central Europe in the 19th and 20th Centuries</u> and coauthor of many monographs on modern Hungarian economic and political history.

ROBERT SHARLET, Chairman and Associate Professor of Political Science at Union College, was Joint Senior Fellow of the Research Institute on Communist Affairs and of the Russian Institute at Columbia University in 1973-74. He is coauthor of <u>The Soviet Legal System and Arms Inspection</u> and has written on Soviet political and legal development in scholarly periodicals and books.

OTTO ULC is Associate Professor of Political Science at the State University of New York in Binghamton. He is the author of <u>The Judge in a Communist State</u> and has published on Eastern European politics in scholarly periodicals and books.

IVAN VOLGYES is Associate Professor of Political Science at the University of Nebraska. He is the author of <u>Political Socialization in Eastern Europe</u> (Praeger, 1974), <u>The Hungarian Soviet Republic</u>, coauthor of <u>Czechoslovakia, Hungary, Poland</u>, editor of <u>Environmental Deterioration in the Soviet Union and Eastern Europe</u> (Praeger, 1974), <u>Hungary in Revolution 1918-1919</u>, coeditor of <u>On the Road to Communism</u>, and has published on Eastern European politics in scholarly periodicals and books.

RELATED TITLES
Published by
Praeger Special Studies

CHANGE AND ADAPTATION IN SOVIET AND EAST EUROPEAN
POLITICS
edited by
Jane P. Shapiro
Peter J. Potichnyj

CRISIS IN SOCIALIST PLANNING: Eastern Europe and
the USSR
Jan Marczewski

THE FUTURE OF INTER-BLOC RELATIONS IN EUROPE
edited by
Louis J. Mensonides
James A. Kuhlman

MODERNIZATION IN ROMANIA SINCE WORLD WAR II:
A Socioeconomic and Political Analysis
Trond Gilberg

POLITICAL SOCIALIZATION IN EASTERN EUROPE:
A Comparative Framework
edited by
Ivan Volgyes

SOCIAL CHANGE AND STRATIFICATION IN EASTERN EUROPE:
An Interpretive Analysis of Poland and Her Neighbors
Alexander J. Matejko

THE SOCIAL STRUCTURE OF EASTERN EUROPE: Transition
and Process in Czechoslovakia, Hungary, Poland,
Romania, and Yugoslavia
edited by
Bernard Lewis Faber

TECHNOLOGY IN COMECON: Acceleration of Technological
Progress through Economic Planning and the Market
J. Wilczynski

MASSACHUSETTS